HOMESCAPING

Designing

Your Landscape

to Match

Your Home

ANNE HALPIN

Principal photographer, Jerry Pavia

HOMESCAPING

RODALE

The information in this book has been carefully researched, and all efforts have been made to ensure accuracy. Rodale Inc.
assumes no responsibility for any injuries suffered or for damages or losses incurred during the use of or as a result of following this
information. It is important to study all directions carefully before taking any action based on the information and advice presented
in this book. When using any commercial product, always read and follow label directions. Where trade names are used,
no discrimination is intended and no endorsement by Rodale Inc. is implied.

Printed in the United States of America on acid-free ∞, recycled paper ♻.

Book design by Carol Angstadt
Illustrations by Anthony Sidwell

Photo credits can be found on page 259.

Library of Congress Cataloging-in-Publication Data

Halpin, Anne Moyer.
    Homescaping : design your landscape to match your home / Anne Halpin.
        p.   cm.
    Includes bibliographical references (p.   ) and index.
    ISBN-13 978–1–57954–903–9   hardcover
    ISBN-10 1–57954–903–9   hardcover
    1. Gardens—Design.   2. Landscape gardening.   3. Garden structures.
    4. Garden ornaments and furniture.   I. Title.
    SB473.H2965   2005
    712'.6—dc22   2004027361

Distributed in the trade by Holtzbrinck Publishers

2 4 6 8 10 9 . 7 5 3   hardcover

RODALE
LIVE YOUR WHOLE LIFE™

We inspire and enable people to improve their lives and the world around them
For more of our products visit **rodalestore.com** or call 800-848-4735

[FOR BRANDON]

[Contents]

Acknowledgments
viii

Creating the Perfect Fit
ix

CHAPTER 1: Garden Styles and Home Architecture
1

CHAPTER 2: Color-Coordinating House and Garden
53

CHAPTER 3: Hardscaping and Space Management
87

CHAPTER 4: Garden Structures
131

CHAPTER 5: Decorating the Great Outdoors
167

Plant Finders
209

Recommended Reading
253

Resources
255

Photo Credits
259

Index
263

USDA Plant Hardiness Zone Map
276

[Acknowledgments]

This book could not have come together in the way that it did without the input of a number of people. First of all, I want to thank Jerry Pavia for his glorious photographs that capture so beautifully both the spirit and the details of so many diverse gardens. Thanks to my editor, Chris Bucks, for her guidance and her unending encouragement, and for being so great to work with. Thanks to my agent, Jeanne Fredericks, for her insight and feedback, and for all her efforts on my behalf.

Thank you also to Helen Lober of Hampton Nursery and Landscapes, in Hampton Bays, New York, for sharing information on pavement plants, and to Joe Tortorella, of J. Tortorella Swimming Pools, in Southampton, New York, for information on patio surfaces.

Finally, to my husband and son, John and Brandon White, my thanks for their love and support, and for putting up with me at deadline time.

CREATING THE PERFECT FIT

Investing time and money into the grounds around your home is well worth the cost and effort. Not only does good landscaping enhance the appeal of any home and create a beautiful setting for it, a well-designed landscape will also work for you, making it easier to get around to all parts of your property and to do the things you like to do outdoors. The landscape helps support your lifestyle and interests. There are economic benefits, too. Landscaping has been shown to boost resale values and overall property worth. But perhaps above all, your landscape simply can improve the quality of your life in many ways.

Improving Your Quality of Life

Well-designed outdoor space increases your total living space for at least part of the year. In warm climates, you can use your outdoor space for many months. And even in cold climates, you can enjoy outdoor living not only in the summertime but in spring and fall, too, if you have a patio heater or outdoor hearth.

The home is the center of family life and the place where many of us like to entertain friends. Spending time with friends and family outdoors can

A well-designed landscape invites you to spend time outdoors, especially when there is a comfortable place in which to sit and survey the flowers—in this case, white marguerites and blue lithodora.

be among life's great joys, and it's so much simpler to be able to socialize right at home. Gatherings can be spontaneous and low-key in a well-equipped backyard. Many pleasures are to be had outdoors, and spending time in your landscape helps you to forge a connection to nature. Spending time outdoors also reveals to us the many sensual delights of the garden. We are rewarded with the colors of foliage and flowers, and often with fragrance as well; with textures both visual and tactile; with the movement of swaying branches and fluttering moths; with the songs of birds and the rustling of leaves in the breeze. And there are psychological benefits, too.

Spending time outdoors, just *being* in nature, can be soothing, inspiring, and invigorating if we open ourselves to perceiving its many moods. You can design a garden to create or enhance different feelings, too, by choosing particular plants, styles, color schemes, and accessories. Formal gardens, for example, are serene and peaceful. Cottage gardens are cheerful places. Informal gardens can be casual and friendly or, sometimes, dynamic and exciting, depending on how they are put together and what's growing in them. Japanese-style gardens are meditative and tranquil.

In your garden, you can help to nurture wildlife—birds, bees, and butterflies; fish and frogs; and beneficial insects like ladybugs and praying mantids. And you can enjoy their presence.

If you design your landscape to support the things you like to do and to look beautiful at the same time, spending time in your backyard can feel like taking a vacation without ever leaving home. It is my hope that this book will show you a way to do that.

Enhancing Functionality and Utility

The right landscaping around your home makes the house look grounded and complete, integrated into its setting. The house just looks like it belongs there. Plantings, hardscape, and structures can also work, individually or in concert, to welcome visitors and direct them to your door, or to provide privacy screening or a security barrier that keeps the world at bay. Landscaping can camouflage eyesores, blocking from view the street, the compost pile, or your neighbor's garage. You can landscape to create just the right setting for outdoor activities such as dining, playing sports and games, exercising or doing yoga, or just plain relaxing. Thus, the landscape works on many levels.

Boosting Property Values

Any real estate agent can tell you that a well-designed landscape increases property values and the resale value of a home. Studies have shown that landscaping returns 100 to 200 percent of the investment you make in it. Houses with "curb appeal" are the easiest to sell and command the highest prices. Besides keeping the house well maintained and painted, surrounding it with an attractive landscape is the best way to create curb appeal. And designing the landscape to coordinate with the house in terms of both style and color creates the most curb appeal of all. Even if you plan never to sell your house, the kind of landscaping described in this book will enable you to have outdoor space that appeals to your senses, supports your lifestyle, and expresses your personality like no other. You'll feel truly at home in your yard and garden.

How to Use This Book

This book presents a different way to arrive at a garden or landscape design. Instead of starting with abstract principles of design and applying them to your property, I encourage you to think about how you use the space outside your home, or how you'd like to use it. Approach planning and decorating your landscape as you do the interior of the house. Just as different rooms indoors have different functions—eating, dining, leisure pursuits, sleeping—so, too, do the spaces outdoors in your landscape. You can have spaces outdoors for eating, leisure, and even sleeping.

If you think about working outward from the house, extending the decorative style and the colors of the house into the outdoors, the indoor and outdoor spaces will flow into one another in a seamless, unified whole—a true homescape. This book takes a decorator's approach to color, form, and space and applies it to the yard and garden, and the space between house and garden (the deck or patio). You will be able to express your tastes and your lifestyle outdoors to create new living space that perfectly suits the look of the house. Begin with the kind of house you have and select a garden style, colors, and plants that coordinate with it. (This book will be most useful for properties of an acre or less, where the gardens are close to the house and the landscape immediately adjoins it. The broader concerns involved in designing a landscape for a large estate go beyond the scope of this book.)

Chapter 1 deals with style and how particular garden styles work with different styles of home architecture. Use this chapter to find the best style for your landscape. Chapter 2 deals with color and shows how to create garden color schemes that coordinate with the colors used on and in your home, and which colors work best with different-colored houses. Chapter 3 considers hardscaping and space management issues and offers guidance on finding paths, walls, fences, and hedges that work with the style of your house and garden. Chapter 4 explores structures—decks, patios, arches, arbors, pergolas, gazebos, and sheds—and how they can contribute to and be integrated into the overall design of the property. Finally, Chapter 5 surveys the universe of outdoor accessories: furniture, lighting, water features, statuary and ornaments, and pots and other containers, and it offers tips on how to work them into your outdoor setting.

My goal in writing *Homescaping* has been to enable you, the homeowner, to modify your existing landscape or create a new design to enhance your outdoor activities, increase your property values, and beautifully complement your home, whether you do much of the work yourself or hire professionals to create and execute the design. I hope that this book will prove an easy-to-use guide, showing you how to tailor your outdoor space to fit your house as well as your clothes fit you.

Informal plantings perfectly suit the feeling of this tiny, rustic guesthouse. When your landscape is in tune with the style of your house, the result is a garden that feels like home.

CHAPTER 1

[Garden Styles and Home Architecture]

Gardens are as wonderfully diverse as the people who create them and the places they inhabit. Every garden is unique, and the best ones reflect the personalities of their gardeners. But with such a vast range of styles to consider and a nearly endless universe of plants from which to choose, where do you begin? There are loads of books on garden design, and the subject can seem overwhelming. But there are some helpful guidelines you can follow to narrow down your choices. The complicated universe can be simplified. In fact, the art of designing a garden can be broken down very simply into three broad approaches: formal, informal, and naturalistic. And there are particular plants to suit each kind of garden. Many variations exist within the three categories,

◄ This exuberant informal garden wraps around the house like the porch.

Far left: Formal gardens are laid out with straight lines and precise geometric shapes. *Left:* In an informal garden, plants billow in drifts and intermingle their colors in relaxed groupings. *Right:* Naturalistic gardens evoke plant communities found in wild places, such as woodlands, meadows, or deserts.

istic garden is to look at it as a community of plants adapted to a specific set of conditions. Meadow plantings, woodland gardens, and desert gardens are three examples of naturalistic gardens. In a naturalistic garden, as in a natural environment, the plants are not simply laid out in rows or clumps. They fill a variety of niches. A woodland garden, for instance, combines tall trees with smaller understory shrubs and ephemerals (herbaceous perennials that come and go throughout the growing season). Low groundcovers carpet the soil beneath the other plants.

The style of garden that will best suit your house depends, of course, on your own personal sense of style and the kind of look that appeals to you. But some types of homes are more readily suited to particular garden styles. Some houses just look best when surrounded by a formal garden, while others are better complemented by a naturalistic landscape. The architectural style of your house, the materials from which it is constructed, and its location and setting all play a role in determining what sort of landscape will suit it best. A brick Colonial in an eastern suburb would probably look strange with a desert garden out front, while formal beds with topiaries and boxwood hedges would look odd next to a log home.

In this chapter we will take a look at the three basic approaches to garden design and what kinds of houses they suit best.

but the basic design concepts apply to all gardens in each of the three.

Formal gardens represent an idealization of nature, and they clearly show the hand of the gardener. In a formal garden, beds and borders are precisely shaped, plants are clipped into perfect forms, and maintenance is meticulous. Like classical paintings, formal gardens convey a feeling of serenity and repose. The landscape is well ordered and controlled. The very discipline of a formal garden can be reassuring. The stability of the design can give you a sense of calm and balance.

Informal gardens are less precisely structured, but they are still carefully thought out and organized.

Their effect is very different from the quiet order of a formal garden. Informal gardens have lots of dynamic curves and flowing lines, and the plants are allowed to assume more or less their natural growth habits. Informal landscapes are relaxed and easygoing, and they convey a happy exuberance. The plants lean into one another to mingle their colors, and they spill over the edges of containers and onto walkways. Informal gardens are full of movement.

Naturalistic gardens attempt to mimic or evoke a particular natural environment. The goal of a naturalistic garden is to come as close as possible to recreating the way plants grow in the wild. One of the most important considerations in creating a natural-

The rectangular spaces of this courtyard garden echo the grid of streets and buildings in the city outside the walls. Neatly clipped Korean boxwood (*Buxus microphylla* var. *koreana*) enhances the formality of the design.

Urban Settings

If you live in town, your house is probably part of a grid of streets, sidewalks, and buildings. City buildings tend to be built of formal materials such as brick or limestone. Stucco can appear formal or informal, depending on the design of the house.

A grid of streets and buildings is full of hard edges and straight lines. To integrate your house into this kind of environment, you can echo the shapes of the neighborhood in your garden. A formal garden with geometric beds arranged along axial paths would effectively connect the house to the setting.

Older subdivisions and planned communities were sometimes laid out in grids, with houses situated on nearly identical rectangular lots. The houses, though, were usually modestly sized and rather informal in design and materials. The strict geometry of the setting lends itself to a formal design, but the informal nature of this kind of house suggests that a modified version of a formal garden (as described on page 18), a sort of hybrid between formal and informal style, would work better than a pared-down version of Versailles. (See page 6 for more on formal gardens.)

Where Do You Live?

The very first step in designing a garden tailored to your home is to take some time to think about where you live. Consider the location and setting of your home, and the landscape that surrounds it. You can take cues from the landscape (natural or constructed) around your house when you begin to think about your garden's design.

In the Country

In the wide-open spaces of rural communities, development is often more informal. Roads wind and curve, and properties are not necessarily carved into neat square or rectangular lots.

Suburban and farther-from-town exurban housing developments that are not close to city centers and

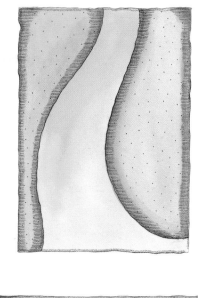

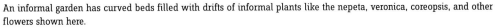
An informal garden has curved beds filled with drifts of informal plants like the nepeta, veronica, coreopsis, and other flowers shown here.

downtowns often have winding streets and homes in a variety of architectural styles. This kind of setting could inspire informal designs that also employ sweeping curves and flowing plantings. For instance, beds of colorful flowers could ramble around the edges of an elliptical or irregularly curved lawn. If the lawn is large enough, there could be one or more island beds, perhaps kidney-shaped or more amorphously curved.

If you have a rectangular or square lawn and want to keep that shape for easier mowing, you could soften the geometry by bordering the lawn with gracefully curved beds. Let the outer edges of the beds, along the property line, house, driveway, or sidewalk be straight, and curve the edges along the side adjacent to the lawn. Allowing some plants to spill over the edge of the garden further softens the look. Installing mowing strips of brick or stone along the edge of the garden and flush with the lawn surface will allow you to mow the lawn without hacking up the plants along the edge (and it will eliminate time-consuming edging of the garden beds, too).

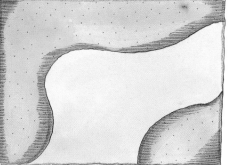

Here are two ways to soften the look of a rectangular lawn by using curved garden beds along the perimeter. The backs of the beds conform to the straight edges of the lawn, but the front edges of the gardens trace graceful, soft curves.

In many newer developments, big formal houses are the order of the day, and formal gardens often suit them best, even when they sit on a curved street. Using circular forms in the garden would help connect the house to the winding street. You might, for instance, design circular garden beds bisected by a straight axis that could be a walkway leading to the house.

Natural Settings

In a truly rural location, the beauty of your home's natural setting can inspire your designs. A naturalistic garden that echoes the surrounding landscape can smoothly integrate your house into its environment. Making a naturalistic garden doesn't mean that you have to try to duplicate what's already there. You need not feel limited to recreating a woodland in a forested setting, or planting beach grass in a seashore garden. If you want to have a more structured garden or grow particular plants that you love, such as roses or cutting flowers, you can create conventional garden beds close to the house, and let your plantings become looser and more natural as you work outward from the house. For example, planting native shrubs and wildflowers toward the edges of your property can help make a graceful visual transition from the garden to the woods beyond. If open fields lie next door, a planting of ornamental grasses and meadow or prairie flowers along the property line can link your property to the surrounding environment.

Transitional plantings can link your house and garden to a beautiful view. The trees planted just beyond this deck help to create a visual transition between the house and the woodlands beyond the property.

The Formal Garden

Formal gardens were traditionally the province of the aristocracy, who had the land available and the wherewithal to employ the legions of gardeners needed to tend them. Formal gardens have taken different forms in different eras. In the 17th century, knot gardens and parterres were popular, with low, clipped hedges tracing elaborate patterns on the ground. Parterres were designed to be viewed from above—from atop a slope, a balcony, or the upper floors of the house. In the 18th century, people went romantic, building mysterious grottoes and imitations of classical ruins, with statuary and pillars amid the plants. A bit later, the "landscape" movement dominated by the indomitable English landscape designer Lancelot "Capability" Brown swept away the grottoes and ruins and aimed instead to create perfected landscapes of grassy slopes, groves and clumps of trees, and large pools or ponds. These landscapes often required much moving of earth to reshape the terrain; the existing natural setting was unimportant. Flowers, topiaries, statuary, and other embellishments were considered frivolous and vulgar, and they were banished from the scene.

Over time, homeowners began to model their smaller landscapes after the large, lavish estate gardens of the wealthy. Carpet beds of low plants laid out in intricate, colorful patterns inspired by oriental rugs were popular among the 19th-century Victorians, although some of them opted for planting "wild" gardens instead.

In this formal garden, rectangular beds of Iceberg roses are surrounded by meticulously sheared boxwood hedges.

In our own time, formality fell out of favor during the mid-20th century, as American life became less structured and more relaxed. We became a casual society, and our gardens reflected our free and easy lifestyles. But the pendulum of public taste has swung back the other way to an extent. Formal designs have made something of a comeback in recent years, perhaps because we no longer feel as safe and confident as we used to. People tend to be drawn to formality when they feel a need for more stability and order in their lives, and we seem to be in such a period now. When so much of the world seems out of control, it is reassuring to seek the shelter of a structured, peaceful home ground. But whatever the motive for creating them, formal gardens work best with formal architectural styles.

House Styles Suited to Formal Gardens

Formal houses look most at home in formally styled landscapes. For instance, Colonial and Federal-style houses built of brick or stone are well served by formal gardens. Urban townhouses and row homes, especially older or historic homes, are often constructed in formal architectural styles such as Second Empire, Georgian, or Greek Revival.

Houses in these styles would be well served by a formal landscape.

Colonial, Federal (feature stone or brick construction, little ornamentation)

Italianate (features curved eyebrow lintels, protruding stoop—classic New York City brownstone)

Greek Revival (features fluted columns with Doric or Ionic capitals)

Second Empire (features mansard roof)

Romanesque (features rounded arches, Byzantine leaf details)

Renaissance, Italian Renaissance (feature limestone or light-colored brick construction, ornate pilasters)

Queen Anne, Victorian (feature big porches, gables, decorative woodwork)

Gothic Revival (features gables; turrets; pointed, arched windows)

Contemporary, modern (feature spare and unadorned, clean lines)

QUEEN ANNE

The three kinds of houses shown here would be nicely complemented by a formal garden.

COLONIAL

GREEK REVIVAL

Landscapes for Victorian houses can be formal or informal, depending on the location and color scheme of the house. A Victorian home in an urban area, painted in the classic Victorian manner with doors, shutters, and other trim done in two colors that contrast with the wall color, would look right surrounded by formal gardens. On the other hand, a Victorian-style wood shingle home near the water also would look good with formal gardens if the house sits amid sweeping, well-manicured lawns dotted with majestic old shade trees. But the same house could be suited to a less formal landscape if the lot is smaller or laid out differently. If the house sits at the end of a winding driveway, perhaps sheltered or screened by a clump of trees, a less formal garden might work better.

Elements of Formal Gardens

When you think "formal garden," do you think "old-fashioned, confining, boring"? You wouldn't be alone, but actually, formal gardens can be bold and dramatic. Not all formal gardens are classical or take their cues from palatial or historic gardens such as those of Versailles or Monticello. Formal gardens can be as current as today's news. They can be coolly minimalist or sleekly contemporary. Such updated formal styles are the perfect garden partners for modernistic houses.

In short, there are many kinds of formal gardens. They can be large or small, or even done entirely with containers in tiny city courtyards. But whatever their dimensions or location, formal gardens have certain qualities in common. Balance and symmetry are two hallmarks of formal design. These elements, along with the crisp perfection of the plant forms, and the way the structural lines (called axes) bring the eye to rest where they intersect, give formal landscapes their sense of stability and serenity. Formal gardens look and feel peaceful and calm.

Left: Matched pairs of urns planted with red geraniums add color to a formal brick walkway. *Above:* A Victorian house painted white is nicely complemented by formal clipped shrubs.

THE FORMAL GARDEN

These design elements are the hallmarks of formal gardens:

- Space divided by straight axes

- Beds in neat geometric shapes, in proportion to the house and one another

- Symmetrical layout and balanced plantings

- Formal paved surfaces

- Low, clipped hedges or other neat edgings around beds

- Simple color scheme

- Neatly maintained plants

- Topiaries and clipped shrubs

- Water features—pools, fountains

- Statuary, urns, bowls and other containers, geometric accent pieces

Here's a rundown of the basic components of formal garden design.

The beds in a formal garden are designed along axes—straight lines of sight that lead to prominent features in the landscape, such as the house. All the elements of the landscape are organized around the axes. The axes and garden beds together form a pattern, and the spaces in the pattern are where the plants go.

Designers have used axes to give structure to landscapes for hundreds of years. Axes can be seen in Italian gardens of the medieval period, and in Moorish gardens even earlier. Typically, a formal landscape has two axes perpendicular to one another: the main axis and the secondary axis. Often, the axes take the form of linear paths or walkways (called axial paths). The main axis path is wider than the secondary path that crosses it, giving the main axis visual prominence.

Formal beds and borders are laid out in neat, precise geometric shapes that usually have straight edges—rectangles, squares, or even triangles. It's also possible to have circular beds, especially in combination with other shapes as part of a larger pattern. Circular beds are more difficult than straight-edged beds to lay out and plant well, but they are easier to handle when you divide them into quadrants or wedges.

The secondary axis crossing the main path at a 90-degree angle is part of what gives a formal landscape its feeling of quiet. Your eye travels along the main axis, then stops when it reaches the intersection of the secondary axis. The junction is a good place for a focal point, perhaps a sundial, water fea-

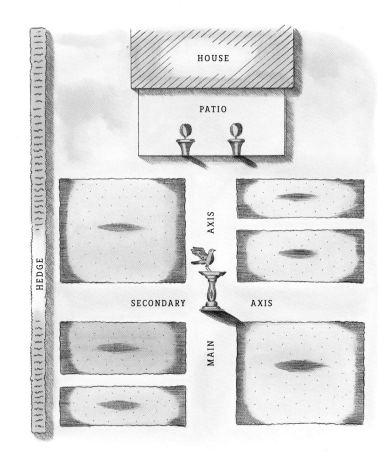

In this formal garden, several rectangular beds are arranged along two axes. The main axis leads to the house and is wider than the perpendicular secondary axis.

ture, or piece of sculpture. The focal point gives the eye a place to rest. The illustration shows a square garden divided into four geometric beds by intersecting paths. The gardener has placed a fountain in the center where the paths cross. Notice how all four beds are the same size and echoing shapes.

In this formal design, the main axis path, paved in herringbone brick, leads to the gate at the far end of the garden.

In this circular garden, semicircular beds curve around a central bed ornamented by an armillary sphere.

Neat edgings and carefully plotted paths help to define the planting areas in formal gardens.

Formal Pavements

The best surfaces for paths in formal gardens are neat and orderly. Brick, concrete pavers laid in formal patterns, and bluestone are three good examples. You can also use grass for paths if you keep it mowed and cleanly edged, but grass likes to spread and creep into adjacent garden beds, so it's more work to maintain. (See Chapter 3 for more information on designing and making paths.)

If there are changes of level in the garden, you'll also need steps. In a formal garden, steps are wide and solidly constructed of stone, brick, or other formal pavements.

Balanced Plantings and Symmetrical Beds

Balance and symmetry are essential qualities of formal gardens. The beds on both sides of an axis path should be balanced. In many gardens, the beds are mirror images of one another, at least in terms of their shape. You don't have to put exactly the same plants in the same places in each bed—that can be boring and overly static. But repeating some plants from bed to bed and using the same color scheme throughout will help to unify the garden and add rhythm to the plantings.

To emphasize and clearly define the shapes of the beds, you may want to outline them with a low, clipped hedge of boxwood, santolina, or another plant that takes shearing well, or install neat edgings of brick. (You can find information on hedges and edgings in Chapter 3.)

In any case, try to balance the beds in the garden, whatever their size and configuration. For example, if you want to have gardens on each side of your front door, make both beds the same size and shape. It also helps if your beds are of pleasing proportions (see "Working with Proportion" on the opposite page for information).

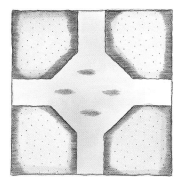

Here, four symmetrical, geometrically shaped beds make a neatly controlled formal statement. The beds are bisected by two perpendicular axis paths. Repeating plants from one bed to another enhances the well-planned formal look.

Paths surfaced with brick are in keeping with the formal character of this garden. Build on the formal style of this simple four-bed garden by surfacing the paths with brick (shown here), flagstone, or neatly laid pea gravel.

Clipped low hedges of boxwood or other low shrubs enhance a formal garden by outlining the geometric shapes of the beds. A sundial or other ornament in the center of the garden, where the paths intersect, completes the design.

WORKING WITH PROPORTION

One way to really tie your garden to your house is to relate the size of the beds to an architectural feature of the house or a prominent feature of the surrounding landscape. You might use the width of your front door, the house itself, or maybe the garage. The bed could be one-third or one-half the width of the garage, or twice as wide as the front door.

When you have determined one dimension of the bed, you can take advantage of another simple designer's trick to choose the other dimension: You can use Fibonacci numbers. Fibonacci numbers are a numerical sequence devised by a 13th-century mathematician named Leonardo Fibonacci. The sequence is created by adding together the two numbers preceding the next one in the sequence: 1, 2, 3, 5, 8, 13, 21, 34, 55, and so on. Any two adjacent numbers in the sequence can be used to create a space of pleasing proportions. Thus, if you design a garden bed of 3 by 5 feet, or 21 by 34 feet, you will automatically have a well-proportioned bed.

Interestingly, patterns based on Fibonacci numbers can be found throughout the natural world. The regular spiral of the chambered nautilus shell and the curved pattern of seeds in the head of a sunflower are just two patterns in nature that are related to the sequence of Fibonacci numbers.

Using Fibonacci numbers in your landscape design is a subtle trick, but it really will lend polish to your designs. You'll be using 800-year-old principles to design your 21st-century garden.

WIDE HOOP

TALL HOOP

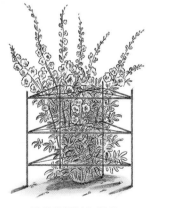

TRIANGULAR GRID

TWIG STAKES

Many tall or bushy plants need staking to support their long stems or heavy flowerheads. Unobtrusive means of support include hoop supports, which work well for tall, straight stems; twig stakes, for floppy stems; and round or triangular grids, which are helpful for bushy and clump-forming plants.

Neatly Groomed Plants

Formal gardens reflect human control over the natural world—the civilizing of nature—so it's essential that the plants look neat and well maintained. Floppy, overgrown plants make the garden look dishevelled, and disorder is not what you want in a formal garden. If you don't have time to do a lot of staking and pruning, choose plants that are naturally neat in habit, such as irises and peonies. Make sure that other tall plants are securely staked so they stand up straight and don't lean into their neighbors.

Shrubs and hedges in formal gardens are carefully clipped into idealized shapes.

The fresh, white Iceberg roses in this garden are accented with pink geraniums in the urn.

If you want to use more than one color in a formal garden, keep the combination simple for the best effect. Blue and white is a classic mix, as is red and white with lots of green. Also, don't forget to consider the color of the house when working out a color scheme for the garden. (See Chapter 2 for more on working with color.)

Idealized Plant Forms

Some plants possess a natural grace that's in keeping with the elegance of a formal garden. Other plants achieve a formal look with careful pruning. Some can even be turned into living works of art. At the very least, you want any hedges to be sheared into neat planes. Evergreen shrubs will, at their simplest, be clipped into neat cones or balls, or even squared-off boxes. But you can turn them into green sculptures, too, by training them as topiaries.

Topiary belongs in a formal garden. It's perhaps the ultimate expression of human control over plants. Through the painstaking training and pruning of topiary, plants can be turned into all sorts of things they are not—spirals, the lollipop forms known as standards, even animals. Through the art of topiary, plants can achieve a perfection of form they could never attain in their natural state. Whether such idealization is a worthwhile goal lies at the heart of the argument for or against formal design. In any case, if you're going to have topiaries, a formal garden is undeniably the place to display them. They would look hopelessly out of place in any other kind of landscape.

Some of the plants in formal gardens help define the underlying structure and accentuate the lines. Carefully clipped hedges delineate the edges of beds or paths when they are kept low. They make boundaries without obscuring the plants in the beds. Tall hedges act like walls and screens, marking property boundaries (and thus, the edges of the landscape) or, within the landscape, serving as the walls of garden rooms, dividing separate areas within the garden.

Restrained Color Scheme

A riot of colors won't work well in a formal garden. That's not to say that a formal garden has to be all green or have flowers of only one color. But a simple color scheme generally works best in a formal setting. In a formal garden, structure is important. A lively mix of colors can detract attention from the structure of carefully shaped and sized beds and paths.

A garden of all white flowers can feel refreshing and crisp, especially with the addition of some well-placed accents in another color. If you opt for a monochromatic scheme, whether you use white or another color, give special consideration to varying the forms of the plants and flowers in it. Another way to add interest to a single-color garden is to use different tones of the color. Combine several shades of pink, for instance, or use a range of yellows from ivory to soft lemon to rich gold.

Choosing Plants for Formal Gardens

The best plants for formal gardens are naturally neat of habit or amenable to pruning and shaping. Boxwood is a classic example: It grows slowly and stays compact, and it also takes shearing beautifully. You can use individual boxwoods as focal points or specimens, especially when you clip them into neat cones or ovals. Or you can plant a row of them and shear the group into a diminutive hedge. When left unpruned, boxwood eventually becomes rather billowy—a soft, appealing shape that's lovely in more informal gardens.

There are many plants whose timeless elegance have given them a classic quality that's perfect for a formal garden. If flowers are your fancy, you'll probably want to grow delphiniums, lilies, irises, and peonies. See "Plants for Formal Gardens" on page 210 for more suggestions.

Lilies, like the Asiatic lily 'Malta', are lovely in formal gardens.

Bearded iris (this one is 'Conjuration') is another classic.

Water Features

Water has traditionally been a part of formal gardens. The grand palatial landscapes created in Italy during the Renaissance often had fountains and jets of water that danced high into the air. Water, whether moving or still, is a delightful addition to a garden today, too, although on a more modest scale. There are many ways to bring the quiet beauty and gentle music of water into your garden. You might place a fountain in the intersection of two axial paths to provide a focal point. In a quiet nook or corner, a small trickling basin or waterspout makes soft, soothing sounds. In an open area, a rectangular or round pool quietly reflects the sky above. (See Chapter 5 for more information on water features.)

Statuary and Ornaments

Ornamental pieces add a finishing touch and extra visual interest to formal gardens. Urns, bowls, and other containers can play an important supporting role in the design, especially if they are large and impressive looking. Containers are great additions to all kinds of gardens, but in a formal garden you want to show off the container rather than the plants. In fact, you don't need to put plants in your containers at all. If you do plant them, choose neat, upright plants that won't spill romantically over the edges and obscure the shape and pattern of the pot. A neatly clipped boxwood or dwarf Alberta spruce would fit the bill nicely, as would a spike dracaena for a single season.

Urns, bowls, troughs, and boxes can all add a decorative note to formal gardens. You can use them as focal points, place them on steps or atop a wall, or set them on a patio, next to a bench, or in a quiet corner. A pair of containers can flank the front door or the entry to the garden.

Urns have a classic look that's well suited to formal gardens, and you can find them with or without a footed base. You can purchase urns made of terra-cotta, stone, faux stone, glazed ceramic, and even fiberglass finished to look like antique cast iron or stone. Plain urns are nice, but you can also find them decorated with garland or basketweave patterns, or with fluted, scalloped, or incised designs. For more height, you can place an urn on a pedestal made of stone or cement.

For a contemporary garden, seek out sleek, glazed ceramic containers or straight-sided ones made of zinc or brushed aluminum. For a Japanese-

A beautiful container,
with or without plants,
can provide a lovely accent
in a formal garden.

style garden, oriental ceramic pots with colored glazes or painted patterns work beautifully.

If you live where winter temperatures are below freezing and you want to leave your containers outdoors year-round, the best materials to choose are fiberglass or a faux stone material that has been fired in a kiln. Terra-cotta and ceramic pots are likely to crack if they are exposed to repeated freezing and thawing temperatures, especially if you leave the soil in them all winter.

Other kinds of ornaments for formal gardens include obelisks and sundials. Obelisks are useful for vertical accents. They may be made of solid stone or have trelliswork sides of wood or metal. You can set a trelliswork obelisk atop a planter and use it as a tuteur to support vines or upright plants. You can also place an obelisk on a base, or directly on the ground. Pyramids fill a similar niche where you need less height than an obelisk would provide.

Spheres provide another sort of geometric accent. Small stone balls can serve as finials on pillars or walls. Larger balls can simply sit on the ground. If you want a lighter look, there are glass balls and reflective gazing globes to set on a pedestal or tuck into a garden bed.

Sundials and armillary spheres remind us of a time when there were no mechanical clocks and the hours were measured by the movement of the sun across the sky. They make charming focal points and garden accents. For a formal landscape, set the sundial on a pedestal of classic design—garlanded, fluted, or with a pattern of drapery.

Finally, statuary and sculpture make lovely accents for formal gardens. You might choose classical

In this garden, a piece of statuary in a classical style is displayed in front of a dark gray pillar.

or mythological figures, cherubs, or saints, and you can find them in cement, stone, or lighter-weight fiberglass resin. In a contemporary garden, abstract pieces of stone, bronze, and other materials can add the right touch.

Modifying Formal Designs

If your home lends itself to formal landscaping but you find the precision of a formal garden too stuffy or confining, consider a compromise. Instead of creating a purely formal garden, you could structure the garden in formal beds, then plant informally within them. That way, the garden has good strong bones, but the skeleton can wear looser, more comfortable clothes.

Many of the great British country gardens have informal plantings in formal beds. This modified formal style affords both a strong, sturdy structure and the lushness of plants allowed to grow in a more natural manner. The plants intermingle their colors and spill over the edges of the beds, softening the lines of the composition without losing the underlying structure. A modified formal garden is the ideal style for many situations.

The celebrated 19th-century English garden designers William Robinson and Gertrude Jekyll were instrumental in developing this kind of modified formal garden style. These two people, more than anyone else, were instrumental in moving English gardens away from the rigid formality of carpet beds and toward a freer style. Robinson was a plantsman, and he argued for a more natural use of plants in the garden. Jekyll was a painter, and her greatest contribution was to bring her painterly sense of color to the garden.

The Victorian carpet beds of the day used strong color contrasts to emphasize the fussy patterns of the designs, but Jekyll brought a much more subtle and harmonious color palette to the grand borders she created. Her method was to modulate colors over the length of the border and to make subtle transitions from one color to the next.

A border might begin with reds, then move into yellows, blues, violets, and purples, then back again through the palette to close with reds at the other end of the garden. The plants were grouped into irregular masses called drifts, and the color was softer and paler toward the edges of each drift to allow it to blend better with the color of the next drift. Jekyll placed the most intense color in the center of the drift. Thus, she could connect intense red with rich purple by having a light pink at the edge of the red drift next to a pale lavender at the edge of the purple drift.

Bear in mind that these borders were executed on the grand scale. Some of them were hundreds of feet long, and few were less than 4 feet wide. Few of us today have enough space for a border that modulates through the entire color spectrum, but we can certainly take inspiration from Gertrude Jekyll's work, on a smaller scale.

The Informal Garden

Some houses look best with informal gardens. The straight lines and strict geometry of formal landscape styles just seem to fight the architecture of many popular house designs. Informal gardens are generally suited to farmhouses, ranch-style houses, bungalows and cottages, saltboxes, and log homes. Victorian homes can also be well served by informal gardens if they are located in rural areas or small towns. Check "Would an Informal Garden Suit Your House?" on page 21 for a list of architectural styles that usually look best paired with informal landscaping.

If your home doesn't fit into any of the obvious types, or if you're not sure what style you have, look at the materials from which it is constructed. If your house is made of wood siding, wood shingles, or logs and it is not contemporary or modern, chances are an informal garden would be appropriate. Adobe and stucco homes are also often suited to informal gardens. Look at your home's facade, too. If the facade is asymmetrical, with the door off center and unequal numbers of windows on either side, your house would probably look good with an informal garden.

Informal plants spilling onto pathways soften the hard edges of a formally structured garden.

Drifts of perennials curve along the pathway to the woodshed in a country garden.

Elements of Informal Gardens

What makes a garden informal? The simple answer is curves and diagonals. Beds and borders designed in flowing, organic-looking shapes are inherently informal. There are no straight axes neatly organizing the space, no precise geometric shapes, and no required symmetry of elements. Within the garden, plants are grouped into flowing drifts that undulate through the bed or border like ribbons blowing in the breeze. Instead of lining up in neat rectangles along the sidewalk or around the edges of the property, beds and borders might snake their way diagonally across the lawn toward the house instead of leading directly to it in a straight line running perpendicular to the street.

The curves and diagonals of informal gardens give them a more dynamic visual quality than formal landscapes possess. Informal gardens are active, often playful. Your eye follows the curve of a path until it disappears around a screen of shrubs, and you naturally want to go exploring to see what else is around the corner. Informal gardens invite explo-

Informal gardens are perfectly at home with these kinds of houses:

Bungalow, cottage

Ranch

Dutch Colonial

Farmhouse

Log home

Saltbox

Stucco, adobe, Pueblo Revival

Post-and-beam or artisan wood house

Wood-shingle house

Craftsman

Postmodern

BUNGALOW

DUTCH COLONIAL

An informal landscape suits an informally styled house, such as those shown here.

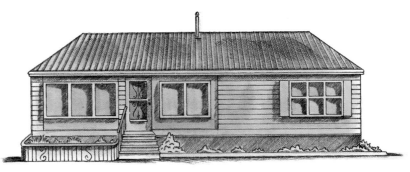

RANCH

ration; they make you want to move through them. Even in a small garden, your eye is drawn to follow the curve of the bed or border toward its end.

Although they lack the strict geometry of formal landscapes, informal gardens are neither haphazard nor messy. They are just as carefully designed, and they need regular maintenance to look their best.

(*Note:* Although you can plant informally within a formally structured garden, the reverse is not true. Planting in formal patterns within an informally shaped garden would probably look silly.)

Informal garden beds complement this casual ranch house.

For many of us, though, informal landscapes perfectly suit our homes and our casual lifestyles. An informal garden is often a good solution for a house on a sloping lot or a property with irregularly shaped boundaries. If your lot is a typical suburban rectangle, you can adapt it for an informal garden by planting around the border to conceal the straight edges. Garden borders along the edge of the property can be straight along the back and curved along the front.

Informal gardens are also ideal for creating transitions between a formal home and a natural land-

USING VINES FOR SPECIAL EFFECTS

Vines are the special-effects department of the garden, able to fill any number of design roles.

You can use vines architecturally, to supply a vertical line to direct the eye upward or to contrast with the horizontal planes of lawn and garden. Vines planted in a row and supported on trellis or lattice panels can make a screen to provide shade or privacy, or divide one part of the landscape from another. A screen of vines is friendlier than a wall, more colorful and private than a fence, and less work to maintain than a tall hedge.

Vines trained around a strategically placed arch can frame a view of the garden or of distant scenery, or quietly draw attention to a sundial, birdbath, or prized specimen plant. The vine-covered arch can provide a charming entry into the garden, or in a large garden can serve as a transition from one garden area to another. Trained to cover an arbor, gazebo, or pergola, vines create a cool, leafy hideaway or dining nook.

Vines can soften the severe lines of walls, fences, and buildings and make them more attractive by adding their colorful flowers, interesting foliage patterns, and appealing textures.

Of course, vines can be purely decorative, too. Use a few vines as ornamental accents on porch posts or railings. Let them climb a lamppost or twine around the post supporting the mailbox.

For a more formal look, some woody vines, such as trumpet creeper (*Campsis radicans*), can be espaliered; others may be trained as standards to produce balls of foliage and flowers atop tall, straight stems. Standards of ivy or golden trumpet vine (*Allamanda cathartica*) can provide seasonal vertical accents in the garden or even take the place of small trees in a tiny garden.

Don't overlook vines when you're looking for ways to add more levels of interest to your landscape.

scape beyond the property. If, for example, you have a formal home that happens to be located next to a woodland, open fields, or along the seashore (lucky you!), you can connect the house to the nearby wild landscape by putting formal gardens close to the house and an informal garden farther out, separated by a low hedge, wall, or fence. The farther reaches of the garden could be naturalistic, including elements echoing the untamed areas that are visible beyond your property.

Naturalistic gardens are a particular kind of informal design in which the garden is designed to recreate the feeling of a natural habitat—a woodland, desert, prairie, meadow, bog or wetland, rocky mountainside, or seashore. We'll look at some of them more closely in a few pages.

If it's a forest that's beyond your borders, you might plant some native shrubs and wildflowers in the outer parts of your landscape. If you look out toward a meadow or prairie, plant ornamental grasses to make a visual transition.

Not all informal gardens are naturalistic. Many of us just want a relaxed, easygoing look to our gardens, without the meticulous fussiness of formal parterres and hedges. Besides employing curves and diagonals in their underlying designs, informal gardens, with one exception, do not require plants to be meticulously groomed and trained into idealized shapes. That is not to say that informal gardens are necessarily low-maintenance propositions, although they can be, depending on what you plant in them. In most cases, though, you will still have to pull the weeds, deadhead the flowers, and stake floppy plants to keep the garden looking neat. But plants in

AT A GLANCE

THE INFORMAL GARDEN

Informal gardens have the following characteristics:

- **Curved beds**
- **Borders with undulating edges**
- **Diagonal lines**
- **Winding paths**
- **Plants in flowing drifts**
- **Tree, shrubs, and herbaceous plants that assume natural habits**
- **Plants that spill over edges of pots and beds**
- **Color scheme that is soft or bright**
- **Informal hedgerow rather than clipped hedges**

informal gardens are allowed to assume their natural growth habits.

Hedges or screens of shrubs or trees need not be clipped into sheer vertical planes or tight globes, buns, or pyramids. Instead, the "walls" of informal

garden rooms are allowed to billow or fountain according to their natural bent. Trees and shrubs in informal landscapes still need to be pruned to remove dead or damaged growth, and perhaps to direct their growth while they are young, remove crossed branches, or improve their shape, but they are not sculpted into fanciful or geometric forms.

Vines can work wonders in informal gardens. Let them climb trellises or even tree trunks, cover arbors or pergolas, clamber over fences, walls, or shrubs, or ramble about on the ground at the feet of taller plants.

One special kind of informal garden in which great care is taken in placing and shaping plants, rocks, and other garden elements, and in creating balance—albeit an asymmetrical balance—is the Japanese-style garden. Japanese gardens may appear to be classically formal in their mannered serenity, but they are not, as I explain on page 29.

Laying Out Informal Beds and Borders

After you choose a site for the garden and come up with a design on paper that you like, you are ready to begin laying out your garden. Before you put shovel to earth, create the outline of the garden on the ground. The easiest way to "draw" the garden is to lay out a length of garden hose or rope on the ground. Adjust the line of the hose or rope until you arrive at a shape you like. Then you can either dig right alongside the hose to mark out the shape, or you can mark the lines by sprinkling lime or spraying landscape paint (which comes in cans that can be sprayed downward instead of sideways), then remove the hose and dig along the line you drew. When the garden area is delineated, you can go on to remove the sod, if you are carving the garden out of existing lawn, or till and prepare the soil.

Planting in Drifts

When you are planting in curved or undulating beds and borders, you don't want to line up the plants like rows of little soldiers. Plants in informal gardens aren't planted to form patterns or designs as in a knot garden or carpet bed. Instead, the goal is to create a more natural look, and the best way

to achieve that is to group the plants into drifts. A drift is simply an elongated, gracefully rounded clump of plants, as shown in the illustration below. Planting in drifts creates more visual impact than simply dotting plants in ones and twos all over the garden.

The size of a drift depends upon the size of the garden and how many kinds of plants you are working with. In a very small garden, the drifts will probably be clumps. But whatever the scale of your garden, bear in mind that it's easiest to achieve a natural look with an uneven number of plants in each drift. With an even number of plants, there's more of a tendency to put them in pairs, circles, or squares.

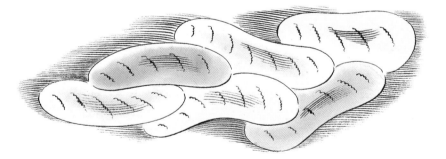

For the most natural look in a bed or border, organize the plants into drifts instead of setting them out in rows or blocks. A drift is simply a flowing, elongated grouping of plants with somewhat irregular edges. Plants from adjoining drifts can intermingle along the edges to soften the effect.

Working with Color

Color schemes for informal gardens can be subtle or dramatic, depending upon the colors of your home's exterior, the colors you like, and the effects you want to create.

Garden designers use color in combinations that are appealing in different ways. Color can be softly pretty, clean and refreshing, or dramatic and arresting. Color can manipulate the sense of space in a garden, and it can influence our mood when we are in the garden, creating a particular feeling.

Warm colors—reds, oranges, yellows, and hot pinks—appear to come forward in space. They are attention-getters and can be used to draw our eye toward a structure, ornament, or important specimen plant in the garden. Red flowers advance visually in space, and they foreshorten distance. A garden planted in warm, bright colors will feel lively and energizing. Soften the colors to pastels—warm pinks, peach, salmon, and light yellow—and the effect will be happy and friendly in a gentle, non-threatening way.

Cool colors, on the other hand—blues, greens, purple, and violet—are calming and restful. Cool colors appear to recede in space, and they create a feeling of serenity and repose. Planting blue and purple flowers in the back of a garden can make the garden seem larger than it is, the back of the garden farther away. A garden of blues and purples seems cool even in hot sun. Deep blues and purples bring a sense of mystery, too, like the depths of a still pool or the sky at twilight. Blue flowers and foliage can create the feeling of an island of serenity, especially

Warm yellows, reds, and oranges make a lively, energetic garden.

around a small pool or fountain or in a seating area. Cool pinks are lovely with blues and purples in the garden, especially when accompanied by silvery foliage. When these colors are softened to lavender or mauve, you get a gentle, misty effect. (Chapter 2 delves more deeply into color combinations for gardens and the effects you can achieve with different colored plants.)

This is a lovely example
of how informal plantings of flowers
(here, white calla lilies and osteospermum)
can soften a formal structure of straight
paths and clipped shrubs.

Choosing Plants for Informal Gardens

Most plants fit well into informal gardens. The neat, well-mannered irises and lilies that look so elegant in formal gardens look just fine in less formal settings, too. But informal gardens are ideal for less restrained plants as well. Asters and goldenrods, globe thistles and goat's beard, black-eyed Susans and baby's breath are all good choices for informal gardens. Ornamental grasses can be enchanting additions, swaying and sighing in the summer breeze. (See page 216 for a list of plants for informal gardens.)

Feathery astilbe blooms in early summer in shady gardens.

Coreopsis blooms all summer when you deadhead it regularly.

The Cottage Garden

Among the most informal of all gardens, cottage gardens have a special charm. These lively, colorful combinations of old-fashioned plants are the very essence of informality, growing together in happy abandon, spilling onto pathways, leaning on fences, and generally creating a feeling of exuberance.

Cottage gardens originated in England and Europe, where the "cottagers" who worked on the estates of the aristocracy grew their own food and medicinal herbs in small plots near their dwellings. They surrounded the gardens with fences to keep out wandering livestock. Settlers brought the cottage garden tradition with them to America, growing vegetables, herbs, and flowers used to make dyes and medicines in dooryard plots enclosed by picket fences.

Today's cottage gardens have evolved to suit different parts of the country, but all of them are built around old-fashioned and regional plants. Most cottage gardens include different kinds of plants—perennials, annuals, bulbs, herbs, vines, and even shrubs—all planted together. Fragrant plants are especially welcome in a cottage garden.

When choosing plants for your cottage garden, be sure to include some that have special meanings or associations for you. My own garden includes old-fashioned bleeding heart (*Dicentra spectabilis*) because I was enchanted by its dangling lockets in a neighbor's garden where I played as a child. I grow a particular kind of lantana because my grandmother always grew it. A cottage garden is also a good place for gift plants and "pass-alongs," cuttings and seedlings given by gardening friends and neighbors. Self-sowers such as Johnny jump-ups (*Viola tricolor*) are fun to include, too—let them come up where they will and introduce a delightful bit of serendipity to your garden. Whichever plants you select for your cottage garden, choose them on the basis of their individual qualities rather than the contribution they would make to the total design. Try to assemble a pleasing assortment of colors, but don't be a slave to a color scheme. Also be sure to include some tall and big plants, too, so you don't end up with a collection of little things.

Enclose the garden with a low picket fence or hedge to give a bit of order. When planting, it's still best to have more than one of each kind of plant—small clumps of three or five will keep the garden from looking entirely random or scattershot.

Choosing Plants for a Cottage Garden

When choosing plants for your cottage garden, look for heirloom and old-fashioned varieties and species rather than relying on lots of modern hybrids. Older varieties of plants like heliotrope and sweet peas are often more fragrant than newer cultivars bred primarily for color or larger size. Plants that self-sow, such as Johnny jump-ups and forget-me-nots, add to the serendipitous charm of a cottage garden as they seed themselves about and pop up in unexpected places. Regional natives can also play a role in cottage gardens, especially where the climate and the site make for difficult growing conditions. (See page 221 for more on plants for cottage gardens.)

THE COTTAGE GARDEN

Here are the basic elements of a cottage garden:

- Garden enclosed by picket fence

- Old-fashioned plants

- Plants chosen for personal preference and meaning rather than design qualities

- Fragrant plants

- Mix of colors

- Individual and small groups of plants, not large clumps or drifts

The Japanese-Style Garden

If you had to pick one word to describe a Japanese garden, that word would be *tranquil*. This serene landscape is designed to facilitate meditation and contemplation, to put the visitor in a mood of peaceful awareness. The goal of a Japanese garden is to interpret the natural world in an abstract, symbolic way. These gardens are inspired by natural settings—woodlands, seashores, windswept mountainsides—and seek to invoke the essence, the spirit, of the wild places without literally recreating them.

The plants and other elements of Japanese-style gardens are used metaphorically: A small pool of water may represent a lake, a single pine tree might evoke a forest, a rock may symbolize an island in the sea. The features in oriental gardens may look as though they just happen to be there, that they have been located accidentally, but in reality each element of the garden has been painstakingly planned and placed with great care.

Central to oriental gardens is the concept of the "borrowed landscape," which originated in China. The Japanese were inspired by paintings they saw on Chinese scrolls to develop garden-making to a high art. By carefully locating and training plants to frame and draw the eye toward a natural feature outside the garden, such as a distant mountain peak, the gardener in a sense makes that feature part of the garden. The effect is enhanced by planting to camouflage less desirable views while highlighting the desired one.

The principles of Japanese garden design can be adapted to create American versions of these refined, serene landscapes. Japanese-style gardens have a minimal look. Plantings are generally spare so that each plant receives its own attention. Evergreens play an important role, although there is also room for deciduous trees and shrubs. Ferns and mosses carpet the ground. When flowering plants are included, they are chosen to bloom one at a time so that each plant has its turn to be a star. Oriental gardens are not riots of color; the effect is far more subtle.

The apparent simplicity of Japanese-style gardens nicely complements the clean, minimal lines of many contemporary homes. But an oriental garden would look out of place next to a more traditionally styled house, such as a formal Colonial or a rustic bungalow.

Do not be deceived by the spareness of Japanese gardens into thinking that they are simple

A JAPANESE-STYLE CONTAINER GARDEN

If you have no ground space, you can create an oriental-style garden in pots. Choose imported oriental pots glazed in muted, earthy colors—pale green, ocher, umber, wine red, and deep gold. Rounded shapes with a rolled or flat rim are best; avoid square or angular shapes. You can even turn a pot into a water feature if you like.

For the most gardenlike look, group several pots of varying sizes and shapes, in all one color or in two or three colors that harmonize nicely. You might want, for example, to set a tall, narrow pot of bamboo or maiden grass (*Miscanthus sinensis*) behind a large, round pot containing a small, neatly pruned azalea or Japanese maple, or a waterproof tub holding some Japanese, yellow flag, or blue flag iris in very moist soil. Add several pots of ferns around and in front of the large pot. In front, place a shallow bowl or some small, low pots of different sedges (*Carex* spp.). If the container garden is on the ground, perhaps next to the entrance to the house or alongside a patio, set the pots on a base of gravel or pebbles to create an effect of islands in a sea.

THE JAPANESE-STYLE GARDEN

These design elements typify the Japanese style:

- Design inspired by site

- Careful asymmetrical balance

- Boulders to suggest mountains and rock formations

- Massed pebbles and stones that evoke water

- Winding paths for strolling past garden features

- Water, still or in motion

- Screened plantings to enclose garden

- Trees pruned to emphasize natural form

- Plants treated like works of art

to create. The features of the garden are carefully chosen and positioned to work in harmony with one another. The careful, balanced use of space and spareness of the elements would seem to make these gardens formal, but they are not. They are, in fact, informal, though in a calculated way. The balance is asymmetrical. The paths wind and curve. The artful pruning of the trees and deliberate placement of rocks, plants, and water are meant, in the end, to evoke the spirit of nature, not artifice. Nature is idealized and reinterpreted by the mind, eye, and hand of the gardener. It's a reverence for nature that finds expression here, and a seeking to be at one with the natural world.

Japanese gardens are not about lanterns and little bridges. They take their inspiration from the natural landscape, refining and distilling its essential spirit into simple combinations of stone, water, and plants. These combinations of elements create a balance of opposing forces: rough textures balance smooth, dark colors balance light, the mass of rock or tree balances open space.

Balance is an essential part of Japanese gardens, but it's an asymmetrical balance. Balance in a Japanese garden is not created by intersecting axes, as in a western-style formal garden. The paths do not lead directly toward focal points in a straight line. Instead, they weave and meander past the features of the garden. This kind of asymmetric balance is difficult to understand at first, and it's more difficult to create than the symmetrical balance of a formal garden. The same principle can be seen at work in the stylized arrangements of ikebana, the Japanese art of flower arranging.

If you do want to include stone lanterns in your garden, use them for lighting, or place them where you'd need to illuminate a path if you were walking in the garden at night. Place a bridge where you need to cross a stream.

If you decide to design your own Japanese-style garden, let the site itself and the surrounding landscape inspire your design. Try to capture the essence of the landscape in your garden. Use local stone and regional plants as much as possible. (If you live in a developed area with little open space, look for vestiges of the wild landscape, and do some research to find out what the area was like before it got built up.) Also consider in your planning the needs of those who will visit the garden, and provide walkways for

easy, secure strolling, and benches on which to sit for a rest or to take in the scene.

Elements of a Japanese-Style Garden

These are the elements from which to shape an oriental garden.

Rocks

Rocks are the bones of the earth itself. Large rocks bring a sense of stability, of enduring strength, to the garden. As rock weathers or as moss grows on it, it reflects the passage of time even as it endures. Rocks in a Japanese garden speak all these messages, but they have practical roles to play, too.

Large boulders can be placed to divide space, to serve as a backdrop for plants, to screen the curve of a path from view, or to prevent erosion on a slope. Placing a smaller stone behind a larger one helps create an illusion of depth, especially if the smaller rock is darker in color.

When choosing rocks for your garden, try to use local stone that looks like it belongs there. Don't mix different kinds of stone; use all granite rocks, for example. Choose rocks that are similar to one another in color, with interesting shapes and textures.

Place rocks so that they look natural, as if they were deposited by an ancient glacier or heaved out of the nearest volcano. Aim for a naturalistic angle. You want the rocks to help create the overall look of a natural setting—a boulder in the woods, or a pebbly mountain scree. Position large rocks to balance other elements in the garden or to call attention to something you want to be noticed.

Masses of small stones and pebbles create effects on the ground. A sea of raked gravel can appear to flow and eddy around the large boulders, or it can evoke a river flowing down a hill. Rivers and seas of stone are especially useful in dry climates where water is scarce, and they can soothe and refresh the spirit as water can.

Paths

Paths lead visitors through the garden and enable them to observe all of its features. The paths wind their way past the rocks, plants, and water features and pace the journey. Consider the comfort of visitors when planning your paths. Make the paths wide enough for two people to stroll comfortably side by side. Place stepping-stones a comfortable distance apart. If you want people to look around them as they walk, make the path smooth and even. If you want them to look down and notice something on the ground, make the path uneven by adding stepping-stones or an uneven (but not hazardous) pavement.

Surface the paths with natural materials. You can, if you like, use different materials in keeping with different parts of the garden. A path through a grove of trees could be covered with shredded leaves or a woody mulch. Next to a pool, try paving the path with pebbles raked into rippled patterns. You can use a different kind of pattern or pavement near a plant or object to which you want to call the visitor's attention. It's common for Japanese gardens to employ several different kinds of paving on paths.

Water

Water brings a particular grace to any garden, but it is an especially important component of a Japanese garden. Water trickling from a bamboo spout into a stone basin creates a gentle music that is soothing and calming. Bubbling, gurgling water is cheering and uplifting. Moving water also helps mask ambient noise in the neighborhood.

Still water in a pond or pool quietly mirrors the sky above, inspiring contemplation. Gazing at the changing reflections of passing clouds and birds in flight puts the visitor in a meditative mood.

Try to include a water feature in your oriental garden, even if it is as small as a water spout trickling into a stone basin equipped with a recirculating pump. You can make a small pool with a preformed or flexible plastic liner.

A bridge over a pond in this Japanese-style garden features a seat that invites a visitor to pause for a moment to take in the scene.

Choosing Plants
for a Japanese-Style Garden

Oriental gardens are self-contained places screened off from the rest of the busy world. Boundary plantings of trees and shrubs are essential for enclosing the garden. Inside the garden, place plants to frame a desirable view or hide an eyesore, to draw attention to a water feature or interesting rock, or to balance other elements in the garden. Plant trees as individual specimens or in small groups to convey a feeling of strength and stability as a large boulder would.

Each plant in a Japanese garden is treated as a work of art, given its own importance. Trees are pruned and trained to emphasize their natural form, especially when that form is contorted or imperfect. (See page 226 for plants for Japanese-style gardens.)

Variegated sedge (*Carex siderosticha* 'Variegata') is a good choice for an oriental garden.

If you decide to include azaleas or other flowering shrubs when you are choosing plants to screen the garden, try to select varieties that will bloom in succession rather than all at once so that each plant will have its moment of glory.

Evergreens are important for providing year-round structure and color. Japanese black pine (*Pinus thunbergii*) is classic, but in some places, such as on Long Island where I live, they are dying as a result of borer invasion. Other good choices include Scotch

HOW TO DO IT

PRUNING TIPS

Careful pruning is essential in a Japanese-style garden, but that does not mean carving plants into topiary lollipops, globes, and pyramids. Instead, strive for forms that are inspired by nature but in an idealized way. Above all, aim for smooth, flowing lines.

Prune trees, especially featured specimen trees, to point out their interesting lines and to make them look windblown and ancient. An S-shaped trunk is especially desirable; you may be able to find a tree with a curved trunk, but more likely you will have to train a young tree yourself to get this shape.

Remove selected branches to allow space between branches, so that each branch is easy to see. If your tree has an S-shaped trunk, remove branches growing from the concave, or incurved, parts of the trunk, and leave in place branches on the outcurved parts of the trunk. Encourage the branches to droop downward slightly by attaching weights

or cables staked to the ground. Prune to create a rounded, cloud-shaped head of foliage at the end of each branch (see the accompanying illustration).

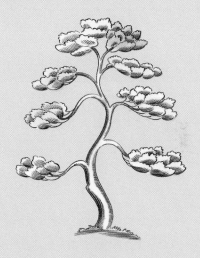

Trees in Japanese-style gardens are meticulously pruned into idealized forms. One technique, cloud pruning, creates rounded, cloudlike clumps of foliage at the ends of well-spaced branches. Prune shrubs into smooth, hemispherical shapes. Try to avoid turning them into buns or globes.

pine (*P. sylvestris*), white pine (*P. strobus*), and shore pine (*P. contorta* var. *contorta*). Look for interesting, irregular shapes with a rugged, windblown appearance. Evergreens will probably require special pruning to bring out their best characteristics (see "Pruning Tips" on page 33 for more information).

Different trees work best in different locations. For instance, weeping trees are often planted near water to reinforce the feeling of the water's flow. Generally, small to medium-size trees work best in oriental gardens, although large gardens will include some taller trees. Japanese cherries are appropriate because they offer spring flowers, shade in summer, and colorful fall foliage. Japanese maples also have multiseason interest. Plums, apricots, crabapples, dogwoods, and willows are other good choices.

Under these trees, you can carpet the earth with ferns, mosses, or groundcovers. Native wildflowers and other perennials can play a role, too, if you use them sparingly for accents.

Bamboo provides a quintessential oriental look, but many bamboos spread aggressively and are hard to contain. Unless you are willing to do battle, plant your bamboos in large pots.

Ornamental grasses bring movement and sound to the garden as their stems sway and rustle in the breeze. Some of them, such as the popular *Miscanthus sinensis*, can spread to the point of being invasive, so find out if the grass you choose is problematic in your area before you plant it.

Keep the garden neat and clean at all times. Remove any dead or damaged growth when you notice it, and keep the weeds pulled. Remember, the garden is an idealization of nature.

The Naturalistic Garden

Many houses in rural areas or at the edges of the suburbs are blessed with beautiful views of unspoiled countryside, or even farther-off natural areas. You might see woodlands or meadows from your backyard, or glimpse a distant mountain peak from the living room window. Naturalistic gardens often work quite well in such settings. If the style of your garden echoes the look of the surrounding (or distant but visible) landscape, your garden will look like it belongs there. It will help to anchor your house in the landscape and give it a feeling of place.

Like Japanese-style gardens, naturalistic gardens are inspired by nature. But naturalistic gardens are more literal renderings of natural environments, suggesting more directly the look of woodlands, deserts, seashores, meadows, prairies, bogs, or rocky mountainsides. Naturalistic garden styles often tie into geographic regions—prairies, for example, are indigenous to the midwestern United States. Plantings in naturalistic gardens mimic what exists in nature. In designing the garden, you will create a community of plants—an ecosystem, although an edited one.

Most naturalistic gardens combine native plants with nonnatives from similar habitats in other parts of the country or the world. A woodland garden, for instance, has tall canopy trees, understory trees and shrubs, herbaceous foliage and flowering plants, and low groundcovers, just like a natural forest. But the woodland garden is tamed. Improved cultivars grow alongside wildflowers, and undesirables like poison

ivy and oriental bittersweet are nowhere to be found. Instead of dense, twiggy brush, the woodland garden's understory contains organized plantings of spicebush, rhododendrons, and other attractive shrubs. Naturalistic gardens are not splashy and showy like traditional perennial borders; their beauty is quieter. But they look "right" for the region and are easier to care for.

Naturalistic gardens look good in a variety of situations. Contemporary houses are often well served by naturalistic landscapes, as are log homes, rustic

This meadow garden combines native wildflowers, including golden black-eyed Susans (*Rudbeckia*) and purple-pink coneflowers (*Echinacea*), with grasses.

cabins, and houses in a distinct regional vernacular, such as stone farmhouses in Pennsylvania, clapboard saltboxes in New England, and adobe homes in New Mexico. The type of naturalistic garden you can create will depend upon the growing conditions on your property. A woodland garden would be ideal for a shady property in the Northeast, for example, while a prairie garden would work well on a sunny midwestern lot.

If you are looking for inspiration in designing a naturalistic garden, try to spend some time in the kind of natural environment that's like the landscape you want to have. Hike through the woods and learn what grows there. Observe how the plants grow together in the desert. Explore the seashore. Read about the natural history of your area.

If you want a truly regional naturalistic garden, grow native plants. Natives will be naturally suited to your local growing conditions and they will never look out of place. They will be better able than imported plants to tolerate extremes of cold, heat, drought, or moisture that are likely to occur in your area. They will also suffer less damage from pests and diseases. Many native plants are quite beautiful, and increasing numbers of them are becoming available from reputable nurseries. Seek out local or regional growers to find native plants for your area. Be sure to ask whether the plants have been propagated and grown by the nursery. Some native plants on the market are illegally collected from the wild and will become endangered if too many are removed from natural habitat areas, which are shrinking everywhere. Wild collection is a problem in some southwestern desert areas, for example, where slow-growing cacti are stolen from the wild and sold.

Naturalistic gardens should look as "un-gardeny" as possible. You will want to add paths for access to the plants, and you can also encourage wildlife in the garden. Include bird feeders and water sources, and grow some plants attractive to birds, bees, and butterflies. Use natural materials to surface walkways. It's best to develop your naturalistic garden gradually. Start with a basic framework of trees and shrubs, then add more plants and other elements as you become more familiar with the ecosystem.

Once established, naturalistic gardens require less maintenance than conventional beds and borders. Let plants assume their natural forms. Don't bother to deadhead spent flowers unless you really find them unsightly. Some will produce seeds that birds will eat, and others will self-sow to produce new generations of plants. Don't prune trees and shrubs except to remove dead or damaged growth.

The Woodland Garden

If you have mature shade trees in your yard, a woodland garden could be a good choice. The ideal site for a woodland garden is under trees that cast dappled shade, but work with what you have. It's not a good idea to cut down healthy, big trees to let in more light. You could remove some low branches and have an arborist selectively thin branches higher up, but further intervention could affect the woodland ecosystem. The most difficult site for a woodland garden would be under mature conifers, which cast very dense shade year-round. In such a location, only the most shade-tolerant groundcovers may grow.

To understand the woodland environment, think in layers, both above and below ground. Plants in a woodland grow in several different layers, which you will need to copy in your garden. The topmost layer is called the canopy, and it is made up of the crowns of the tallest trees. The kinds of trees in the canopy, their forms and the density of their foliage, and how close together they grow determine the amount of light reaching the lower layers of vegetation. The next layer in the woodland is the understory, made up of smaller trees, shrubs, and young saplings.

THE WOODLAND GARDEN

You'll find the following elements in a woodland garden:

- Layered plants: canopy trees, understory, shade-tolerant herbaceous flowers and foliage, groundcovers

- Humusy soil

- Plants that assume natural forms

- Winding paths surfaced with shredded leaves, wood chips, or other natural materials

Below the understory are herbaceous plants—wildflowers, ferns, perennials, and annuals. The soil is carpeted with spreading and trailing groundcovers and mosses.

There are also layers in the ground. The forest floor is covered by several inches of loose, humusy soil that is rich in organic matter from leaves that fall from the trees each autumn and decompose on the ground. Below this layer of loose soil is a layer of denser soil, and below that lies the subsoil. If your property lacks the loose, humusy top layer, bring in 4 to 8 inches of good topsoil mixed with generous amounts of compost before you do any planting. If your native soil is sandy or heavy clay, adding organic materials will improve its texture and make it more hospitable to a wider variety of plants.

If you are not in a hurry, you can improve the soil over the course of a year, or even two, by spreading a few inches of shredded leaves over the ground and letting them decompose. Many municipalities have shredded or unshredded leaves available free for the asking after annual leaf collections. Keeping the leaves damp will hasten the decomposition process. You can also mix them with compost or soil to introduce microbes that will help decay.

The soil in woodlands is generally acidic, except where the underlying bedrock is limestone, and most of the plants suited to woodland gardens grow best in soil with a mildly acidic pH. Usually, soil pH is more acidic where rainfall is abundant. Decomposing leaves and pine needles also make for acidic soil.

Soils in the eastern part of the United States are usually acidic, and those in the western and mid-

DIGGING DEEPER

TYPES OF SHADE

Not all shade gardens are the same as shade varies greatly in quality and duration. Shade patterns shift with the seasons and time of day as the sun moves across the sky. Morning shade is cooler than afternoon shade. Many plants appreciate some afternoon shade in summer, especially in southern climates where the sun is intense. Study the type of shade on your property when planning a woodland garden. Here are descriptions of different kinds of shade.

Partial shade, semishade: A site that receives sun for 2 to 6 hours a day. The location may be sunny in either morning or afternoon, with shade the rest of the day, or it may have lightly dappled shade, with patches of sun on the ground all day.

Light shade, thin shade: A bright, airy location that may receive an hour or two of sun a day. Light shade is found under young leaves that let a good amount of light reach the ground.

Medium shade, half-shade, high shade: A location that may receive some sun early or late in the day but is shady at midday. Found under trees with a somewhat open canopy and branches high above the ground (20 feet or more), or where there is reflected sunlight.

Full shade: A place under mature deciduous trees with large leaves and a dense canopy, where no sunlight directly strikes the ground.

Deep shade, heavy shade: The most difficult environment for plants: cool and dim, constantly shadowed by tall evergreens, a nearby building, or dense forest.

western parts of the country tend to be neutral or alkaline. Shade-tolerant plants that will grow in nonacid soils include arrowwood and cranberry viburnums, red-twig dogwood, and hellebores.

If you will be taming an existing woodland to make your garden, you will need to remove some vegetation to allow access and make room for desirable plants. Dig up most of the small saplings, and pull out tangled, dense undergrowth and weeds. Getting rid of invasives such as bittersweet and poison ivy will require sustained vigilance until they stop reappearing. Pull up bittersweet wherever you see it. Poison ivy can be pulled, too, if you wear rubber gloves and long sleeves, or you can keep cutting it down as soon as it pops up and it will eventually disappear.

If you wish to thin some branches from the canopy, hire a certified arborist to do the work.

When choosing plants for a woodland garden, make sure that you understand the kind of shade you have to work with (see "Types of Shade" on page 37). Also consider plant growth habits and blooming times.

Design Tips

When choosing plants for the woodland garden, try to include some white-flowered perennials and golden- or variegated-leaved perennials or shrubs to bring light into the dimness. A group of yellow flowers can look like a shaft of sunlight when glimpsed through the trees.

Many woodland wildflowers bloom in spring before the deciduous trees leaf out, and quite a few are ephemerals that go dormant after they bloom. Be sure to include some plants for summer bloom and also for autumn color. In addition to fiery autumn foliage, you can have fall and winter color from shrubs and groundcovers that produce lots of bright berries.

Add mystery: If you want to make a small woodland garden seem bigger, lay out winding paths and position some of the understory plants to screen parts of the garden from view. Visitors will be drawn to stroll the paths and explore parts of the garden they can't see. When you can't see the entire garden at once, it creates intrigue and mystery, and the garden feels more spacious than it is.

Another consideration in choosing plants is their root systems. Deep-rooted trees are easier to plant under than shallow-rooted trees. In a natural forest, plants with different rooting patterns grow close together, making efficient use of underground space. Analyzing rooting patterns is more work than most home gardeners will want to do, but at least find out about the root systems of existing trees, and try to choose deep-rooted trees if you are planting new specimens. Besides being easier to work around, deep-rooted trees will not compete with shallower-rooted shrubs, ferns, and flowers for space, water, and nutrients.

Trees with small leaves and branches high above the ground cast lighter, more dappled shade than large-leaved shade trees such as Norway maple. If you will be planting new trees, birches, oaks, and honey locust are some good candidates. (See "Good Trees for a Woodland Garden" on page 39 for more possibilities.)

Paths wind through wild sweet William (*Phlox divaricata*) and maidenhair fern (*Adiantum capillus-veneris*) in a woodland garden.

Planting and Care Tips

When planting under trees, dig holes between large, shallow roots instead of chopping out pieces of the roots to make planting spots. In more open areas, dig planting holes only as deep as the plant's rootball so the plant will sit at the same depth it was growing at the nursery. You can plant trees and shrubs with the top of the rootball slightly above ground level

GOOD TREES FOR A WOODLAND GARDEN

These beautiful trees are all good choices for woodland gardens. Some offer the bonus of pretty flowers; others sport colored leaves or attractive bark.

Acer ginnala, Amur maple

A. griseum, paperbark maple

A. palmatum, Japanese maple

Betula spp., birches

Cercis canadensis, redbud

Cladrastis lutea, yellowwood

Cornus kousa, Chinese dogwood

C. xrutgersensis, hybrid dogwood

Gleditsia triacanthos var. *inermis,* honey locust

Halesia carolina, Carolina silverbell

Liquidambar styraciflua, sweet gum

Magnolia spp., magnolias

Metasequoia glyptostroboides, dawn redwood

Quercus spp., oaks

Sorbus spp., mountain ashes

Stewartia pseudocamellia, Japanese stewartia

Styrax japonicus, Japanese snowbell

TREES NOT SO GOOD IN A WOODLAND GARDEN

These trees have shallow or wide-ranging roots that will compete with garden plants for moisture and nutrients.

Acer negundo, box elder

A. platanoides, Norway maple

A. saccharinum, silver maple

A. saccharum, sugar maple

Aesculus spp., horse chestnuts

Fagus spp., beeches

Juglans nigra, black walnut

Liriodendron tulipifera, tulip tree

Pinus strobus, white pine

Platanus spp., sycamores

Ulmus spp., elms

(mulch well to conserve moisture) to allow for settling. Plant in clumps for the most natural look, and allow enough space for plants to mature to their full width without crowding.

After the plants are in place, try to disturb the soil as little as possible. Don't till or cultivate. Pull weeds by hand until the groundcovers fill in. Mulch with an inch or so of shredded leaves or compost to conserve soil moisture and protect new roots. If no rain falls, water if the soil dries out while plants are establishing themselves during the first few weeks. You'll also need to water new trees during drought periods throughout their first year in the garden.

When the autumn leaves fall, you can simply leave them in place. If you prefer a neater look, rake up the leaves and shred them, then spread them back on the garden as mulch. Allowing the leaves to decompose in the soil will probably eliminate any need for future fertilizing.

Spread any mulch only 3 or 4 inches deep. A deeper layer of mulch will encourage tree and shrub roots to grow up into it, and those shallow roots would be vulnerable during times of drought or intense heat. Don't bring mulch right up to the bases of trees and shrubs, and don't bury the crowns of herbaceous plants. Mulch can trap moisture that can rot bark and plant crowns, and it can also provide winter shelter for rodents that might gnaw on tree bark and cause damage.

Helleborus 'Tom Wilson' blooms in spring in woodland gardens.

Wild sweet William (*Phlox divaricata*) bears lavender-blue flowers in spring.

Meadow and Prairie Gardens

In the wild, meadows and prairies are grasslands with no trees or sizable shrubs. Meadows are found where land that was once cleared, usually for farming, has been left to revegetate on its own. Natural meadows are temporary; in time, trees and shrubs will start to grow there, and eventually the meadow will become a forest. Meadows can be moist or dry, but they are almost always sunny places because there are no trees to cast shade.

Prairies are endemic to the flat plains of the midwestern United States and Canada, where buffalo once roamed. Plants native to prairies are able to tolerate cold winters and hot, dry summers. Prairies are a mix of wildflowers and grasses, but the plant communities vary with the amount of rain that typically falls in the region. Tallgrass prairies, which are home to taller-growing grasses such as big bluestem (*Andropogon gerardii*) and switch grass (*Panicum virgatum*), get more moisture, which allows the plants to grow taller. Shortgrass prairies are drier, and they host shorter grasses such as side-oats grama (*Bouteloua curtipendula*) and buffalo grass (*Buchloe dactyloides*). Both kinds of prairies include both cool-season and warm-season grasses.

In nature, prairies were kept free of trees by periodic fires started by lightning strikes. The fires destroyed trees and shrubs before they could become well established, but the seeds of the grasses and wildflowers were able to survive the flames and germinate with the spring rains.

MEADOW AND PRAIRIE GARDENS

The following are features of meadow and prairie gardens:

- Mix of grasses mowed just once a year

- Regional, native annual and perennial wildflowers

- Paths mowed through plantings

- Boundaries fenced or mowed so that plantings look like a garden

- Flat, treeless, and sunny

If you have a relatively flat, sunny expanse—a former farm field, perhaps, or a vacant lot—a meadow or prairie garden might provide a nice complement to your house, integrating the building into its setting with plants native to or suited to your region. In fact, these kinds of gardens work best with regional plants that are native to or naturalized in your area. Meadows and prairies take some work to become established, but once they settle in, you won't have to do much more than mow them once a year (or, if your municipality allows it, burn off the plants).

Establish the Garden

The best site for a meadow or prairie garden is open, flat or gently sloping, and receives at least 8 hours of full, unobstructed sunlight a day. Average soil is best; rich soil will only encourage more weeds to grow.

If you will be creating the garden in an area that is now a lawn, it helps to plan ahead. If you can wait a couple of years to plant the garden, stop fertilizing the lawn and just mow it for a year to allow extra nutrients that have built up in the soil to be used up (they'd help weeds more than your meadow or prairie plants). Then, cover the lawn with a heavy sheet of black plastic or several layers of newspaper for a year to smother the sod. Leaving the plastic in place for an entire year should get rid of both cool-season and warm-season grasses. To get the job done more quickly, skip the plastic and rent a sod cutter.

Choose Plants for Meadow and Prairie Gardens

Seek out plants that are suited to your climate and soil type, and aim to have flowers blooming throughout the growing season. Meadow and prairie

flowers suited to the East and Midwest are largely perennials, but in the Southwest many of the best natives are annuals or short-lived perennials, such as Texas bluebonnet (*Lupinus texensis*), that don't, as a rule, do well in other regions. Indian paintbrush (*Castilleja parviflora*) is another good example of a southwestern wildflower that is nearly impossible to grow outside its native region.

Including annuals in the garden will ensure plenty of color in the first year, when perennials have not yet reached blooming size. You may need to reseed with annuals for the first 2 or 3 years as the perennials become established, or else the young perennials will be overrun by weeds.

To learn more about plants that would be appropriate for your area, observe what grows wild in undeveloped places and along roadsides. A good guidebook can help you determine which of these are native and noninvasive. (See "Recommended

---

MAINTAINING A MEADOW OR PRAIRIE

To keep a meadow from following its natural tendency to progress toward becoming a forest, you need to prevent woody plants and vigorous weeds from becoming established in the garden. Annual mowing is one useful technique for meadow management. To mow a meadow or prairie, set the mower blades to high to avoid harming plant crowns, and mow in fall, the second year after you plant the meadow. Before

mowing, you may wish to collect seedheads from plants you'd like to spread in the garden, and sow the seeds after mowing or save them for spring planting. Rake up the clippings after mowing the garden.

You may also need to go into the garden occasionally through the growing season and pull or dig out troublesome weeds to keep them from colonizing the planting.

Reading" on page 253.) If you find other meadow or prairie gardens locally, ask the gardeners/home-owners which plants work well for them. You could also contact your local Cooperative Extension office for more information.

Indian grass (*Sorghastrum nutans*) is a lovely native grass for prairie gardens.

An improved form of Joe Pye weed (*Eupatorium maculatum* 'Gateway') blooms in late summer in meadow gardens.

Buy Good Seeds

Most meadow and prairie gardens are started from seed. Purchasing enough plants to cover a large area becomes expensive, although if your meadow will be quite small you could start with plants. If at all possible, buy plants from local growers—they will be better adapted to local conditions than plants grown in other places. Local nurseries can tell you whether the plants they sell are from local sources. Otherwise, look for a regional seed mix from a good mail-order nursery, such as the ones listed in "Resources" on page 255. You want to find a nursery that propagates its own seeds or plants rather than collecting from the wild. Also be aware that "meadow-in-a-can" mixes may contain a large proportion of annuals. Your meadow will have lots of color the first season, but you may be left wondering why your pretty meadow has become a weed patch the next year. Inexpensive seed mixes are also more likely to contain less-desirable, weedier species than high-quality blends.

Pull the Weeds

Speaking of weeds, you will need to remove them during the garden's first few years, until the perennials become well established (most of them need 3 years to bloom from seed). Otherwise, the more aggressive weeds will crowd out the young perennials. A shortcut to keep the weeds under control is to mow the meadow to a height of 6 inches, at least in the first year. It will keep the tall weeds from going to seed but shouldn't hurt the still-small perennials.

If your seed mix contained annuals that are likely to self-sow, learn what their seedlings look like by observing carefully during the garden's first season so you don't pull up annual seedlings in subsequent years. Once the meadow or prairie becomes established, you will need to weed only occasionally to remove large, unattractive invaders or tree seedlings that come up.

Mow Paths

To really enjoy your garden, mow some paths through it, and keep them mowed. Mowing around the perimeter of your meadow or prairie will keep it looking well tended and more like a garden, and should help to appease any neighbors who object to your garden.

Once your meadow or prairie becomes established, it will become a largely self-sufficient community of wildflowers, grasses, and wildlife. Birds and butterflies, crickets and katydids, even small animals will visit your garden—especially if you provide sources of water for them.

The Rock Garden

A rock garden is often ideal in a place where conventional beds and borders would be difficult to create and maintain—on a sloping lot, for instance, where the soil is already stony, where an ancient glacier deposited some large boulders, at a high elevation where the summer sun is intense and winters are quite cold, or in a woodland with rock ledges or outcrops. A rock garden also affords a perfect opportunity for plant fanatics to indulge their appetites for beautifully gemlike or interestingly shaped specimens in a small space. The term "rock garden" may conjure up for you images of windswept mountainsides, but rock gardens can look quite refined, despite their stony underpinnings. Many—though certainly not all—rock garden plants are native to the mountainous regions of the world. Most of them are compact in size and, given just the right conditions, extremely tough.

A rock garden's design is built on the cultural needs of the plants growing in it. A true rock garden is not just a garden with some artfully placed rocks set into it. Instead, the rock garden aims to recreate, or more accurately, to evoke the look and feeling of a particular habitat rather than being a purely aesthetic mix of forms and colors.

Types of Rock Gardens

Here are the basic features of some different kinds of rock gardens.

Alpine meadow. If you read *Heidi* as a child, you probably carry inside you a mental image of a mountain hillside covered with soft grass and spangled

A rocky slope is an ideal location for a rock garden.

with wildflowers, where little goats graze happily. True alpine meadows are found in nature at high elevations, between alpine forests of spruce and fir and the higher, colder, more barren zones closer to mountain peaks. Alpine meadows are open, treeless areas of small grasses and sedges mixed with flowering plants. You can create your own version of an alpine meadow in an open area that is level or gently sloped by planting a mix of grasses and small bulbs such as crocus, small-flowered narcissus such as *Narcissus cyclamineus* and *N. bulbocodium*, and little irises such as *Iris reticulata* and *I. cristata.* The effect works best if the "meadow" lies next to a rocky outcrop or some large boulders that give it a boundary and context.

Rock outcrops, boulders, and crevices. Outcrops are simply large rock formations that jut out of the ground. You can tuck plants into the soil around the base of such rocks, in pockets of soil in depressions in the rock, or in crevices in the rock (small spaces that go all the way through the rock to the ground). European rock gardeners like to pile up smaller rocks in order to create lots of crevices between them that can be filled with soil and planted. Crevice plants are generally accustomed to having their heads in the sun and their roots in the cooler, moister spaces between stones.

Dry stone walls. Dry stone walls have become wildly popular in the northeastern United States, where I live. When they are planted, they become charming little gardens in themselves, as well as space dividers or retainers for slopes. Walls can be constructed with small, soil-filled pockets for planting in between the stones, or you can stuff soil mix into

Saponaria is an excellent plant for rock gardens and stone walls. Like other rock garden plants, it needs lots of sun and excellent drainage.

gaps between stones. As plants grow, their roots will anchor the soil, but in the beginning you will need to water very carefully to avoid washing away the soil. In time, the plants will spill out of the soil pockets and cascade over the stonework. See "Plants for Walls and Crevices" on page 46 for some suggestions for planting in a dry stone wall.

Screes. A natural scree is a sloping area at the base of a cliff or a steep hillside that is covered with loose stones carried there by erosion or landslides. In the garden, a scree bed is simply a raised bed filled with a gravelly soil mix. This kind of bed will have the kind of excellent free drainage that is essential for the survival of so many rock garden plants. If you live in a humid, rainy climate, a scree bed is probably the best kind of rock garden to have.

A raised bed is simply a garden bed that's created on top of the existing soil. You can build sides for the bed of stone, brick, or wood to contain the soil mix. Position these beds where you would otherwise put a bed or border in the ground: right next

THE ROCK GARDEN

Here are some common characteristics of rock gardens.

- Well-drained, rocky environment: boulders, crevices, dry stone walls, scree beds, alpine meadows, rocky woodland

- Often on sloping ground

- Work well in well-drained soil and low humidity

- Plants that need lots of sun

- Paths surfaced with stone

- Small, drought-tolerant plants

to the house, along a driveway or walkway, off a deck or patio. Fill your bed or beds with a blend of 4 parts gravel in mixed sizes, ½ part crumbled compost, and ½ part good, loamy soil.

Rocky woodland. More and more housing lots are being carved out of forested areas these days, as our suburbs stretch ever farther from our city centers. That means an increasing number of homeowners find themselves faced with the need to create a landscape where there's plenty of shade, and sometimes rocks. A rocky woodland is not a rock garden in the traditional sense. The plants grown there are woodland wildflowers and ferns, rather than the customary alpines and sun lovers.

But if you have big rocks in your backyard, it's easier to work with them than to move them. A woodland rock garden offers an interesting alternative for a shady site. This kind of garden will be cool and green, lusher than most rock gardens, and enticing on a hot summer day.

Site Considerations

For the most part, rock gardens work best in dry climates, where humidity is low and the soil is loose and gravelly. Places where the soil is heavy clay and summer air is often torrid—the southeastern United

PLANT FINDER

PLANTS FOR WALLS AND CREVICES

These small plants like good drainage and plenty of sun. Tuck them into pockets of soil in a dry-laid stone wall, or in crevices in or between large rocks.

Anacyclus pyrethrum var. *depressus*, Mount Atlas daisy

Arabis caucasica, wall rock cress

A. procurrens, running rock cress

Armeria juniperifolia (A. caespitosa), sea pink

Aubrieta x*cultorum*, purple rock cress

Aurinia saxatilis, basket-of-gold

Campanula carpatica, Carpathian harebell

C. cochleariifolia, fairies' thimbles

C. portenschlagiana, Dalmatian bellflower

Erinus alpinus, alpine liverwort

Geranium sanguineum var. *striatum*, Lancaster geranium

Gypsophila repens, creeping baby's breath

Iberis sempervirens, perennial candytuft

Laurentia fluviatilis, blue star creeper

Lewisia cotyledon, L. 'Cotyledon Hybrids'

Mentha requienii, Corsican mint

Phlox subulata, mountain pink

Saponaria ocymoides, soapwort

Saxifraga callosa, limestone saxifrage

S. cochlearis, snail saxifrage

S. longifolia, Pyrenean saxifrage

S. paniculata, livelong saxifrage

Sedum acre, golden carpet sedum

S. kamtschaticum, Kamschatka or Russian stonecrop

S. spathulifolium, Pacific or broadleaf stonecrop

States, for example—can be challenging for rock garden plants. That doesn't mean you can't succeed there, but it probably does mean that you will have to experiment to find the plants that will fare best in your conditions. And creating the right kind of soil mix for them to grow in will also be key to success.

Look past the borders of your property when choosing a site for your rock garden. That doesn't mean you should put the garden in your neighbor's yard, but it's ideal when the surrounding landscape is compatible with the style of your garden. If you have a view of distant mountains, try to site your garden to take advantage of the view, and use the mountains as a backdrop. If a rocky ledge or large boulders adorn your property, try to build the garden around them rather than moving them. A rock garden on a half-acre lot in town is going to look artificial, at least up to a point. But a screen of evergreen trees along the property line can provide a sense of enclosure that allows you to create your own little world.

A location in full sun is best for most kinds of rock gardens in cooler northern climates and coastal areas where the sun is less intense. In the arid West and Southwest, some afternoon shade is usually beneficial. When assessing sun/shade patterns in your prospective garden spot, pay attention to shade cast by large rocks and by walls. Plants growing on the north side must be able to tolerate the cool, shady conditions they will find there. Around the south side of the rock, the hotter, sunnier microclimate will call for different plants.

Paths Are Important

Paths are a necessary part of the rock garden. You must never step on the growing beds, or you will compact the soil and restrict the drainage capacity that is so critical for the health of rock garden plants. To surface a path through your rock garden, choose gravel or paving stones that are the same type as, or similar to, your other stone garden features (such as boulders or walls). In a woodland rock garden, you could instead use wood rounds, bark mulch, or wood chips to cover paths.

Soil

The one element of a rock garden that is crucial for success, above all others, is the right kind of soil. Rock garden plants must have excellent drainage if they are going to thrive. In wet, heavy, or compacted soil, they will rot. The soil must be loose, porous, and well aerated. When blending your soil mix, gauge the proportions of the components on the wettest part of the year where you live. You can always water if you have to during a dry summer, but you can't siphon away excess water in winter or spring. Make sure the soil will drain well during the wettest season.

HOW TO DO IT

TIPS FOR WORKING WITH ROCKS

■ Large rocks are better than small ones. They require heavy equipment if you want to move them, but they are easier to work with visually. It's easier to achieve a naturalistic look with a few large rocks than with a lot of smaller ones.

■ Rocks in a garden should all look similar to one another. Don't mix limestone with granite with sandstone. You want the rocks to look as if they all came from the same underlying bedrock.

■ Local stone, if you can get it, is ideal. It will naturally look right in your area.

■ Set the rocks into, not on top of, the ground. Bury the base of the rock to its widest point, to anchor it securely and achieve a natural look.

■ Gravel has a multitude of uses. Blend pea gravel into soil mixes, and use mixed gravel in scree beds. Using a gravel mulch after you've planted your garden reduces maintenance—it prevents soil from eroding or compacting, keeps dirt from splashing up onto plants during rain (which could cause rot), and keeps down weeds.

See "Soil Mixes for Rock Gardens" below for some good soil blends. In addition, here are some tips for customizing the soil mix to suit your conditions.

If your soil is low in phosphorus (a soil test will show you), add some rock phosphate to the soil.

HOW TO DO IT

SOIL MIXES FOR ROCK GARDENS

Here are two recipes for rock garden soils. Use the scree bed mix for plants that need absolutely perfect drainage.

Basic Soil Mix

1 part gravel or coarse sand

1 part crumbled compost

1 part topsoil or loam

Mix together well.

Scree Bed Mix

4 parts gravel in mixed sizes

½ part garden loam

½ part crumbled compost

Mix together well.

If the pH is acidic, add ground limestone periodically to raise the pH to near neutral.

If your climate is rainy or humid, increase the proportion of gravel or sand, and decrease the proportion of soil and compost in the mix.

If you plan to create an alpine meadow, you will probably need to do some special soil preparation work. Begin by removing any existing sod (follow the procedures described for meadow gardens on page 42). When the sod is gone, pull out any stones or roots left in the ground, and break up clods and clumps of soil. If the soil is clayey or very sandy, work in some compost or other organic matter. Rake well to create a fine texture. Then, spread a thin layer of soil mix on top, and work it into the top of the existing soil. Finally, spread several inches of soil mix over that, and do not mix it in.

Choosing Plants for a Rock Garden

When the rocks and paths are in place and you've prepared the soil, it's time to plant. Use larger plants—dwarf evergreens and small shrubs—to reinforce the basic structure provided by the rock features and paths. Choose these larger plants for their form and texture; bloom is ephemeral and is a secondary consideration. For the greatest visual impact, plant them in groups at the back of the garden, along the sides, and in the foreground to create a feeling of greater depth. Use plants to enhance large rocks or outcrops. For example, placing a low mounding or spreading shrub on top of an outcrop will emphasize the horizontal line, while a narrow, upright shrub would fight the line of the rock and stick out like a lonely sentinel

Basket-of-gold (*Aurinia saxatilis*) brings its bright yellow flowers to spring rock gardens.

Deutzia crenata var. *nakaiana* 'Nikko' is a dwarf shrub that works well in rock gardens.

in the landscape. On the other hand, planting that same upright shrub in front of the outcrop would provide a contrasting line that is visually pleasing.

Remember when placing structural plants that they will grow over time, and it's important to allow room unless you want to redo the garden every several years. Even dwarf evergreens grow, however slowly. Don't plant too many of them or too close together, or the garden will get crowded after a while.

When the structural plants are in place, you can add smaller perennials, bulbs, and groundcovers. Choose these plants according to the growing conditions in particular spots of your garden. Tuck crevice plants into rock crevices and walls. Plant alpines in scree beds. In an alpine meadow, set small bulbs, grasses, and sedges. In a rocky woodland, plant small ferns and shade-loving wildflowers. For the most authentic look, put larger plants in lower parts of the garden and around the bases of large rocks, where soil washed down by rain would tend to accumulate in the kind of natural environment your garden seeks to emulate. These larger plants might include *Alchemilla, Aurinia, Bergenia, Heuchera,* and even dwarf bearded iris cultivars. Around and in front of the larger plants, in the foreground of the garden, place smaller flowers such as *Campanula carpatica,* small bulbs, and mat-forming groundcovers such as thyme or mountain pinks (*Phlox subulata*).

The Desert Garden

Deserts are places that get little rainfall. They are often windy places where the sun blazes in the sky and summer days are extremely hot. The soil might be sandy or it might be gravelly, but it usually drains quickly, and what little rain does fall doesn't stay long in the soil. Certain times of year bring fierce storms that may drop a lot of rain, even floods, but the water drains away quickly. The low rainfall allows salts to build up in the soil—they do not leach away—and consequently, desert soils tend to be alkaline, some

extremely so. The low humidity allows for sharp temperature swings; while days can be hot, nights can be cold, especially at higher elevations. The desert is a tough place for plants and people to survive. But as more people gravitate to the Sun Belt regions of the United States, more and more houses are being built in desert areas made habitable by irrigation and air conditioning.

Plants that survive in the desert without irrigation have adapted to the particular conditions found there and don't grow well in wetter, more humid environments. Above all, desert plants have to be able to tolerate drought. They have evolved special ways to store water, in the sap of thick, succulent stems and fleshy leaves. Many have long taproots that dive deep into the soil to access moisture down below (this makes them difficult to transplant). Many plants have waxy coatings that slow transpiration. Leaves are often small, another means of reducing transpiration, and some plants shed their leaves in dry seasons. Cactus spines and hairs on the leaves of other plants trap drops of dew and rain, and they also cast shade on the leaves. If those hairy leaves are silver, they also reflect some light, and thus heat, off the plants. Aromatic plants such as santolina and lavender contain volatile oils in their leaves that in very hot weather form a halo of fine droplets around the plant that cuts the glare of the sun.

Most desert plants grow slowly, so they don't require large amounts of water to fuel their growth. They wait to bloom until enough rain falls—some plants can wait years. During the wet season, the desert bursts into bloom—a tapestry of color so rich you have to see it to believe it's possible. When the

This cactus, *Mammillaria zeilmanniana*, produces a ring of red-violet, pink, or white flowers in summer.

This bright-flowered plant is an aloe, from a genus of succulents that store moisture in their fleshy leaves.

THE DESERT GARDEN

Here is a list of elements to include in your desert garden:

- Succulents, cacti, and other drought-tolerant plants

- Compositions of plant form

- Well-drained soil

- Shade provided by regional trees or structures

- Minimum of pavement; paths surfaced with loose gravel or other porous material

- Gravel mulch

rains are over, the flowers disappear and the desert floor turns brown or gray once more.

With irrigation, you can grow lots of plants that would never survive in the desert under natural conditions. You can grow roses or classic English perennials, and plenty of people do. But a landscape of natives and other desert plants can provide a real sense of place, and it can make your house look at home in its surroundings. And it allows you to conserve that most precious of resources in an arid climate: water. Also, desert plants that are naturally suited to your growing conditions will be far easier to maintain than exotics from other kinds of climates, and they'll probably last longer.

Design Tips

Sources of shade and protection from wind are welcome elements in desert gardens. There aren't a lot of shade trees to choose from for a desert garden, but you can make good use of lattice screens, arbors and pergolas, and even lath houses. If you decide to incorporate strategically placed walls or fences to serve as windbreaks, make sure they are of an open construction that allows air to pass through. Solid barriers will create odd wind patterns, drafts, and eddies that could be as damaging to plants as the unobstructed wind.

Deer and rabbits can be problematic, especially if you live outside of town, and you may need fencing to keep them out.

It's best to keep any necessary paved surfaces as small as is feasible so that the ground can soak up the maximum amount of rain when it falls. Runoff water would just be wasted. Use gravel, pebbles, or other porous surfaces on walkways and driveways if you can to permit maximum water absorption.

When choosing plants for your landscape, consider their forms carefully. The bold forms of cacti can be difficult to blend with other kinds of plants. Placing cacti in groups instead of dotting them individually about the garden will help. You might even want to devote a separate bed or area to cacti and other succulents. Tall, columnar cacti look best in the back of the garden, with lower round and barrel-shaped species in front. You will undoubtedly want to include at least some cacti in your landscape because they are so showy when they bloom. Cactus blossoms are often large in proportion to the size of the plant, with satiny, glossy, or diaphanous petals in warm, bright colors.

See "Plants for Desert Gardens" on page 248 for some plants to consider including in your garden. Be sure that you have a good understanding of your climate when choosing plants. Desert conditions vary widely with location and elevation. If you live where the temperature usually stays above 50°F, you can grow practically any desert plant. But plants that would be hardy in such a mild climate at a low elevation might not survive in a high desert garden, where temperatures dip much lower in winter. Local nurseries and garden clubs can be good sources of information on plants that grow well in your area.

Planting and Maintenance Tips

The most important consideration in a desert garden is drainage. Good drainage is critical for the success of desert plants. Some of the hardier plants, such as yuccas, can tolerate some cold, but they can't withstand cold and wet conditions—they'll rot. If your soil has an underlying layer of hardpan or if the subsoil is just heavy, it would probably be best to make raised beds for the garden. Make the beds a foot high and spread a 3- to 4-inch layer of gravel on the bottom to provide drainage before filling them with soil. If the soil is very alkaline, you may need to flood the soil with clear water that is not too soft to flush out the accumulated salts before planting, and perhaps periodically thereafter as well. High levels of mineral salts that build up in the soil can be toxic to plants.

When you do plant, set plants at the same depth they were growing in the nursery pot. Mulch with a layer of fine gravel to conserve moisture. Water every few days after planting to help plants settle in. As the plants grow, water only when the soil is dry. It's best to water early or late in the day, when the strong rays of the sun will not be focused through water droplets and cause burned spots on the leaves. Many plants go dormant in winter; at that time, water only enough to keep them from shrivelling.

CHAPTER 2

[Color-Coordinating House and Garden]

When you've decided on a stylistic direction for your garden and laid out basic structural plans for the locations, shapes, and dimensions of beds, borders, and other plantings, it's time to consider color. In this chapter, we'll look at how to work with color and how to relate the colors of the garden to the colors of the house exterior.

There are all sorts of ways to coordinate the colors in your garden with the colors you choose for both the exterior and interior of your house. You can use colors to echo, or repeat, from house to garden, or to harmonize with one another. Or, you can juxtapose colors that contrast and intensify when you place them in proximity to each other.

◄ Flaming fall foliage in this garden echoes the warm orange shutters.

Ways to Work with Color

You can approach color choices for your garden in a number of different ways. You can, for instance, design your garden so that some of its colors echo or pick up colors from your house. The colors in your garden can harmonize with the colors of the house, or the garden can contrast with the house. Either of these approaches can work if you take some time to think about your color possibilities.

As you think about potential color schemes for your garden, consider the way you personally respond to color, and the kinds of colors you like in other areas of your life, such as your clothes and the interior decor of your home. Do you generally prefer bright, warm reds, oranges, and yellows; or cool, peaceful blues, greens, and purples? Are you drawn to subtle, harmonious blends of colors or to lively, contrasting mixes? Rich, deep tones or soft pastels? Do you like the serenity and cleanness of white instead of other colors?

Always remember that your garden should please you, first and foremost. Use whatever colors you like to look at. Although a well-designed landscape will add significantly to the value of your home, it should also reflect your personality. The design of your landscape should not be strictly a business decision. The true value of a garden resides in the way it speaks to your soul. If you don't like or re-

Notice how the orange-tipped flowers of red-hot pokers (*Knifophia*) pick up the color of the salmony orange shutters on the house in the background.

spond to the colors and plants in your garden, there's little point in having one. You might as well just put in some hedges and foundation shrubs and call it a day. But if you are taking the time to read this book, you undoubtedly already appreciate how beautiful and satisfying a thoughtfully executed garden can be. The best gardens reflect the tastes and sensibilities of their owners just as surely as do the furnishings and decorative objects inside the home. See "The Psychological Dimensions of Color" on page 56 for information on using your personal response to colors in choosing colors for your garden.

Qualities of Colors

Color theory is complex, and it can take years of study to fully understand it. But there are guidelines you can follow in mixing and matching colors to arrive at pleasing combinations. It helps to understand some basic properties of color.

First of all, colors are not simply colors. What most of us think of as "colors" are more correctly called *hues*. A hue is pure color—red, yellow, blue, orange—as generated by a particular wavelength of light and perceived by our eyes and brains. Hue is the first aspect of color to consider. Another is the color's value—its lightness or darkness. Value is altered by adding white to the hue to lighten it (the resulting colors are called tints), or by adding black to darken it (these colors are called shades). For example, adding white to red creates pink. The amount of white you add determines the lightness of the pink. Adding black to the red gives you deep maroon shades. The third aspect of color is intensity—the

Pink, purple, and white flowers combine in a soft, pleasing color scheme. Pink and white roses anchor the garden, accented with purple Siberian iris.

brightness or dullness of the color. Intensity is a result of the color's saturation—how much of the color is present.

All artists are familiar with these terms, but it's helpful for gardeners to know them, too. Choosing flowers of different values and intensities brings more variety and interest to the garden, and being sensitive to value and intensity can make the difference between colors that fight one another and colors that create a pleasing contrast or harmony.

The Psychological Dimensions of Color

In addition to its visual qualities, each color of the visible spectrum has its own emotional and psychological qualities, which may determine, in part, which colors appeal to different people. Colors provoke responses in us, and you can use these responses to add an extra dimension to your garden.

Blue creates a peaceful, restful feeling. This color of the sea and the sky calms us and makes us feel cool. A blue garden seems somehow cool even in hot sun. Blue flowers and foliage can create the feeling of an island of serenity, especially around a small pool or fountain, or in a seating area.

Purples and violets possess a sense of mystery; these deep, rich tones appear to soften and recede in the distance, and they appear blurred and dark and misty when seen from across the lawn. Purple is also impressive and majesterial, the color of royalty. Deep purples look luxuriant in the garden and feel somehow confident and assured.

Cool blues and purples, executed here with *Salvia* 'Victoria' and verbena, bring a peaceful feeling to the garden. Pink petunias add a soft, bright note.

Green is the most restful color to the human eye. Pure greens, deep forest greens, and bluish greens are cool and rich, and they bring a feeling of elegance and formality to garden settings. Imagine being in a cool, leafy woodland glade as opposed to a brightly colored flower garden in the sun. Pale greens and yellow-greens, on the other hand, feel lighter, brighter, and more informal.

White, the other cool, calm color (which in terms of light is really a combination of all the colors in the spectrum), creates a sense of openness and space in the garden, and can make a small garden feel bigger. White also looks clean and fresh, the color symbolic of innocence and purity. Cool, bluish white flowers shimmer and sparkle in the shade and glimmer gently at dusk. Warm, creamy whites glow in dim light and add soft warmth to a garden of blue and violet flowers.

Gray is said to promote creativity, offering a blank slate upon which to let the mind play. For a garden

White calla lilies (*Zantedeschia aethiopica*) outside a gray-trimmed window look cool and calm, and might spark your creativity.

to fire your imagination, plant lots of gray and silver-leaved plants to create a neutral background against which to dream dreams and foster the flow of ideas.

The colors from the warm part of the spectrum are the fiery attention-getters that create an entirely different mood in the landscape.

Red is the boldest and most exciting. It demands our attention, and seems to stride purposefully toward the eye across space. Red in the garden can call attention to a focal point or draw the eye away from a less-than-desirable view. This color feels warm and energizing and stimulates conversation. Red flowers surrounding a picnic table or other outdoor dining area will tend to make it seem as if the food tastes better, increasing the pleasure in an already delightful experience. Red is intensified when surrounded by its complement, green (see "Contrasting Color Schemes" on page 64). When lightened with white, red softens into pink; with a bit of blue and gray it turns to mauve. Pinks and mauves are soft, soothing colors, warm and friendly. They promise to be somehow fragrant or sweet to the taste. Pinks and mauves in the garden bring feelings of peace and gentleness, harmony and joy.

Yellow is the color perceived most readily by the human eye (which explains why we have yellow taxis and school buses). It, too, draws attention and can be used to emphasize features in the garden and draw attention away from eyesores. Yellow is cheerful and happy, glowing rather than smoldering. Pale yellows and greenish yellows are light and bright without being hot; they bring a sense of freshness and a quality of spring to the garden. They create a feeling of quiet excitation and can help make

a small garden feel bigger. Golden yellows are warmer, deeper and richer; they glow where the pale greenish yellows gleam.

Orange is the color of impulse. In the garden, it glows warm like a candle flame or the embers of a fire. Orange feels energetic and positive, and is good for emphasis in the garden. In its pastel forms—apricot, salmon, and peach tints—orange is cheerful, friendly, and welcoming and brings a pleasant feeling to the garden.

Hot colors are bold and dramatic, and they demand attention. In this garden, red bougainvillea looks even redder next to the ferns in summer. As the ferns yellow in fall, they add a warm, softening glow to the garden.

Developing a Color Scheme

There are four basic ways to work with color to build color schemes in the garden. You can rely on a single flower color contrasted against foliage; you can combine harmonious or analogous colors, or contrasting or complementary colors; or you can plant in an assortment of mixed colors.

An artist's color wheel is an invaluable guide to understanding the relationships between colors and how they work together. Refer to the illustration below as you read about the different ways to combine colors in the garden. Don't feel that you have to be a slave to the color wheel. If you have a strong sense of color, follow your own inner light. But if you feel at a loss when you try to mix colors, the color wheel can be a useful tool.

A garden executed in one color does not have to be boring. Monochromatic does not necessarily equal monotonous. This all-pink garden gains interest from different shades and tints of the color, as well as a variety of flower forms.

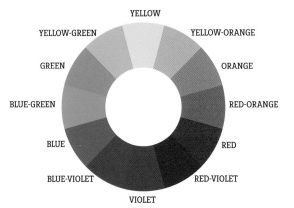

An artist's color wheel is a great help in planning color schemes. Colors close to one another on the wheel form harmonious combinations, and colors farther apart contrast with one another. Colors opposite one another on the color wheel are called complementary, and they create the strongest contrasts of all.

Monochromatic Gardens

The simplest color scheme of all is built on a single color, perhaps expressed in several different shades and tints, and perhaps with a small amount of a second color added as an accent. Monochromatic gardens can be quite soothing to the eye, and their simplicity can work extremely well in a formal setting.

You might like a garden of all white flowers, or red, or yellow. Or you could combine several shades of pink.

Single-color gardens need not be boring, either. You can include a variety of flower forms, plant heights, shapes and textures, flower sizes, and color values and intensities (pale, bright, or dark). Or you can mix in some plants with variegated or colored foliage for added interest.

FOLIAGE EFFECTS

Foliage plays an important role in any garden. Flowers, especially perennials, come and go, but leaves are in place throughout the growing season. When considering plants for your garden, try to have a variety of leaf sizes, shapes, and textures. From rounded to spiky to feathery, leaves come in many forms.

You can also use foliage color in the garden to add interest and to create special effects. Here are a few points to consider about leaves.

Deep, rich green leaves are a terrific backdrop or companion for red or white flowers. Deep greens make reds pop and whites sparkle.

Grayish green or silver leaves, such as those of artemisia, achillea, nepeta, and lamb's ears (*Stachys*), act as blenders or harmonizers. You can plant them among bright-colored flowers to tone down and help blend the colors. Grayish or silvery foliage softens sharp lines and hard edges—they can give a formal garden a softer, less austere look. Gray leaves can also diffuse bright, strong light, a plus in climates where the sun is intense and glaring.

Golden leaves light up shady corners like a shaft of sunlight. In a humid,

A composition of foliage can be as beautiful as flowers. Hostas in the background combine with ferns, purple-leaved heucherella, and golden filipendula in a grouping that looks good all season.

cloudy climate, golden foliage lends a warm glow. But in places where the sun is quite strong, yellow leaves can look pale and washed out.

Red and purple leaves add dramatic accents to the garden.

Variegated foliage (striped, streaked, spotted, edged, or splashed with one or more other colors) can add depth and richness to the garden, but it works best when used sparingly. Too many patterned leaves create chaos in the garden and detract from the flower colors. Use just one or two variegated plants in your composition.

Evergreen foliage contributes to the garden year-round. Be aware that evergreen foliage may look different in winter than in summer. Some evergreens, such as creeping juniper (*Juniperus horizontalis*) and inkberry (*Ilex glabra*), take on purplish tones in cold weather. Others, including littleleaf boxwood (*Buxus microphylla*), eastern red cedar (*Juniperus virginiana*), and arborvitae (*Thuja occidentalis*), turn bronzy or yellowish. The plants return to their usual green when the weather warms up in spring.

PLANTS FOR AN ALL-WHITE GARDEN

Monochromatic gardens can have plenty of interest. Even a garden of all white flowers can display a diversity of forms, textures, and gradations of color, from pearly grayish tones to warm, creamy ivories. One of the most famous gardens in the world is the white garden created by Vita Sackville-West at Sissinghurst Castle in England.

Here is a sampling of white flowers to give you an idea of the variety that is possible in single-color gardens.

Spring Bloomers

Korean forsythia (*Abeliophyllum distichum*) is a shrub with many small, 4-petaled white flowers in early spring.

Grecian windflower (*Anemone blanda*) is a low-growing bulb plant with many-petaled daisy flowers close to the ground.

Lily-of-the-valley (*Convallaria majalis*) has dangling little bells with a beguiling fragrance that bloom on thin stems in late spring.

Perennial candytuft (*Iberis sempervirens*), a perennial, and sweet alyssum (*Lobularia maritima*), an annual, both produce clusters of tiny white flowers. Sweet alyssum will keep blooming all summer, and the blossoms are honey-scented.

Iris cvs. have elegant flowers with 3 upright and 3 drooping petals, some with contrasting patches or spots.

Narcissus cvs. have a central cup backed by flat or backswept petals and come in a range of sizes.

Pieris spp. are shrubs with clusters of small, urn-shaped flowers at the ends of stems lined with dark green leaves.

Solomon's seal (*Polygonatum* spp.) has dangling greenish white tubes on arching stems.

Azaleas and rhododendrons (*Rhododendron* cvs.) have clusters of funnel-shaped flowers with ruffled petals.

Trees, including magnolias, crabapples, and flowering cherries, also can contribute white flowers to the spring landscape.

Summer Bloomers

Snapdragons (*Antirrhinum majus*) have spikes of tubular, 2-lipped flowers.

Marguerites (*Argyranthemum frutescens*) have daisy flowers all summer.

Columbines (*Aquilegia* spp.) have graceful, spurred blooms with petals gathered into a central cup.

Astilbe spp. have fluffy plumes of tiny white blossoms.

Clematis cvs. have large single or double, flat-faced, bell-shaped, or tubular flowers.

Dahlia cvs. come in a variety of forms from daisies to pompoms, and in tones from pure white to creamy.

Dianthus spp. have small flowers with fringed petals, some spicily fragrant.

Baby's breath (*Gypsophila paniculata*) has delicate sprays of tiny flowers.

Daylilies (*Hemerocallis* cvs.) and lilies (*Lilium* cvs.) have trumpet flowers that may face upward or droop.

Hydrangea spp. bear large clusters of flowers in a round snowball or flat "lacecap" form.

Shasta daisy (*Leucanthemum* x*superbum*) is the classic, yellow-centered white daisy.

Peonies (*Paeonia* spp.) have bowl-shaped single or full, double flowers; many are fragrant.

Summer phlox (*Phlox paniculata*) has round heads of fragrant, disc-shaped flowers.

Lilacs (*Syringa vulgaris*) have cone-shaped clusters of sweetly fragrant, 4-petaled flowers.

White-flowered trees include sourwood (*Oxydendrum arboreum*), Franklin tree (*Franklinia alatamaha*), and Japanese stewartia (*Stewartia pseudocamellia*).

Fall Bloomers

Japanese anemone (*Anemone* x*hybrida*) has 5-petaled discs in clusters atop slender stems.

Asters (*Aster* spp.) have daisy flowers with many narrow rays (petals) and yellow centers.

Boltonia (*Boltonia asteroides*) is a tall, rangy plant with lots of daisy flowers with many thin petals.

Chrysanthemums (*Chrysanthemum* or *Dendrathema* cvs.) can range from single daisies to full pompoms.

Bugbanes (*Cimicifuga* spp.) have tall, slender wands of tiny white flowers in late summer and fall.

Sweet autumn clematis (*Clematis terniflora*) is a vigorous vine covered with foamy masses of small, white, fragrant blooms at the end of summer.

A well-designed monochromatic garden incorporates a variety of flower shapes and textures. This sparkling all-white composition combines the varied forms of tulips, azaleas, and another shrub, *Deutzia gracilis*.

PLANT AND FLOWER FORMS

Flowers can be daisylike discs, round globes, stars, cups, bells, trumpets, vertical spires, wands, fluffy plumes, or airy sprays. The plants that produce them may have bold, sculptural leaves, such as canna or castor bean; angular, sword-shaped leaves, like those of iris and gladiolus; delicately cut and divided foliage, such as that of yarrows and astilbes; or glossy leaves, like gardenias and English ivy. Plants themselves can be low and sprawling, bushy, or upright and angular; trees and shrubs may be rounded, pyramidal, spreading, narrowly upright, or weeping. Mixing different forms and textures will make your landscape more interesting, even if your designs focus on one color.

HARMONIOUS COLOR SCHEMES

Here are some color combinations for harmonious gardens:

- Blue, cool pink, purple, and silver
- Pink, mauve, and purple
- Rose-pink, lavender, and purple
- Rose, pink, and blue
- Rose-pink, pink, and silver
- Orange, gold, and cream
- Red, orange, and gold
- Crimson, rose, and pink
- Red, scarlet, and gold
- Scarlet, yellow-orange, and yellow
- Deep red, pink, and lavender
- Warm pink, orange, yellow, and cream
- Orange, salmon, and yellow
- Red and pink
- Pink and purple
- Pink and blue
- Pink, peach, and deep orange
- Deep purple-black, cool pink, and silver
- Maroon and pink
- Red, red-violet, and purple

Pink and blue is a lovely, soft harmony of colors for flower gardens. Here, pink geraniums keep company with the blue blossoms of borage.

Harmonious Color Schemes

Harmonious, or analogous, colors are related; they are located near one another on the color wheel, and they blend smoothly with one another. Examples of harmonious color schemes are red, orange, and gold; or blue, purple, and pink. Harmonious color schemes are often quiet and subtle, as in the case of a blend of pastel shades of pink, rose, and lilac petunias. But they can also be surprisingly dramatic, as in a bed of orange and yellow cosmos and marigolds, red salvia, golden achillea, and *Canna* 'Rosemond Coles' (red-and-yellow flowers), 'Pretoria' (orange flowers and yellow-striped leaves), or 'Red King Humbert' (red flowers and purple-red leaves). These combinations of closely related colors are most appealing to the eyes of some people. For others, contrast is needed to bring more life to the composition.

An easy way to get a harmonious combination of colors is to plant several varieties or cultivars of one type—or better yet, one species—of flower. You might want to plant several kinds of celosia, for example, or astilbe, or daylilies. The colors of the different cultivars may be different in hue and intensity, but they will usually harmonize with one another. Consider the many colors of bearded iris, for example. It is difficult to find varieties whose colors truly clash with one another. Individual cultivars within a hybrid series, such as Super Elfin hybrid impatiens, Dreamer primulas, or Rocket snapdragons, are especially compatible.

Contrasting color schemes often work best when you plant lots of one color and smaller amounts of a second color, as seen in this blue and yellow garden.

Contrasting Color Schemes

Contrasting colors are farther apart on a color wheel, and placing them next to each other emphasizes their different qualities. Complementary colors lie opposite one another on the color wheel, and they contrast more intensely than any other juxtaposition of colors. Examples of complementary colors include blue and orange, purple and yellow, and red and green. Complementary colors of the same value and intensity placed next to one another tend to intensify one another. The 19th-century English landscape painter John Constable placed small strokes of red amid expanses of foliage in his paintings to make the greens look greener. If you look closely, you may perceive the same effect in a garden.

If you want to plant a garden of complementary colors, you will probably find the most pleasing results by planting the softer of the two colors over a larger portion of the garden and using the brighter color sparingly, as an accent. For example, if you want to combine deep blue salvia with bright orange marigolds, plant lots more salvia than marigolds. If you plant more marigolds and fewer salvia, the orange will overwhelm the blue.

Another way to tone down a contrasting scheme is to soften the shade of the brighter color. Instead of using orange marigolds with the salvia, you could instead plant salmon-colored geraniums or petunias. Conversely, with a strong orange such as geum, you might opt for a softer blue, such as that of willow blue star (*Amsonia tabernaemontana*) or peach-leaved bellflower (*Campanula persicifolia* 'Telham Beauty'). A third option would be to plant soft blue with salmon and inject some livelier notes by adding deeper blue accents. Imagine a planting of soft peach daylilies or bearded iris, with light blue delphinium and Siberian iris, and spires of deep violet-blue salvia interjected.

A third way to soften intensely contrasting colors is to introduce some neutral tones—white flowers or silver foliage—to blend the colors, or to surround the contrasting hues with lots of green foliage to absorb some of the color and allow the viewer's eye to rest.

AT A GLANCE

CONTRASTING COLOR SCHEMES

Here are some contrasting color combinations for the garden:

- Blue and orange (complementary)
- Blue-violet, salmon, and apricot
- Red, yellow, and blue
- Red, white, and blue
- Red-violet and yellow-green
- Blue and yellow
- Purple and yellow (complementary)
- Purple and gold
- Lavender, purple, and yellow
- Peach, lavender, and purple
- Pink and yellow

- Pink, yellow, and purple
- Purple and orange (intense)
- Red and purple (very intense!)
- Magenta and orange (whew!)
- Blue and white
- Red and white
- Yellow and white
- Deep purple-black and orange
- Violet and pale yellow
- Rose-pink, violet, and cool greenish yellow
- Magenta, violet, and yellow-green
- Purple, chartreuse, and gold

Contrasting color schemes can be quite beautiful, but you may find that you like them best in a garden that will be viewed from a distance—from across the lawn, perhaps—rather than up close, such as in a container garden on a patio.

Polychromatic Gardens

In a multicolored, or polychromatic, garden, the variety of colors included depends entirely on your preference. Multicolored gardens can be blindingly brilliant if all strong colors are used; they can be cheerful and festive if you mix pastels with a few bright tones; or they can be surprisingly subtle when soft, pale colors are used.

A polychromatic garden generally works best when one color is dominant to bring a sense of cohesiveness to the overall scheme. And don't sprinkle the plants of each color throughout the garden like so many pieces of confetti; you will lose the visual impact, and your garden will look more like a motley collection of plants. Instead, plant in color groups, in bands or drifts or clumps.

To get the best effect from a multicolored garden, surround it with lots of green to provide some visual relief. Set your flowers of many colors in front of evergreen shrubs or a hedge, or in a bed in the middle of a lawn.

Drifts of spiky blue salvia, feathery love-in-a-mist (*Nigella damascena*), orange poppies (*Papaver somniferum*), and other flowers combine in a lively multicolored garden.

Color Palettes

The following color palettes for plants contain trees, shrubs, vines, foliage plants, and grasses in addition to flowers. The listings are not exhaustive, but you'll find plenty of great plants to use in building your garden. If you are seeking particular tints or shades of color—say, salmon or peach—try to buy plants locally. Visit nurseries and garden centers and look at the plants. Mail-order catalogs may afford a broader choice of plants, but the colors in the photos are often deceiving. There's no substitute for seeing plants in person. Besides visiting retail outlets to look at plants, you can gain a wealth of insight into flower colors and how they work together by visiting botanical gardens and other public gardens, by taking tours of private gardens when they are offered in your area, and simply by looking at gardens as you walk around your neighborhood.

Plant Palette: Reds

Perennials, Bulbs, and Annuals

Alcea rosea, hollyhock

Antirrhinum majus, snapdragon

Aquilegia spp., columbines

Aster spp.

Astilbe spp.

Begonia spp.

Bougainvillea spp.

Caladium cvs.

Calibrachoa cvs., million bells

Callistephus chinensis, China aster

Celosia cvs.

Centranthus ruber, red valerian

Chrysanthemum (*Dendrathema*) cvs., garden chrysanthemums

Coleus (*Solenostemon*) cvs.

Crocosmia cvs., montbretias

Dahlia cvs.

Dianthus spp., garden pinks

Fritillaria imperialis cvs., crown imperials

Fuchsia cvs.

Geum cvs.

Gladiolus cvs.

Gomphrena globosa, globe amaranth

Helleborus cvs., hellebores

Hemerocallis cvs., daylilies

Heuchera sanguinea, coral bells

Hibiscus rosa-sinensis, Chinese hibiscus

Hyacinthus orientalis, hyacinth

Impatiens cvs., bedding impatiens, balsam impatiens

Ipomoea spp., morning glories

Iris cvs., bearded irises

Kniphofia cvs., red-hot pokers

Lathyrus odoratus, sweet pea

Lilium spp. and cvs., lilies

Lobelia cardinalis, cardinal flower

Lupinus cvs., lupines

Lychnis chalcedonica, Maltese cross

Mimulus ×*hybridus*, monkey flower

Monarda didyma, bee balm

Nicotiana cvs., flowering tobacco

Paeonia cvs., peonies

Papaver spp., poppies

Pelargonium cvs., geraniums

Pennisetum setaceum 'Rubrum', fountain grass

Penstemon cvs.

Petunia cvs.

Phlox paniculata, summer phlox

Primula spp., primroses

Salvia spp.

Tropaeolum majus, nasturtium

Tulipa cvs., tulips

Verbena cvs.

Viola ×*wittrockiana*, pansy

Zauschneria californica, California fuchsia

Zinnia elegans

Trees, Shrubs, and Vines

Acer palmatum cvs., Japanese maples

Camellia cvs.

Campsis radicans, trumpet vine

Clematis cvs.

Cotoneaster spp. (fruit)

Ilex spp., hollies (fruit)

Lagerstroemia indica, crape myrtle

Lonicera sempervirens cvs., trumpet honeysuckles

Rhododendron cvs., azaleas, rhododendrons

Rosa cvs., roses

Plant Palette: Pinks

Perennials, Bulbs, and Annuals

Achillea cvs., yarrows

Alcea rosea, hollyhock

Allium spp., flowering onions

Anemone spp.

Antirrhinum majus, snapdragon

Aquilegia spp., columbines

Arabis spp., rock cresses

Argyranthemum cvs., marguerites

Armeria spp., sea pinks

Aster spp.

Astilbe spp., false spireas

Astrantia major, masterwort

Begonia spp

Bergenia spp.

Bougainvillea cvs.

Caladium cvs. (foliage)

Callistephus chinensis, China aster

Calluna vulgaris, heather

Catharanthus roseus, Madagascar periwinkle

Celosia cvs., cockscombs

Centaurea spp., bachelor's buttons, sweet sultans

Centranthus ruber, red valerian

Chelone spp., turtleheads

Chrysanthemum (*Dendrathema*) cvs., garden mums

Cleome hassleriana, spider flower

Colchicum autumnale, autumn crocus

Consolida ambigua, larkspur

Coreopsis rosea, tickseed

Cosmos bipinnatus

Cyclamen spp., hardy cyclamens

Dahlia cvs.

Delphinium cvs.

Dianthus spp., garden pinks

Dicentra spp., bleeding hearts

Digitalis purpurea, foxglove

Epimedium spp., fairy wings

Erigeron spp., fleabanes

Erythronium spp., dogtooth violets

Filipendula spp., meadowsweets

Fuchsia cvs.

Geranium spp., cranesbills

Gladiolus cvs.

Gomphrena globosa, globe amaranth

Gypsophila paniculata, baby's breath

Helleborus cvs., hellebores

Hemerocallis cvs., daylilies

Heuchera sanguinea, coralbells

Hibiscus spp.

Hyacinthus orientalis cvs., hyacinths

Iberis umbellatus, globe candytuft

Impatiens spp.

Ipomoea spp., morning glories

Iris spp. and cvs.

Lathyrus odoratus, sweet pea

Lilium spp. and cvs., lilies

Limonium sinuatum, statice

Lupinus cvs., lupines

Lychnis spp., campions

Lycoris spp., magic lilies

Malva moschata, musk mallow

Monarda didyma, bee balm

Nicotiana alata, flowering tobacco

Oenothera speciosa

Peonia cvs., peonies

Papaver spp., poppies

Pelargonium cvs., geraniums

Penstemon spp.

Pentas lanceolata, star cluster

Petunia cvs.

Phlox spp.

Physostegia virginiana, false dragonhead

Primula spp., primroses

Saponaria spp., soapworts

Saxifraga spp., saxifrages

Scabiosa columbaria 'Butterfly Pink', pincushion flower

Sedum spp., stonecrops

Sidalcea malviflora, prairie mallow

Thalictrum spp., meadow rue

Tradescantia Andersoniana Group, spiderwort

Tulipa cvs., tulips

Verbena ×*hybrida*

Veronica cvs.

Viola ×*wittrockiana*, pansy

Zephyranthes spp., zephyr lilies

Zinnia elegans

Trees, Shrubs, and Vines

Abelia floribunda

Camellia cvs.

Clematis cvs.

Erica spp., heaths

Hydrangea macrophylla, bigleaf hydrangea

Kalmia latifolia, mountain laurel

Lagerstroemia indica, crape myrtle

Lonicera spp., honeysuckles

Magnolia ×*soulangiana*, saucer magnolia

Malus cvs., crabapples

Potentilla fruticosa, cinquefoil

Prunus spp., flowering cherries

Rhododendron spp. and cvs., azaleas

Rhododendron spp. and cvs., rhododendrons

Rosa cvs., roses

Spiraea japonica, spirea

Weigela cvs.

Plant Palette: Oranges

Perennials, Bulbs, and Annuals

Achillea 'Paprika'

Alcea 'Peaches 'n' Dreams', hollyhock

Antirrhinum majus, snapdragon

Asclepias tuberosa, butterfly weed

Begonia tuberhybrida, tuberous begonia

Calendula officinalis, pot marigold

Canna 'Pretoria'

Celosia cvs.

Chrysanthemum cvs., garden mums

Coleus cvs.

Cosmos sulphureus

Dahlia cvs.

Eschscholzia californica, California poppy

Fritillaria imperialis, crown imperial

Fuchsia 'Coralle' and 'Hidcote'

Geum cvs., avenses

Gladiolus cvs.

Helenium cvs., sneezeweeds

Hemerocallis fulva, *H.* cvs., daylilies

Hibiscus rosa-sinensis, Chinese hibiscus

Impatiens cvs.

Iris cvs., bearded iris

Kniphofia cvs., red-hot pokers

Lantana 'Tangerine'

Ligularia dentata 'Desdemona'

Lilium cvs., lilies

Osteospermum cvs.

Paeonia 'Coral Charm', peony

Papaver spp., poppies

Pelargonium cvs., geraniums

Petunia cvs.

Physalis alkekengii, Chinese lantern (seed capsules)

Portulaca grandiflora, rose moss

Potentilla 'Tangerine'

Pyracantha spp., firethorns (fruits)

Tagetes cvs., marigolds

Thunbergia alata, black-eyed Susan vine

Trollius 'Orange Globe', globeflower

Tropaeolum majus, nasturtium

Tulipa cvs., tulips

Viola ×*wittrockiana*, pansy

Zinnia haageana 'Orange Star'

Trees, Shrubs, and Vines

Bougainvillea cvs.

Campsis 'Indian Summer', trumpet vine

Hamamelis 'Jelena', witch hazel

Lonicera spp., honeysuckles

Rhododendron cvs., azaleas

Rosa cvs., roses

Plant Palette: Yellows

Perennials, Bulbs, and Annuals

Achillea cvs., yarrows

Alchemilla mollis, lady's mantle (greenish yellow)

Anthemis tinctoria, golden marguerite

Antirrhinum majus, snapdragon

Aquilegia chrysantha, *A.* cvs., columbines

Argyranthemum cvs., marguerites

Aurinia saxatilis, basket of gold

Begonia ×*tuberhybrida*, tuberous begonia

Calendula officinalis, pot marigold

Carex elata 'Aurea', Bowles' golden sedge (leaves)

Celosia argentea, cockscomb

Centaurea moschata, sweet sultan

Chrysanthemum (*Dendrathema*) cvs., garden mums

Chrysogonum virginianum, green-and-gold

Coleus (*Solenostemon*) cvs. (leaves)

Coreopsis spp., tickseeds

Cosmos sulfureus

Crocus cvs.

Dahlia cvs.

Doronicum spp., leopard's banes

Epimedium spp., fairy wings

Eranthis hyemalis, winter aconite

Eremurus spp., foxtail lilies

Erythronium spp., trout lilies

Forsythia spp.

Fritillaria imperialis, crown imperial

Gaillardia spp., blanket flowers

Gladiolus cvs.

Helenium autumnale, sneezeweed

Helianthus spp., sunflowers

Heliopsis spp., ox-eyes

Hemerocallis cvs., daylilies

Hibiscus rosa-sinensis, Chinese hibiscus

Hosta cvs., plantain lilies

Inula spp.

Iris cvs.

Kniphofia cvs., red-hot pokers

Lantana camara cvs.

Lilium cvs., lilies

Limonium sinuatum, statice

Linaria spp., toadflaxes

Linum flavum, yellow flax

Lupinus cvs., lupines

Lysimachia nummularia 'Aurea', golden creeping Jenny

Melampodium (*Leucanthemum*) *paludosum*

Mimulus spp. and cvs., monkey flowers

Narcissus spp. and cvs., daffodils

Nemesia strumosa cvs.

Oenothera spp., evening primroses, sundrops

Opuntia spp., prickly pears

Papaver nudicaule, Iceland poppy

Primula spp., primroses

Ranunculus spp., buttercups

Rudbeckia spp., black-eyed Susans

Solidago spp., goldenrods

Tagetes cvs., marigolds

Thermopsis villosa, false lupine

Thunbergia alata, black-eyed Susan vine

Trollius spp., globeflowers

Tropaeolum majus, nasturtium

Tulipa cvs., tulips

Uvularia spp., merrybells

Verbascum spp., mulleins

Viola ×*wittrockiana*, pansy

Zantedeschia elliottiana, golden calla lily

Zinnia spp.

Trees, Shrubs, and Vines

Allamanda cathartica, golden trumpet vine

Corylopsis spp., winter hazels

Hamamelis spp., witch hazels

Hypericum spp., St. John's wort

Jasminum nudiflorum, winter jasmine

Kerria japonica, Japanese kerria

Laburnum ×*watereri*, golden chain tree

Lonicera spp., honeysuckles

Potentilla spp., cinquefoils

Rhododendron cvs., azaleas

Rosa cvs., roses

Sambucus racemosa 'Plumosa Aurea', elder (leaves)

Plant Palette: Blues and Violets

Perennials, Bulbs, and Annuals

Aconitum spp., monkshoods

Adenophora spp., ladybells

Agapanthus spp., African lilies

Agastache 'Licorice Blue'

Ageratum houstonianum, flossflower

Amsonia spp., blue stars

Anemone blanda, Grecian windflower

Aquilegia caerulea, Rocky Mountain columbine

Aster spp.

Baptisia australis, false indigo

Browallia speciosa, bush violet

Brunnera macrophylla, Siberian bugloss

Callistephus chinensis, China aster

Campanula spp., bellflowers

Centaurea cyanus, bachelor's button

Ceratostigma plumbaginoides, leadwort

Chionodoxa luciliae, glory-of-the-snow

Consolida ambigua, larkspur

Delphinium cvs.

Echinops ritro, globe thistle

Echium candicans, pride of Madeira

Elymus magellanicus, wild rye (leaves)

Eryngium spp., sea hollies

Exacum affine, Persian violet

Gentiana spp., gentians

Geranium spp., cranesbills

Heliotropium cvs., heliotropes

Hosta cvs., plantain lilies (leaves)

Hyacinthoides spp., bluebells

Hyacinthus cvs., hyacinths

Hyssopus officinalis, hyssop

Ipomoea tricolor 'Heavenly Blue', morning glory

Iris spp. and cvs.

Limonium sinuatum, statice

Linum perenne, perennial flax

Lobelia spp.

Lupinus cvs., lupines

Mertensia virginica (*pulmonarioides*), Virginia bluebells

Myosotis spp., forget-me-nots

Nigella damascena, love-in-a-mist

Omphalodes spp., navelworts

Phlox spp.

Platycodon grandiflorus, balloon flower

Plumbago auriculata, Cape leadwort

Polemonium caeruleum, Jacob's ladder

Primula spp., primroses

Pulmonaria spp., lungworts

Salvia spp.

Scabiosa cvs., pincushion flowers

Scaevola aemula, fanflower

Scilla siberica, Siberian squill

Stokesia laevis, Stokes' aster

Torenia fournieri, wishbone flower

Trachelium caeruleum, blue lace flower

Tradescantia Andersoniana Group, spiderwort

Veronica spp.

Viola spp., violets, pansies

Trees, Shrubs, and Vines

Buddleia davidii 'Darkness', 'Empire Blue', 'Nanho Blue', butterfly bushes

Caryopteris ×*clandonensis*, blue mist shrub

Clematis cvs.

Hydrangea macrophylla, bigleaf hydrangea

Rosmarinus officinalis, rosemary

Plant Palette: Purples

Perennials, Bulbs, and Annuals

Acanthus spp., bear's breeches

Ageratum houstonianum, flossflower

Ajuga 'Catlin's Giant', 'Valfredda', bugleweed

Allium spp., flowering onions

Aquilegia cvs., columbines

Astilbe cvs., false spireas

Aster cvs.

Bougainvillea cvs.

Campanula spp., bellflowers, harebells

Centaurea cyanus, bachelor's button

Chrysanthemum (*Dendrathema*) cvs., garden mums

Cleome hassleriana, spider flower

Colchicum cvs., meadow saffrons

Consolida ambigua, larkspur

Crocus cvs.

Dahlia cvs.

Delphinium cvs.

Digitalis purpurea, foxglove

Echinacea purpurea, purple coneflower

Erigeron cvs., fleabanes

Erythronium spp., dogtooth violets

Eupatorium purpureum, Joe Pye weed

Fuchsia cvs.

Geranium spp., cranesbills

Gladiolus cvs.

Gomphrena globosa, globe amaranth

Heliotropium arborescens, heliotrope

Helleborus cvs., hellebores

Hesperis matronalis, dame's rocket

Heuchera 'Palace Purple', alumroot (leaves)

Hosta cvs., plantain lilies

Hyacinthus cvs., hyacinths

Iberis umbellata, globe candytuft

Impatiens cvs.

Ipomoea cvs., morning glories

Lathyrus odoratus, sweet pea

Lavandula spp., lavenders

Liatris spp., gayfeathers

Limonium sinuatum, statice

Lupinus cvs., lupines

Penstemon spp.

Pentas cvs.

Perilla frutescens, shiso (leaves)

Perovskia atriplicifolia, Russian sage

Petunia cvs.

Phlox spp.

Phormium tenax cvs., New Zealand flax

Primula spp., primroses

Pulmonaria spp., lungworts

Ricinus communis 'Impala', castor bean (leaves)

Salvia spp.

Scabiosa spp., pincushion flowers

Thalictrum spp., meadow rue

Tradescantia pallida 'Purpurea' (*Setcreasea purpurea*), purple heart (leaves)

Trillium erectum, purple trillium

Tulipa cvs., tulips

Verbena bonariensis, *V.* 'Homestead Purple'

Viola spp., violets, pansies

Zinnia elegans

Trees, Shrubs, and Vines

Buddleia spp., butterfly bushes

Callicarpa spp., beautyberries (fruit)

Clematis cvs.

Cotinus coggygria 'Royal Purple', smoke tree

Dolichos lablab (*Lablab purpurea*), hyacinth bean

Erica cvs., heaths

Rhododendron cvs., azaleas, rhododendrons

Syringa vulgaris, lilac

Vitex agnus-castus, chastetree

Wisteria spp.

Plant Palette: Whites

Perennials, Bulbs, and Annuals

Achillea millefolium, yarrow

Actaea alba (*A. pachypoda*), white baneberry

Agapanthus cvs., African lilies

Ageratum houstonianum 'Hawaii White', flossflower

Allium spp., flowering onions

Anaphalis margaritacea, pearly everlasting

Anemone spp., windflowers

Antirrhinum majus, snapdragon

Aquilegia spp., columbines

Arabis caucasica, wall rock cress

Argyranthemum spp., marguerites

Armeria spp., sea pinks

Aruncus dioicus, goatsbeard

Aster spp.

Astilbe spp., false spireas

Baptisia alba, false indigo

Begonia cvs.

Boltonia asteroides

Caladium cvs.

Callistephus chinensis, China aster

Calochortus spp., fairy lanterns

Campanula spp., bellflowers, harebells

Catharanthus roseus, Madagascar periwinkle

Centaurea cyanus, bachelor's button

Cerastium tomentosum, snow-in-summer

Chelone spp., turtleheads

Chrysanthemum (*Dendrathema*) cvs., garden mum

Cimicifuga spp., bugbanes

Clematis cvs.

Clethra alnifolia, sweet pepperbush

Consolida ambigua, larkspur

Convallaria majalis, lily-of-the-valley

Crocus spp.

Cyclamen spp.

Dahlia cvs.

Delphinium cvs.

Dianthus spp., garden pinks

Dicentra spp., bleeding hearts

Dictamnus albus, gas plant

Digitalis purpurea, foxglove

Disporum spp., fairy bells

Epimedium grandiflorum, fairy wings

Eremurus himalaicus, foxtail lily

Erythronium spp., trout lilies

Filipendula spp., meadowsweet

Fuchsia cvs.

Galanthus nivalis, snowdrop

Galium odoratum, sweet woodruff

Gardenia augusta, Cape jasmine

Geranium spp., cranesbills

Gladiolus cvs.

Gypsophila spp., baby's breath

Helleborus cvs., hellebores

Hemerocallis cvs., daylilies

Hesperocallis undulata, desert lily

Hibiscus spp.

Hyacinthoides cvs., bluebells

Hyacinthus orientalis, hyacinths

Hydrangea spp.

Iberis spp., candytufts

Impatiens cvs.

Iris spp.

Jasminum spp., jasmines

Lamium maculatum cvs., deadnettles

Lathyrus odoratus, sweet pea

Leucanthemum spp., daisies

Leucojum spp., snowflakes

Liatris cvs., gayfeathers

Lilium spp. and cvs., lilies

Limonium sinuatum, statice

Lonicera spp., honeysuckles

Lupinus cvs., lupines

Lysimachia clethroides, gooseneck loosestrife

Malva moschata 'Alba', musk mallow

Narcissus cvs., daffodils

Nemesia strumosa cvs.

Nicotiana spp., flowering tobacco

Nierembergia caerulea 'Mont Blanc', cup flower

Nigella damascena, love-in-a-mist

Ornithogalum spp., stars-of-Bethlehem

Paeonia cvs., peonies

Papaver spp., poppies

Pelargonium cvs., geraniums

Pentas lanceolata cvs., Egyptian star clusters

Petunia cvs.

Phlox spp.

Platycodon grandiflorus, balloon flower

Polygonatum spp., Solomon's seals

Primula spp., primroses

Pulmonaria cvs., lungworts

Salvia spp.

Sanguisorba canadensis, Canadian burnet

Saponaria cvs., soapworts

Saxifraga spp., saxifrages

Smilax racemosa, false Solomon's seal

Stokesia laevis, Stokes' aster

Thalictrum cvs., meadow rue

Tropaeolum majus, nasturtium

Tulipa cvs., tulips

Verbena cvs.

Veronica cvs.

Viola spp., violets, pansies

Yucca spp.

Zantedeschia spp., calla lilies

Zephyranthes spp., rain lilies

Zinnia spp.

Trees, Shrubs, and Vines

Abelia ×*grandiflora*, glossy abelia

Abeliophyllum distichum, Korean forsythia

Aesculus parviflora, bottlebrush buckeye

Bougainvillea cvs.

Camellia cvs.

Cladrastis kentukea, yellowwood

Cornus spp., dogwoods

Deutzia spp.

Erica spp., heaths

Fallopia aubertii (*Polygonum aubertii*),
    silver lace vine

Lonicera spp., honeysuckles

Magnolia spp.

Malus spp., crabapples

Philadelphus spp., mock oranges

Pieris spp.

Potentilla fruticosa cvs., cinquefoils

Prunus spp., flowering cherries

Rhododendron spp. and cvs., azaleas,
    rhododendrons

Rosa cvs., roses

Spiraea spp.

Stewartia pseudocamellia, Japanese stewartia

Styrax spp., snowbells

Syringa cvs., lilacs

Viburnum spp.

Weigela 'Snowflake'

Wisteria cvs.

Coordinating Garden Colors with Your House

In coordinating your garden with your house, you will need to consider the colors of various parts of the house. Many houses use a three-color scheme. The main color is the color of the walls, the body of the house. The primary trim color goes on the window and door frames, porch, columns, lintels, and perhaps trellises attached to the house. The third color, the accent color, is used on the front door, shutters, and perhaps under the eaves.

Bear in mind that daylight affects color. Colors look brighter on a house in a sunny location than they look on chips in a paint store. On a shaded house, the colors will look darker than on the paint chips. So, if your house is on a sunny site, you might pick a color slightly darker than the tone you want. On a shady site, go a bit lighter. Check the color by buying a small can of the color you've chosen, painting a couple of boards, and propping them up in your yard to see how the color looks.

Here's another tip: Bright colors work best on small houses—they are overwhelming on big houses. A large house looks best in neutrals or soft

COLORS FOR DIFFERENT ARCHITECTURAL STYLES

If you want to be historically accurate, consider using these colors for particular house styles.

Colonial, Federal, Georgian, Greek Revival: Simple colors, not bright—slate blue, gray, gold, yellowish or grayish green, white

Victorian, Gothic: Earthy colors—brown, terracotta, brick red, burgundy, dusty rose, navy, bluish green, forest green, gold, plum, beige

Arts and Crafts, Bungalow: Simpler earth-toned palette, rich and saturated—earthy brown, burgundy, golden brown, brownish gold, gray, sea green, teal, tan, taupe

Modern (post-World War II): Similar to historic colors, but brighter—beige, gold, gray, blue, tan

Here's a thoughtful coordination of colors. The deep green color of the house trim is repeated on the stair risers, the plant stand, a lattice screen, and the antique pump in the garden, tying the landscape to the house.

pastels, although it can handle more trim colors than a small house. Victorian houses are often painted in several different colors to emphasized their ornate gingerbread trim. A small house is best with a simple color scheme.

Now, the first step in coordinating your color schemes is to go outside and take a good look at your house.

Start with the Walls

Most obvious, because they're the biggest, are the walls of the building. Wall color is created by building materials, such as brick, stone, or wood, and by colored paint, siding, or stucco applied to the walls.

If the walls of your house are a neutral color, such as off-white, gray, taupe, or even sage green, your garden can be practically any color. But if your house is a stronger color, such as yellow or red, you will probably want to avoid colors such as cool pinks or magentas that would clash.

Look at the Trim

One of the best ways to link house and garden is through the trim around windows and doors, or the colors of doors and shutters. You might prefer to see all the trim and doors in the same neutral color, or a closely related color, such as beige trim with a white door. Or you might like the look of a different color for doors and shutters—perhaps, for instance, a slate blue door with cream trim, or a red door with gray trim. Good trim colors that go with a variety of flower colors include white, cream or ivory, beige, slate blue, sage green, dark green, and black.

Make a color link between house and garden by picking up the colors of the door and shutters in your garden colors. Colors can coordinate by echoing, harmonizing with, or contrasting with one another, as described under "Ways to Work with Color," on page 54.

Here's an example of how it can work. Suppose your house has taupe or tan walls, with beige trim and a salmon door and shutters. A garden of warm sunset colors—oranges and yellows—would coordinate beautifully with the house. You could echo the door and shutters with salmon impatiens and coleus if the garden is shady, or salmon petunias and bearded iris in a sunny garden. Deeper oranges, russets, and golds would harmonize with the salmon, and adding some red accents would enrich the palette. Other sources of warm colors include shrubs such as Japanese kerria (*Kerria japonica*), witch hazels (*Hamamelis* spp.), roses, bougainvillea, and St. John's worts (*Hypericum* spp.); vines such as honeysuckles (*Lonicera* spp.) and trumpet vines (*Campsis* cvs.); and the autumn foliage of deciduous trees. See "Flowers for a Sunset Garden" on page 76 for some plants that would work in this kind of garden.

Use the information in "Color Schemes for Different Houses" on page 78 to get started thinking about possible color combinations for your house and landscape. When you've settled on a color scheme, the "Color Palette Tables" beginning on page 66 will give you a starting point in your search for plants in the colors you want.

The glowing sunset colors of this autumn garden are beautiful against the pale, neutral backdrop provided by the house. Tawny maiden grass (*Miscanthus sinensis* 'Variegatus'), *Hosta* 'Gold Drop', and barberries (*Berberis thunbergii* 'Rose Glow') in their full fall color contribute a range of warm tones.

FLOWERS FOR A SUNSET GARDEN

If you love sunset colors, plant some of these in your warm-toned garden.

Salmons

Bougainvillea spp.

Coleus (*Solenostemon*)

Gladiolus spp.

Hemerocallis, daylily

Impatiens spp.

Iris cvs., bearded iris

Paeonia 'Coral Charm', Coral Charm peony

Papaver orientale cvs., oriental poppies

Pelargonium cvs., geraniums

Petunia cvs.

Phlox drummondii 'Light Salmon', annual phlox

Tulipa cvs., tulips

Oranges

Achillea 'Paprika'

Asclepias tuberosa, butterfly weed

Bougainvillea spp.

Calendula officinalis, pot marigold

Campsis radicans, trumpet vine

Canna 'Pretoria', 'Rosemond Coles'

Celosia 'Apricot Brandy'

Eschscholzia californica, California poppy

Hemerocallis, daylily

Kniphofia cvs., red-hot poker

Lantana 'Tangerine'

Ligularia dentata 'Desdemona', golden groundsel

Lilium spp. and cvs., lilies

Lonicera spp., honeysuckles

Potentilla 'Tangerine'

Portulaca grandiflora, rose moss

Tagetes spp., marigolds

Tropaeolum majus, nasturtium

Tulipa cvs., tulips

Russets

Chrysanthemum cvs.

Coleus (*Solenostemon*)

Sedum 'Autumn Joy'

Golds

Achillea 'Coronation Gold', 'Gold Plate'

Allamanda cathartica, golden trumpet vine

Antirrhinum majus, snapdragon

Aurinia saxatilis, basket of gold

Calendula officinalis, pot marigold

Canna 'King Midas'

Celosia 'Century Yellow'

Coreopsis spp., tickseeds

Helianthus spp., sunflowers

Hemerocallis cvs., daylilies

Lantana camara cvs.

Ligularia 'The Rocket'

Lilium spp. and cvs., lilies

Narcissus spp. and cvs., daffodils

Oenothera spp., evening primroses, sundrops

Portulaca grandiflora, rose moss

Rosa spp. and cvs., roses

Rudbeckia spp., black-eyed Susans

Tagetes spp., marigolds

Tropaeolum majus, nasturtium

Viola ×*wittrockiana*, pansy

Reds

Achillea 'Fire King'

Antirrhinum majus, snapdragon

Astilbe spp.

Calibrachoa cvs., million bells

Canna 'Red King Humbert'

Chrysanthemum cvs.

Dahlia cvs.

Helenium cvs., sneezeweeds

Hemerocallis cvs., daylilies

Hibiscus rosa-sinensis, Chinese hibiscus

Lilium spp. and cvs., lilies

Monarda didyma 'Cambridge Scarlet,' beebalm

Penstemon spp.

Paeonia cvs., peonies

Papaver orientale, oriental poppy

Pelargonium cvs., geraniums

Rosa spp. and cvs., roses

Zauschneria californica, California fuchsia

Other Details to Consider in Color Planning

In addition to the walls and trim of the house, consider the color of the roof. Many roofs are neutral colors—tan, brown, gray, or black—but a roof might also be red tile or green shingles, which merit consideration in planning your landscape color scheme.

Also think about accents and accessories on the property: railings, fences and gates, retaining walls, sheds and outbuildings, gazebos, arbors, pergolas, even pots and window boxes. Creative use of color can transform a gate or a gazebo into an active ingredient in the garden, turning a ho-hum part of the landscape into an *aha!* experience for the eyes.

Pavement plays a color role, too. The surfaces of driveways, sidewalks, and paths also figure into the overall landscape color scheme. A blacktop driveway is going to look harsh and strident; it will always call attention to itself. To make such a drive less noticeable, you could create screens along the edges with tall flowering perennials or ornamental grasses, a vine-covered fence, a clipped hedge, or a border of shrubs. The screening will block the view of the driveway from the lawn or inside the house.

A gravel or bluestone driveway is less obtrusive, and concrete pavers are also available in a range of neutral colors. (See Chapter 3 for more information on surface materials for driveways and walkways.)

Finally, look at the color of the soil in your garden. This may seem like a silly detail, but consider that all your plants are seen against the backdrop of the soil in which they grow. Red clay looks different from dark brown loam or light, sandy soil. If your soil is red

clay, or if you are fond of dyed red cedar mulch, this color is well worth thinking about when you work out flower colors for the garden. You will probably want to avoid planting cool pink and deep red flowers against these orangey red backgrounds. A dark-colored shredded mulch, on the other hand, provides a perfect foil for flowers of all colors.

Inspired use of color on architectural elements in the garden, as seen in these examples from a painter's garden, can turn everyday details into stunning accents and can also link the garden to the house if you echo trim colors.

Color Schemes for Different Houses

Armed with some understanding of basic color theory and a good sense of the colors you have to work with on your house, it's time to put all the parts together and begin to zero in on a color scheme for your garden. This section will give you a place to start in considering possible colors for your garden.

Gray Houses

Practically any garden color scheme will look good with a gray house. Whether the house is built of stone, sided, or painted, gray walls afford a broad choice of trim colors around which to build a garden color scheme. For example, a grayish rose or claret trim might suggest pinks and purples for the garden. Slate blue trim would work beautifully with a blue, orange, and salmon theme. Pinks would work well with a plum-colored trim.

Since gray is a cool color, you may find that you prefer cool pinks and lavenders instead of warm, peachy pinks. Or you might like the added warmth better. Some trim colors to consider for a gray house include pale gray, cool white, claret (purple-red, a bit lighter than burgundy), plum, slate blue, dark green, taupe, beige, and desert shades—terra-cotta or salmon, dusty rose or grayish rose, and gray-green.

Garden Colors for Gray Houses	
Blue, pink, and silver	Rose-pink, lavender, and purple
Blue and white	Red, white, and blue
Blue and peach	Red, yellow, and blue
Blue, orange, and salmon	Crimson, pink, and lavender
Purple and orange	Maroon and chartreuse
Lavender and peach	Deep purple-black and pink
Pink and blue	Magenta and orange
Pink and white	
Pink and purple	Red and white
Pink, blue, and purple	Blue and yellow
Pink, rose, and silver	

Many flower colors work beautifully with a gray house. In this garden, soft pink roses, red climbing roses, and silvery artemisia gleam against the gray walls.

Taupe and Tan Houses

Taupe and tan houses, too, can be well served by a host of different color schemes. Taupe is a grayed brown, which puts it in the cool family. Pinks, blues, and lavender look great with taupe, as do orange, salmon, peach, apricot, and white. If the house has a rich green trim, red flowers will really pop in the garden. Tan houses are a warmer, more golden brown, but many of the same colors will work with it, too. Warm color combinations can harmonize nicely with a tan house as well.

Good trim colors for taupe and tan houses include beige, tan, green, cream, and white. Many flower colors work well with taupe, but warm colors look best with tan.

Garden Colors for Taupe and Tan Houses

Rose, pink, and lavender

Blue, orange, and salmon

Blue-violet, coral, and apricot

Lavender, peach, and orange

Pink and blue

Pink and purple

Rose, pink, and blue

Rose-pink, lavender, and purple

Pink, blue, and purple

Pink, blue, and silver

Orange, apricot, and yellow

Red and white

Crimson, pink, and lavender

Maroon, chartreuse, and yellow

Blue-violet, chartreuse, yellow, and a touch of magenta

White, Off-White, and Beige Houses

If your house is white, off-white, or beige, with a neutral-colored roof and trim, the universe of garden color schemes is yours. About the only caveat is this: If you want an all-white garden, make sure you surround it with plenty of greenery so the flowers show up. A clipped hedge would provide a fine backdrop for white flowers in a formal garden, and a grouping of unpruned evergreen shrubs would do the same in an informal landscape. Just be sure the background planting is positioned to the north of the flower garden so it doesn't block the sun.

Trim colors to consider include slate blue, navy, black, green, gray, taupe, or various shades of beige. Flower choices are practically limitless for white houses.

Garden Colors for White, Off-White, and Beige Houses

Purple and pink	Blue-violet, orange, and apricot	Red and white	Red, rose, and pink
Purple, pink, and yellow	Rose, pink, and blue	Red and yellow	Yellow and orange
Pink and yellow	Pink, light blue, and orange	Red and pink	Yellow, orange, and salmon
Purple, blue-violet, and soft yellow	Rose, lavender, and purple	Red, orange, and yellow	Yellow, gold, and scarlet
Purple and yellow	Warm pink, orange, gold, and cream	Red, scarlet, and gold	Deep purple-black and pink
Blue and pink	Pink, blue, and purple	Red, white, and blue	Maroon and chartreuse
Blue and yellow		Red, yellow, and blue	
Blue and orange			

Brown Houses

Brown houses may be the honey color of logs or other natural woods, or the gray-brown of weathered wood shingles. Or they may be painted a color as dark as chocolate. What sort of brown your house is will naturally affect your choice of colors in the garden. A natural-colored wood house can support a wide variety of color schemes in the landscape. Darker brown homes look especially good with bright, warm sunset colors—orange, gold, yellow, salmon, and cream. Red flowers would look fine with a light wood, but would tend to get lost against dark chocolate browns. You can, however, create interesting effects by mixing some dark red-brown foliage into a garden of brighter yellows, from plants such as *Heuchera* 'Chocolate Ruffles', *Cimicifuga simplex* 'Brunette' or 'Hillside Black Beauty', sunset hibiscus (*Hibiscus acetosella* 'Coppertone'), and the unusual reddish brown flowers of Carolina allspice (*Calycanthus floridus*).

Good trim colors for brown houses include white, beige, brick red (for a lighter brown or natural wood), terra-cotta, salmon, and green.

Garden Colors for Brown Houses

Pink, blue, and purple	Maroon and chartreuse
Red, pink, and rose	Blue and white
Red, orange, and yellow	Red-brown, cream, and yellow
Blue and yellow	Orange, gold, yellow, and salmon
Blue and peach	Blue, orange, and salmon
Purple and yellow	
Pink, lavender, and silver	

Good flower colors for a brown house depend upon the tone of the brown. The pale brown stone of this home is beautifully complemented by the warm pink geraniums and roses in the garden.

Green Houses

Green houses, whether a grayish sage color or a deeper forest green, are nicely complemented by a host of different schemes in the garden, especially if the house trim is a neutral white or beige. Blues, purples, pinks, and rose-pinks contrast beautifully with a green house. Yellows and oranges work well with a dark green house but are less appealing (to my eye, at least) next to a sage green house. Rich, deep reds, on the other hand, work better with a lighter or grayish green house than with a dark green home, where the contrast could be too jarring.

Trim colors to consider for a green house include beige, cream, white, mauve, deeper green (on a sage house), and gray.

Garden Colors for Green Houses

Purple and yellow	Rose, pink, and blue
Purple and cream	Rose, pink, and silver
Purple, lavender, and yellow	Rose, lavender, and purple
Purple, pink, and yellow	Crimson, pink, and lavender
Pink and yellow	Deep purple-black and pink
Blue, pink, and silver	Red and white
Pink and blue	Green and white
Pink, rose, and purple	

This green and white garden echoes the colors of the siding and trim on the house. Introducing some rich reds adds a dramatic accent to the quiet scheme.

Red Houses

A garden for a red house, whether of brick, redwood (or a redwood-colored stain), or red siding, bears some careful consideration. For a harmonious scheme, yellows, oranges, and golds can work quite well. For a pleasing contrast, consider blue and yellow, or blue and peach. Deep red flowers can work, too, such as chocolate cosmos or *Knautia macedonica*. But you will probably want to avoid using magenta, cool pinks, bright reds, and strong purples next to a red house, unless you have an adventurous spirit.

A red house needs trim colors that don't fight the walls. White, cream, and beige are good choices.

Garden Colors for Red Houses

Yellow, orange, and gold	Blue and yellow
Yellow and white	Blue and peach
Yellow, orange, and salmon	Blue, orange, and salmon
Orange, gold, yellow, and creamy white	

A garden with warm-toned flowers in yellows and reds, along with plenty of green foliage, beautifully complements a brick house.

Blue Houses

Gardens that include some rich, deep blues and violets create a pleasing harmony with a blue house. Whether you combine analogous lavenders and pinks with the blues or contrast them with yellow or peach, the effect can be lovely. In a formal setting, consider a blue-and-white or, for more drama, a red-and-white scheme. If the trim is accented with a burgundy-red, you can echo that color in the garden with deep purple-red foliage such as that of 'Bloodgood' Japanese maples or a purple-leaved alumroot such as *Heuchera micrantha* 'Palace Purple'.

Some good trim colors for blue houses would be beige, white, gray, cream, or burgundy.

Pinks are lovely in gardens to accompany blue houses. Here, a Japanese cherry tree is underplanted with foamy white snow-in-summer (*Cerastium tomentosum*). Spiky New Zealand flax (*Phormium tenax*) provides a dramatic contrast with the China Doll rose behind it.

Garden Colors for Blue Houses

Pink, blue, and silver	Pink and blue
Blue and white	Rose, pink, and blue
Blue and yellow	Pink, blue, and orange
Blue and peach	Orange, gold, yellow, and cream
Blue, orange, and salmon	Red, white, and blue
Blue-violet, orange, and apricot	Red, yellow, and blue
Violet, lavender, and yellow	Yellow and white
Purple, blue-violet, and cream or light yellow	Maroon, pink, and white
Pink and yellow	Maroon, yellow, and gold

Yellow Houses

A yellow house can support any number of outdoor color schemes. Warm reds, oranges, and yellows will harmonize with it. Cool blues and purples will contrast. You can add a sophisticated touch to the garden by including some yellow-variegated foliage in your planning. Leaves splashed, streaked, or spotted with gold, such as those of gold dust plant (*Aucuba japonica*) or hosta cultivars, echo the house in a rich and subtle way. Imagine a garden of blues and yellows with some gold-splashed leaves incorporated into it—the foliage will enrich the whole garden. White is the most-often-used trim color for yellow houses.

Garden Colors for Yellow Houses

Blue, pink, and silver	Pink and yellow
Blue and white	Pink and blue
Blue and yellow	Rose, pink, and blue
Blue and peach	Warm pink, orange, gold, and cream
Blue, orange, and salmon	Red and yellow
Blue-violet, orange, and apricot	Red, orange, gold, and salmon
Purple and yellow	Red, orange, and yellow
Purple and cream	Red, scarlet, and gold
Purple, pink, and yellow	Red, yellow, and blue
Purple, blue-violet, and pale yellow	Yellow and white

Warm pinks, salmons, oranges, and reds harmonize readily with a yellow house.

CHAPTER 3

Hardscaping and Space Management

Just as a well-built house needs a strong foundation, a well-designed garden needs a sound structure. In addition to trees, shrubs, and hedges, the more-or-less permanent plants in a landscape, the constructed elements in the garden—paths and walkways, walls and fences—form the garden's underlying structure, what garden designers like to call its "bones." These parts of the landscape are visible year-round, and they become prominent in winter, when the charming distractions of flowers and foliage are less in evidence or absent altogether except in the warmest climates. The constructed elements of the garden—the walls, fences, and paths—are called *hardscape* in the landscaping industry. Patios are hardscape, too, but in this chapter we are concerned with hardscaping that is used

◄ Walls, paths, and pavement are essential structural elements of the garden. The hard edges of formal walls and paths can be softened with loose plantings, as seen here.

to manage space and movement through the garden. Hedges are also included because they work much like walls and fences. (You can find information on decks and patios in the next chapter.)

Before you put a plant in the ground, you would do well to plan for the structural elements of the landscape. Use walls, fences, and hedges to define spaces, delineate boundaries, and create privacy. Set paths and walkways to get from one place to another. When these elements are laid out in a way that both enables them to serve their intended functions and makes visual sense, and when they are constructed of materials that complement the materials, colors, and style of your house, the entire property works as one, a single coordinated design. Here is where the unified landscape begins.

On a formal property, the design usually works as a grid, with paths laid in straight lines and decks and patios in neat rectangular or geometric shapes. Informal landscapes make more use of flowing curves and undulating lines.

The way you manage space in your landscape determines the locations of beds and borders and provides the basis for your plantings. If you have an existing landscape, study it in winter to assess where improvements and redirections might bring more logic to the underlying structure, improve the flow of traffic, and generally make it more comfortable and easy to use.

In this chapter, we will look at creating good bones for your landscape, and we'll explore options for paths and walkways, walls and fences, and hedges and screens of plants. The next chapter will go on to address structures.

Paths and Walkways

Paths are essential on most properties. They get you from one place to another, enable the mailman to find your front door, allow you to push cartloads of compost to the beds and borders where you need it, and show visitors how to move through your garden to enjoy its beauty without getting their feet wet or muddy. Paths connect house and landscape into a unified property. They link the house to the street and all the outdoor spaces you use—the garage, a shed, a gazebo, a patio. From the routes you normally take to reach these places, you can start to build a pattern with paths.

Paths move you through the landscape both physically, as you walk on them, and mentally, as your eyes follow their lines across the land. Try to put in the fewest paths you need to get from place to place. You don't want to carve up your property with a maze of paths running here, there, and everywhere. Instead, leave the space in bigger chunks and use it for garden beds and borders, or for lawn or other plantings. Whether your landscaping plans involve renovating an existing garden or starting a new one, it pays to understand the characteristics of your property before you begin. You will want to construct pathways and other structural features where they will serve their purpose most effectively and play a visually pleasing role in the overall design, of course, but you also need to take into account the land itself.

You need to know, particularly where paths are concerned, where water collects after heavy rain, where ice is likely to form, and where snow lingers in spring. It's also wise to find out the path water follows when it runs off during a storm.

It's best to avoid putting paths or walkways in poorly drained locations. Water will puddle up on the paths during heavy rain and freeze over in winter, making walking difficult in both cases. If you have no alternative to making a walkway in a wet spot, you will need to either install drainage tiles or pipes underground or build a raised boardwalk to keep your feet dry.

Where to Put Paths

When you moved into your house, it probably already had a walkway from the street or driveway to the front door. But there are numerous other places where paths are useful. You will need paths to link different parts of the landscape. You'll also need to have access to beds and borders to maintain the plants, you'll have to put out the trash, and you'll need to get to the garage (if it's not attached to the house) and to wherever you park your car in the driveway. A path can lead to a gazebo, arbor, or other outdoor structure; to a swimming pool or a pond; to a bench or swing; or to a special area for children's play or sports. You might want a path that leads past a piece of art, a birdbath, a sundial, or some other ornament. A path can lead past garden beds and borders (an edging of bricks laid flat and flush with with the ground makes a handy mowing strip so you won't have to edge the path). Look for places people naturally walk, where the grass is worn from foot traffic. There might be a shortcut you habitually take across the lawn to get to your car, for instance. You probably need paths in these places, too. If these tracks don't fit well into your design, you can put in

Plan paths for ready access to outbuildings.

Formal paths are smooth and level, and they lead straight to their destination.

Informal paths can wind and meander through the landscape.

a few less noticeable stepping-stones instead of a path to save the grass.

If your garden is formal, you will want to create a grid of straight paths that are smooth and level. If your property slopes at an angle of 30 degrees or more, you will need to build a series of terraces in which to garden, in order to maintain the straight lines and sharp edges of a formal design. You might include a path running horizontally across the face of the hillside to enhance the controlled, contained look of the garden.

Paths in an informal garden can wind and curve as they meander through the landscape, following the line of a bed or border and tracing gentle undulations in the terrain, where steps are not needed. Paths that twist and turn bring a touch of mystery to the garden, and a sense of discovery—you never know what you will find around the next bend. Winding paths also make a small garden feel bigger. Even in an informal garden, though, you will probably want to make some paths straight. Routes to destinations you need to reach in a timely manner, such as those to the garage or the trash bin, for instance, are usually best laid straight to their goals.

On the other hand, a path that leads to a shady bench or a secluded pool, or past a piece of sculpture or a breathtaking specimen tree, can meander a bit to allow strollers to take in more of the garden along the way. You will walk more slowly on a winding path, and you will have more time to look around you.

The surface materials of a path also affect the speed at which you will traverse it. Rough, uneven surfaces demand more care of the walker. Smoother surfaces encourage a speedier pace. You can factor ease and speed of travel into your path planning, and you can even use surface pavements to manipulate how fast people walk in your landscape. Switching from smooth, even flagstone stepping-stones to rougher fieldstone as the path approaches a garden feature will cause strollers to slow down to notice the feature. Just don't make the pavement so uneven that people will need to look down at their feet in order not to trip.

You can also use different path surfaces in different parts of the landscape to call attention to transitions from one area to another, as, for example, between one garden room and the next, or between a sunny flower border and a shady woodland garden. In Japanese gardens, different pavements are often used to denote different parts of the landscape and to highlight specimen plants and carefully orchestrated views.

Paths should be wide enough to comfortably accommodate the people and accessories passing over them, but they need not all be the same width. A primary path, one that leads to an important destination, such as the front door, the swimming pool, or into the garden, should be 3 to 4 feet wide so two people can comfortably walk side by side. You might even prefer the walk to the front door to be wider still—4 or 5 feet—to give it maximum importance and also to visually balance the volume of the house. Also take into account whether you will need to push a lawn mower, garden cart, or baby stroller along the path—such needs help determine the best pavement material for the path.

Secondary paths that allow you to get behind beds and borders to maintain the plants, fill birdfeeders, or find your way to a hidden hammock should be narrower than the primary paths; 2 to 3 feet is usually sufficient.

STAIR TIPS

If you need to make steps in a hillside path, be aware that outdoor steps are different from stairs indoors. Outdoor steps should be broader and lower, for a more gradual climb (or descent).

Make the treads (the top part of the step, where you place your foot) at least 12 inches wide. Make the risers (the front, vertical part of the step) 5 to 6 inches high.

If you will need more than a dozen steps to reach the top of the slope, it's a good idea to add a broader landing halfway up.

On a steep hill, or wherever you need more than a few steps, install railings for your safety and comfort.

Consider, always, the comfort and safety of those who will use the paths. Make all paths a bit wider where they curve. If the path will climb a slope, plan to add steps if the grade exceeds 4 or 5 percent. A path used often by young children (to reach a play area, for instance) needs a soft surface. Where older people or others not always sure-footed will walk, avoid using surface materials—such as wood and smooth slate—that become slippery when they're wet. Finally, keep paths at least 2 feet away from the foundation of the house, walls, hedges, and large trees.

Path Styles

Paths look best when they are planned to blend in with the house and other elements of the landscape. Lots of different materials will serve to surface a path—some formal, others informal; some hard, others soft. Your goal is to choose a path style that will work with the house and look at home on your property.

One way to connect paths to the look of the house is to repeat some of the same materials used on the house and elsewhere in the landscape. If your house is brick, consider using brick for the main paths. If you have a flagstone patio, you can also use flagstone on your paths. If your house is sided with wood shingles, look for gravel, fieldstone, or concrete pavers of a similar color. If your house is stuccoed, you could pave paths with light sandstone of a similar hue. In a woodland garden, surface paths with shredded bark or another woodsy material to keep them unobtrusive and let the soft colors of your shade-tolerant wildflowers and bulbs shine through.

Brick, flagstone, and concrete pavers all can work beautifully for paving paths in formal gardens. Tile creates a Mediterranean look. Gravel comes in a variety of colors and is versatile in its applications, but it is an especially good choice for paths in a rock garden or a desert garden. You can get creative with

A path of pebbles, brick, and stepping-stones.

paths, too, and make mosaics of tile, pebbles, marbles, or even pieces of broken flowerpots or old dishes set in cement. You can even cast your own stepping-stones (kits are available) and memorialize children's footprints, favorite sayings, important dates, and other items with personal meanings.

Surface Materials

Path materials are either hard and solid or soft and yielding underfoot. Hard surfaces—brick, flagstone, and concrete (poured or in the form of individual paving blocks)—work well in formal gardens. They,

along with less-formal fieldstone, are expensive and time-consuming to install, but they are durable, hold up well under traffic, are reasonably permanent, and don't require a lot of maintenance. Soft surfaces—gravel, pebbles, wood chips, shredded bark, pine needles, and grass or groundcovers—are inherently informal, for the most part. They are inexpensive and quick and easy to install, but they need periodic maintenance and replenishment. Gravel and pebbles scatter and work their way down into the ground over time. Mulches, wood chips, and pine needles decompose. Grass has to be mowed and groundcovers weeded, at least once in a while. It's also difficult to push a wheelbarrow over a soft-surface path. Stepping-stones have a hard surface, but they are set into the lawn or a base of loose stones; they are really a category of their own.

Consider your site as well as your house when choosing path materials. Such practical considerations as the terrain and the amount of traffic the path will bear need to be taken into account. If you live in a rainy climate, a hard-surfaced path in a low spot is an invitation to standing puddles after rain. A porous, loose surface of gravel or mulch will allow rainwater to soak into the ground rather than run off and is a better choice. But on a slope, a loose surface such as wood chips or pebbles will be likely to wash downhill during heavy rains. A much-traveled path between the house and garage will provide the surest, safest footing if it is paved with a smooth, hard material.

Any path needs to be well prepared before the surface is laid if it's to function well over time. Hard surfaces are best laid on a base of gravel and sand to

ensure good drainage and stability. The last thing you need is a large, lingering puddle or a sheet of ice in the middle of the walkway. Stepping-stones need to be set into the ground so that their faces are even with the surface. When just set on top of the ground, they can tip over if you step on their edges. Even a simple path of shredded bark will stay in place better if you prepare the ground first and install an edging. No matter what kind of surface you use, try to make the path very slightly higher in the center (about ¼ inch) and slightly lower at the edges, so water will not collect on the path.

Here is a rundown of possible path materials and their applications.

Brick

A traditional and popular paving material, brick makes an attractive, durable path with an even surface. A brick path looks formal, especially when set in mortar; unmortared paths can also work in informal settings. The classic brownish red color of brick is warm and appealing, but bricks come in a range of tones, including beige, tan, pale orangey pink, and deep red-brown. Brick is readily available and comes in a range of sizes. It's expensive, but a well-laid brick path will last a lifetime. You might be able to find used brick, or odds and ends left over from patios or paths installed by professional contractors that you can purchase for less. But find out what kind of brick it is before you buy.

Wherever the ground freezes (in much of the United States, in other words), you will need to use paving brick, which is sometimes called *water-struck*

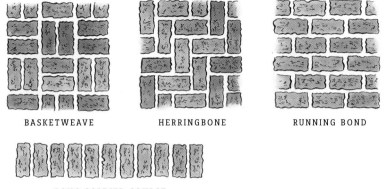

BASKETWEAVE   HERRINGBONE   RUNNING BOND

LONG SOLDIER COURSE

You can lay bricks in simple or complex patterns in a path or patio. The long solider course is simplest and will direct attention along the line of a path. Basketweave is complex and interesting, and herringbone is elegant and formal. Running bond is straightforward and can also be used for a sturdy wall.

Railroad ties serve as steps in this basketweave brick path on a slope.

brick. Severe-weather brick is toughest but most expensive. Moderate-weather bricks are less expensive but are not as uniform in size. They are also more porous, and they will weather over time. Moss will grow on moderate-weather bricks in shady, moist locations, which creates a beautifully antique look but can make for slippery walking when wet. Antique and old salvaged brick looks wonderful, but it will not hold up well in winter weather. Moisture will get into the bricks and freeze, repeated freezing and thawing will crack them, and eventually the bricks will break apart. Facing brick is also available, but like old brick, it is liable to crack under winter conditions. Glazed brick, too, is problematic. The glaze can be damaged by salts contained in sidewalk de-icers or fertilizers, and moisture may penetrate the damaged surface, causing cracking and eventual crumbling over time.

Lay your brick path on a base of sand and gravel, as described in "How to Lay a Path" on page 101. You can lay brick in any of a variety of patterns, from a simple running bond laid in sand to more formal and elaborate basketweave and herringbone patterns set in mortar. See the illustration above for a selection.

The best way to keep a brick path free of weeds is to lay it in mortar. Another way to minimize weed growth is to use plastic brick-laying guides; you position these atop the gravel and sand base, and simply set the bricks into the spaces. If an unmortared path is what you want, you will just have to resign yourself to doing some occasional weeding. If the path is well edged, you can pour a concentrated vinegar solution over the bricks to eliminate weeds.

Flagstone

Flagstones are not made of any particular mineral—they're simply pieces of quarried stone that are split into fairly thin sections and used for paving. Flagstone makes a beautiful path: smooth and even to walk on, extremely durable, long-lasting, and relatively easy to install. It is also the most costly paving material commonly used for surfacing walkways.

The quarried stone is cut into various-size rectangles for very formal, elegant pavement, or into irregular shapes for less-formal pavements (sometimes called random paving or crazy paving). To make a flagstone path, you can use all cut or all irregular flags, or you can mix the two types. You can also mix colors, if you wish.

Flagstones are made from various types of rock and come in several colors. Sandstone flags are shades of tan, buff, pink, or red; bluestone (which is actually a kind of sandstone) is gray, deep slate blue or, alternatively, tan or brown; and limestone is white or pinkish to gray. Slate (a metamorphosed form of shale) is dark gray to black or shades of red. It is sometimes used for paving, although unless the surface is rough it becomes very slippery when wet. Some slates also may be prone to flaking and chipping in cold-winter climates. Slabs of marble also become slick when wet and are not recommended for paving (they're also prohibitively expensive).

Limestone is a soft, porous rock that you might consider using for paths if you live in an area with a dry climate. Limestone comes in a range of light colors and is attractive, but it stains readily. Because of its porosity, limestone is not a good choice for humid and wet climates unless it is coated with a sealant after installation.

Granite is sometimes used for flagstones, but it is more often used as cobbles, Belgian block, or other thick paving and building stones.

When you select flagstones for a path, don't choose the thinnest ones you can find. To bear the weight of people and equipment, paving flags should be at least 2 inches thick. Thinner stones are more likely to crack.

A straight, smooth axis path in a formal garden.

Fieldstone

Fieldstone is dug from the ground of fields and prairies, not quarried from solid rock like flagstone. It is sturdy and durable, and it is expensive, though a bit less so than flagstone. Fieldstone comes in many shapes and sizes and in a range of colors that varies from one region of the country to another, depending on the kind of rock it is. Fieldstones are irregularly shaped and have a rough, rustic look that works quite well in informal gardens.

Stepping-stones lead through a chamomile lawn.

For use in a path, look for relatively flat pieces of fieldstone. You can use fieldstones as stepping-stones or fit them together to make a continuous path. Because the stones are irregular, plan on burying them partially to create a reasonably level surface that will be even enough to walk on.

Poured Concrete

Concrete sidewalks are ubiquitous in American towns and cities. More sidewalks are made of concrete than of any other material. There are reasons why concrete is so popular; it's inexpensive and durable, making an even, long-lasting walkway. On the downside, though, concrete absorbs heat and often becomes too hot to walk barefoot on in summer. It can crack if it is not properly installed, and it's boring and looks intrusive in the landscape.

There are ways to make concrete look better, so that you can have a sturdy path that's not a glaring ribbon of white. Instead of just pouring a procession of white slabs, you can tint the concrete to a darker, less unnatural color. You can use wood edgings between slabs and arrange them to create interesting patterns. You can brush or rake out the wet surface to expose the rough-textured pebbled aggregate beneath. Or you can have concrete that is stamped or otherwise textured to resemble stone. Textured concrete is less expensive than real stone, but it costs more than ordinary poured concrete.

Concrete pavers combine with smooth river rock in this path.

Concrete Pavers

Concrete paving blocks are available in an ever-expanding selection of sizes, styles, and colors. They come in beige or tan, brick red, various shades of gray and blue-gray, and brown. Some are made to look like bricks or cobblestones. Others look decidedly unnatural. Some pavers interlock and some do not.

Concrete pavers make a durable, permanent walkway, and they are easy to install. You can lay them in any number of different patterns and even combine two or more colors, although a multicolored design would work better in a larger area such as a

driveway, parking area, or patio. Pavers are sold by the piece, and they produce a path with a finished look and an even surface.

Pavers are not inexpensive. They cost less than brick or flagstone, but more than gravel and other loose surfaces. One caveat where pavers are concerned is that weeds can squeeze up between them. It can be difficult to pull weeds from the tiny spaces between the blocks; a dousing with concentrated vinegar solution might be a better way to get rid of any weeds that pop up. Also, you will need to shop around to find the best variety of styles; not all local retailers carry a big selection.

Gravel, Pebbles, and Crushed Rock

Loose stone is versatile and easy to install. If you lay a gravel path on a good base (see "How to Lay a Path" on page 101) and install an edging to hold the stones in place, a gravel path will last reasonably well. Without an edging, the stones will spread and scatter, and some will work their way down into the soil. Some of your path will end up in the garden, where it will be nearly impossible to remove without a soil sieve. In a year or two, you will have to put down more stone. Still, if your soil is dense enough and you don't mind replenishing the stone on a regular basis, it's possible to lay a crushed stone path right on top of the ground. It's better to create a base, though.

Gravel and crushed stone come in a range of colors from white to black. There are cool grays and blue-grays, and warm buffs, tans, browns, brick reds, and beiges.

Crushed gravel or bluestone
can surface a path in a formal
or informal garden.

White pebbles and marble chips, which are popular in some seashore areas, can be unnatural looking and glaring in their brightness. The path's brilliance can detract from the garden. But if a white path is what you want, these are obvious choices. An old-fashioned white paving material sometimes seen where I live on eastern Long Island is crushed oyster shells. In coastal areas, where seashells are readily available, they afford another pavement option.

Dark-colored gravel is adaptable and can work in many different situations, even formal landscapes. A brick or cobblestone edging looks more finished and sophisticated than gravel by itself, so be sure to use this kind of neat, precise edging in a formal situation. Dark stone will be unobtrusive in the landscape and will not compete with garden plants for attention—you will hardly notice it. You can choose the color to harmonize with your house. If the house is a warm color, brown or brick red gravel would be a good choice. For a cool-colored house, you might opt instead for gray or blue-gray stone. You can also mix two or more colors together.

Loose stone is sold in bags or in bulk. One 50-pound bag of pea gravel will cover an area of 5 square yards to a depth of 2 inches. Unless your path is very short, it's better to buy by the cubic yard. (People in the nursery business tend to refer to a cubic yard of material simply as "a yard.") Gravel is less expensive than fieldstone, flagstone, or brick. Loose pebbles or other stone with rounded edges is reasonably comfortable to walk on, as long as you are not wearing high heels. Crushed stone with jagged edges is less comfortable to step on, at least initially, but over time the pieces of stone will pack together more tightly than rounded stone and they will eventually form a more solid, cohesive surface. Rounded stone will stay looser.

A gravel path is pretty easy to install. Once the base is prepared and the edging is in place, all you have to do is dump and spread the stone. Bear in mind, however, that even if you put down a layer of landscape fabric to keep out weeds, eventually weeds will get into the path, especially as the layer of stone thins over time. You will need to remove the weeds to keep the path looking neat.

Tile

If you love a Mediterranean or Southwest look and your home reflects it, you might consider paving a path with quarry tile or other ceramic tile. A tiled path can work if it leads from a tiled patio to another part of the landscape. Tiles are best in warm climates where winter freezes and thaws are not an issue. They look elegant and polished and produce a smooth, even surface, but they can crack if you don't install them properly or if you drop heavy objects on them. Purchase tile intended for outdoor use. You can choose among an array of colors and select tones that echo or harmonize with your house. Or you might like to inject a note of contrasting color in selected spots, such as on stair treads or risers.

Another type of tile to consider if you have young children is the spongy rubber tile meant to provide a soft surface for play areas. These tiles come in dark colors, and although they are not cheap, they do prevent injuries on paths where kids run and play.

Recycled Glass

Recycled tumbled glass is starting to show up in gardens. The glass, tumbled smooth and in a host of colors, looks like beach glass. A patch or "river" of recycled tumbled glass adds a fanciful color accent in a concrete path. Or scatter it into a pebbled walkway; it has no sharp edges and will not hurt bare feet. One caveat: If you want to use glass in a path that will be heavily traveled, seal it with a waterproof resin to extend its life.

Natural Materials

For a natural-looking path in a woodland garden or other informal shade garden, you can spread a layer of bark nuggets, wood chips, shredded bark, pine needles, or other materials used for mulching gardens. Although they don't last very long and need to be replenished every year or two, these mulches have a lot to recommend them for surfacing paths, especially in a shady environment. They are inexpensive, for one thing; they add organic matter to the soil as they decompose; and, except for pine needles, they are readily available in bags at garden centers and nurseries or in bulk (delivered) from tree care companies and nurseries. You may also be able to get chipped or shredded wood for free at construction sites or at municipal waste disposal facilities. One cubic yard of mulch will cover an area of 140 square feet, to 2 inches deep.

You can spread mulch materials right on the ground to make a path, although to keep the material in place you need to recess the path a few inches

Above: Fieldstone stepping-stones provide solid places to step in an informal mulched path. *Right:* Sawn wood rounds surface another informal garden path.

Grass

A neatly mowed swath of grass makes a pleasant path, especially between garden beds and borders, if you are willing to do the work to maintain it in good condition. A grass path won't cost a lot, and with good care it will be pretty permanent. But you will need to mow it and topdress it with compost every year. In dry weather you'll need to water the path, and you may have to deal with an assortment of pest and disease problems, depending on where you live. Lawn grasses spread, too, and unless you edge your path regularly you will find it creeping into your flowerbeds.

Still, grass beautifully sets off the colors of the garden, and it's lovely to walk barefoot on in summer. You can use grass paths in either formal or informal gardens. Installing a mowing strip of bricks set flush with the ground along the edge of the garden will allow you to mow the path without hand-edging.

or install edging. If the location is poorly drained and the ground is often wet, spread a layer of gravel before you lay the mulch, to provide drainage. Soggy mulch is uncomfortable to walk on and decomposes faster than drier material.

Give your path a generous layer of mulch—2 inches or more. The material will compact over time and with foot traffic. Because you want to get the organic matter back into the soil as the mulch decomposes, do not lay landscape fabric over the soil before laying the path. That means you will have to do some periodic weeding, but the mulch will prevent a lot of weeds from sprouting and the work should not be too onerous.

A path of lawn grass is attractive and long lasting and provides a pleasant walking surface. It will, however, need regular maintenance to look its best.

Groundcovers

Some groundcover plants can stand up to light foot traffic and can be used to surface paths in areas that don't get walked on a lot. Some of these plants are fragrant when stepped on—an added bonus. Groundcovers are spreaders by nature, and they will want to wander into your garden, too. You can let them intermingle a bit along the edges of beds and borders to integrate path and garden; just clip them or pull up unwanted strays when they spread too far. Or, to keep the path separate, install an edging that extends several inches underground along the path

and a mowing strip along the front of the garden (whether or not you have grass between the garden and the path) to discourage spreading. (See "Groundcovers for Paths" on page 99 for examples of plants that can stand up to light foot traffic.)

Edgings for Paths

To keep the surface of your paths in place, you will need to install edgings. A number of materials can serve as edgings, among them wooden boards, short posts or stakes, bricks, and stones. You can also buy edging strips of plastic or metal.

Brick or stone. Bricks or stone blocks, such as Belgian block or cobbles, are easy to use for edging curved paths, but they work well for straight paths, too. Although expensive up front, paving brick or stone provides a stable, permanent edging. You may mortar them in place if you wish, or simply stand them on end next to one another. Set brick or

stone edgers in place after you have excavated the path area but before you lay the base materials. If you will be edging a hard-surface path, unless your bricks or blocks are 9 or 10 inches long, you may need to excavate a shallow ledge along the edges of your paths so the edgers will sit a little higher than the base of the path. See "How to Lay a Path" on page 101 for information on recommended excavation depths.

One note about brick paths: Include the edging when you plan the width of your path so that both the bricks laid flat in the path and the bricks stood on end for edging will fit in the space. This way, you won't have to cut bricks to fit.

Concrete and cultured stone. If your path will be surfaced with concrete pavers, you can purchase edgings to match them. You will find both individual blocks that interlock at the ends and edging strips with a flat bottom and scalloped top, in straight or curved sections.

(continued on page 101)

A path of ajuga and golden nummularia.

A TEMPORARY PATH

In a pinch, you can simply lay bricks or stone, or spread mulch or gravel, right on top of the ground to make a path. It will look decent for a season, but don't count on it as a long-term solution. That's because the path will spread when it's walked on, wash away in intense rain, and heave and buckle in cold winter weather when the ground repeatedly freezes and thaws.

GROUNDCOVERS FOR PATHS

The plants listed here can all tolerate light foot traffic.

PLANT	DESCRIPTION	GROWING CONDITIONS	COMMENTS	GROWING RANGE
Ajuga reptans, bugleweed	Creeping perennial to 6 in. high, with glossy deep green, purple-bronze, or variegated spoon-shaped leaves and, in late spring to early summer, spikes of deep violet flowers.	Partial to medium shade; adapts to a range of soils.	Attractive and free-spreading, especially in moist soils.	Zones 3–9
Alchemilla alpina, alpine lady's mantle	Spreading, mat-forming perennial 4 in. high, with rounded leaves divided into 5 to 7 slender lobes and, in summer, loose, airy clusters of tiny chartreuse flowers.	Full sun to partial shade; moist, humusy soil.	Deadhead if you want to prevent self-sowing.	Zones 3–7
Antennaria dioica, pussytoes	Mat-forming, semi-evergreen perennial 2 in. high, with spoon-shaped, hairy, gray-green leaves and, in early summer, clusters of fluffy white to pinkish flowers.	Full sun to light shade; well-drained soil of average fertility.	Thrives in dry conditions.	Zones 5–9
Cerastium tomentosum, snow-in-summer	Mat-forming perennial to 6 in. high, with woolly silver-gray leaves and, in early summer, masses of small, starry white flowers.	Full sun; well-drained, sandy soil of average or poor fertility.	Good choice for poor soils; spreads very vigorously elsewhere.	Zones 2–7
Chamaemelum nobile, Roman chamomile	Sprawling, mat-forming perennial 1 ft high, with apple-scented, bright green, divided threadlike leaves and, in summer, small white daisy flowers.	Full sun to partial shade; light, well-drained, sandy soil of average fertility.	Vigorous spreader. Cultivar 'Treneague' does not bloom.	Zones 3–10
Chrysogonum virginianum, goldenstar	Spreading, mat-forming perennial to 12 in. high, with hairy, toothed, heart-shaped to oblong leaves and, in spring and early summer, star-shaped golden yellow flowers.	Full sun to light shade; moist but well-drained, humusy soil.	Nice in woodland gardens.	Zones 5–9
Cotula (*Leptinella*) *squalida*, New Zealand brass buttons	Creeping perennial to 6 in. high, forms a dense mat of divided, fernlike, oval to oblong green leaves and, in late spring and early summer, small yellow-green flowers.	Partial shade; moist but well-drained soil of average fertility.	Does well in wet places.	Zones 4–7
Cymbalaria muralis, Kenilworth ivy	Vining perennial to 3 ft long, with small, lobed, kidney-shaped leaves and, in summer, small light purple flowers.	Partial shade to full sun; moist but well-drained soil of average fertility.	Small but vigorous.	Zones 4–8
Dichondra micrantha	Prostrate, spreading, tender groundcover to 1½ ft high, with small, rounded green leaves and tiny white or yellow flowers in summer.	Full sun to partial shade; well-drained soil of average fertility, with mildly acid pH.	Sometimes used as a lawn substitute.	Zones 10–11; elsewhere as annual
Euonymus fortunei 'Kewensis', wintercreeper	Mat-forming evergreen shrub about 4 in. high, with oval, dark green leaves on slender stems.	Full sun to light shade; well-drained soil of average fertility.	Protect from cold, drying winter winds.	Zones 5–9

(continued)

PLANT	DESCRIPTION	GROWING CONDITIONS	COMMENTS	GROWING RANGE
Lysimachia nummularia, creeping Jenny	Prostrate trailing perennial 2 in. high, with small, rounded leaves and yellow flowers in summer.	Full sun to partial shade; moist, humusy soil of average fertility.	Cultivar 'Aurea' has golden leaves.	Zones 4–8
Mazus reptans	Mat-forming perennial 2 in. high, with small, toothed, oval leaves and, in late spring to early summer, small, lipped, purple flowers.	Full sun; moist but well-drained soil of average fertility.	Good choice for a path in a rock garden.	Zones 5–8
Mentha requienii, Corsican mint	Prostrate, mat-forming perennial about ½ in. high, with small, round, intensely mint-scented leaves of rich green and, in summer, clusters of small, tubular, lavender flowers.	Partial to light shade; moist, humusy soil of average fertility.	Releases its fragrance when stepped on.	Zones 6–11
Ophiopogon japonicus, dwarf mondo grass	Clumping perennial to 1 ft high, with narrow, arching leaves and, in summer, spikes of small, bell-shaped white flowers followed by deep blue-black berries.	Full sun to partial shade; moist but well-drained, humusy soil of good fertility, with mildly acid pH.	Nice lining a path as well.	Zones 7–10
Sagina subulata, Irish moss	Mat-forming perennial ½ in. high, with small, narrow leaves and, in summer, tiny white flowers.	Full sun to partial shade; moist but well-drained soil of poor to average fertility, with acid to neutral pH.	Dainty plant with tiny leaves.	Zones 4–7
Sedum acre, goldmoss sedum	Mat-forming, trailing perennial to 4 in. high, with succulent, triangular leaves and, in late spring and summer, clusters of tiny greenish yellow flowers.	Full sun to partial shade; well-drained, humusy soil of average fertility.	Good plant for dry soils.	Zones 3–9
Soleirolia soleirolii, baby's tears	Diminutive, trailing, mat-forming perennial 2 to 4 in. high, with tiny round leaves and minute white flowers in summer.	Partial to full shade; moist but well-drained soil of average fertility.	Can be invasive in good soils.	Zones 9–11
Thymus pseudolanuginosus, woolly thyme	Creeping perennial 3 in. high, with small, aromatic, oval leaves and, in early summer, light pink to mauve flowers.	Full sun; well-drained soil of average fertility, with neutral to alkaline pH.	Attracts lots of bees when blooming, so don't walk barefoot.	Zones 5–9
Thymus serpyllum, mother-of-thyme	Mat-forming perennial to 6 in. high, with aromatic, oval leaves and, in early summer, clusters of tiny lilac to rose flowers attractive to bees.	Full sun; well-drained soil of average fertility, with neutral to alkaline pH.	Tolerates drought.	Zones 4–9
Waldsteinia ternata, barren strawberry	Vigorous, spreading perennial to 4 in. high, with lobed semi-evergreen leaves and, in late spring to early summer, clusters of 5-petaled yellow flowers.	Full sun to partial shade; adapts to a range of soils of average fertility.	Nice in woodland gardens.	Zones 3–8

Wood. Wood boards are the easiest kind of edging to use for straight paths. Use rot-resistant wood such as redwood, cypress, or cedar in planks an inch thick. You can also make a stockade edging for a curved or straight path by hammering in a line of short wooden posts.

Excavate the path as described in "How to Lay a Path" below. If your soil is loose and sandy, put your edging in place before you lay any of the base materials for the path. Hold the boards in place with short stakes every few feet. If your soil is dense clay, lay the gravel base first and set the edgers on top of it, then lay the sand base. In either case, the top of the edging boards should be even with the top surface of the path when it is complete. You can let a stockade-type edging show above the path surface if you like the look.

Metal and plastic. You can use inexpensive metal edging strips to hold a loose-surface path in place, if you wish. Stake the edging to hold it in place. Plastic edging strips can work, too, although they don't always stay in place around curves.

After the path edgings are in place, fill in behind them with soil excavated from the path to fill any gaps and firm the edging into place.

How to Lay a Path

A stable, long-lasting path starts with good site preparation. Here's how to make a basic, unmortared path.

First, lay out the course of the path. Use stakes and string to mark off a straight path, or set out lengths of rope or garden hose for a curved walkway.

Adjust the lines until they please you. Measure the width you want and lay out the other side of the path.

Excavate the area between the two sides 8 inches deep for a hard-surface path, or 6 inches deep for a loose-surface path. Try to get the bottom of the excavated area as level as you can.

If you are making a hard-surface path or if your soil is sandy, install the edgings at this stage.

Cover the ground with landscape fabric or perforated plastic cut to fit, or with several layers of newspaper, to keep down weeds. Tuck the fabric under the edging if it's already in place.

Next, spread a 4-inch layer of crushed stone or coarse gravel in the bottom of the path. Walk on the stone to pack it down, then lay a spirit level on top and rake as needed to get a level surface.

Spread a 2-inch layer of builder's sand or stone dust on top of the gravel. Tamp down the sand to pack it and remove air pockets. Then pull a board across it, edge down, to level the sand.

For a hard-surface path, lay bricks, stones, or pavers on top of the sand, with the edges touching. Tap each one into place with a rubber mallet. When all the pavement is in place, cover it with a thin layer of medium-grade builder's sand. Sweep the sand over the path surface to fill the cracks between pavers. Sweep off the excess, then spray with water to settle the sand into the cracks. Let the sand dry, then repeat the process as needed until all the holes are filled with sand.

For a loose- or soft-surface path, spread 2 inches of gravel, pebbles, mulch, or whatever surface you are using on top of the sand. Try to make the center of the path slightly higher than the edges so that water will drain off. Walk over the surface material to pack it down.

A RIVER OF STONE

A course of stones laid down a gentle slope or at the bottom of a hill can suggest the look of a river where none exists. In a dry desert garden, the stone can evoke a wash, where water flows in certain seasons. In a Japanese garden, raked stones can call to mind a flowing river or a still pool.

Use smooth, rounded stones for your river to evoke the look of water; after all, the stones once were in water—they got their rounded edges from the action of water flowing over them.

When you lay stepping-stones in a path, it's important to set them at a comfortable stepping distance from one another. Walk the path before installing the stones to find the best spacing for them.

Walls and Fences

Walls and fences are indispensable in most home landscapes. Their vertical lines mark property boundaries, define spaces in the landscape, afford privacy and shade, and buffer the wind. You also might need walls to retain soil on a slope, transform a steep, unusable hillside into space-efficient terraces, or support raised garden beds.

Although walls and fences perform many of the same functions, they look and feel very different from one another. Whether you build a wall or a fence depends largely on your personal preference—what you want to see in your landscape. But the kind of wall or fence you put up is influenced by the purpose it is to serve in the landscape, the style of your house and garden, the regional vernacular, and the look of your neighborhood.

Enclosing your yard or part of your garden with a wall or fence creates a private space that can be your own secret realm, a peaceful or happy escape from the rest of the world. Inside the enclosure, you are free to design the surroundings in any style you choose. You can plant a tropical paradise for a summer in New England if you want to, or have a Japanese-style garden behind a Brooklyn brownstone. Completely enclosing a small yard or garden would seem perhaps to create a claustrophobic environment, but in truth, the opposite often happens. Because the enclosed space is all immediately visible, every inch of it becomes more important, and it can actually feel bigger than it really is.

You might not want this degree of enclosure, though. You might want to just screen off the

How to Lay Stepping-Stones

Whatever you use as stepping-stones—flagstone, fieldstone, concrete or wood rounds, groups of bricks—place them a comfortable stepping distance apart. If they're set too close together, you will have to take mincing little steps that don't permit a comfortable walking rhythm. If the stones are too far apart, you will find yourself leaping from one stone to the next. Try them out before you install them, and move them around until you can walk comfortably over them.

When the stones are in position, outline each one by digging the tip of a trowel into the ground around the edges of the stone. Then, move the stone and excavate the area inside the outline. Excavate to a depth equal to the thickness of the stone, so it will sit flush with the ground, plus 2 inches to allow for a stabilizing sand base. Smooth the bottom of the hole, spread a 2-inch layer of sand in the hole and level it, then set the stepping-stone in place.

swimming pool or separate the driveway from the yard.

Walls and fences, like paths, are part of the landscape's basic structure. Building walls and fences will change the look of your property, so it's important to consider them just as carefully as you do other kinds of structural alterations.

Walls

Don't decide to build a wall on a whim—it's a big investment and a permanent structure that will not be easily moved if you realize later on that you put it in the wrong place or that you don't like the material it's made of and the way it looks. Start your planning process with the reason you want a wall and where you think one is needed.

When European colonists settled in the future United States, the settlers built walls primarily to keep livestock from wandering into their food and medicinal gardens. They built them from materials that were available locally. Over time, regional styles developed that are still popular today. When you think of a dry-laid stone wall, for instance, you probably think of New England. These walls were born of necessity; farmers dug stones from their fields so they could grow crops, and they just piled the stones around the edges of the fields. In the cities of the Southeast, brick walls enclose private, elegant courtyards with formal gardens inside. In the Southwest, stucco is the material of choice for walls that complement the adobe and stucco houses.

A wall can organize space, demarcate boundaries, and provide a vertical element in the landscape. It can enclose a space, set it apart, and invest it with added importance. It can give you privacy or serve as a backdrop for a flower garden. A retaining wall can hold soil on a slope. A low wall can edge formal beds and borders or contain raised planting beds. A masonry wall, if it faces south, can create a warmer microclimate in part of your garden. Masonry heats up earlier in spring and stays warmer longer in fall than a wood fence or bare soil, and it can extend the growing season in its immediate area. This heat-absorbing ability can be problematic in areas prone to late spring frosts, where it can encourage plants to start sending out buds only to have them zapped by a frost. Where summer weather is quite hot, a masonry wall can hold too much heat and prevent the area behind it from cooling off after sundown.

One thing that's important to understand about walls is the way they affect wind patterns. When wind strikes a solid wall, it swirls up the face of the wall and can come forcefully back down on the other side. If you want a wall to serve as a windbreak and moderate the force of prevailing winds that blow across your property, choose a design that incorporates screening blocks (with patterns of holes cut into them) to allow air to pass freely through it, or erect an open-style fence or a hedge instead.

Before you build any wall, especially along property boundaries, check local building codes and ordinances. They often specify setbacks for walls on property lines or near the street, and they may include requirements for wall height, depth, and type of foundation, and required reinforcement. Building a wall that is strong takes skill and know-how; unless you are an experienced do-it-yourselfer, you would do well to have a professional do the job for you.

Freestanding Walls

Freestanding walls that do not have to retain a slope afford a wealth of design possibilities. Walls can work in many different places, but by all means put them where they make sense and serve some useful purpose. A wall usually needs to connect to something else—the house, or perhaps itself if it encloses an area. If you want to screen off just part of the yard, you'd do better to plant a row of shrubs or tall perennials instead of erecting a wall or fence.

Freestanding walls, like this one of mortared stone, have a variety of uses in home landscapes. This wall was built to create a raised bed for planting. The neat, geometric shape of the bed and the clean look of the stone are formal in style.

If you want a wall for privacy, you will need a high one. But if you have security concerns, bear in mind that just as the wall will allow you to enjoy your yard in private, it will also conceal from passersby anyone who might enter your property when you are not at home. For outlining formal garden beds, a low wall is what you want. Low walls are also good for containing raised beds and built-in planters in formal landscapes. Walls for dividing spaces may be short or tall, depending on whether you want to see what's beyond the walls or whether you want the space inside to be private.

You can add decorative features to non-retaining walls to make them more interesting. A brick or stone wall needs a cap of flat slabs called *coping,* to keep water from getting inside the wall where it could freeze and cause damage in winter, and to give the wall a finished look. Some walls, particularly brick ones that run over a long distance, incorporate pilasters (columns) for added support. You can make the pilasters more ornamental by spacing them at regular intervals.

If your wall does not need to provide privacy, consider incorporating open spaces into the design. Walls with open construction appear lighter and less formidable than solid walls. They let in air and can serve as windbreaks, and they also allow summer breezes to pass through—a welcome relief on a hot day. An open wall also lets in light, which is important if plants are to grow behind it. A wall more than a foot or so high that is located to the south of a garden will block at least some light from reaching the plants.

Both brick and concrete block walls can incorporate open spaces. The usual way it's done is to set screen blocks or open fretwork designs in the center of the wall between pilasters, with solid block or brick above and below. A coping of stone or cement slabs laid on top of the wall finishes the structure.

For stability and strength, a wall must be thick enough to support its height. The ratio of thickness to height varies with the type of soil upon which you are building, the depth of the frost line (how deep the soil freezes in winter), and, of course, how high the wall will be. A good foundation will keep the wall stable and prevent it from shifting as a result of frost heaving. The foundation must be sunk below the frost line, and in any climate it should be at least 3 feet deep in sandy soil and 2 feet deep in clay soil. Make the foundation twice as wide as the thickness of the wall.

If your wall will be taller than 3 feet, it will need to incorporate interior vertical rods of rebar or built-in support columns to brace the structure and hold it upright.

Retaining Walls

A retaining wall is built to hold back the soil on a slope to keep it in place. You may need to build a retaining wall at the bottom of a hill. Or you can use retaining walls to create terraces on a steep slope that would otherwise be unusable for gardening and both difficult and dangerous to mow as a lawn. Terracing creates level areas that step down the slope. How many terraces you will need depends on how high and steep the hill is. If you are going to create ter-

Retaining walls need to be very sturdy to withstand the pressure of the soil behind them. Mortared brick is one good type of construction for a retaining wall.

races, you will also want to have access paths with steps made of materials similar to those of the retaining walls.

You may need a building permit to put up a retaining wall, so check local building codes and ordinances for requirements before beginning construction.

A retaining wall must be very strong to bear the weight of the tons of soil that will be pushing against it. When soil is wet, it becomes more unstable and even heavier. Your retaining wall will need a deep, strong foundation, located below the frost line and made as thick as the wall and twice as wide. Provide for drainage by installing behind the wall perforated drain pipes surrounded by gravel.

You can build a retaining wall of brick, concrete blocks with a stucco covering, poured concrete, precast concrete blocks, cut stone, or fieldstone. Brick, poured concrete, and concrete block, reinforced with rebar or pilasters, make the strongest walls. Mortared block or brick are strongest of all and are the best choices where you need a wall 4 feet or higher. Dry-laid stone walls, although they are quite strong when built well, are best used on a gentle slope where only a low wall is needed.

Wall Materials

Whether you need to build a freestanding wall or a retaining wall, you can choose among a variety of materials. Choose the material for the wall based on the purpose of the wall and its height, and also with the style and colors of your house and garden in mind. Mortared brick and stone walls are the most formal-looking; dry-laid stone the least.

Brick

Brick is a traditional and widely used material for walls. It's an excellent choice in a formal setting, but it can also work in less-formal landscapes if the bricks are aged. Brick is versatile; you can choose among a range of bond patterns and a variety of colors, too. Depending on how they are fired, bricks may be red, yellow, gray, blue, or mixed tones. The classic brownish red color harmonizes or contrasts nicely with many flower colors, especially yellows, oranges, and blues. A brick wall is expensive, but if properly built, it will last a lifetime.

There are three grades of brick among which to choose when building a wall: common brick, facing brick, and engineering brick. Engineering brick is the highest grade. It is the hardest, most weather resistant, and most expensive. The middle grade is facing brick, so-called because the edges (or faces) are given a weather-resistant finish. The bricks weather slowly when set with their faces outward. Common brick is the cheapest kind of brick. It is not given a finish and will show the effects of weathering, which in less formal situations is probably just the look you want for your landscape.

There are a number of bond patterns in which you can lay bricks to build a wall. The most widely used—and simplest—is the running bond, in which all the bricks are laid with the long faces showing. In an English bond wall, courses of brick alternate, with

A brick wall of open construction allows light and air to reach garden plants growing behind it.

one layer having the long faces exposed and the next layer having the short faces exposed. In a Flemish bond, each course of bricks contains alternating long and short faces. A fourth pattern, the stack bond, has bricks laid directly atop one another with all the mortared joints aligned vertically. This kind of wall is the least sturdy and is best used only for low walls of 3 feet or less.

If you would like your brick wall to be more decorative, consider using a more ornate pattern such as basketweave, and top off the wall with an attractive coping. The coping will also serve the practical function of keeping water from getting down inside the wall where it could freeze and cause cracks in winter.

Stone

Stone walls are beautiful additions to the landscape. If you build a wall of local stone, it will look most at home in its setting. Mortared stone looks more formal than dry-laid stone, and mortared cut stone is the most formal and elegant of all. Blocks of stone cut at the quarry in regular, even sizes with smooth surfaces are called ashlar. Fieldstone, which is dug rather than quarried and has rough surfaces and uneven shapes and sizes, is also called rubble stone. Fieldstone or cobbles are more informal looking. Both ashlar and fieldstone are usually sold by the cubic yard at quarries and stone yards.

Mortared stone walls are not as strong as mortared brick or concrete block walls. In fact, they are not substantially stronger than dry-laid stone walls, which are long-lasting when well built. One advantage a mortared stone wall has over a dry-laid wall is that it will stay in place when it is sat upon or bumped, and you can better incorporate irregular pieces of stone in building it.

A mortared stone wall needs a footing built below the frost line, as deep as the wall is thick and twice as wide as the wall's thickness. In building a stone wall, the largest stones go in the bottom courses (layers) and the flattest stones in the uppermost courses. Square stones make the sturdiest, most stable corners.

Dry-laid, or unmortared, stone walls are intricately composed piles of stone with no mortar to hold the pieces together. They are inherently less formal than mortared walls and they are quite beautiful. So ubiquitous in New England, dry-laid stone walls were born of necessity as farmers dug stones out of the ground to prepare cleared fields for planting. Dry-laid walls are very difficult to build—their construction is an art. Just stacking flat stones more or less on top of one another won't make a stable wall. But when well built, dry stone walls can last for a century or more. Even the best-built wall should not be too high, though—3 feet is about the limit. A 3-foot-high wall should be at least 2 feet wide at the base. Local stone looks best in a dry-laid wall.

A dry-laid wall does not require concrete footings. Instead, you can prepare a base similar to that for a path. Excavate an 8-inch-deep trench where the wall will go, lay landscape fabric in the bottom and

If you want to build a wall with irregular pieces of stone, mortared construction works best. Here, the stones are arranged in interesting patterns, and the wall looks neat and finished.

A well-built dry-laid stone wall is put together like an intricate puzzle. Building one is an art.

Concrete Block and Stucco

Old-fashioned concrete blocks, although not much to look at, make a strong, stable wall when mortared together. Concrete blocks are less expensive than brick and stone. And covering the wall with stucco vastly improves its appearance. A stucco wall looks best with a stucco house. You can use stucco in its natural color or tint it with colored pigments. If your house is stucco or adobe, you can have your wall tinted to match.

Even if you do not build the wall yourself, it's helpful to understand the process. Here is the basic procedure for erecting a concrete block wall.

The wall will need to be laid atop a concrete foundation, as described on page 104. Let the footings dry and cure before starting to set the blocks. For strength, the wall should be braced with rebar rods laid horizontally between courses of block. Lay the first row of blocks on a bed of mortar, and put a ⅜-inch-thick layer of mortar between the rows of block. While the mortar is still wet, use a spirit level to make sure each block is sitting straight. Set the blocks so the vertical joints between them are staggered, not aligned, for maximum strength. You can finish the top of the wall with a coping of stone slabs or brick, or you can cover it with stucco.

When the mortar is dry, you can stucco the wall to cover the concrete blocks. First, spread an adhesive concrete binder to help the stucco stick to the concrete blocks. Then, apply two or three coats of stucco. The first coat, called a scratch coat, should be ⅜ inch—just shy of ½ inch—thick. Start troweling on the stucco at the bottom of the wall, and work

up the sides, then spread 4 inches of gravel for drainage. Tamp and level the gravel, and lay the stones on top, starting with the largest stones on the bottom course of the wall.

To build a dry wall, make two vertical stacks of stones, one in back of the other, linked by long "bond" stones running front to back between the two piles and placed every few feet along the length of the wall. Building a dry-laid wall is like putting together a puzzle of stone—you hunt for stones to fit snugly in the spaces between other stones. Expert masons know how to split and shape stones with a hammer and chisel to fit the available spaces. It is a painstaking, time-consuming process. As the wall is built, you fill in behind and between stones with soil. If you want to make pockets for plants, which charmingly soften the look of a dry-laid wall, use good soil amended with compost between the stones. Gently tuck small plants in the pockets of soil and work the soil around the delicate roots with your fingers. Mist well to thoroughly moisten the soil without washing it away. (See "Plants for Walls and Crevices" on page 46 for a list of plants that do well in rock crevices and dry stone walls.)

Finish the wall with a coping of flat capstones. You may want to have the coping mortared in place to hold the capstones in place and prevent moisture from getting down into the wall.

MAKING PLANTING POCKETS IN A WALL

To create planting pockets in a dry-laid stone wall, fill the joints between stones with good garden soil amended with compost, or with a loose, porous, all-purpose potting mix. Use a pointed trowel and your fingers to work the soil into each pocket, and pack in as much as you can. Moisten the soil with a fine spray of water until it's damp throughout.

Next, remove a small plant from its nursery pot or flat, make a hole in the soil with your fingers, and tuck in the plant. Gently cover the roots, and firm the soil around them with your fingers. Mist the new plant with a fine spray of water from a plant mister until the soil is thoroughly wet. Tuck some small pebbles or stone chips around the plant to help hold the roots in place.

Mist with water every couple of days for the first 2 weeks (unless it rains), until the transplant sends new roots out into the soil. If any soil has fallen out of the pocket, tuck it back in. As the plant grows, its roots will eventually hold the soil in place.

Plants among the stones soften the look of a rock garden or dry-laid stone wall in a most delightful way. Rock cress (*Aubrieta xcultorum*), wallflower (*Erysimum cheiri*), and *Sedum spathulifolium* grow here.

your way up. Let the stucco cure by spraying it with a gentle mist from a garden hose twice a day for the first 2 days, so it dries slowly. After that, let the stucco dry naturally.

You can apply a second scratch coat of stucco, if you wish, when the first coat has dried most of the way. Before the second scratch coat is completely dry, brush it with a wire brush to rough up the surface and encourage the top coat to adhere better. Moisten the surface of the scratch coat by misting it with water. Then spread the top coat of stucco in a thin layer just ¼ inch thick. Spray it with water twice a day for the first 2 days so that the stucco can cure properly.

Concrete Wall Blocks

Not concrete blocks in the traditional sense, these wall blocks, like concrete pavers, are textured to resemble stone. They come in various sizes, some similar in size to bricks, and others more like cobblestones. Colors include tan, gray, brown, and multicolored red and gray. Coordinating copings are also available for these blocks.

Concrete wall stones are best suited to low walls of 2 feet or less. They are easy to work with, and do-it-yourselfers can build their own walls with them. You can use the stones for both straight and curved walls. A low wall built from these blocks does not require a concrete footing. Instead, prepare a gravel/sand base as described in "How to Lay a Path" on page 101. The depth of the excavation depends on the height of the wall. For a wall 10 inches high or less, dig deep enough to halfway bury the first course of stones, plus allow 2 inches for the gravel/sand base. For a higher wall, completely bury the first course of blocks. In addition, excavate out to 1 foot behind the stones to allow for backfilling with an aggregate. This will help stabilize the wall and provide drainage. Compact the base with a tamper, and be sure that the base is level before you begin to lay the blocks. Backfill behind each course of blocks with a drainage aggregate.

A stuccoed wall looks elegant next to a stucco or adobe house, especially when it is tinted the same color. Decking the wall with brilliant bougainvillea adds a breathtaking finishing touch.

HOW MUCH WILL YOU NEED?

Here are some guidelines for calculating how much material you will need for different kinds of walls.

Stone: Multiply length of wall in feet × height of wall × width of wall to get cubic feet.

Cubic feet divided by 27 = Cubic yards.

If you are using cut stone (ashlar), add 10 percent to cover breakage and waste. If you are using rubble stone, add 25 percent.

Concrete blocks, wall blocks, brick: Length of wall divided by length of 1 block, wall block, or brick = Number of blocks in each course

Height of wall divided by height of one block, wall block, or brick = Number of courses

Number of pieces × number of courses = Total blocks, wall blocks, or bricks needed

Get some extra blocks, wall blocks, or bricks to cover damage and waste.

Fences

Fences mark off space just as walls and hedges do, and you can use them in many of the same ways. Fences are faster, easier, and less expensive than walls, and they take up a lot less space than either walls or hedges. You can use fences to define property boundaries, divide space, contain pets, exclude wildlife, create privacy, make shade, slow the wind, or separate the lawn from the driveway. A fence can provide a backdrop for a flower border or enclose a cottage garden. It can support flowering vines or climbing roses. Fences can be strictly utilitarian, or they can be very decorative additions to the landscape. You will probably want to use a fence where a wall would block the light or a nice view, or where space is at a premium.

You can choose from a host of fence styles, from simple turkey wire fencing to keep out wildlife to delicate bamboo screening to enclose a Japanese tea garden. Many fences are made of wood, but there are also wrought-iron fences, and vinyl fences made to mimic the look of painted wood.

The function of the fence will determine, at least in part, its design. Generally, boundary fences are sturdier and more utilitarian, and interior fences can be more decorative. For privacy, you need a fence that is tall and of a construction that shields whatever is behind it from view, and you need to position the fence carefully so that it obscures the area you don't want to be seen. For year-round privacy, board-

Vines and fences make good partners. Fences support vines and display their flowers to great effect, while vines decorate fences and soften their lines. Here, *Clematis* 'Nelly Moser' weaves its stems through a lattice panel fence.

on-board and close-board fences (described on page 114) are two options. For seasonal privacy, perhaps next to a deck used for summer sunbathing, you might consider trellis or lattice panels with vines or climbing roses trained on them.

To define property boundaries, use a fence that is not terribly expensive because you will need a lot of it. Stockade and picket fences are two possibilities. Another is a simple post-and-rail style; this kind of fence works especially well in the country because it will not block your view and it is easy to install. If you live on a large, formal property and are not constrained by budgetary limitations, a stately wrought-iron fence could serve you well. To enclose a cottage garden, a white picket fence is traditional and still hard to beat. You can also have a fanciful fence made of peeled poles, natural branches, bamboo poles, ocotillo stakes (in the Southwest, where this shrub grows), or log sections stood on end. Unless you want privacy, a fence around the yard is fine at about 3 feet high.

In a windy location, a fence can serve as a windbreak to slow the force of prevailing winds. The goal of a windbreak is not to stop the wind but to diffuse it and reduce its speed. An open fence that has space between the boards allows air to circulate freely and minimizes wind damage. Board-on-board, lattice or trellis panels, and louvered and basketweave fences can all work as windbreaks. One note: To be sure that you know where you need the windbreak, observe on which side or sides of your house the prevailing winds blow in winter and in summer.

A fence can create shade, too, but if it is located to the south of a garden area, use an open construction that will let in some light for the plants.

On a more practical level, if you need a fence to keep children or the dog in the yard, it must be high enough that the kids can't climb it and the dog can't jump over it (height will vary with the size of the dog or the climbing ability of the child). If the dog is a digger, the fence will need to extend far enough underground that the dog won't be able to tunnel underneath it. If you need to keep out deer, your fence ought to be 10 feet high—deer are impressive jumpers. Hungry rabbits and groundhogs can be kept at bay with a wire mesh or chicken-wire fence 3 feet high and extending 6 inches underground.

Design Considerations

When you set about choosing a fence, you will need to consider materials, heights, construction styles, and colors. In addition to fulfilling its intended purpose, you will want your fence to complement the architecture of your house. You might even echo or copy a design detail of the house, such as shaping pickets like the balusters supporting a porch rail, or cutting the tops of fenceposts to match the angle of a roof peak. Factor into your thinking the style of your neighborhood and your region, and plan a fence in keeping with the vernacular. That way, your fence will look like it belongs there. If you've never really thought about these kinds of style issues before, drive around your town and look at houses, gardens, fences, and walls, to see what other people have done. Careful observation of one's surroundings can be very instructive.

To unite house and garden, you might want to paint the fence to match the trim on the house. If it's a subtle color, you can probably get away with painting the whole fence. But if the color is bright, try instead painting gates or end posts flanking an entry point for color accents that refer back to the house but are not visually distracting or overwhelming.

If you want your fence to be less apparent, paint it a dark neutral color—brown, gray, dark green, even black. You might want a fence to not call attention to itself if a particularly lovely garden or an inspiring view lies beyond it. If, on the other hand, you want a fence that draws the eye, whose lines are immediately visible in the landscape, white is a classic color to use. White also has the advantage of being able to reflect light into a shady garden, but it may be too glaring in a very sunny site. When you start to think about colors, it may be helpful to factor in that white fences need repainting every couple of years to keep them looking clean and fresh. Darker-colored fences need less frequent maintenance.

Dark-colored fences need less maintenance than white ones.

BOARD-ON-BOARD FENCE

PICKET FENCE

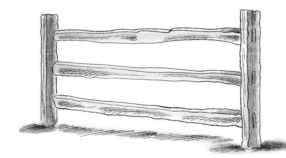

POST-AND-RAIL FENCE

Here are three popular fence styles. All have an open construction that allows wind to pass through easily without creating odd currents and eddies. A board-on-board fence affords the greatest degree of privacy. Picket fences are generally informal but can be given a touch of class with shaped pickets and decorative posts topped with finials. Rail fences are beautifully suited to rural properties where the goal is to define boundaries without concealing what lies within them.

A fence needs to have a logical beginning and ending point—it needs to make sense for it to be where it is. Try to connect the fence to an architectural feature—a deck or the garage, for instance. Or run it completely around an area to enclose it and connect the fence to itself. If you want to screen a limited area, you might do better to plant a row of shrubs in front of it instead of erecting a fence.

Kinds of Fences

Wood is the most widely used material for building fences. Wood fences come in many styles: picket, stockade, woven, post and rail, close board, board on board, grapestake, lattice, and more. You can allow a wood fence to weather naturally, stain or waterproof it for a natural look, or paint it in the color of your choice.

There are metal fences, too, including wrought iron, chain link, turkey wire, and welded creations.

Picket Fences

Arguably the most popular fence style of all, the picket fence consists of two or more horizontal rails with vertical flat boards called pickets, or palings, spread evenly along them. Picket fences are classic enclosures for cottage gardens and informal herb gardens. They can edge a property or define space without totally blocking the view. They also do a reasonable job of containing kids and pets. Picket fences are not terribly strong, but they are decorative and can be downright charming.

Picket fences are usually no more than 6 feet high, usually less, and they are not too difficult to build. There are lots of designs for pickets, from simple ones with pointed tips and straight sides to fancier styles with shaped sides and decorative tips. Adding ornamental finials to the tops of the fence-posts gives a simple picket fence more flair.

Traditional picket fences are made of wood, but there are also vinyl picket fences that look pretty good and need no maintenance. Vinyl picket fencing comes in just a few neutral colors: white, gray, and brown. You can have a builder construct a picket fence from scratch if you want custom-shaped pickets, or you can purchase partly assembled panels at a building materials store.

Most picket fences are made of wood (*left*), but easy-care vinyl fences are available, too (*far left*). Install your fence with the rails on the inside of the pickets.

An open-grid panel fence divides space without hiding what's behind it. It's an ideal place to grow climbing roses or flowering vines.

set very close together, with little or no space between the boards. The boards may run vertically or horizontally. This kind of fence looks less welcoming than a board-on-board or louver fence of looser construction. It also can cause odd wind currents and eddies that may damage plants growing near the fence.

When stood on end and angled, the boards become louvers. Louver fences make good windbreaks, letting air and light into the yard while still affording privacy.

Thin boards may be woven over and under one another, the way a basket is woven, for a different kind of look. A woven fence affords a great deal of privacy, but it can be problematic if the wood is woven so tightly that air cannot penetrate the wood readily. A tight fence is not recommended for a windy location.

Panel Fences

Panel fences go up faster than most other kinds of fences. A panel fence is constructed of panels that are put together in units up to 8 feet wide. Each panel runs from one post to the next. The panels may be closed board, trelliswork or lattice, or other designs. Trelliswork panels are a grid of wood or plastic bars set in a frame. Lattice panels are made of flat strips of wood arranged in a diagonal grid. Both of these kinds of panels are ideal for supporting flowering vines such as honeysuckle or morning glories, which bring color and softness to the fence. Prefabricated fence panels are widely available at building supply stores and lumberyards.

Board Fences

In a board fence, individual boards are nailed next to one another on the rails, with less space between them than in a picket fence. Each board is usually less than 6 inches wide; wider boards are likely to warp. The boards can run vertically, horizontally, or diagonally. For more variety, you can alternate panels of vertical and horizontal boards.

A board-on-board fence has two rows of staggered boards. It looks good from either side, and the staggered design lets in light and air while still affording privacy. This kind of fence can serve as a windbreak if you need it to.

In a close-board fence, a single row of boards is

A board-on-board fence affords maximum privacy while still admitting light and air.

To make a board fence higher, or just to add a decorative touch, run lattice or trellis panels along the top. You may even be inspired to train flowering vines to grow up the fence and along the lattice or trellis—it's a lovely effect.

Post-and-Rail Fences

A post-and-rail fence is composed of vertical posts and two or more horizontal rails (the number of rails is determined by how high the fence needs to be). Post-and-rail fences are seen all over the American countryside. They are easy to put up and not terribly expensive. A low, two-rail fence about 3 feet high can mark property boundaries or serve as a linear accent in the landscape. Higher rail fences can hold livestock.

Stockade-Type Fences

A stockade fence can take any of a number of forms, but it is basically a row of slender stakes attached to horizontal rails, with no space between them. A fence of very slender posts is sometimes called a grapestake fence. A palisade fence is similar, except it has no horizontal rails. You can make a palisade from a line of tall stakes, bamboo canes, log sections, poles, or even crooked branches. Regional materials can work, too, such as the ocotillo fences seen in the desert Southwest. A palisade fence is very easy to make—you simply pound the upright posts into the ground. But don't depend on it to last for many years—palisades can be whimsical and fun, but they are not very strong, especially when they are of any appreciable height.

A stockade fence is made of narrow, upright stakes attached to horizontal rails and very closely spaced. A palisade is similar but has no strengthening rails.

Metal Fences

Wrought iron is a traditional and very formal fencing material that looks at home enclosing elegant city properties or large country estates. Widely used in the 19th century, wrought iron is still employed for fences today, though less frequently. Wrought-iron fencing is usually simple, but the gates can be elaborate and beautifully detailed. Wrought iron is usually painted black, although white fences are occasionally used. It is best suited to historic and period homes, and it works well with Victorians, especially those with Gothic detailing.

Wrought-iron fences will rust if you don't keep them painted. If you want the look of wrought iron with lower maintenance, you could look into anodized aluminum fencing, which comes in similar styles.

More contemporary metal fences can be had, too. For the most part they are custom-made art pieces, intriguing and quite beautiful but very costly.

Metal fencing is more often strictly utilitarian. Chain-link fencing shows up in lots of public spaces, but seldom at home. It is expensive, difficult to erect, and too unattractive and institutional-looking for home landscapes. Turkey wire (large-mesh wire fencing often sold with a green vinyl coating) can be used along a driveway or property border, but it's not much to look at and it's not very strong. Still, it has the virtue of being inexpensive and is easily installed; you hang it on metal posts driven into the ground. You can camouflage turkey wire and other less-than-attractive fences by training vines on them. See "Vines to Train on Fences" on page 117 for a list of good candidates.

Wrought-iron fences have a classic, elegant look that is especially fitting for surrounding urban properties. If left unpainted, they will rust.

Vines and fences are natural partners. All the vines described here are good candidates for training on fences.

PLANT	DESCRIPTION	GROWING CONDITIONS	GROWING RANGE
Allamanda cathartica, golden trumpet vine	Tender perennial vine with oblong, glossy green leaves and yellow trumpet flowers in summer.	Full sun; moist, fertile soil.	Zones 10–11; elsewhere grow as annual
Cardiospermum halicacabum, love-in-a-puff	Tendrilled vine with 3-part, toothed leaves and clusters of tiny white flowers; seeds have heart-shaped marking.	Full sun; any average soil.	Zones 7–11; often grown as annual
Clematis cvs.	Woody vines with saucer- to bell-shaped flowers in a spectrum of colors, including shades of purple, blue, red, pink, and white, plus a few yellows, blooming from spring to fall, depending on species.	Sun to partial shade, with roots shaded; fertile, moist but well-drained soil of neutral to mildly alkaline pH.	Zones 3–8; hardiness varies with species
Cobaea scandens, cup-and-saucer vine	Tender, tendrilled vine with oval leaves and, in summer, cup-shaped purple flowers backed by a saucerlike green calyx.	Full sun to partial shade; average soil.	Zones 9–11; elsewhere grow as annual
Dolichos lablab (*Lablab purpurea*), hyacinth bean	Twining vine with oval to triangular leaves and purple pealike flowers followed by shiny red-violet pods.	Full sun; moist but well-drained soil of average to good fertility.	Zones 10–11; elsewhere grow as annual
Fallopia aubertii (*Polygonum aubertii*), silver lace vine	Twining perennial vine with oval to lance-shaped leaves and, in late summer to early fall, sprays of tiny white flowers.	Full sun to partial shade; moist soil of average fertility, tolerates a range of soils.	Zones 5–9
Ipomoea alba, moonflower	Twining tender perennial vine with heart-shaped leaves and large, fragrant, white flowers that bloom at night.	Full sun; light, well-drained soil of good fertility.	Grow as annual
Ipomoea x*multifida,* cardinal climber	Vigorous, tender, twining vine with deeply cut, arrow-shaped leaves and, throughout summer, brilliant red, tubular flowers with a pentagonal face.	Full sun; light, well-drained, fertile soil.	Grow as annual
Ipomoea purpurea, I. tricolor, morning glory	Vigorous twiners with heart-shaped leaves and funnel-shaped flowers in white, pink, purple, violet, sky blue, and crimson.	Full sun; light, well-drained soil of average to good fertility.	Grow as annual
Ipomoea quamoclit, cypress vine	Delicate twining vine with feathery leaves and star-shaped bright scarlet flowers.	Full sun; moist, light but well-drained soil of good fertility.	Grow as annual

(continued)

PLANT	DESCRIPTION	GROWING CONDITIONS	GROWING RANGE
Jasminum spp., jasmines	Perennial vines with glossy green, oval leaves and star-shaped, tubular, richly fragrant white flowers.	Full sun to partial shade; moist but well-drained soil of average to good fertility.	Zones 8–11, varies with species
Lonicera spp., honeysuckles	Vigorous perennial twiners with oval leaves and 2-lipped trumpet flowers, some fragrant, in red, orange, pink, yellow, and white.	Full sun; moist but well-drained soil of average fertility.	Zones vary with species
Mandevilla xamabilis	Tender twining vine with deep green, ribbed, oblong leaves and large, bright pink trumpet flowers all summer.	Full sun to partial shade; light, moist but well-drained, humusy soil of average to good fertility.	Zones 10–11; elsewhere grow as annual
Mina lobata, flag-of-Spain	Tender twiner with lobed leaves and, in summer, sprays of tubular flowers that open red and fade to orange, then yellow.	Full sun; light, well-drained soil of good fertility.	Zones 10–11; elsewhere grow as annual
Passiflora spp., passionflowers	Tendrilled vines with lobed leaves and saucer-shaped flowers with a crown of long filaments, in shades of blue, purple, red, pink, and white.	Full sun to partial shade; moist but well-drained, humusy soil.	Zones vary with species; many grow in Zones 8–11
Rhodochiton atrosanguinea, purple bell vine	Tender perennial vine with heart-shaped leaves and tubular, deep purple flowers extending from drooping, bell-shaped calyces of dusky pinkish maroon.	Full sun to partial shade; well-drained soil of average fertility.	Zones 10–11; elsewhere grow as annual
Rosa cvs., climbing roses	Long-stemmed woody plants with oval toothed leaves and, in summer, single to double flowers, many fragrant, in shades of red, pink, yellow, orange, and white.	Full sun; moist but well-drained soil of good fertility.	Zones vary with cultivar
Thunbergia alata, black-eyed Susan vine	Tender twining vine with triangular toothed leaves and gold, orange, or ivory flowers with wide, flat petals and a dark center.	Full sun to light shade; moist but well-drained soil of good fertility.	Zones 10–11; elsewhere grow as annual
Thunbergia grandiflora, Bengal clock vine	Twiner with large, oval leaves and funnel-shaped sky blue flowers.	Partial to light shade; moist but well-drained, humusy soil of good fertility.	Zones 10–11; elsewhere grow as annual
Tropaeolum peregrinum, canary creeper	Twining vine with light green lobed leaves and, throughout summer, small, bright yellow, fringed flowers that resemble tiny birds.	Full sun to partial shade; moist but well-drained soil of average fertility.	Annual

If you live in deer country—and more and more of us do—fencing your property is almost obligatory unless you don't mind dealing with serious limitations in the kinds of plants you can grow. Fencing to exclude deer may be of wire mesh or plastic netting, or you can use a fence of electrified wire strands. Deer fencing must be high: 10 feet is usually recommended. Fences this high are difficult to install. Another option is to erect two 4-foot fences, one inside the other, about 3 feet apart. Deer usually will not jump a fence when they see another one beyond it. Camouflage the inner fence from your view by planting shrubs in front of it inside the yard or by training vines on the inside of the fence. To use the double-fence method, you need to have a lot of unused space around the perimeter of your property.

You can use vines for camouflage, too, turning an ordinary fence into a spectacular accent in your landscape.

Fencemaking Guidelines

Fences need more maintenance than walls. Painted fences need repainting periodically. Unpainted wood will eventually weather to the point at which boards will need to be replaced. Fences built of rot-resistant redwood, cypress, or cedar need the least maintenance, but they are also expensive. Look for lower grades of these woods for fencing—knots are usually not a problem in a fence. To minimize water damage, provide for drainage below the posts, and bevel or round the tops of the posts, or put metal caps on them. Vinyl fencing needs no maintenance.

Don't forget to consult your local building codes before beginning construction of a fence along property boundaries. Your community may have rules about required setbacks and height restrictions.

Lay out the line of your fence with stakes and string. Then walk along the fence line and examine the site. If you find a big rock where you plan to put a fence post, you may have to adjust the course a bit.

If the fence will be more than 3 feet high, you will need to sink the supporting posts into concrete footings to hold the fence securely upright in strong winds. Footings need to go below the frost line and be at least 18 inches deep for a 3- to 6-foot fence, or 30 inches deep for a fence higher than 6 feet. Make the holes three times the width of the fence post. Dig the post holes 2 inches deeper than required, and spread 2 inches of gravel in each hole for drainage before you pour the footings.

When the posts are in place and dry, the horizontal rails can be attached. Attaching the rails between the posts can create a fence on its own, or the rails can support pickets, boards, or panels.

One last note about installation: If your fence is not double-sided, erect it with the best side facing out. The side with the visible rails should face in toward your property so you are always putting your best face forward. If you don't like the idea of looking at the back of the fence, look on the bright side: The rail gives you a place to park your water bottle while you are working in the garden.

HOW TO DO IT

HOW TO TRY OUT A FENCE

Here's a way to try out a fence (or a wall or hedge) before you build it to make sure it's going to work the way you want it to and that you are putting it in the right place. Put up a series of poles as high as the fence will be, and run a line between them (like putting up a clothesline). Drape old sheets, tarpaulins, or garden row covers over the line to approximate the fence. Then step back and examine the drape from different angles. If necessary, you can adjust the line and position of the fence-to-be until you are satisfied with the way it looks.

TROUBLESHOOTING FENCING PROBLEMS

If you need a fence over uneven or sloping terrain, you have three options:

1. Build the fence in panels that step down the hill. The usual solution, this kind of fence looks neat and controlled.

2. Have the bottom of the fence follow the contours of the ground, but keep the top line of the fence straight by cutting posts and upright boards to different lengths as needed. A very time-consuming way to go.

3. Make a stockade or palisade fence that simply follows the land or slope, so both top and bottom have a slanted or wavy look.

Fence posts are usually set 6 to 9 feet apart, depending on the weight of the materials used to build the fence and the windiness of the site. If the space between fence posts works out unevenly over the length of the fence, go back and slightly shorten the distance between all the posts to absorb the difference. To do this, of course, you have to plot the locations of all the posts *before* you install any.

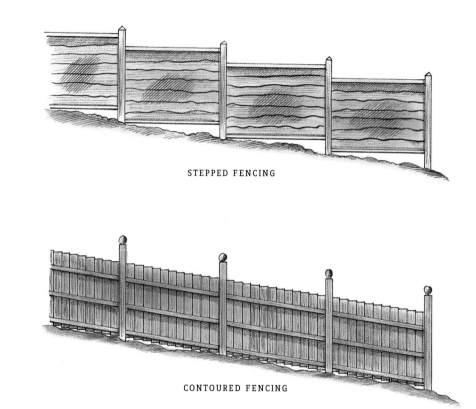

STEPPED FENCING

CONTOURED FENCING

Installing a fence on uneven ground presents an interesting challenge. One way to negotiate a slope is to install the fence in panels that step down the hill. The top and bottom of each panel remain straight for a neat, clean line. On rolling ground, it may work better to contour the fence so both the top and bottom follow the terrain.

Gates

Fences and walls that enclose things need gates, and choosing a gate style lets you exercise a little creativity. A gate has decided psychological connotations. An open gate invites you to come in. A closed gate suggests privacy and also mystery; you naturally wonder what's behind it. On a practical level, a gate shows visitors where to enter your property. In the landscape, gates enable you to travel from one discrete place to another—from the street to your front walk, from the front yard to the back, from one part of the garden to another, from outside a hedge, wall, or fence to inside.

Gates provide a definite transition from the outside world into your garden and from one part of your property to another. Going through a gate gives you a distinct sense of passage, of going someplace else. You can do a lot with gates. A gate can be as high as the wall (or hedge, or fence) into which it is set, or it can be shorter or taller. But however high the gate, it will visually divide space and mark a boundary and point of transition. You can add an arch or arbor above the gate and train climbing roses or flowering vines over it, to give the gate more prominence and call attention to it. Just make sure the arch is high enough for tall visitors to comfortably pass underneath. An arch over a gate, lush with flowers and greenery, welcomes you

What is as welcoming as a gate under an archway of flowers? Brilliant bougainvillea creates an enticing entry to this southwestern home.

home and gives passersby a delightful spill of color to enjoy.

Gate styles are as varied as the imaginations of the people who create them. You can have a gate of pickets, close-board construction, louvers, or a trellis panel. A gate made from a section of stockade works in a stockade fence. Japanese moon gates have a cut-out circle that can be left open or criss-crossed with a fretwork of wood bars or slats. The circle symbolizes the full moon. Despite their oriental origins, moon gates adapt to a range of styles. In a rustic fence, make a rustic gate with unpeeled branches, Adirondack-style.

Wrought-iron gates look very elegant and formal; consider the imposing coolness of the great iron gates seen on large estates. You can use wrought iron for a Victorian house in the city, especially one with Gothic detailing. A wrought-iron gate also looks good in a stucco wall or a brick wall. Metal gates also can be works of art, welded in one-of-a-kind designs by a skilled sculptor or metalworker.

If you don't want to interrupt the line of a fence but still need to have access to a fenced area, you can turn a panel of the fence into a gate with unobtrusive hinges and latches.

A gate is a good place to inject a note of color into your landscape. A light-colored gate contrasts effectively with dark foliage, such as that of a hedge or a screen of evergreens. Conversely, a dark-colored gate shows well against a light background—a light-colored house, the sky, a wheat field. A dark green or dark blue gate will not interfere with the view of the landscape behind it; it is a good choice for a place with a view. A white gate will tend to stop the eye and discourage looking past it. A blue gate can make

The lattice-grid gate works beautifully with this trelliswork fence. Climbing roses spill over the fence and arch, and forget-me-nots bloom in front.

reference to a nearby body of water, or to the sky, especially in a western landscape where the sky seems so amazingly blue.

You can paint a gate to echo, harmonize with, or contrast with your home's trim. You could paint gates the same color as shutters or the front door or another architectural detail to tie it to the house. (See Chapter 2 for more information on working with color.)

When planning a gate, whether you buy or build one, consider its function when you decide on the right height and width. Make it wide enough to allow passage of garden equipment if that is necessary. A front gate needs to be given more importance so it is easy to find, while a gate on a narrow path leading to a hidden bench can be smaller. There are many kinds of latches, fasteners, and hinges, and you can choose a style in keeping with the style of your gate—period pieces for historic settings; sleek, modern designs for contemporary models. Don't forget childproof latches or automatic openers if you need them. A counterweight allows the gate to close automatically.

Hedges and Plant Screens

A hedge or hedgerow is a living screen of plants that serves the same purposes as a wall or fence. Neatly sheared hedges are at home in formal landscapes with their straight lines and careful geometries of form and space. In an informal setting, a screen of shrubs and trees left to assume their natural form, or a hedgerow of mixed trees and shrubs, does the job in a less structured way.

Like walls and fences, hedges, screens, and hedgerows play a number of important roles in the landscape. You can use them to create privacy, mark property boundaries, define space, serve as the walls of garden rooms, slow the wind, hide something you don't want to see, buffer noise from traffic or neighbors, and provide a neutral backdrop for a flower garden. A hedge can also create a warm microclimate in the garden—as much as a whole zone milder—where you can experiment with plants that are not normally hardy in your area.

A hedge is a row of plants growing together to form a smooth, unbroken plane. Hedges need to be carefully clipped at least twice a year to maintain their straight lines. Low hedges enclosing a formal garden bed or forming the design in a knot garden need clipping whenever new growth sprouts out of the top or sides. That makes them fairly labor intensive.

A hedge usually consists of a single type of plant, although you can mix in different varieties to add subtle interest. One thing all hedge plants must have is an ability to tolerate having the tips of their stems sheared off, and ideally, to sprout from old wood. Plants that cannot grow well from old wood, such as pines, can be pruned into a hedge, but if the hedge suffers damage or grows too large you won't be able to cut it back to rejuvenate it; you will have to remove the plants and start over. A good hedge plant has small leaves closely spaced along the stems, is dense, branches low to the ground, and can be encouraged to grow leaves low on the stems.

An informal screen or hedgerow doesn't need such meticulous maintenance. The plants are allowed to grow normally, and instead of forming a flat wall of greenery, they will billow and fountain for a softer, more natural look. You may want to prune selectively once a year to keep the plants looking neat, and you should remove any dead or damaged growth you find, but otherwise a screen or hedgerow is a fairly low-maintenance proposition. An informal screen can be a row of one kind of plant, such as junipers or bridal wreath spirea (*Spiraea* x*vanhouttei*), or it can combine several different kinds of shrubs. Screens and hedgerows may bring color to the landscape, too. They may bloom in spring or summer, or glow with color in fall (choose varieties that coordinate with your color scheme). Local birds can find shelter and food in your hedgerow.

A neatly sheared formal hedge makes an elegant backdrop for a sumptuous border of flowering perennials and ornamental grasses.

You can create hedges and screens with evergreen or deciduous plants; their height varies according to how you will use them. If you want to have privacy or enclose a garden room, the hedge or hedgerow should be a minimum of 5 feet high; 6 feet or taller is generally best. To screen a sitting area or an in-ground swimming pool, 3 to 4 feet is high enough. If you need a low hedge to outline a formal garden bed, make a pattern in a knot garden or parterre, or edge a path, a foot or so is all the height you need.

If you are deciding between a hedge or plant screen, a wall, or a fence for your property, bear in mind that formal hedges are wider than fences, and informal screens and hedgerows are quite wide indeed. They are not the best choices for small properties where space is limited. If you do want a hedge or plant screen on a small lot, seek out columnar plants that stay narrow as they mature, such as 'Sky Pencil' Japanese holly or 'Skyrocket' juniper.

Choosing Plants

There are several issues to consider when choosing plants for a hedge or screen. One consideration, of course, is height. But you also need to think about whether the plant is deciduous or evergreen, how fast it grows, and how low to the ground it will have branches.

This screen of mixed conifers offers an interesting mix of forms, colors, and textures and looks good year-round. Better yet, it requires little in the way of maintenance.

If you want year-round privacy, evergreens are your best bet. A hedge or screen of evergreens will effectively block a view if you use plants that retain branches low to the ground as they grow. Privet, boxwood, and yew are three classic hedge plants that don't develop long trunks. For informal screening, you could consider white spruce (*Picea glauca*) or eastern hemlock (*Tsuga canadensis*), although hemlocks suffer from a pest called woolly adelgid in some places. The downside of using evergreen trees like these for screening is that they grow slowly.

Gardeners in northern climates need to consider that evergreen hedges are more susceptible to damage from winter snow and ice than are deciduous plantings. Pruning the top of the hedge in a rounded or pointed shape rather than flat will help it to shed accumulating snow, but you will inevitably have to go out and knock off heavy snow and ice from time to time.

If you need screening mostly during warm weather when you're outdoors in the yard, or if you want your hedge to have flowers or colorful fall foliage, deciduous plants will serve you well. Planting dense, twiggy bushes or two staggered rows of plants will provide reasonable coverage even in winter. Another instance in which a deciduous hedge may be better than an evergreen one is on a small property where a tall evergreen hedge, especially on the north side, would cast considerable shade over the yard. Deciduous plants, including columnar varieties of trees such as maples or hornbeams, will let in more light than evergreens, especially in winter. You could even consider a seasonal planting of tall annuals—a row of hollyhocks, sunflowers, or castor bean, perhaps, or tall perennials such as *Heliopsis* 'Summer Sun' or *Rudbeckia* 'Herbstonne'.

Whether you opt for an evergreen or deciduous screen, you'll have to choose between fast-growing plants and slower growers to create the hedge or screen. It can be tempting to plant fast growers such as privet, especially if you want privacy *now*. But bear in mind that fast growers are likely to keep on going past the size you want your hedge to be, and they will require more work to keep in line. Fast growers are often spreaders, too (consider the wandering ways of golden bamboo), and in the end they may be more trouble than they're worth. Also, many fast growers are short-lived and will need to be replaced or rejuvenated after several years.

Slow-growing plants such as boxwoods and hollies are usually easier to care for, but they take a lot longer to reach an appreciable height. You can purchase larger plants, but they're expensive and harder to transplant.

One possible solution is to plant a row of fast growers and a row of slow growers alongside, and plan to remove the fast growers when the slow growers are big enough. This will be a lot of work. If you choose this approach, plant two separate hedges instead of interspersing fast and slow growers in the same line, or the faster plants may crowd and shade out the slower-growing plants and you will lose the very plants you want for the long term.

You might instead plant the fast growers, but space them farther apart than the usual hedge spacing, allowing them more room to expand and lengthening their serviceable life. Or just selectively remove some plants from the hedge when necessary to eliminate overcrowding.

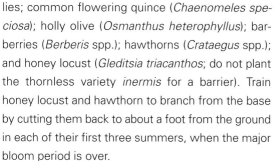

HOW TO DO IT

PLANNING A WINDBREAK

To use an evergreen hedge or screen as a windbreak, position the planting between the house and the wind, and align it perpendicular to the direction from which the prevailing winter (or summer) winds blow. A rule of thumb for gauging windbreak effectiveness is that the windbreak will provide good protection over an area 5 to 10 times its height, and less protection over a distance 20 times its height. Make sure the windbreak is long enough: It should extend beyond the house for about 50 feet on both sides, or you may get problematic wind currents in the protected area.

Thorny shrub roses make a beautiful and very effective barrier planting if you have enough space and plenty of sun.

Barrier Screens

Plant screens can afford security as well as privacy; thorny plants will keep out intruders of both the two- and four-footed varieties. Good plants for barrier screening include rugosa roses (*Rosa rugosa*) and other shrub roses, which offer the bonus of their wonderfully fragrant flowers in summer; Chinese holly (*Ilex cornuta*), *Ilex* 'Dragon Lady', and other hollies; common flowering quince (*Chaenomeles speciosa*); holly olive (*Osmanthus heterophyllus*); barberries (*Berberis* spp.); hawthorns (*Crataegus* spp.); and honey locust (*Gleditsia triacanthos*; do not plant the thornless variety *inermis* for a barrier). Train honey locust and hawthorn to branch from the base by cutting them back to about a foot from the ground in each of their first three summers, when the major bloom period is over.

Here is a sampling of plants suitable for clipped hedges.
There are numerous hollies, privets, yews, and arborvitaes that would also serve well.
Plants are evergreen unless otherwise noted.

PLANT	COMMENTS	GROWING RANGE
Buxus sempervirens, boxwood	Slow growing to 15 ft tall by 15 ft wide, long-lived. Deer resistant.	Zones 6–8
Cephalotaxus fortunei, Chinese plum yew	Slow growing to 30 ft by 15 ft. Expensive but lovely. Deer resistant.	Zones 6–9
x*Cypressocyparis leylandii*, Leyland cypress	Fast growing to 60 ft by 10 ft. Tolerates partial shade.	Zones 7–10
Feijoa sellowiana, pineapple guava	Medium to fast growing, to 12 ft by 10 ft. Start training when young for best density. Moderate deer resistance.	Zones 8–10
Ilex cornuta, Chinese holly	Slow growing to 8 ft by 10 ft. Dense and rounded. Need male pollinator within 30–40 feet of female for berries.	Zones 7–9
Ligustrum ovalifolium, California privet	Fast growing to 12 ft by 10 ft. Evergreen or semi-evergreen, deciduous in colder parts of range.	Zones 5 or 6–8
Lonicera nitida, boxleaf honeysuckle	To 8 ft by 7 ft. Evergreen to semi-evergreen. White flowers. 'Baggesen's Gold' has yellow-green foliage.	Zones 6–9
Podocarpus macrophyllus, yew pine	Slow growing to 30 ft by 15 ft. Tolerates some shade. Good for the South.	Zones 7–10
Taxus x*media*, yew	Medium growth rate, size varies with cultivar. Shade tolerant but deer love it. Prone to windburn in exposed locations.	Zones 5–7
Thuja occidentalis, American arborvitae	Slow to medium growth rate, to 40 ft by 12 ft. Overused, but reliable and adaptable.	Zones 2–7

SCREENING PLANTS

These plants all make good informal screens. Additional species and varieties
of false cypress, pine, and viburnum will also work well.

Deciduous Screens

PLANT	COMMENTS	GROWING RANGE
Abelia ×*grandiflora*, glossy abelia	Medium to fast growth rate to 6 ft by 6 ft. Evergreen in the South. Can be sheared as hedge, but white flowers will be lost.	Zones 6–9
Acer campestre, hedge maple	Slow growing to 30 ft by 30 ft. Adapts to wide range of soils, acid to alkaline.	Zones 5–8
Berberis ×*mentorensis*, Mentor barberry	Medium growth rate to 5 ft by 6 ft. Good barrier.	Zones 5–8
Carpinus betulus 'Fastigiata', fastigiate European hornbeam	Slow to medium growth rate to 40 ft by 25 ft. Adapts to wide range of well-drained soils.	Zones 4–8
Clethra alnifolia, sweet pepperbush	Slow to medium growth rate to 7 ft by 6 ft. Fragrant white flowers. Best in moist soil.	Zones 3–9
Cotoneaster multiflorus	Medium growth rate to 10 ft by 12 ft. White flowers in spring, red berries in fall.	Zones 4–7
Euonymus alatus, burning bush	Slow growing to 15 ft by 10 ft. Brilliant red fall foliage.	Zones 4–9
Maclura pomifera, Osage orange	Fast growing to 40 ft by 35 ft. Tolerates difficult conditions.	Zones 5–9
Spiraea ×*vanhouttei*, bridal wreath	Fast growing to 6 ft by 6 ft. Gracefully arching branches; abundant white flowers in spring. Tolerates some shade.	Zones 4–9
Stephanandra incisa, cut-leaf stephanandra	Fast growing to 5 ft by 6 ft. Elegant and dense, with arching branches.	Zones 5–8
Viburnum plicatum var. *tomentosum*, doublefile viburnum	Medium growth rate to 9 ft by 10 ft. Flat-topped white flower clusters in spring; birds love the red fruit.	Zones 4–8

Evergreen Screens

PLANT	COMMENTS	GROWING RANGE
Calocedrus decurrens, incense cedar	Slow to medium growth rate to 50 ft by 9 ft. Dense and columnar, formal-looking.	Zones 5–8
Chamaecyparis nootkanensis, Nootka false cypress	Medium growth rate to 50 ft by 15 ft. Native to coastal Northwest and thrives in those conditions.	Zones 4–7
Ilex spp., hollies	Slow growing.	Zones vary with species
Juniperus spp., junipers	Slow to medium growth rate.	Zones vary with species
Myrica cerifera, wax myrtle	Medium to fast growth rate to 15 ft by 15 ft. Aromatic oval leaves.	Zones 6–9
Nerium oleander, oleander	Medium to fast growth rate; size varies with conditions. Summer flowers in red, pink, or white.	Zones 8–10
Pinus cembra, Swiss stone pine	Slow growing to 50 ft by 20 ft. Deer resistant.	Zones 3–7
Prunus laurocerasus, cherry laurel	Medium growth rate to 10 ft by 15 ft or more. Large, glossy leaves; tolerates shade. Hardiest cultivar: 'Schipkaensis', skip laurel.	Zones 6–9
Rhododendron spp., rhododendrons	Slow growing.	Zones vary with species

CHAPTER 4

[Garden Structures]

Paths, walls, fences, and hedges define space in the garden and regulate movement through it. Other structural elements become part of the landscape's spaces and enhance the space in any number of ways. Patios and decks provide outdoor living space, whether they are attached to the house or located some distance away from it. Arbors and pergolas create shade and enclosure overhead. Gazebos give you a delightful place in which to just enjoy the garden, to be among the plants. Sheds are for storage, of course, but they, too, can become design elements. In this chapter, we'll look at ways to tie these outdoor structures into your landscape.

◄ Gazebos, arbors, and other structures make it a pleasure to spend time in the garden.

Here's a great example of how you can integrate a patio into your landscape for maximum enjoyment. The rustic furniture really suits the informal style of the garden.

Patios

A patio helps to connect the house with the landscape. Because it sits at ground level, or sometimes slightly below, a patio feels more like part of the garden than part of the house. Patios can be formal or informal, depending on their shape and the materials used to construct them. When choosing a site for a patio, think about how you will be likely to use it and at what time of day.

The most popular place for a patio is right off the back of the house, with access through a door at ground level. This kind of convenient location, directly off of a room that you use a great deal, will make your patio a comfortable extension of your living space. If the patio is equipped with the right amenities, you will naturally gravitate to it in pleasant weather. If you expect to dine *al fresco* on the patio, locate it off the kitchen. Consider on which side of the house the patio will be located, too. A western exposure can be perfect for outdoor dinners because it will stay warmer in the evening. It may, however, be unpleasantly hot in the afternoon. In a warm climate, a patio with a northern exposure will be cooler and not so sunny.

There are other places to consider putting a patio besides near the kitchen or dining room. You might put a small, private patio off a first-floor master bedroom, with access through French doors or sliders. Screen the patio with lattice or trelliswork and you have a cozy, protected spot where you can relax with a cup of tea and the Sunday papers.

Away from the house, you could construct a patio in a flat, shady spot in the center of the garden, or in a secluded corner behind a screen of shrubs. You can also turn awkward, little-used space such as a narrow side yard or driveway into a patio, perhaps closed off from the street by a wall or fence. You can make a sunken patio in the foundation of an old barn or garage that was torn down, turning an eyesore into attractive, usable space. A sunken patio is especially nice in a cool northern climate because it will collect heat from the sun while providing shelter from the wind, making it warmer than a patio in a more exposed location.

How big your patio should be depends primarily on how you will use it, although you will also want to keep it in scale with the size of your house and property. If you want to create a private retreat, a small patio will feel cozier and more personal. If you want a space for family activities such as dining, relaxing, and recreation, think about the number of people in your family and what kinds of furnishings you will need in order to accommodate what they like to do. What size straight lines make them feel a lot like an outdoor room. For a patio not connected to the house, you could also consider a round or oval shape if it would fit into your overall landscape design.

Features for Patios

Installing an awning or other covering over the patio will enable you to use it on rainy days if you want to. If you live in a warm climate, you will almost certainly want to incorporate some sort of overhead shade structure, perhaps an arbor. Train vines on the arbor to create a lovely, leafy canopy that shields you from the hot summer sun and lets in soft, dappled light.

If you will be using the patio at night, you will need to plan for lighting. See Chapter 5 for a discussion of outdoor lighting options. A patio used for entertaining will probably need to incorporate a serving area, a barbecue grill, and perhaps a more extensive outdoor cooking area. Electrical outlets will be necessary, too. You may also want to include a bar. Comfortable, serviceable furniture will add to your enjoyment of the space. To use the patio earlier in spring and later in fall, include an outdoor fireplace, a fire pit, or a chiminea for heat. Many different styles are available.

Flagstone patio with New Dawn roses and fragrant potato vine (*Solanum jasminoides*).

table will you need, and how many chairs? Will you want *chaise longues*? How about a pint-size picnic table and a sandbox in a corner for children's use?

If you want to use your patio for entertaining friends and extended family, consider the number of people you usually entertain. You will need space for a big table and enough chairs to accommodate everyone, plus room for your guests to move about and converse.

Square and rectangular patios are the easiest shapes to lay out and construct, and they are traditional shapes for patios adjacent to the house. The

An outdoor heater allows you to use the patio in cool weather.

If you plan to install a hot tub on the patio, you will need to consider plumbing and electrical requirements, and privacy screening.

A patio can be a fine place for a fountain or other water feature. A small pool or fountain, or even a simple water spout, enhances the tranquil serenity of a formal patio.

Having garden beds around the patio enhances its connection to the landscape. Repeat plants from other beds and borders in planting areas close by the patio to further unify the property. Installing planter boxes or raised beds will emphasize the lines of a formal patio, in addition to providing space for plants. Or you could create a formal look with a low, clipped hedge running along the perimeter. Germander (*Teucrium chamaedrys*), santolina (*Santolina chamae-cyparissus*), lavenders (*Lavandula* spp.), and littleleaf boxwood (*Buxus microphylla*) all can be used for low hedges.

Small trees are especially welcome near a patio, where they supply shade and greenery, and perhaps flowers, too. You might even construct a patio around one of your favorite trees and incorporate it right into the design.

Fragrant plants are delightful next to a patio, where you can enjoy their special qualities. If you plan to use the patio a lot in the evening, consider planting a garden of night-blooming flowers, or a moonlight garden of white flowers that will glow as the light fades at dusk.

A small fountain or other water feature is a delightful addition to a patio. This one is framed by fragrant lavender and aromatic boxwood, and carpeted with ajuga and golden creeping Jenny (*Lysimachia nummularia* 'Aurea').

Fragrant plants to grow on or near patios include roses, white sweet alyssum (*Lobularia maritima*), and boxwood.

FRAGRANT FLOWERS

The flowers listed here are all fragrant. Consider including some of them in containers on patios and decks, and in garden beds nearby.

Annuals, Bulbs, and Perennials

Abronia villosa, sand verbena

Agastache spp., anise hyssops (scented leaves)

Allium tuberosum, garlic chives

Brugmansia spp., angel's trumpets (poisonous if eaten)

Centranthus ruber, red valerian

Centaurea moschata, sweet sultan

Convallaria majalis, lily-of-the-valley

Crinum spp.

Dianthus spp., clove pinks, carnations

Dictamnus albus, gas plant

Erysimum cheiri, wallflower

Filipendula rubra, queen-of-the-prairie

Gladiolus callianthus, acidanthera

Heliotropium arborescens, heliotrope

Hesperis matronalis, dame's rocket

Hosta plantaginea, fragrant plantain lily

Hyacinthus orientalis, hyacinth

Hymenocallis spp., Peruvian daffodils

Iberis umbellata, rocket candytuft

Iris reticulata, netted iris

Iris cvs., bearded irises (many are fragrant)

Lathyrus odoratus, sweet pea

Lavandula spp., lavenders

Lilium spp. and cvs., lilies (many are fragrant)

Lobularia maritima, sweet alyssum

Lycoris squamigera, magic lily

Matthiola incana, stock

Monarda didyma, beebalm

Muscari spp., grape hyacinths

Narcissus spp. and cvs., daffodils (some are fragrant)

Paeonia cvs., peonies

Petunia cvs.

Phlox paniculata, garden phlox

Polianthes tuberosa, tuberose

Reseda odorata, mignonette

Tropaeolum majus, nasturtium

Viola odorata, sweet violet

Yucca spp.

Shrubs and Vines

Akebia quinata, five-leaf akebia

Anredera cordifolia, madeira vine

Beaumontia grandiflora, Easter lily vine

Buddleia davidii, butterfly bush

Ceanothus spp., California lilacs

Chimonanthus praecox, wintersweet

Choisya ternata, Mexican orange

Clematis terniflora, sweet autumn clematis

Clethra alnifolia, sweet pepperbush

Corylopsis pauciflora, buttercup winterhazel

Daphne spp.

Dioscorea batatas, cinnamon vine

Fothergilla major, large fothergilla

Gardenia jasminoides, gardenia, Cape jasmine

Gelsemium sempervirens, Carolina jessamine

Hamamelis spp., witch hazels

Itea spp., sweetspires

Jasminum spp., jasmines

Lonicera spp., honeysuckles

Mandevilla laxa, Chilean jasmine

Nerium oleander, oleander

Osmanthus fragrans, sweet olive

Philadelphus spp., mock oranges

Pittosporum tobira, Japanese mock orange

Rhododendron spp., deciduous azaleas

Ribes odoratum, flowering currant

Rosa cvs., roses

Schisandra chinensis, Chinese magnolia vine

Stephanotis floribunda, Madagascar jasmine

Styrax obassia, fragrant snowbell

Syringa vulgaris, lilac

Trachelospermum jasminoides, Confederate jasmine

Viburnum spp. (several are fragrants)

Wisteria floribunda, Japanese wisteria

Surfaces for Patios

Like walls and paths, patios can look formal or informal, depending on the surface material used in their construction. Mortared brick and flagstone cut into uniform paving blocks are the most formal surfaces for patios. Tile, too, makes an elegant, formal patio surface in warm climates. Poured concrete (especially when the surface is textured), cultured stone pavers, irregularly cut flagstone, fieldstone, and unmortared, weathered, or antique brick have an informal look.

Most patios are made of some sort of masonry—poured concrete that can be textured or colored, concrete paving blocks, brick, manufactured or cultured stone, flagstone, or fieldstone. The basic characteristics of most of these materials are discussed in the section on paths in Chapter 3. Here are some considerations for using different kinds of masonry for patios. There are styles and colors to suit all types of houses.

Poured Concrete

A smooth concrete slab is probably the most widely used kind of patio. Concrete has much to recommend it as a patio surface—it is durable, not terribly expensive, and easy to have installed. But these days, a concrete patio can be a lot more interesting (and less slippery) than the traditional smooth, white slab. One simple technique is to rake or brush the surface while it is still wet to expose the pebbly aggregate underneath. You can have a contractor imprint the surface with a textured pattern to look like

PLANT FINDER

PATIO TREES

These compact trees are good candidates for planting near patios and decks. Some may drop fruit; if you want to avoid cleanup chores, steer clear of fruiting trees such as crabapple and serviceberry.

Acer griseum, paperbark maple, Zones 4–8

Acer palmatum, Japanese maple, Zones 6–8

Amelanchier canadensis, serviceberry, Zones 3–7

Cercis chinensis, Chinese redbud, Zones 6–9

Cercis occidentalis, western redbud, Zones 6–10

Chilopsis linearis, desert willow, Zones 8–9

Chionanthus retusus, Chinese fringe tree, Zones 6–10

Chionanthus virginicus, fringe tree, Zones 5–9

Cornus kousa, Chinese dogwood, Zones 5–8

Cornus x*rutgersensis*, hybrid dogwood, Zones 5–8

Cotinus coggygria, smoketree, Zones 5–8

Crataegus laevigata, English hawthorn, Zones 5–8

Franklinia alatamaha, Franklin tree, Zones 6–9

Laburnum x*watereri*, golden chain tree, Zones 6–8

Leptospermum scoparium, New Zealand tea tree, Zones 9–11

Magnolia x*soulangeana*, saucer magnolia, Zones 5–9

Magnolia stellata, star magnolia, Zones 5–9

Malus cvs., crabapples, Zones 5–8

stone or brick, or tint the concrete in a color that complements your house.

Concrete can be colored either by adding pigment to the wet concrete mix or by treating the surface of the cured and dried slab with a paint stain or an acid stain. Paint stains come in more than 20 colors, including browns, greens, reds, blues, and tans; you roll them on with a paint roller. Blue stains generally tend to wear less well than other colors. Acid stains react chemically with the minerals in the concrete to etch the color right into the surface. The resulting finish resembles stone. Both these methods can be used on a newly constructed patio or to renovate one that already exists.

Another way to make concrete more interesting is to use strips of rot-resistant wood, or bricks, to di-

Concrete or cultured stone pavers come in a host of styles, shapes, and colors for use in patios, paths, driveways, and walls. These paving blocks look like bricks.

A poured concrete patio is more attractive when the surface is divided into segments, textured, or tinted.

vide up the patio into squares and then dress up the squares by exposing the aggregate, pressing colored pebbles into the wet surface, coloring them, or stamping them with textured patterns. Available patterns include limestone, slate, cobblestone, and brick. You can also make an outer edge of brick around the perimeter of a patio to give a concrete slab a more finished look.

Finally, you can pour a thinner slab—3 inches instead of the usual 4—and use it as a base for flagstones, tiles, crushed stone, or other kinds of masonry.

Paving Blocks

Pavers may be made of real stone or of manufactured or cultured stone, which is actually a blend of cement and lightweight aggregates molded, colored, and textured to look like stone or brick. Cultured stone can look amazingly naturalistic, and while it isn't cheap, it is less expensive than natural stone. Pavers vary in thickness. Cultured stone is just a couple of inches thick, with a textured face and a flat back side. It weighs less than a real stone or brick.

For a patio, you will probably want a relatively smooth, even surface that will allow you to roll out the gas grill and lounge chairs easily. But in an informal situation, pavers resembling cobblestones can work, if they're sunk into the ground so that their surface is at ground level. You might want to try this with Belgian block (or the cultured stone equivalent, called Brussels block) or fieldstone. As is the case with paths, to really make a stone patio look like it belongs in the landscape, it's best to use local stone, or something that looks like the local stone.

If you are after a more formal look, choose pavers cut in rectangular or square shapes and set them in a regular, straight pattern. Arced and curved designs are better for less-formal patios. Pavers come in different shapes, sizes, and colors. Some pavers are cut to interlock with one another, while others you simply lay next to one another like bricks or stones.

There are also larger paving slabs that are molded with textures such as irregular flagstones (crazy paving), cobblestones, or bricks.

Brick

Brick makes a durable, good-looking patio that beautifully complements a historic or formal home. You can lay a brick patio in the same kinds of patterns you use for brick paths. A mortared brick patio will look more formal than an unmortared one. Like a path, a brick patio can be laid on a sand and gravel base instead of on concrete or mortar. See the paths section on page 91 for more information on choosing and working with brick.

Flagstone

Bluestone flags that are quarried and cut into regular rectangular shapes in uniform sizes make the most formal patio of all. Irregularly cut flagstone is a bit less formal. Flagstone is durable and beautiful, but it is also expensive. It comes in a range of colors from deep gray to blue-gray to brownish red, tan, and beige. The lighter colors tend to get dirty easily and can be difficult to clean. If you want to use limestone for your patio, use the hardest available kind. Limestone is porous and does not hold up terribly well in climates where rain is plentiful and winters are cold. Wisconsin limestone is generally harder and less porous than Indiana limestone. If you opt for a light-colored limestone or sandstone, it's best to apply a sealant to protect the stone after the patio is in place. The sealant will help prevent staining and protect the patio from winter damage. You can choose a matte, dull, satin, or gloss finish. Let the patio cure for a month before you use it.

Fieldstone

Stone dug from fields and prairies can be used to make charming informal patios. Because fieldstone is irregularly sized and rounded rather than flat, you will need to partially bury the stones to create a surface even enough to walk on. Even a relatively flat field-

A patio of cut bluestone is perfect in a formal garden. The white wicker furniture and graceful wood bench enhance the elegant look.

A mortared brick patio
is durable and attractive.
This one incorporates a
built-in planting bed.

stone surface will not be smooth, though, and you may find it difficult to wheel patio furniture and the barbecue grill across it. Still, it makes a beautiful, rustic-looking patio, and it is less expensive than flagstone.

The fieldstones in this charming patio are interplanted with thyme and creeping rosemary, whose rich scents are released by the sun's heat or when stepped upon.

Tile

In the Southwest, a tile patio can elegantly complement a stucco or adobe home with a tiled roof. Add a fountain or small pool to further enhance the Spanish feeling. Tile looks classy, even formal, and is especially nice for a patio off a living or dining room. For a patio, you need to purchase tiles intended for outdoor use—ideally a frost-free, nonskid tile. Tile is durable, wears well, and needs little maintenance. The earthy colors harmonize well with gardens. Tiles come in a wide range of colors and designs, and prices vary significantly. Hand-painted imported tiles can be quite costly, but they are undeniably beautiful.

PLANT FINDER

NIGHT-BLOOMING FLOWERS

Flowers that bloom at night are a special treat. If you use your patio or deck a lot in the evening, plant some of these beauties to bring some magic to your summer nights. All of them either open at the end of the day or remain open at night. Most are sweetly fragrant to help attract their nocturnal pollinators.

Abronia fragrans,
white sand verbena

Datura metel,
thornapple (poisonous)

Gaura coccinea,
scarlet gaura

Gaura lindheimeri,
white gaura

Gladiolus tristis

Hemerocallis citrina,
citron daylily

Hemerocallis lilioasphodelus,
lemon lily

Hesperantha spp.,
evening irises

Hesperocallis undulata,
desert lily

Hosta plantaginea,
fragrant plantain lily

Ipomoea alba,
moonflower

Matthiola longipetala subsp.
bicornis, evening stock

Mentzelia decapetala,
evening star

Mirabilis jalapa,
four o'clock

Nicotiana alata, N. suaveolens, N. sylvestris, flowering tobacco

Nymphaea cvs.,
night-blooming tropical waterlilies

Oenothera biennis,
evening primrose

Oenothera caespitosa,
gumbo lily

Pardanthopsis dichotoma,
vesper iris

Saponaria officinalis,
soapwort

Silene alba,
evening campion

Silene noctiflora,
night-flowering catchfly

Yucca spp.

Mixed Media

You can combine different materials for an especially interesting design. You could, for example, use a border of Belgian or Brussels block around the perimeter of a patio made of concrete or flagstone. Or you could create a grid pattern of concrete squares outlined in brick, or combine brick with squares of mortared pebbles. Or let grass or, if your conditions are right, moss grow between paving stones. (See "Planting in the Patio" on page 143 for information on how to plant in between stones.)

Above: A patio of irregular flagstones interplanted with blue star creeper (*Laurentia fluviatilis*) has a casual charm. *Left:* An interesting mixed-media patio combines brick with concrete panels inlaid with cobbles.

Patio Construction Tips

For a sturdy patio, you need a flat, even surface that drains well. This will avoid puddles on the patio after rain, and ice buildup and cracking in winter. Prepare a good base of gravel and sand 4 to 8 inches thick. If the patio is adjacent to the house, water should drain away from the house. Grading the patio site very slightly—about ¼ inch per foot is considered acceptable in most conditions—will permit water to drain off, but you won't notice the grade when you are using the patio.

If the patio is located away from the house, make it slightly higher in the center and slope it ever so gently out toward the edges.

The basic procedure for building a patio goes like this: First, lay out the outline, marking it off with stakes and string. Then, excavate to a depth of 6 inches, plus the thickness of the paving material you will be using. Grade the area as described above, to provide for drainage. Put down landscape fabric to keep out weeds. Spread 4 inches of gravel in the excavated area and tamp it down. Spread 2 inches of sand on top of the gravel and level it. Then, you are ready to proceed with a concrete slab or base, or installing pavers, bricks, or other paving materials.

PLANTING IN THE PATIO

If you are making a patio from pavers or dry-laid brick, flagstone, or fieldstone, you can leave some spaces empty and plant in them. Or you can leave extra space between some of the stones or pavers and tuck small plants into the little niches. Remove the base sand and gravel in each planting space and fill in with a light, porous, fertile potting mix. One good planting mix to use in patio pavements is a blend of 2 parts finely crumbled compost, 1 part sharp (builder's) sand, and 1 part peat moss or vermiculite.

You can choose from the plants listed in "Groundcovers for Paths" (see page 99) for your patio. All of those will tolerate being stepped on. You can also use the plants listed here, although it would be best to plant these in corners where they won't likely be walked on.

Brachyscome iberidifolia, Swan River daisy

Diascia spp.

Helianthemum nummularium, rock rose

Lobularia maritima, sweet alyssum

Portulaca grandiflora, rose moss

Thymophylla (Dyssodia) tenuiloba, Dahlberg daisy

Viola tricolor, Johnny jump-up

Decks

Decks are informal places that are perfect for casual outdoor living. Like patios, decks connect the house to the garden. But because decks are usually attached to the house and are built above the ground, they feel more like part of the house than the garden. A deck can really expand your living space in nice weather, and it provides a comfortable transition between the indoors and the yard. You can socialize with friends and relatives there, or have open-air meals with your family. You can birdwatch, sunbathe, or read. Kids can play there, and you can easily keep an eye on little ones. A deck visually opens up your house, too, and makes it feel bigger—an especially valuable amenity for a small house.

When deciding where to put a deck, think about how you want to use it, and think about the environmental qualities of possible locations, too. It makes sense to put a deck outside the rooms of the house in which you do the same things you'll want to do on your deck. For instance, if you want an outdoor dining area, put the deck off the kitchen—it'll be easier to carry food, dishes, and utensils back and forth. If you want to kick back with a good book, you might put a small deck off a bedroom. For a place to watch the birds, an upper-level deck on a tree-shaded side of the house is ideal; installing feeders, a birdbath, and birdhouses in the landscape nearby will help attract your feathered friends. If you want to sunbathe or fill the deck with pots of flowers, a sunny southern or eastern exposure is best.

You can use a deck to solve design problems, too. Decks are great facilitators on sloping and uneven lots, where they allow you to use otherwise wasted space. You can build a deck around a favorite

tree you want to keep; if the deck has an upper level, it can feel a little bit like a treehouse. Or you can construct a deck around a spa or aboveground swimming pool to make the tub or pool feel built in rather than plunked on the ground.

Site your deck where the conditions will be most comfortable for you. Study the patterns of sun and shade around your house during the times of year when you will use the deck. If you live in the North, you will probably enjoy a sunny location. But in the South, shade will be a must, at least in the afternoon, and preferably between 10 A.M. and late afternoon. Think, too, about the direction from which the prevailing winds blow. Will you want to catch the cooling breezes in summer? Or does your area get blustery winds from which you'd like to be sheltered?

A deck located on the north or east side of the house will be cooler and will get less sun than one on the south or west side. The north side may not get any direct sun at all, and the east side will get morning sun, the coolest sun of the day. A deck on the south or west side of the house will be sunnier and warmer. The south side will be sunny all day, and the west side will get the hot afternoon sun. Depending on where you live, you may want all the heat you can get, or as little as you can arrange.

Whatever exposure you have to work with, you can adapt it to your needs. You can moderate the environment for the deck in a number of ways. Overhead awnings provide shelter from sun and rain. Screens, sunshades, and arbors can create shade. Well-placed deciduous trees will give you shade in summer but let in the sun during winter. Hedges and fences can buffer the wind.

If you will be building a big deck that runs across a whole side of the house, that has multiple levels,

An umbrella provides shade when the sun gets too hot on this pleasant deck. The porch roof also affords shelter from sun and rain.

Bird feeders hung near the edge of the adjacent woodland provide hours of entertainment when the homeowners sit quietly on the deck and observe.

or that extends some distance out into the yard, you would be wise to develop an overall site plan for your property before you build. Start by making an enlarged photocopy of your property survey, which will show the location of your house and the boundaries of your property. Use overlays of tracing paper to indicate the positions of utility lines, paths, walls and fences, trees and large shrubs, and garden beds and borders. Then use additional overlays to try out different locations and shapes for your deck (this method works for patios, too).

When you've chosen a place for the deck, take a close look at it. Unlike patios, decks are especially well suited to uneven ground. But even on level terrain, it's important to have a well-drained location for a deck, because if water collects under the deck and around the supporting posts there will eventually be problems with rotting of the wood. The ideal situation is land that slopes gently away from the house. If your ground is flat, however, you can dig a drainage channel before beginning construction, to siphon off excess water.

Before you go any further in your planning, find out what local building codes specify regarding deck construction, and get the necessary building permits. Decks are considered accessory living space, and most towns regulate how they can be built.

How Big Should You Build?

How big the deck should be depends on how you are going to use it and how many people you will need to accommodate. The deck must be large enough to serve your needs, but at the same time, you don't want it to overwhelm the house visually. One way to come up with a good size is to make the deck as big as the largest room in your house.

Along with deciding on how big to make the deck goes figuring out whether you want to have one or more levels, and how high off the ground you want the deck to be. One important consideration is to make the deck where it joins the house the same height as the floor inside, so you can cross the threshold smoothly without needing to step up or down. For a smooth passage, you should need only to step over the doorsill.

Building a deck on two or more different levels can be a great way to get more usable space on a sloping property, and it can also make a flat site more interesting and varied. If you have a great view, designing your deck on multiple levels can help you make the most of it. Raising part of the deck up to the second story on a hillside property might allow you to look over the treetops for a view of distant water or mountains. On the other hand, to preserve a nice view you already have from your windows, you might want to drop the deck down a few steps so you don't have to look past tables, chairs, and the barbecue grill for the scenery.

You can also design a multilevel deck to accommodate different activities on different levels. A sunny upper level might be ideal for sunbathing, while the main level closest to the house could become the dining area. A barbecue grill and other cooking facilities could be tucked into a lower level.

If you do decide on a second-story deck, don't let the space underneath go to waste. One option is to use it for storage, and screen it off with lattice or trel-liswork. Plant vines at the bottom of the screen and train them to climb up to the deck, and they will visually connect it to the yard. Add garden beds around the edges to further integrate the deck into the landscape.

Another possibility is to build a patio under the deck and turn it into a cool, shady hideaway.

Shapes and Surface Patterns

You can make a deck in pretty much any shape you want. Most decks are rectangular or square, and those shapes are easiest to plan and build, but you could also have a deck that is pentagonal or hexagonal, round or oval. Bear in mind that straight sides are a lot easier to build than curves, if you are doing it yourself, and they are also less expensive to pay someone else to build.

Because decks are made of individual planks rather than sheets of wood, the decking can be laid in interesting patterns. The usual method is simply to run the boards parallel or perpendicular to the side of the house on which the deck is built. But you can also take a more creative approach and lay the boards diagonally or in a V-shaped pattern. The V-shape performs the subtle trick of drawing the eye toward the point of the V; it can be used to direct the attention or the feet of visitors toward stairs or the door to the house. You can also lay the boards in a herringbone pattern, a diamond design, or in blocks like a parquet floor. These last three designs will require a lot more measuring and cutting than the others. The illustration on page 146 shows several different flooring patterns you might consider for your deck.

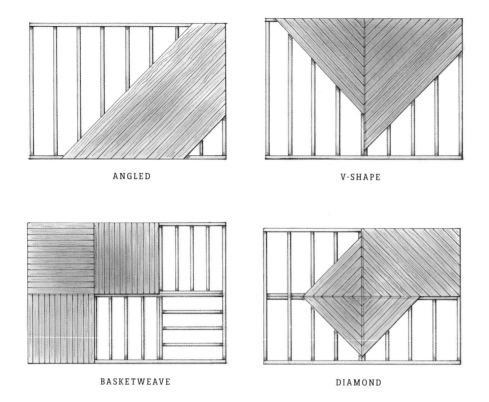

ANGLED

V-SHAPE

BASKETWEAVE

DIAMOND

You can lay a deck floor with the boards running simply parallel or perpendicular to the house, or you can opt for a more interesting or creative pattern. Possibilities include angling the boards for a diagonal line, a V-shape that points toward or away from the house, a basketweave pattern like a parquet floor, and a diagonal scheme built around a central diamond shape. Basketweave and diamond patterns involve the most labor to measure and saw.

One problem in adding on a deck is making it look like it belongs to the house and fits comfortably there. Many decks look like they are just tacked on as afterthoughts and bear no relation to either the house or the garden. However, there are some things you can do to integrate the deck with the house and landscape.

If your house is made of wood, a wood deck will be a natural complement. In any case, you can stain the deck to match or to harmonize with the color of your house. Stain railings to match the deck, or let the railings or railing posts pick up one of the trim colors of the house. Stair risers are another place to echo trim colors. Another technique is to repeat in the deck a line or architectural detail from the house. For example, you could design an arbor to cover part of the deck, with a peaked top that echoes a roof peak of the house. Repeat the garden's color scheme in pots and plants placed on the deck, and in outdoor furnishings. You'll find more suggestions for coordinating furnishings and accessories in Chapter 5.

Decks are inherently informal, and they usually work best with houses of informal design. But if you want to achieve a more formal look for a deck, build it in a pleasingly proportioned rectangle that's in scale with the house, and consider using a detailed surface pattern such as a diamond or parquet design, or painting (rather than staining) the deck to match the house walls. Or, instead of a wood floor, surface the deck with smooth-surfaced recycled plastic decking that is a neutral gray color (see "Deck Construction Tips" on page 148 for more information on this material).

Steps and Railings

All decks need at least a few steps to enable you to get from the floor to the ground. Steps also connect the different platforms of multilevel decks. For comfort and ease of use, make the steps broad and low. Steps for decks are often built to be 4 to 6 feet wide, with low, easy-to-climb risers. A good ratio of riser height to tread width is 6:12; the wider the tread, the lower the riser. That means a step with a 12-inch-wide tread needs a 6-inch-high riser. A step with a 14-inch-wide tread gets a 5-inch riser. Steps onto the deck should represent a gracious welcome, not an athletic event.

The risers for the stairs may be either closed or open, though closed risers are easier to negotiate for people of all ages, and for pets, too. Closed risers can be painted a different color than the treads and the deck flooring, perhaps to match a trim color of the house.

Railings are an important part of any deck. Your town's building code may include specifications for deck railings, such as what is considered acceptable spacing between railing posts. On a high deck, and wherever young children or pets are present, railing posts need to be close together so that none and nothing can slip between them. Railing posts can be simply straight with vertical sides, or they can be shaped for a more decorative look. Most deck railings are made of wood, but if you build a deck from recycled plastic planks (described on page 148), you can get railings to match. Railings for decks on contemporary homes are often made of sleek tubular steel.

You can choose either built-in or freestanding benches for your deck, or a combination of the two. Built-in benches with hinged seats can provide handy storage space.

Features and Accessories for Decks

Your deck is going to need plenty of seating, and one great way to provide it is to build in benches along the railings around the edges of the deck. Built-in benches make very efficient use of space, especially if you build them as boxes and hinge the seats to serve as lids. The benches then do double duty as storage space. Add color-coordinated cushions for comfortable seating. Another place to consider placing benches is along the house wall, where the deck meets the house. Putting benches in a corner of the deck, where two sides come together, creates a perfect little conversation nook.

Along with benches, consider including some built-in planter boxes that make it easy to have flowers and foliage close at hand. You can locate planters on either side of the entrance to the deck, along the wall of the house, in corners, and alongside steps to mark changes in level. With a wide rim, a planter box also could serve as auxiliary seating. Mounting window boxes on deck railings adds a bit of romance. Fill them with flowers, and be sure to include some cascading plants and vines to tumble over the edges. The plants recommended in "Hanging Basket Plants" on page 150 are some good choices. See "Window Box Plants" on page 148 for more suggestions.

WINDOW BOX PLANTS

These plants are all good choices for window boxes.

Antirrhinum majus, snapdragon

Arctotis stoechadifolia, African daisy

Argyranthemum frutescens, marguerite

Begonia Semperflorens Group, wax begonia

Browallia speciosa, sapphire flower

Buxus microphylla, small-leaved boxwood

Caladium xhortulanum, fancy-leaved caladium

Catharanthus roseus, Madagascar periwinkle

Celosia cristata, woolflower

Cineraria maritima, dusty miller

Coleus hybrids

Dahlia cvs., dwarf dahlias

Dianthus chinensis, China pink

Ferns

Gerbera jamesonii, Transvaal daisy

Gomphrena globosa, globe amaranth

Helichrysum petiolare, licorice plant

Heliotropium arborescens, heliotrope

Impatiens walleriana, bedding impatiens

Lobelia erinus, edging lobelia

Nicotiana alata, flowering tobacco

Nierembergia hippomanica, cupflower

Pelargonium spp., geraniums

Petunia xhybrida

Phlox drummondii, annual phlox

Portulaca grandiflora, rose moss

Primula spp., primroses

Salvia spp., sages

Tagetes spp., marigolds

Tropaeolum majus, nasturtium

Verbena canadensis, V. xhybrida

Zinnia angustifolia, narrow-leaved zinnia

Most decks are used for dining and cooking, too. Options for tables and chairs are discussed in Chapter 5. If you're going to have a barbecue or cooking area, it would be wise to provide fireproofing in the vicinity so that you don't inadvertently set the deck on fire. Set the grill on a fireproof surface, keep it well away from railings, and of course, never leave it unattended when it is in use.

A deck is a good place for an outdoor spa or hot tub. You might even build the deck around the tub. Locate a bench close by, where bathers can toss towels and sandals.

To create a delightfully shady seating area, consider erecting an arbor over a portion of the deck. You'll find information on arbors in the next section of this chapter.

Deck Construction Tips

Decks are exposed to the weather year-round, so use rot-resistant wood to build them. Cypress, cedar, and redwood all weather to silvery gray if left unpainted. You can leave the wood its natural color or stain it a color that harmonizes with the house. Neutral browns, grays, and tans work with a range of house colors. Bear in mind that darker-colored stains will show wear sooner than lighter colors. For the longest life and best wear, use a finish that will penetrate the wood and make it water repellent. If you want to paint your deck to match your house, use the color on stair risers and railing posts instead of the flooring, and key it to the house's trim.

An alternative to the traditional wooden deck is one built of a material made of a combination of recycled wood and plastic grocery bags, called Trex. This material costs about one-third more than wood, but it offers a lot of advantages. It doesn't rot or splinter, it needs no stains or sealants, and it resists moisture and sun damage. It does not get slippery when wet. The material is available in two textures, one resembling wood and the other smoother and more akin to stone. Five colors are available—three brown shades and two grays. You can also get coordinating railings and edgings. This decking is widely available and, while it doesn't look exactly like natural wood or stone, it is attractive and very durable. It lends itself to both traditional and contemporary designs.

Landscaping for Decks

One problem with decks is hiding the space underneath them. You can screen off the bottom of the deck with lattice panels or trelliswork. But often, a better option is to create garden beds around the deck's perimeter. Plantings not only add color to the deck area, they also help tie the deck into the landscape. For continuity, use the same colors you've used in your other beds and borders.

Shrubs can provide excellent screening around a deck. If the deck is very close to the ground, use spreading junipers, cotoneasters, carpet roses, or other sprawling plants. Use upright but relatively low growers such as azaleas, spiraea, barberry, daphne, potentilla, hypericum, and hydrangeas around decks of modest elevation. For higher decks, plant taller shrubs such as rhododendron, viburnum, upright varieties of yew or juniper, hollies, lilacs, shrub roses, or even small trees. You can choose shrubs for spring or summer flowers, ornamental berries, colorful fall foliage, or a combination of attributes. Tall ornamental grasses are another option; you can let them stand all winter if they don't get blown over in stiff winds or bent under heavy snow and ice; then, simply cut them back close to the ground in early spring. If the deck is on the second story, consider including trellis panels on which you can train honeysuckle, clematis, or other vines to ascend to the deck.

For more color, plant perennials and annuals in front of the shrubs on the side toward the lawn. If lower maintenance is what you need, plant easy-care groundcovers instead.

Of course, a deck wouldn't be complete without some potted plants. Deck containers can hold lots more than a few geraniums or petunias, and they can create or at least contribute to the deck's ambience. You can combine lots of plants in large tubs, bowls, and planter boxes, or group smaller pots together for visual impact. For a lush look, combine tall centerpiece plants with bushy plants for volume, then add smaller filler and accent flowers, and include cascading and trailing plants to spill over the edges of the planters.

Key the pots and plants to your garden's color scheme, picking up colors from the house trim and beds and borders. Container plants can produce all sorts of looks. You could create a tropical paradise (many tropical plants can overwinter in bright windows indoors in cold climates), a meadowy wildflower feeling, oriental serenity, cottage gardenlike charm, or bold, contemporary drama. When you go to the garden center or nursery, mix and match

Decorate your deck with lots of plants in containers. You can place potted plants on tables, on and at the top and bottom of stairs, and in window boxes mounted on railings. Group containers together for greater visual punch.

plants on a cart or in a corner out of the way, setting the nursery pots together in groups until you come up with a combination you like. You will need to consider your color scheme and also your growing conditions: Is the deck sunny or shady? Will you be there to water every day, or do you need very drought-tolerant plants in your pots?

In addition to placing pots and planters on the deck and filling built-in planter boxes along the railings, you can add color on more levels with hanging baskets mounted on wall brackets and arbors, and window boxes attached to the railings. See Chapter 5 for suggestions on how to decorate with containers.

Use cascading and trailing plants in hanging baskets to create a leafy, flowery screen for the deck. Suspend baskets at varying heights for greater density and interest.

HANGING BASKET PLANTS

These plants are all good choices for hanging baskets. (Partial to light shade is best for plants listed here for shade.)

Sun

Brachyscome iberidifolia,
Swan River daisy

Calibrachoa cvs.,
million bells

Cobaea scandens,
cup-and-saucer vine

Felicia bergeriana,
kingfisher daisy

Helichrysum petiolare,
licorice plant

Ipomoea batatas,
sweet potato vine

Lantana cvs.

Lobularia maritima,
sweet alyssum

Lysimachia nummularia 'Aurea',
golden creeping Jenny

Nierembergia hippomanica,
cup flower

Pelargonium peltatum,
ivy geranium

Petunia integrifolia, violet-flowered petunia

Petunia, Wave cultivars

Portulaca grandiflora, rose moss

Scaevola aemula,
fanflower

Thunbergia alata,
black-eyed Susan vine

Tradescantia purpurea 'Pallida',
purple heart

Tropaeolum majus,
nasturtium

Verbena canadensis,
rose verbena

Shade

Begonia Tuberhybrida Group,
tuberous begonia

Fuchsia ×*hybrida*

Impatiens walleriana, bedding impatiens

Lobelia erinus,
edging lobelia

Plectranthus forsteri 'Marginatus',
variegated Swedish ivy

Sun or Shade

Browallia speciosa,
sapphire flower

Hedera helix cvs.,
English ivy

Vinca major 'Variegata'

CONTAINER PLANTS FOR SHADE

These plants will tolerate partial to dappled shade, and they grow well in containers.

Annuals, Bulbs, and Perennials

Ajuga reptans, bugleweed

Alternanthera spp., Joseph's coats

Aquilegia cvs., columbines

Bamboos

Begonia Semperflorens Group, wax begonias

Begonia Tuberhybrida Group, tuberous begonias

Bellis perennis, English daisy

Browallia speciosa, sapphire flower

Caladium ×*hortulanum*, fancy-leaved caladium

Campanula carpatica, Carpathian harebell

Campanula medium, Canterbury bells

Carex spp., sedges

Catharanthus roseus, Madagascar periwinkle

Chasmanthium latifolium, spangle grass

Clivia miniata, kaffir lily

Colocasia esculenta, elephant's ear

Cuphea cvs.

Cyclamen hederifolium, hardy cyclamen

Digitalis purpurea, foxglove

Exacum affine, Persian violet

Ferns

Fuchsia cvs.

Galanthus nivalis, snowdrop

Hakonechloa macra 'Aureola', hakone grass

Hedera helix cvs., English ivy

Hosta cvs., plantain lilies

Hypoestes phyllostachya, polka dot plant

Iberis umbellata, globe candytuft

Impatiens cvs., bedding and New Guinea impatiens

Lamium spp., deadnettles

Lobelia erinus, edging lobelia

Lobularia maritima, sweet alyssum

Mentha spp., mints

Mimulus ×*hybridus*, monkey flower

Mirabilis jalapa, four o'clock

Muhlenbeckia complexa, wire vine

Myosotis sylvatica, annual forget-me-not

Narcissus cvs., daffodils

Nemophila menziesii, baby blue-eyes

Nicotiana alata, flowering tobacco

Primula spp., primroses

Salvia spp., sages

Strobilanthes dyerianus, Persian shield

Torenia fournieri, wishbone flower

Vinca major 'Variegata', *V. minor*, periwinkles

Viola cornuta, horned violet, tufted pansy

Viola ×*wittrockiana*, pansy

Shrubs

Aucuba japonica, gold dust tree

Berberis thunbergii, barberry

Buxus microphylla, small-leaved boxwood

Euonymus fortunei, wintercreeper

Fatsia japonica, Japanese aralia

Picea glauca var. *albertiana* 'Conica', dwarf Alberta spruce

Pittosporum tobira, Japanese mock orange

Rhododendron cvs., azaleas

Taxus cvs., yews

Screening Decks and Patios for Shade and Privacy

It's nice to have some shade on a deck or patio, and in warm southern climates it's essential. If your patio or deck does not get much shade from nearby trees, you can create some shade with a combination of structures and plants. Shade screening has the added benefit of affording you some privacy on your deck or patio.

You can create screening overhead, or alongside the area you want to protect. For overhead screening, put up an arbor or pergola. A pergola, which is more tunnel-like than an arbor, works best when attached to the wall of the house. An arbor makes sense right next to the house, too, but an arbor is also quite wonderful over a freestanding patio. You can also use one in a corner of a deck, or on an upper or lower level to create a shady bower. See page 154 for more information on arbors. If you want protection from the rain, a canopy, awning, or tent will serve better than an open structure. If you want to have the option to provide overhead shade some of the time but not necessarily always, consider retractable awnings.

To hide the deck or patio from view, you need to create screening alongside it. If you want shade, too, put the screen on the south side. If you don't want to block the sun, put the screen on the north side. Screening for a deck or patio can take any number of forms. You could use a hedge or informal screen of shrubs, as described on page 123. A row of tall

A solid fence provides privacy screening for this patio, with a porthole window that allows a view of the world outside.

shrubs would work, too, but it's important to position any of these permanent plantings carefully, so that you don't end up with more shade than you want. Find out how tall the plants will be when they mature; taller shrubs may need to be planted some distance away from the deck to cast their shadows where you want them. If you are not sure whether or where you want to put in a permanent screen, you can try out a temporary screen planting of hollyhocks or sunflowers for a season to see how it works.

You can also use structures for screening. Instead of planting shrubs, put up panels of lattice, grid-type trelliswork, or horizontal lath strips. Train vines to grow on the screen and you'll have the bonus of flowers and foliage. The plants recommended in the list of vines to grow on fences (see page 117) are also good candidates for growing on screens.

Make space for planting around the support posts of the screen, or create planting beds along the outer edge of the deck or patio under the screen. If you opt for an overhead structure, you can also hang baskets of cascading or trailing plants for extra color. Use shade-tolerant plants if you will have vines over the top of the structure.

Here are some examples of how to pull together land-scape elements to work with different houses.

Colonial/Federal

Garden: formal, with geometric beds

Fences (if used): close-board or panel, painted to match house trim

Walls: brick, with wrought-iron gates

Paths: brick, mortared or dry-laid

Patio: brick

Bungalow, Cottage, Saltbox

Garden: informal

Fences: picket (painted to match door, shutters, or trim), or post-and-rail

Paths: flagstone, fieldstone, or dry-laid brick

Patio: irregular flagstone, fieldstone, or informal pavers

Deck: natural wood; if house is painted, pick up trim color for railing posts

Formal Victorian

Garden: formal

Fences: wrought-iron

Paths: brick or flagstone

Patio: brick, perhaps with fountain

Informal Victorian

Garden: informal

Fences: Gothic picket

Paths: dry-laid brick, gravel, or irregular flag-stone

Patio: irregular flagstone, dry-laid brick, or gravel

Ranch

Garden: informal

Fences: board-on-board or stockade

Paths: pavers, poured concrete, dry-laid brick, or gravel

Patio: textured or stained concrete, or pavers

Deck: natural or stained wood

Contemporary

Garden: naturalistic

Fences: board-on-board or panel

Paths: flagstone or gravel

Patio: flagstone

Deck: wood stained to match house; tubular steel railings; clean, minimalist lines

Porches

A porch is the perfect place to put your feet up and watch the world go by. And because it has a roof, you can use it in rainy weather. Porches with comfortable furniture are great places to socialize with family, neighbors, and friends. They extend a warm welcome to visitors. In my neighborhood growing up, a bunch of kids used to while away entire summer afternoons on our front porch playing games. On the Fourth of July, my whole family used to watch the local fireworks show from my grandparents' front porch, comfortably ensconced in rocking chairs, a big glider, and a porch swing. It was one of the highlights of summer, at least for us kids.

A well-equipped porch can become an airy outdoor living room to which your family will naturally gravitate. You can screen it to keep out bugs, and add a ceiling fan to keep the breezes moving. If you want a more private porch, you can build one onto the back or the side of the house instead of the front.

A traditional porch has wood flooring made with narrow boards and painted in a neutral color (glossy gray is a classic). The ceiling is also of narrow wooden boards, often beadboard. White is a traditional color for porch ceilings and it is a classic look, but it can seem a bit severe. Sky blue is another popular choice. You might consider instead painting the ceiling in a pastel tint of one of your home's trim colors, then picking up that color in pillows and other furnishings.

Customize your porch to suit your location and your lifestyle. If the porch has a southern exposure, make some shade with trellised vines or hanging baskets suspended on several different levels. For more privacy, install lattice or trelliswork panels on the sides of the porch. If you want a wood screen across the front of the porch, cut out some large circles so that it looks more friendly and less forbidding.

Containers of plants on the steps extend a welcome to visitors. You can place matched containers on either side of the front door, at the top of the steps, or at the foot of the stairs. Neatly clipped evergreen shrubs or topiaries, or hibiscus or other flowering shrubs trained as standards, look quite elegant in front of a formal house.

For a less formal look, it's hard to beat pots overflowing with colorful flowers. Line them up on one side of the stairs, or group them together at the top or bottom. Tie the plantings and pots to the landscape by repeating colors and plants used in garden beds and borders.

If your house and landscape are formal, you can construct your new porch to match. Supporting the roof with columns topped with Doric or Ionic capitals adds a formal touch. So does the white beadboard ceiling. If the steps up to the porch are made of wood, you could paint the risers white to match the ceiling and the treads to match the color of the porch floor. Or, if your front walk is made of flagstone or brick, you could repeat that material on the stair treads. Wicker furniture in crisp white completes the elegant formal look.

For a less formal porch, use simpler posts to support the roof, and keep the furnishings casual. You might want to include comfortable lounge chairs and rockers and perhaps a glider or swing. Natural wicker and rattan are perfect on a porch, and Adirondack chairs bring a country cabin kind of feeling.

If you lay a carpet on the porch, coordinate the colors of pillows, tablecloths, and other accessories with it. Add a small dining table and chairs if you want to use the porch for dining, or just include some small tables next to chairs to hold books and drinks conveniently. Make sure there is adequate lighting for nighttime use.

Arches, Arbors, and Pergolas

Arches, arbors, and pergolas add character to the garden. They are permanent presences, not just seasonal performers. They interact with plants throughout the growing season and stand through the winter, too, when all the non-woody plants have died back and the deciduous trees have lost their leaves. Arches, arbors, and pergolas become part of the landscape's bone structure.

These structures are all a bit different from one another, but they are used in similar ways. Arches are the simplest of the three, and they have simple curved tops and straight sides. Arbors are supported by four or more legs, and their tops may be curved, peaked, or flat. Pergolas are much the same, but a pergola implies more of a tunnel. A pergola is longer than an arbor, and it is meant to be walked under.

All three structures are basically open. They suggest a sense of shelter, but they don't really offer protection from the elements. You can use arches, arbors, and pergolas purely for their architectural value and leave them free of plantings. In some landscapes, this kind of clean line is just what is needed to fit a minimalist design, or to offer visual relief in an intensively planted garden. But these structures all make excellent supports for vines, and they are entirely charming when covered in foliage and flowers. You can buy these structures in kit form, build them yourself, have them custom-built, or purchase finished pieces.

There are lots of ways to use arches, arbors, and pergolas to create special effects in the landscape. Their vertical lines contrast with the horizontal lines of lawns, paths, and garden beds, and they can make interesting accents. Training vines on them enhances the vertical effect; the vines draw the eye upward and can help a small garden to feel bigger.

Place an arch or arbor over a path to mark its beginning or to define the entrance to a special part of the garden or another "room" in the landscape. You can use an arch to frame a view to which you want to call attention—perhaps a piece of statuary or a prized specimen plant across the lawn, or maybe some spectacular distant scenery.

Arbors and pergolas are perfect for creating shady little bowers or for roofing outdoor dining or sitting areas. Put an arbor over a patio or part of a deck to create an outdoor activity (or inactivity) center with a dining table and chairs, a hammock or swing and lounge chairs, benches with comfy pillows, and a children's play area.

Another bonus of an arbor or pergola is that when you cover the sides and top with vines, you gain privacy, blocking the view from upstairs windows and your neighbor's yard. Back up a pergola against a fence or wall, or attach it to the back of the house, for a shady, relaxing, self-contained seating gallery.

An arch covered with climbing roses and large-flowered *Clematis* 'Henryi' marks the beginning of a path in a most beguiling fashion. The arch draws your eye and entices you to walk along the path.

An arbor backed up against a fence becomes a comfortably enclosed gallery. Located at the end of an axis path, it is an essential component of the garden's design.

However you plan to use arches, an arbor, or a pergola in your landscape, choose their locations with care. For these structures to really work, they need to make sense where you put them. Just plopping one in the middle of the lawn won't take advantage of its old-fashioned charm. Get the most from arches, arbors, and pergolas by making them part of the total landscape design. Make sure there is a path leading to the structure, if not through it.

Structure Styles

Your outdoor structures should, of course, be compatible with the style of your home and the rest of your landscape. If your house is built of brick, use brick support columns for arbors or pergolas. With other formal houses, you could use classically styled columns of fiberglass or concrete, or veneer your columns with cultured stone. If you have a wrought-iron fence or gates, you can repeat the iron supports in an arbor or arch. With a modern house, go for sleek aluminum or steel supports. In an informal setting, use wood.

Consider issues of scale, too. Substantial supporting columns work well in large gardens but would overwhelm smaller ones. If you don't have a lot of space, build an airy, open arbor with more slender, less visually weighty supports. Conversely, in an expansive landscape, a delicate wrought-iron arch could get lost from a distance. In such a spacious setting you can easily use bigger, sturdier posts or columns for the structure.

An arch, arbor, or pergola must be high enough for people to comfortably walk or stand underneath.

The minimum width for a pergola is about 5 feet, which will allow two people to stroll slowly alongside one another with room to spare. They shouldn't feel they need to rush through. You might even add a bench to encourage stopping and resting for a while. When planning size and location, don't forget to think about whether you will need to move lawn equipment or other large objects through the structure. If you need to drive your riding mower through that charming rose-covered arch to get to the backyard, make sure it's wide enough.

If you're going to make the investment and the effort to have an arch, arbor, or pergola, build your structure to last. Make it sturdy enough to bear the weight of mature woody vines growing on it (vigorous growers like wisteria and trumpet creeper will become quite heavy with age). You will also want the structure to stand up to wind, rain, and snow. Set the support posts of arbors and pergolas into concrete footings for stability. The top crossbars can be nailed or screwed to the supporting beams, or the boards can be notched where they cross so that they interlock.

Arches

Arches work best when they mark beginnings and endings. Install one at the entrance to your property, where your sidewalk or path meets the public pavement. Or place an arch at the end of a path through the garden, in front of a hedge or plant screen. You can put an arch at the top of steps, right outside a door, or at the entrance to a garden enclosed by a fence.

Here you can see how to situate an arbor to frame a view. From this arbor your gaze is drawn along the path to the ornament in the center of the garden.

This beautiful rose-covered arch is placed where two paths intersect in this garden. Note how the trelliswork on the sides of the arch provides added support for the roses' long canes.

A flowery arbor with a comfortable seat is the very essence of the romantic garden. This arbor, covered with a noisette rose, 'Bouquet d'Or', frames a view of the landscape beyond.

Arbors

Some arbors are really just widened arches, while others are much roomier. Arbor styles range from rustic structures made of hand-peeled cedar posts to elegant classical designs, which may have Grecian-looking peaked tops reminiscent of pediments, and columns with Doric capitals. The tops may echo a design feature of the house: curved like a Palladian window or peaked like the angle of a roof. It might be flat like a pergola, rounded like a dome, or drawn into a pointed Gothic arch.

An arbor can be a simple framework, or it can be enclosed on one or more sides with decorative lattice or trelliswork panels. If the arbor is a destination in itself, perhaps placed in a nook at the end of a winding path, with benches or seats inside, a more enclosed design might be what you want. Or, to make more of a design statement, consider adding another decorative panel to fan out to either side of the arbor, each attached to an end post with a decorative cap. The extra ornamentation gives the arbor more importance. The construction materials, tops, and supports can be varied and combined in different ways to create various styles. Look through catalogs and visit the Web sites of manufacturers that ship or sell locally, or seek out local artisans who offer different designs or modular units you can combine to customize your own design.

Whether you build or buy, explore different styles to find the direction that works for you. There are always options and variations. For example, a rustic arbor of peeled poles can be put together simply, with straight supports and simple crossbars running

Arches come in many styles, with or without gates, some with built-in benches. An arch combined with a moon gate makes a graceful entry point through a hedge or fence. Arches may be rounded, squared off, or drawn into pointed Gothic forms. You can find them in unfinished wood; stained or natural finish; painted white, green, black, or gray; crafted of rustic peeled poles; or fashioned of tubular steel or wrought iron. The sides may be open, laddered with simple crossbars, filigreed with elaborate scrollwork, or screened with panels of trelliswork or lattice.

This rustic-looking arbor of twined branches was actually created by carefully training living plants to grow into a tunnel-like form. The interesting, gnarled structure contrasts with the formal hedges and lawn.

This charming pergola is lush with vines, creating a shady, flowery bower behind the house.

up the sides and over the top. Or it can be an inspired creation of irregular branches that shoot off on diagonals and come together in interesting patterns.

A Victorian styled arbor might have a Gothic arch top and painted wood posts and sides with gingerbread trim to match the house.

In a formal landscape, you can support a sizable arbor with brick pillars, shaped wood columns, or painted wood posts with detailed caps. If your house and grounds have brick and wrought-iron details, you can support your arbor with wrought-iron poles that have filigrees and scrollwork.

For a more contemporary look, keep the lines of the arbor simple and clean. Forget the gingerbread and lattice trim. Instead, make the sides, if you wish to enclose one or more of them, a simple grid of wooden bars or metal pipe, with larger openings than those found in trelliswork panels. The arbor's vaulted or peaked top can be made with poles or bars running lengthwise, with crossbars as needed for support. If your home has deck railings of tubular steel, make the arbor to match.

Pergolas

Pergolas are much like arbors, and the two terms are often used interchangeably. But whereas many arbors cover an area that is more or less square and contained, pergolas are usually longer than they are wide—they're more tunnel-like. A pergola may have an arched or flat top, and it can be freestanding or attached along its length to the house or another structure. A freestanding pergola has two sides to create enclosure; on a pergola attached to a building, one side is generally left open. Styles and materials are like those used for arbors. The defining feature of a pergola, really, is its length. This kind of structure makes a verdant passageway from one place to another. A pergola might lead from the deck to the yard, from the house to the garage, or across the lawn to a patio.

White is probably the most popular color for arches, arbors, and pergolas. White-painted wood looks clean and crisp in the landscape, and it shows off its decorative details clearly against the green of foliage. White structures will be most visible in the landscape, and in some cases, they may be too visible. They can work in either formal or informal settings, depending on their design. If you are considering using white, bear in mind that the pergola will need repainting at some point, which can be a tricky proposition, to say the least, if vines are growing all over it.

Arbors, arches, and pergolas can be painted other colors, too. Deep neutrals generally work best, such as gray, gray-green, or taupe. These darker colors are more understated and less obvious in the landscape than white-painted structures. Black is often used on metal structures of wrought iron or steel. In a contemporary landscape, shiny aluminum or brushed steel may make the right kind of sleek, high-tech statement.

Natural wood is subtler and less formal than painted wood or metal. In the landscape, structures of natural wood are beautiful in a quiet way; they let the plants be the stars of the show. Natural wood works beautifully in informal and naturalistic gardens. For a really rustic look, you could consider building a structure of natural peeled poles or branches.

Plants for Arches, Arbors, and Pergolas

Outdoor structures really become part of the landscape when they partner with vining plants. These pairings can work in different ways. A simply designed, sturdily built arbor might serve mostly as a support for the plants. A vigorous vine, such as wisteria or trumpet creeper, will completely engulf an arbor over time, turning it into a leafy outdoor room. On an arch or arbor with a more decorative design, you can grow vines of a more delicate texture, such as clematis or annual cypress vine, and let the filigree of stems, leaves, and flowers trace patterns on the structure without obscuring it.

Vines climb in a number of ways, and different vines grow best on different kinds of supports. If you know what kind of vines you want to grow before you install an arch, arbor, or pergola, you can plan the structure to include the best kind of support on the sides and posts. If you put the structure in place first, choose vines that will best take advantage of the way it is built.

There are three basic ways by which vines can climb: Some twine their stems around the support; some twist tendrils or leaf stems around it; and others attach themselves to the supporting surface with sticky aerial roots or pads on leaves or stems called *holdfasts*. Twining vines such as honeysuckle, wisteria, and morning glory need vertical bars or poles to wrap their long stems around. Tendrilled and leaf-climbing vines, such as clematis and sweet peas, find it easiest to twirl around horizontal wires or slender bars. Clinging vines, including climbing hydrangea and Boston ivy, need flat, somewhat rough surfaces to hold on to.

(continued on page 162)

A classic wisteria-draped pergola is breathtaking when the vines bloom in late spring.

VINES FOR ARBORS

Here are some vines to grow on an arch, arbor, or pergola.

PLANT	DESCRIPTION	COMMENTS	GROWING RANGE
Actinidia kolomikta, kolomikta vine	Twiner with tiny white flowers in spring; colorful green, white, and pink leaves; and edible fruit if males and females are planted.	Sun to partial shade.	Zones 4–9
Antigonon leptopus, coral vine	Tendrilled vine with clusters of bright rose-pink flowers and dark green arrow- to heart-shaped leaves.	Sun to partial shade.	Zones 9–11
Aristolochia durior, Dutchman's pipe	Twiner with large, dark green leaves and greenish brown flowers shaped like a clay pipe.	Sun to light shade.	Zones 4–8
Aristolochia elegans, calico flower	Twiner with triangular leaves and white-spotted purple flowers.	Sun to light shade.	Zones 10–11
Bougainvillea cvs.	Scandent climber with tiny flowers surrounded by brilliant papery bracts in shades of red, pink, magenta, orange, gold, purple, and white.	Full sun.	Zones 10–11
Campsis radicans, trumpet creeper	Vigorous clinger with compound leaves and tubular red or orange blossoms.	Sun to partial shade.	Zones 5–9
Clematis spp. and cvs.	Tendrilled vines with saucerlike, bell-shaped, starry, or tubular flowers in many shades of pink, rose, red, purple, violet, blue, and white, plus a few yellows.	Sun to partial shade, with roots shaded.	Zones 4–8; varies with species
Cobaea scandens, cup-and-saucer vine	Tendrilled vine with oval leaves and cup-shaped purple flowers backed by flat green calyces.	Sun to partial shade.	Zones 9–11; elsewhere grow as annual
Fallopia aubertii, silver lace vine	Twiner with oblong leaves and sprays of tiny white flowers.	Sun to partial shade.	Zones 5–9
Gelsemium sempervirens, Carolina jessamine	Evergreen twiner with glossy green leaves and clusters of fragrant, tubular yellow flowers.	Sun to light shade.	Zones 7–9
Humulus lupulus 'Aureus', golden hop vine	Twiner with large, lobed, yellow-green leaves.	Sun to light shade.	Zones 3–9
Hydrangea petiolaris, climbing hydrangea	Clinging woody vine with oval leaves and large, white, flat-topped flower clusters.	Sun to partial shade.	Zones 4–9

PLANT	DESCRIPTION	COMMENTS	GROWING RANGE
Ipomoea spp., morning glories	Vigorous twiners with lobed or heart-shaped leaves and funnel-shaped flowers in shades of purple, pink, red, white, and true blue, some flushed, edged, or streaked with a second color.	Full sun.	Annual
Ipomoea quamoclit, cypress vine	Twiner with delicate, feathery leaves and star-shaped scarlet flowers.	Full sun.	Annual
Jasminum spp., jasmines	Twining evergreen vines with glossy green leaves and clusters of fragrant, star-shaped white flowers.	Sun to partial shade.	Zones 8–11; varies with species
Lonicera spp., honeysuckles	Twiners with oblong leaves and tubular, 2-lipped flowers, some fragrant, in white, yellow, orange, pink, or red.	Full sun.	Zones 5–9; varies with species
Parthenocissus tricuspidata, Boston ivy	Clinging vine with lobed, maplelike leaves that turn red in fall.	Sun or shade.	Zones 3–8
Passiflora spp., passionflowers	Tendrilled vines with lobed leaves and complex, beautiful flowers in shades of red, white, pink, and purple.	Sun to partial shade.	Zones 8–11, some hardier; varies with species
Rosa cvs., climbing roses	Scandent long-stemmed shrubs with toothed oval leaves and flowers, many fragrant, in shades of red, pink, orange, yellow, and white.	Full sun.	Zones 5–9; varies with cultivar
Trachelospermum jasminoides, Confederate jasmine	Vigorous twiner with oblong evergreen leaves and clusters of fragrant, star-shaped white flowers.	Sun to light shade.	Zones 8–11
Tropaeolum peregrinum, canary creeper	Twining vine with light green, lobed leaves and fringed, bright yellow flowers.	Sun to partial shade.	Annual
Vitis coignetiae, crimson glory vine	Ornamental grapevine with large, heart-shaped leaves turning bright red in fall and clusters of dark fruit.	Sun to partial shade.	Zones 5–11
Wisteria spp.	Vigorous, woody twiners with compound leaves and large, drooping clusters of pealike flowers, some fragrant, in lavender, blue, or white.	Sun to partial shade.	Zones 5–10

Climbing roses, which are such favorites for arches and arbors, represent a fourth kind of plant, which are called *scandent*. Climbing roses are not true vines, and they are unable to hold on to their support. They simply lean their long stems on whatever support happens to be nearby. If you want to train roses on your arch, you will have to attach their stems to the structure as they grow. Garden centers sell various kinds of ties and hooks to use. Climbing roses are lovely on arches, but they actually bloom best when the canes are trained horizontally. Make sure you train yours over the top of the arch instead of pruning them back when they reach the top of the vertical sides.

If your arch, arbor, or pergola is of a simple design with open sides, you will probably need to help the vines climb it. You can staple garden netting or hardware cloth around large support posts to give the vines something to climb, or attach some strings or wires among other widely spaced supports. When the vines reach the top of the structure, train them to spread over the top by fastening the stems in place as they grow. See "Vines for Arbors" on page 160 for some plants to grow on arches, arbors, and pergolas.

See "Vines for Arbors" on page 160

SHADE FOR WINDOWS

Here's a way to bring leafy shade to a room inside your home and make it feel like an arbor: Install a trellis made specially to fit over windows. Upright support brackets go on either side of the window, to support horizontal or downward-angled crossbars running above the top of the window frame. Train vines over the trellis for a leafy green screen.

Window trellises are especially helpful for rooms that receive a lot of sun that makes them heat up in summer. The trellises come in various sizes. Install them over one or more windows, over sliding or French doors, or even to dress up the door of a garage or shed.

Gazebos

A gazebo is an outdoor shelter set in a landscape to provide a place from which to look at the garden. The word *gazebo* comes to us from England. It's a faux Latin term (in other words, a made-up word meant to sound like Latin) that is "translated" as "I shall gaze." Gazebos evolved from the follies that were all the rage among the British aristocracy in the 1700s. These were all sorts of outdoor structures that served no useful purpose other than to look exotic. The 18th-century nobility were busy putting up ruined Greek temples, Chinese pagodas, mysterious dark grottoes, Gothic towers on hilltops, and broken marble columns overgrown with vines. The follies were made of stone, wood, or cast iron, and they were open to the air. By Queen Victoria's time, these structures had metamorphosed into ornately constructed open-air rooms that were used for band concerts.

The English gazebo in time made the leap across the Atlantic, and in the 19th and early 20th centuries, the structures were used for band concerts here, too. Eventually, gazebos got smaller, and now they are part of many American gardens.

Gazebos are open and airy; the sides may be screened with lattice or trelliswork, or left unscreened. You can have a gazebo custom-built on your property, buy a kit and assemble the pieces on site, or purchase plans and build one from scratch. There are lots of styles, a range of sizes, and a spectrum of prices. Most gazebos have straight sides that are put together on a base to form a hexagonal or octagonal room with a roof over the top.

The best place for a gazebo is overlooking the garden or a special feature of the landscape. This gazebo has a view of a waterlily pool.

A square gazebo would be simplest to build, but octagonal ones are most popular. You can leave the basic structure undecorated, or you can dress it up with lattice panels, with or without circular cutouts to use as windows or niches for hanging baskets of flowers. You can add gingerbread trim. You can shingle the roof with cedar shakes or asphalt roofing shingles. Or you can have an open roof made of lath strips.

Where to Put a Gazebo

A gazebo can be many things—a picnic place, a summerhouse, a shelter from the sun, a meditation spot. But above all, it is a place from which to enjoy your garden. So, when choosing a location for a gazebo, pick a spot where there's something to look at. Put the gazebo in the center of the garden, surrounded by beds and borders. Put it on a path through a grove of trees or a wooded area, especially if you want a place to watch birds or get away from it all, or if your teenage children want a place to hang out with their friends. You could site a gazebo on top of a hill or rise so that you can look down and survey your domain. Or put it near water—a garden pool or pond or a swimming pool. You could even put a gazebo on a wing of a large deck, to use for entertaining. In a small garden, you can back a gazebo up against a boundary wall and make the back side solid.

Placing a gazebo next to a swimming pool provides a place to stash towels and for parents to watch children.

Gazebo Construction Tips

However you style your gazebo, start with a good foundation. Set the structure on a concrete slab, or at least set the support posts into sturdy concrete footings. After all, you don't want to lose your gazebo to the first big windstorm. As the structure goes up, check to see that it is firmly braced. You should not be able to move the gazebo or make it sway by pushing it or leaning on it. If you can shift it with your weight, try adding more cross braces to shore it up. Otherwise, it'll be likely to blow over. It's better to

start with a strong foundation. And make sure that the ground is level before you start, or the pieces of the gazebo won't fit together properly and the structure will be weak—no matter how much you brace it.

To extend the seasonal use of your gazebo, you can run an electric line to it and install a heater. For nighttime use, put in lights (and light the path to the gazebo, too, so you won't be tripping over roots and stones in the dark). If bugs are a problem, screen your gazebo. You could even add a screen door, although it will probably have to be custom-made.

Many gazebos are natural-colored wood or painted

white. If you want an old-fashioned look, and if you have white fences elsewhere on your property, you will probably be happy with a white gazebo. But you can also paint a gazebo to match the house, or you can paint or stain it a dark neutral color, perhaps gray-green or greenish brown, so that it's unobtrusive in the landscape.

You can take some stylish chances, too. For a contemporary or eclectic house, you might want to have a modernistic gazebo with simpler, cleaner lines.

Furnishings for Gazebos

The idea of a gazebo is to have a comfortable place to enjoy the garden, right *in* the garden. Install comfortable seating: benches or chairs with pillows and footstools. Add a small table to hold glasses, books, and maybe a pair of binoculars for birdwatching. If you want to have picnics there, you'll need a small dining table and chairs. If your gazebo is near a swimming pool, put in a cabinet or shelving unit to hold extra towels. You can lay outdoor carpeting on the floor if it's a plain concrete slab. Put in a hammock or porch swing if you like.

It's lovely to decorate a gazebo with plants. You can train vines up the supporting posts and, if you have screened the sides with lattice, the vines can climb on that, too. Suspend hanging baskets in cutout "windows" or the open sides of the structure. Mount window boxes on the side rails. Put a weathervane on top of the roof. See page 150 for a list of hanging basket plants, and see the list of vines for arbors (page 160) for some vines to grow on your gazebo.

Sheds

If your basement is full, your garage is too small, and you need a place to store the lawn mower, string trimmer, shovels and rakes, and empty pots and bags of potting mix, you need a shed! You could throw up a prefab model from the home center and hide it in a corner behind a hedge or fence. Or you could make that little storage building part of the landscape. A shed can be a garden feature in its own right.

There are endless ways to dress up a shed. One thing you can do is paint it to match the house, even right down to the trim. You can use an appealing material such as cedar shakes on the walls and roof, or mount lattice panels on the walls. Add details such as window boxes (if the shed has windows) and fill them with plants. Hang shutters and curtains. Build an arbor onto the front of the shed, and train vines on it to create a shady little sitting area. You could also extend the roof of the shed on one side to create a sheltered space in which to store firewood or trash cans.

In short, if you want it to, even a mundane storage space can become an attractive addition to the landscape.

Sheds are practical, but they can be decorative features, too. This one looks like a tiny country cabin, complete with a vine wreath on the door and window boxes of bright flowers.

CHAPTER 5

Decorating the Great Outdoors

The best part of having a great-looking landscape is spending time enjoying it. If you make your outdoor space comfortable for the activities you wish to pursue there, you'll find yourself wanting to spend time outdoors. Outdoor living is good for the soul, and it offers endless opportunities for bonding with family and sharing good times with friends. But first, you have to decorate your outdoor space.

Decorating outdoors follows the same basic principles as decorating indoors. The first step is to decide how you want to use the various spaces in your yard. You did that up to a point when you designed your landscape, setting aside places for beds and borders, paths, outdoor seating areas, and lawns. You planned for a

◄ Well-chosen ornaments add the finishing touch to the garden.

patio or deck, and perhaps a gazebo, but you may not have fully decided how to use the amenities. Now is the time to finalize plans, and to add the furnishings that will allow you to use the space and the finishing touches that will make it complete. To turn outdoor space into living space, you will need to add furniture, perhaps some appliances, and various accessories.

For decks and patios, you will probably want a dining table and chairs, perhaps some lounge chairs and rockers, cooking equipment, and various other furnishings: a hammock, a swing, and perhaps a spa or hot tub.

In the garden, you will need benches or other kinds of seating, perhaps some sculpture or other art pieces, birdbaths, sundials, and vertical accent pieces such as obelisks and tuteurs.

For both kinds of environments, you will need lighting if you want to use the space after dark. Water features can be delightful additions to the landscape and to a patio. Decorative pots, urns, olive jars, and other planters can fill dozens of roles on decks, patios, and porches—and out in the landscape, too, whether you leave them empty or fill them with color and greenery.

This chapter offers a range of options to consider when you set out to decorate your outdoor space. It's only a beginning, and you will find a vast array of items available as you follow the direction in which your desires lead you.

As a starting point, when you have settled on the purpose of your various outdoor spaces, you will want to furnish them in a style that is compatible with your house and landscape. Coordinate the colors. Choose materials, too, that fit your style, and that will be practical and functional for the way you will use the space. For example, for a British Colonial look reminiscent of India and other hot places, you could furnish a deck or patio with carved teak garden benches with colorful fabric pillows, a sisal or kilim rug, and some ottomans covered in Indian-print fabric. Add some tropical plants in containers. For a more formal look, consider wrought-iron furniture with decorative scrollwork details, a marble-topped table, and some evergreen topiaries in elegant urns, with hibiscus standards for color.

And don't forget to have a little fun, too. Include some things just for pure enjoyment: Hang wind chimes if you like their gentle musical sounds, set out lanterns to make faces glow, indulge in a piece of sculpture or a fountain.

Furnishing Decks and Patios

Furnishing a deck or patio can be as simple as setting up a barbecue grill and a picnic table, or as involved as installing a complete outdoor kitchen and bar with running water, burners, a rotisserie, a wood-fired pizza oven, and tables and seating for 10 or more. Before you rush out to go shopping, think carefully about how you will most often use the space. Think of the deck or patio as if it were an indoor room with a floor, walls, and a ceiling. Although the outdoor space is not enclosed, it is still a volume of space, and your decorating may be easier to approach if you can think about it that way.

Measure the floor space that's available, and sketch out a seating plan to figure out what kinds of pieces you will need and where they should go. Start with the biggest areas first—a cooking/dining space, if that will be the main feature, or a spa or hot tub. Appliances and devices that need electricity should be located where that is most readily supplied.

In a dining area, you will need to allow enough space for a table and chairs that will accommodate your family or the number of people you most often entertain. Table size can be a determining factor in how much space is left over for other activities.

For example, to accommodate a table and chairs that will seat six people comfortably and allow enough room for them all to pull out their chairs to sit down, you need a space 10 by 10 feet. For a table and chairs to seat four people, you need 8 by 8 feet.

Many patio dining sets are designed for four people, but there is a dizzying array of sizes, shapes, styles, and choices. Extension tables with one or more leaves can stretch to accommodate more people for special events, and stay more compact the rest of the time.

Use tracing paper overlays or a series of diagrams to move the dining table and other large pieces around until you find the best arrangement. Then, see how much space is left and work on the pieces you want to fill it. Will you want to add lounge chairs? Occasional tables? An outdoor hearth or heater to extend the season for outdoor living?

When you have an idea of the kinds and numbers of pieces you want, it's time to think about the materials you want. Outdoor furnishings have to stand up to the weather, of course, but different materials are

Coordinating colors outdoors ties the landscape and living areas together. Here, 'Stella de Oro' daylilies echo the yellow umbrella, and they bloom all summer, too.

more comfortable for different sorts of uses, and materials help contribute to style as well. These days, a lot of outdoor furniture is designed and manufactured to look like indoor furniture. New materials and fabrics are continually expanding the range of looks that are possible in weather-resistant furniture. Here is a quick guide to the materials from which you can choose in selecting furnishings for decks, patios, porches, and other outdoor living spaces.

Outdoor Furniture Materials

If you aren't sure how to judge the quality of furniture as you shop, one useful tactic is to find out what kind of warranty the manufacturer provides on it. The best-quality items will come with a 15-year or longer warranty, while low-end pieces are guaranteed for only a year or two. Buy the best pieces that you can afford.

Vinyl

There's plenty of cheap plastic furniture around, and if you're on a tight budget, you may need to make do with low-end chairs and tables for a couple of years. Do the best you can, and do it with attitude, but understand that inexpensive furniture seldom holds up anywhere near as long as better-quality pieces. If you're going to end up replacing your patio set every few years, it will be more cost-effective in the long run to buy better-quality furniture from the start. Or start with just a couple of good pieces and add a few more each year until you have what you need.

Aluminum

Aluminum is by far the most popular material for outdoor furniture, much of it used as the frame for wood, wicker, fabric, or other materials. Most frames are made of hollow aluminum tubing, but cast aluminum is also widely used. Aluminum is rust resistant, which is a big plus, but tubular aluminum can get dinged up and dented with a lot of use. Cast aluminum is more durable, but it's also more expensive. Aluminum can take on a range of different styles, from casual to elegantly formal to coolly modern.

Wood

Wood is also used in a lot of outdoor furniture. Weather-resistant teak and cedar are most common, but you can also find furniture made of oak and other hardwoods, as well as redwood. Teak furniture is the top of the line. It's the most durable and long-lasting,

Teak is the most durable, longest-wearing wood for outdoor furniture, although it is expensive. It wears to a silvery gray over time and holds up well for many years.

seats, rockers, coffee tables, end tables, dining tables, ottomans, lounge chairs, and armchairs is available. Open-weave patterns are especially decorative; they're light and airy looking.

There are many wonderful antique wicker pieces to be had, but for outdoor use other than a porch, choose a synthetic lookalike called all-weather wicker. The synthetics have the look of traditional wicker and hold up far better outdoors—they stand up to rain and sun and resist mildew. (See "Cushions and Fabrics" on page 175 for more information on all-weather wicker.) If you do want to use old wicker pieces on a porch or other protected area, restore the original finish, rather than stripping and repainting, to preserve the value of the furniture. To save money, you can purchase used unrestored pieces and cover tables with tablecloths to hide their imperfections.

but it is also the most expensive. When left unfinished, teak weathers to a pleasing silvery gray. Oiled teak is a bit darker in color than natural teak, and it retains its original warm brown color. Teak furniture can last 20 years or more—even a lifetime—with little maintenance. You can find many styles and sizes of tables and chairs, lounge chairs, benches, occasional tables, and service pieces made of teak.

Cedar doesn't last as long as teak, but it, too, is rot-resistant, and it is less costly than teak. Treating cedar furniture with a good-quality sealant or wood preservative will extend its life.

In addition to traditional styles of wood furniture,

you can also find flights of fancy such as the chairs, benches, and other pieces by artist Laura Spector, with frames of twined and twisted bittersweet vines.

Wicker

Wicker is a process of weaving rather than a particular material, and the look of wicker is a great favorite for porch furniture. Wicker is also beautiful on a patio, and its old-fashioned charm is synonymous with summer for people who love the look. Wicker can be made of jute, sea grass, or even water hyacinth fibers. A vast assortment of wicker sofas, love

Wrought Iron

Wrought iron was very popular in the 19th century, and it is still used for a significant amount of outdoor furniture. It is sometimes less expensive than aluminum furniture, but it can be heavier to move around. One downside of wrought iron is that it will rust if the paint on its surface chips. For the best durability, seek out pieces with a textured finish that comes from two or more coats of rustproof paint.

Plastics

When you think of plastic deck furniture, you probably think inexpensive, and often tacky, certainly not cutting-edge chic. But plastic is gaining new respect as more innovative, stylish pieces are hitting the market. Even top-drawer designers like Philippe Starck are using plastic, so don't automatically write it off without checking to see what's out there. Today's synthetic polymers are weather resistant and able to tolerate ultraviolet rays without damage.

Another recent innovation in outdoor furniture is the use of a material called Polywood, which is made from recycled plastic bottles, milk jugs, and other containers. You can find tables and chairs, some folding, in white or a brown meant to resemble teak, in a variety of styles. Polywood furniture needs only minimal maintenance and lasts for years.

Choosing Furniture

The universe of outdoor furniture is large, indeed, and it seems to be expanding infinitely. It's impossible to survey the field to any depth in this kind of book, but here are some examples of what's currently out there.

Wicker furniture has an airy, summery look. This set has comfortable chairs, and the round table is space-efficient.

Dining Tables

Dining tables can be made of teak, cedar, cherry, or other woods; cast or wrought aluminum; wrought iron; wicker; or various kinds of plastic. You can find round or oval tables, or square, rectangular, or octagonal tables, in various sizes. Versatile extension tables come with one or two leaves that you can add when you need to accommodate more people. Table tops may be made of solid wood or wood slats; glass; sandstone or limestone; mosaics of ceramic tiles, stained glass, or tumbled stone tiles; slate; faux stone; or patterned cast aluminum. Of course, you can also get a simple, old-fashioned wooden picnic table with attached or freestanding benches.

If space is at a premium for you, it helps to know that a round table takes up less space than a square or rectangular table that seats the same number of people. In really small spaces, a bistro table can provide a place to eat in close quarters. You can find bistro tables in most of the same materials used for larger dining tables.

Some tables come with holes for umbrellas, or plugged holes that you can open up if you decide to use an umbrella. If you plan to have an umbrella in the table to provide some shade for dining on a sunny deck, it's generally best to avoid a glass top. If strong winds should topple the umbrella, the table is likely to flip over, too, and the top could shatter.

Whatever sort of table you choose, if you set it on a carpet, the space will instantly appear more defined. Your outdoor dining area will take on more of the look of a room. Use sisal or another type of carpet suitable for outdoor use.

This elegant cast-aluminum table and chairs set looks just right on the well-built brick patio.

Occasional Tables

On a large deck with several seating areas, or even on a small deck with a few lounge chairs, some small occasional tables will come in handy for holding drinks, books, snacks, or other items. A low coffee table can work well in front of a love seat or settee. If you have a dining set, use occasional tables that match it.

Like dining tables, occasional tables can be square or rectangular, round or oval. You can find tables of teak, mahogany, cedar, or cherry, with frames of tubular or cast aluminum or wrought iron. Tops can be solid, slatted, or latticed wood with a natural finish or in colors including white, black, and forest green. Other choices for occasional table tops include cast aluminum (smooth or patterned), stone (even onyx), faux stone, tile or mosaic, or glass.

Chairs

There are multitudes of chairs for outdoor use, in every imaginable design. Dining chairs, armchairs, lounges, rockers, love seats, sofas, captains' chairs, bistro chairs, and bar stools are all available in many styles and price ranges. For the most pulled-together look, match chairs to the tables you will be using. If a more freewheeling, casual look suits your style, you can mix and match chairs for optimum functionality or just for fun.

Many chairs come with pillows sized to fit. Cushions may be one piece that covers both back and seat, two pieces hinged where they meet, or two separate pieces. Most companies offer pillows covered with a choice of colors and, in many cases, a variety of patterns, too. Or you can have pillows custom-made for your furniture and covered in a fabric of your choice. Unless you want to bring all your pillows indoors every time it rains, choose a weather-resistant fabric. (See "Cushions and Fabrics" on page 175 for information on all-weather fabrics.)

Dining Chairs

Chairs for dining come in all shapes, styles, and price ranges. You can spend $10 for a plastic model from the local discount store, or spring for elegant designer teak chairs or colorful enameled hardwood numbers. Or perhaps you like the idea of sleek cast aluminum pieces, stylish little bistro chairs, or environmentally conscious Polywood designs.

One of the earliest French bistro chairs—and still a classic indoor style—is the graceful bentwood style designed by M. Thonet. Thonet would probably be amazed at the diversity of bistro chairs that have descended from his beloved design. Bistro chairs may be fashioned of teak, cast or wrought iron, tubular or cast aluminum, wicker, polypropylene, cherry wood, enameled hardwood, galvanized steel, or stainless steel. Steel with a weather-resistant polyester coating is available in a variety of colors. There are chairs that fold and chairs that stack for easier off-season storage. Bistro chairs can have seats of metal or wood, with or without cushions. One classic type is a spring steel seat rather reminiscent of a pinwheel or umbrella.

Armchairs and Side Chairs

One of the best-known outdoor chair designs is the Adirondack chair, with its wood slat construction, sloping seat, and arched back. Adirondack furniture was created for the upstate New York fishing camps frequented by the titans of industry in the late 1800s. After the turn of the 20th century, big resort hotels put Adirondack chairs on their broad porches. The Adirondack chair has withstood the fickleness of fashion and become a classic. Today, it's manufactured from a variety of woods, including teak, cedar, and mahogany, and it comes

Adirondack chairs are outdoor classics. You can find them in a range of colors in addition to white. Children's sizes are also available.

not only in natural wood or white but also in such *au courant* colors as lime and turquoise, as well as hunter green, yellow, red, and blue. In addition to chairs, you can get lounges, love seats, gliders, rockers, tables, and foot rests in the Adirondack style. There is also an Adirondack chair made of recycled plastic infused with white coloring and ultraviolet stabilizers.

Teak armchairs are beautiful and long-lasting, and they're available in many styles. Teak also partners well with tubular aluminum. Aside from teak, there are cedar, oak, and even pine chairs for outdoors. There's a faux teak, Chippendale-style chair made of brown-colored recycled plastic. You'll also find aluminum chairs and woven resin chairs, chairs with upholstered cushions, and chairs with sling seats. Sling chairs often have aluminum frames, and they may have a weather-resistant fabric sling of vinyl-coated polyester, which comes in several colors. Matching ottomans are available, too. Some chairs recline; others fold or stack for storage.

When you go shopping for chairs, think about comfort as well as style. Heavy-framed chairs with deep seats and big pillows can look enticing and feel great when you're in them but can be difficult to get into and out of. Details like these bear consideration.

Lounge Chairs

Nothing beats a lounge chair for outdoor relaxation except, perhaps, a hammock. The simplest, most portable kind of lounge chair is the folding kind you take to the beach. A beach chair can be a perfectly comfortable place to spend an hour on a day off. Folding beach chairs generally have tubular aluminum frames, although wooden ones are available, too. Coverings range from narrow vinyl straps (which you'll stick to on a hot day) to 1960s-style woven straps (which can get mildewed in damp conditions) to hard-wearing cottons and canvas or pricey designer fabrics. (See "Cushions and Fabrics" on the opposite page for some tips on good outdoor fabrics.)

These comfortable chairs are solid and sturdy, but readily move around on their wheels. The lounge adjusts to several positions. Weather-resistant fabric covers the cushions.

As is the case with other kinds of outdoor furniture, there's a lounge chair for every style and budget. There are multi-position and fixed-back styles, some with rear wheels and some without. They are made of various woods, metal, plastic, and wicker. Most lounges have one- or two-piece cushions. Some come with extras such as cup holders and collapsible canopies and sun shades. Styles range from old-fashioned to retro to ultra-modern, chunky to sleek, funky to elegant. A huge choice of fabric colors and patterns is available for cushions, including custom-covered pillows in whatever fabric you choose. You can have an elegantly scrolled wrought-iron chaise that looks like a classical recamier and perfectly suits a formal patio. Or you might opt for a modern formal look from a wrought-iron frame with slender, simple lines. Other chaise designs have an oriental or Indonesian feel. Still others have the look of Victorian wicker.

Some designers are translating woodworking techniques to the creation of aluminum-framed furniture. A lounge chair made with these sophisticated techniques, outfitted with upholstery of a durable outdoor fabric, is elegant indeed, and perfect for a formal setting. Powder-coated finishes allow you to choose aluminum frames in a spectrum of colors.

Modular and Convertible Pieces

Convertible furniture pieces can be terrific space savers. For example, one handy system involves two benches that convert to a picnic table when you push them together. They're available in cedar or resin. And just as there are modular living room systems for indoors, you can also purchase modular outdoor pieces to combine in all sorts of ways. One collection has a wrought-aluminum frame and all-weather upholstery. You can mix and match pieces for a chair and ottoman, a sofa, a daybed, a chaise that can double as a bench, and a U-shaped seating unit.

Cushions and Fabrics

Along with outdoor chairs come pillows, and if you cover them with all-weather fabrics, you won't have to rush around and gather them up to carry indoors every time it rains. In fact, the right fabrics can be great problem solvers outdoors. Besides upholstering furniture, they cover umbrellas, create tents and sunshades, clothe dining tables, and serve as decorative drapes and hangings, among other things. You may want to look into outdoor carpeting, too, as you have options besides AstroTurf and rubber mats.

One of the best, and best-known, fabrics for outdoor use is Sunbrella, an acrylic fabric with a soil- and stain-resistant finish; it is similar to the material used for boat covers. This fabric will not fade in the sun, it resists mildew, and it provides 98 percent ultraviolet protection (important for an umbrella or sun shade). It's also machine washable. There are a few different kinds of Sunbrella: one woven of finer-gauge yarn, which is softer, and one that is more water repellent. There is also a fire-resistant version. These fabrics come in many colors and patterns, and they're used by many manufacturers for umbrellas, outdoor upholstery, cushion covers, awnings, and more.

Another textile company, Waverly, makes a line

Coordinate fabrics and colors on decks and patios just as you do indoors. Key accent colors of furnishings to the colors of nearby plants.

of polyester fabrics treated with Teflon that are great for covering outdoor cushions. Vinyl-coated polyester fabrics dry quickly after rain, and they stay cool to the touch in hot weather. All of these fabrics repel water and resist fading. They come in a variety of colors and patterns.

Another popular all-weather material, Hularo, is woven of polyethylene fibers and used to cover all-weather wicker furniture. Other kinds of all-weather wicker are made of woven resins. All-weather wicker resists ultraviolet rays and dampness, and it resists pollution, too. It is colorfast, frostproof, and pretty much maintenance free. If you move the furniture indoors over winter in cold-winter climates, all-weather wicker will last a lifetime.

There are other ways to use fabrics outdoors, of course. You can inject a touch of romance by using sheer curtains or silk saris to enclose a dining area or a pavilion, closing them for intimacy and tying them back when you want to savor the view. Light fabrics like these will drift and billow gently with every passing breeze. Be prepared, however, to bring them indoors or tie them down securely in windy weather.

You can also use hanging fabrics to screen off areas, add accents to tables or sofas, or even to enclose different areas in the landscape to turn them into garden rooms. For temporary effects, let your imagination take flight. Indian bedspreads, tie-dyed shawls, lace curtains, fishnets, and even beaded curtains can all be pressed into service as fanciful and beautiful accents for a special event or to suit a mood outdoors. Bamboo blinds can serve as temporary walls around a deck, porch, or patio that can be raised or lowered as needed.

Most decks and patios need at least one umbrella—and frequently more than one—that can provide an island of shade over a dining or seating area on a bright, sunny day. Market umbrellas are very popular these days; they are octagonal in shape and generally shallower than traditional patio umbrellas, but both styles are available in many colors and patterns. When you shop for an umbrella, choose one that has vents or wind flaps around the top that will allow air to pass through, so that the umbrella is less likely to topple over in breezy weather.

Bases for umbrellas are usually made of metal, either in a flat plate or a domed shape. You can find plain and patterned bases in a variety of colors and patterns. Some bases tilt so that you can easily position the umbrella at the best angle to block the sun. Umbrella poles may be made of wood or metal, and many models tilt to adjust the umbrella's angle. A heavy base is the most stable, but it requires more effort to move into place.

Kitchen and Service Pieces

If you plan to cook on your deck or patio, you will want (at minimum) a decent gas or charcoal grill. Or you might want a high-tech infrared grill. If you will be grilling on a wooden deck, it would be prudent to place a fireproof mat under the grill. And of course, never leave a lit grill unattended.

Outdoor appliances can be as simple or as involved as you want them to be. For example, Kitchen Aid makes a complete outdoor cooking system that combines three burners, a rotisserie and grill, a refrigerator, and a sink in one unit. You may not need such a complete setup, but there are many kinds of stoves, grills, ovens, refrigerators, and other appliances designed for outdoor use.

If you cook outdoors a lot, you will probably want

HOW TO DO IT

KEEPING CLEAN

Here are some tips on keeping your outdoor furniture clean.

Teak and other hardwoods: Wipe down with a damp cloth.

All-weather wicker: Wash with mild, soapy water and a clean cloth or soft brush. Rinse well. Use the same technique for natural wicker and rattan, but let the furniture thoroughly dry in the sun before bringing it back onto the porch.

Umbrellas and other furnishings of weather-resistant acrylic fabrics: Brush off loose dirt periodically. Hose off once a month with clear water. When necessary, wash in lukewarm water with a mild soap solution—the manufacturer of Sunbrella recommends $\frac{1}{2}$ ounce of antibacterial dishwashing liquid to $22\frac{1}{2}$ ounces of water. Removable covers can be washed in a washing machine using this solution. Air-dry; the fabric will shrink in a clothes dryer.

Foam pillows: Hand-wash in soapy water in one piece, without removing the covers. Rinse well and let cushions dry upright, out of direct sun.

If you want to have an outdoor kitchen to use for more than just casual grilling, here are some ideas to consider.

■ Have a stove with some burners, as well as a grill, so you can cook vegetables and other nongrilled foods without having to run in and out of the kitchen trying to cook in two places at once.

■ Put in a source of water (probably, cold water will suffice).

■ Include a small refrigerator, such as an under-the-counter model. Allow for ice, either with a small freezer or an ice chest (there are some really nice-looking ones, including high-end teak models and less costly styles, too).

■ Put in lighting that is bright enough to cook by in the kitchen area; in dining and seating areas, softer lighting is more comfortable and flattering.

■ Place candles in hurricane lamps so that they'll stay lit in breezy weather and create less of a fire hazard.

■ Big potted plants, trellised vines, and small trees in tubs, judiciously placed, can make the kitchen area less obvious and help the outdoor space feel more a part of the garden. Include some night-blooming flowers for a romantic touch.

---

to be able to store dishes, glassware, and utensils nearby. Outdoor bars usually include shelving. Bar units come in a variety of materials, including high-end teak and cast aluminum, and some of them fold for out-of-season storage. A bar also provides an additional countertop on which to set glasses and dishes during a party. If you don't need a bar, there are also various shelving units and storage boxes—many of them quite nice-looking—that are meant for outdoor use. If you opt for shelving, bear in mind that shelves made of slats will allow rainwater to drain through freely rather than collect. If you opt for a storage box, get one with a waterproof liner if you plan to leave things in it all season.

In addition to cooking and storage units, portable service pieces come in handy when you're entertaining. There are various sorts of trolleys and serving carts available, in everything from plastic to teak and aluminum. Some have built-in coolers and cutting boards. There are also elegant beverage stands and tubs to hold wine and other beverages.

See "Tips for Outdoor Kitchens" above for some practical ideas to consider when planning your outdoor kitchen.

Heaters

Having a source of heat on your patio or deck will enable you to use it earlier in spring and later in fall, and on cool evenings during the summer. With many outdoor heaters, you also get to enjoy watching the flames against the night sky.

The simplest type of outdoor heater is a firepit, which is not, as it might sound, a hole in the ground, but a shallow, dishlike vessel on a low metal stand. The dish holds a fire made of real logs, or a gas jet fueled by natural gas or propane that emerges from faux logs. Many firepits are made of metal—particu-

larly, copper or steel—set on a wrought-iron stand. Some firepits are made of cast stone that can be stained different colors, like cultured stone paving blocks. You can purchase screens to prevent embers from blowing around, and caps to cover the firepit when it's not in use. Firepits suit a variety of design styles from informal to formal to contemporary.

Another kind of outdoor heat is the chiminea. With a chiminea, you and your family can sit around a campfire that is contained in a small outdoor stove. You can toast marshmallows or gaze at the flames without worrying about setting nearby shrubs on fire. The most popular kind of chiminea looks like a small, potbellied clay oven with a tall neck. Some are modern-looking and made of steel. Some can convert to grills. The potbellied models, with their old-fashioned look, fit comfortably into informal and rustic, naturalistic settings. The more sophisticated, contemporary-looking chimineas are better suited to more formal or modern settings. What all chimineas have in common is the tall neck—the chimney.

If building a wood fire isn't your idea of fun, you might prefer a more sophisticated outdoor hearth. Patio hearths are self-contained units powered by propane, ethyl alcohol, or alcohol-based gels. Many of them look quite elegant—rather like overgrown, Craftsman-style lanterns, with metal frames and glass sides. Safety features on different models include heat shields that allow the heaters to be used

An outdoor fireplace extends the season of use for a deck or patio, enabling you to enjoy *al fresco* dining or conversation on cool days and evenings in spring and fall.

on decks; electronic ignition; and locks to prevent children from getting at the gas chamber when the hearth is turned off. There's no blowing smoke or sparks, as there can be with open fires. Various finishes are available, including copper, stainless, black, beige, and hunter green. Outdoor hearths raise the temperature 10° to 30°F in the area around them.

Other outdoor heating devices include gas fireplaces and gas log sets that use ceramic logs arranged to look like a campfire. Gas logs usually have a metal base that you can camouflage by surrounding it with bricks or cultured stone paving blocks.

There are also hybrid units that can be used either for grilling or heating. One of these is a portable grate that burns charcoal, wood, or pressed wood logs and comes with a removable grill. Finally, a stainless steel grill designed for use on yachts has a dishlike firebox raised several feet off the floor, on a sturdy metal column.

Furnishing Lawn and Garden Areas

Decks, patios, and porches aren't the only outdoor spaces deserving of furnishings, of course. Furniture and decorative accents out in the garden can make your yard a more comfortable place to be, and they can put just the right finishing touch on the landscape. Garden furnishings can be used in more practical ways, too, such as to mark the start of a pathway or to call attention to a prized specimen plant.

Benches, seats, and stools are ideal places for resting in the shade of an arbor or quietly watching birds eating from a feeder. Hammocks and swings invite you to while away a Sunday afternoon. For the true hedonists among us, there are even beds and daybeds to set outdoors under the stars. For picnics on the lawn, there are tents and sunshades. Vertical obelisks, pillars, and tuteurs (pyramidal columns used to train vines) can inject a welcome counterpoint to the horizontal planes of the lawn and garden. And then there is the universe of garden ornaments to deploy as complements and accents to the plants: statuary, sundials, gazing globes, large stone pieces, water features, decorative containers, antiques, and architectural treasures.

As in interior decorating, it's best to use fewer rather than more pieces outdoors, and to use them thoughtfully. Resist the temptation to overdecorate. Garden furnishings should contribute to the overall design and enhance the plants, not overwhelm them. When in doubt, use one large piece instead of a bunch of small ones. Let each item have its own importance. That said, it's also important to decorate

Gazing globes are silvered glass balls that reflect the garden around them. They come in several colors and are usually displayed on pedestals.

A bistro table and chairs create an intimate dining spot with a close-up view of both the garden and the trompe l'oeil Italian landscape in the alcove.

Sculpture of St. Francis in a garden

in scale with the size of your property and plants. A towering obelisk in a tiny courtyard garden, however magnificent it may be, will look out of place. Choose furnishings and decorative pieces with the style and color scheme of your landscape in mind, too. A classical marble bust would look a little strange in a cottage garden, but an antique bee skep or watering can might be just right. Choose colored pots and other pieces to echo a color or colors of the garden.

Generally speaking, the more colorful the garden, the more colorful the ornaments can be. Some gardens, on the other hand, are quieter and should remain so. In a woodland garden done in a palette of greens, pastels, and white, a vermilion arbor would just scream out. If you have a painterly and very sophisticated eye, you can use color in surprising and revelatory ways. By all means, play around with different ideas. But don't make perma-

nent color changes until you are sure that you'll like them. Before you paint that arbor, try the color on a piece of plywood and prop it up alongside to gauge the effect.

Think about the natural materials in and around your garden, too, when shopping for ornaments and accents. An interesting boulder might work beautifully in that woodland garden. Rough-hewn stone columns could be just right for a desert landscape. A carved wooden sculpture may be perfect for a northwestern shade garden.

Finally, put some of yourself into the pieces you use in your garden. Including things that have personal meaning for you enriches the garden and your connection to it.

Benches and Seats

Seating is important in a garden. For one thing, it gives you a place to go; a well-placed bench can be a destination in itself. A bench invites sitting, so place a bench in a place where you'd want to sit. You might put a bench (or a lounge chair, or other seating) in a private spot enclosed by hedges or screens of plants, as a secret hideaway for times when you just want to relax and leave the world behind. Conversely, a couple of benches on the lawn can become a gathering spot to have a cup of tea and chat with visiting friends. Outdoor seats can provide a place from which to look at the garden, and really, any bench should be sited where there's a view to enjoy when you're seated there. Under an arbor or pergola, benches and chairs offer a rest in the cool shade. Back up a bench against a wall or hedge and you'll gain a feeling of enclosure and protection.

Wherever you decide to place a bench, make sure it rests on level ground. You might want to put down a base of gravel or flagstones to give the bench added stability.

In a very tiny garden, a bench might be out of scale. Instead, look for small, drumlike garden seats or stools, or small folding chairs.

Most benches stay out in the garden year-round, and to hold up for any appreciable length of time, they need to be weatherproof. Choose the style with care—the bench will become visually more important in winter, when leaves and flowers are gone from gardens in all but the warmest climates.

Like most outdoor furniture, benches come in various styles and materials. Here are some examples.

This unusual, built-in stone bench hosts a variety of small plants growing in crevices in the back and under the seats.

Wooden Benches

Teak is the classic wood for benches. A teak bench can last for 20 years or more. Unfinished teak will weather to silvery gray. If you want your bench to retain its brown color, treat it periodically with penetrating oil (the oil will darken the color a bit). You can also find benches made of cedar, mahogany, and other woods. In many gardens, especially with informal and naturalistic designs, a wood bench looks most at home when left unfinished or given a natural stain. In a more formal setting, white often works better. Dark green looks sophisticated without calling attention to itself. You can also turn a bench into a standout accent piece by painting it to match one of the trim colors on your house, or to pick up a color

A wooden bench with a gracefully shaped back offers a place in which to rest and contemplate the beauty of the garden.

A simple slab bench is just the right kind of rustic style for a woodland garden near a 'Pink Opal' azalea and ferns.

from your garden. Such color echoes also help to tie the property together.

Some wood benches have backs to them; others are simple slabs on legs. Some have wheels and are portable. You can buy them in kit form or fully assembled. Styles range from rustic settees made of peeled-pole or twig frames and seats made of natural cedar, willow, or poplar, to the elegant and classic Lutyens bench designed by the renowned turn-of-the-20th-century English architect and landscape designer, Sir Edwin Lutyens. Two other popular traditional styles are the arched-back Empire bench with a gracefully curved top, and the camelback, whose back arcs upward in the center and dips down on either side. There are formal Chinese Chippendale styles and Southeastern wood-slat benches with wrought-iron ends. Some benches have carved backs with motifs of birds, vines, leaves, or flowers. You can also find sleek ergonomic benches with coolly modern lines. Standard benches come in 4-, 5-, and 6-foot lengths, but there are other sizes, too. Some benches are designed to fit under arbors. Some have hinged seats that turn them into handy storage boxes.

Stone Benches

Stone benches convey a sense of stability and repose, and they bring a sense of solidity and age to the garden. A stone bench can make a new garden feel like it's been there a long time. When set under deciduous trees, a stone bench will feel refreshingly cool to the touch on a summer day, but warm and comforting in winter sunshine. A stone bench can be as simple as three slabs of granite, put together post-and-lintel style, that makes you feel as if you are resting on the very bones of the earth. Or it can be richly detailed and ornamented with carved flowers and leaves or scrollwork. One lovely design combines a mosaic seat of stone and stained glass with a frame of wrought iron. Cultured or cast stone benches, particularly, come in a range of elaborate styles, with motifs of vines, grapes, or scrollwork. Stone benches work well with all kinds of plants.

There are also fiberglass benches that look like stone but weigh far less.

Metal Benches

Wrought-iron benches are classic pieces, painted either black or white. They bring an elegant charm to a formal garden, and they look quite at home in city courtyards behind brick walls. Add cushions for more comfortable seating.

These days, cast- or wrought-aluminum benches have become popular—furniture designers have certainly discovered the virtues of aluminum. Aluminum benches can be simple, with clean, sleek contemporary lines, or they can be ornately scrolled, like traditional wrought iron. Cast aluminum has opened up a whole new range of design possibilities, for example, a bench that looks as if it was fashioned entirely of tree branches, detailed down to the bark. Designers working in cast aluminum can create intricately patterned pieces. Tubular and extruded aluminum, because they are hollow, are easy to bend and are used a lot in sleek, modernistic furniture designs.

Hammocks, Swings, and Hanging Chairs

It's hard to beat lying in a hammock as a way to feel that all's right with your world. Lying on your back watching the clouds through the trees, or the play of sunshine and shadow across the lawn, really makes it possible to forget your worries and feel at peace.

There are a few different ways to set up a hammock. You can suspend the hammock between two trees—just make sure the trees are sturdy enough to bear the weight. You can sink a couple of stout posts into the ground and hang the hammock from them. (Again, be sure that the posts are strong enough to hold the weight of the heaviest person who will use the hammock, and anchor the posts securely by using a post hole digger for excavating the holes, and perhaps by pouring concrete footings.) Finally, you can get a hammock with a freestanding frame. Most hammock stands are made of tubular aluminum or steel, but there are wooden stands as well. A hammock frame takes up more space than posts, but it's a less permanent fixture. It also allows you to move the hammock to a different spot if you wish to.

The most popular kind of hammock is made of woven cotton rope. Rope hammocks are comfortable, reasonably long wearing, and easily rolled up for winter storage. They may, however, become mildewed or discolored over time. The easiest ones to get into and out of have a wooden bar across each end to hold the hammock open. In addition to rope hammocks, you can find woven hammocks of nylon and other fibers, and slinglike models made of smooth or quilted cotton or canvas. Lots of colors and patterns are available. For added comfort, you can get pillows that tie onto the end of the hammock and stay put while you're using them.

Sometimes, hammocks are turned into chairs, as in the case of a collapsible double rocker with a frame of oak and a seat and back of mildew-resistant woven rope.

If you don't want to hang a hammock, maybe you'd like to hang a chair. There are hanging chairs that are woven of cotton rope or nylon string like hammocks. Others are made of rattan or wicker and are more like baskets. Still others are fabric slings—vinyl-coated polyester fabric is weather resistant and a good choice for a chair.

Adding pillows makes a basket chair more comfortable, and you also can get quilted pads to fit in some chairs.

Swings are fun to have on a porch, deck, or patio, and in the lawn. Some hang from the ceiling, others from a stand. There are also gliders and double rockers to enjoy. All these pieces have a slow, gentle motion that's pleasant for kids and grownups alike.

And Beds, Too!

For true sensualists, there are even beds meant for outdoor use. Talk about relaxing in the garden! One model of outdoor daybed has a powder-coated steel frame; another has a headboard and footboard of twined bittersweet branches. Outdoor beds are not practical in rainy climates, and they are really probably best kept under a roof or awning. But the idea of sleeping outdoors under the trees in a comfort-

An abstractly styled obelisk adds a vertical accent to a contemporary garden and serves as a foil for the fountainy *Xanthorroea* behind it.

able bed surrounded with gauzy curtains takes camping to a whole new level. And for impromptu campouts, you can always simply set up a couple of folding camp beds equipped with air mattresses and sleeping bags.

Statuary and Ornaments

Including works of art, craft, or just plain whimsy in a garden gives it a special finishing touch that bears the unmistakable imprint of your personality, (or at least it should). The juxtaposition of art and plants can lead to discoveries about both—you may find that you see the plants in a new way when you introduce an ornament into their midst. All sorts of things can serve as garden ornaments. There are works of art both figurative and abstract; architectural pieces such as columns and obelisks; reflective gazing globes, bee skeps, birdhouses, sundials, and armillary spheres; repurposed antique millstones, wagon wheels, chimney flue liners, and wheelbarrows; moving mobiles and stabiles; musical bells and wind chimes; natural objects such as boulders and logs; even large, interesting pots, urns, and cauldrons. Let your imagination be your guide.

Art and ornaments add visual interest and impact to the garden, but they can serve more practical purposes, too. Like structural elements, ornaments capture attention. They can thus be deployed to signal special points of interest in the landscape and pathways to take you there.

You can place art or ornaments at the entrance to a porch, deck, patio, or other outdoor living area. Use them to mark the start or end of a walkway, or a break in a hedge that allows passage through it. At the end of a path, the ornament becomes a destination. Or, place an ornament at the junction where two paths meet, such as in the center of a formal garden laid out in symmetrical geometric beds. Sometimes, an ornament set alongside a path next to a large shrub or small tree gives the plant more weight and visual importance. Figurative sculptures, since they have an obvious front and back, are ideal directional signals. You can position them to face toward a fountain or look toward the end of a path.

Here's a trick to use along a straight path, especially in a small garden. To make the path seem longer and the space bigger, set two ornaments that match but are different sizes—say, two distinctive pots—at either end of the path, placing the smaller of the two objects at the far end of the path. You will create a trick of perspective that makes the path seem longer, because your eye will read the far object as being the same size as the nearer object.

Direct the attention of visitors to a gate or door you want them to use by placing a sculpture, a column, a big rock, or a pair of large pots next to it. This is an especially useful trick if you like to use a side door instead of the front door as the primary entrance to the house.

Placing an ornament in front of a hedge or wall gives the ornament an instant backdrop and makes for a more dramatic presentation.

A statue or ornament set in the middle of a bed or border can visually anchor the garden. If the border is long, add two more of the same or a very similar ornament on either side of the central one, to equally divide the space on each side. Repeating objects at equal distances sets up a visual rhythm. In a border of groundcovers or other low, sprawling plants, the more vertical lines of the ornamental pieces bring welcome visual relief to the horizontal plane of the border.

Garden pools and ponds are other fine places for statuary or ornaments. You might stand a bronze heron in the water on a submerged base, or set a couple of bronze or concrete frogs alongside the pool. A pool is also a terrific place for a fountain or bubbler.

A sundial atop a decorative pedestal marks the intersection of two perpendicular paths in this formal garden.

A birdbath or other ornament correctly placed in a bed or border can serve as a visual anchor for the garden.

Flat surfaces also can accommodate decorative enhancements. Hang a mirror on a wall to surprise visitors (who expects to see a mirror outdoors?) and make the garden seem bigger. Mount an antique sign on the wall of a shed. Put a bas relief or plaque on a brick or stucco wall.

In a clever bit of design, narrow mirror panels read, at first glance, as windows but make the garden feel bigger.

Using Ornaments Well

It's a good idea when you buy an ornament or work of art for the garden to have a place in mind for it *before* you make the purchase. In fact, you can scout potential locations before you go shopping, and try to imagine the sort of thing you'd like to see in a particular spot. (This may disappoint those of us who love the serendipitous experience of happening upon just the perfect ornament, but focused shopping saves time and often yields better results.) Of course, you will want to match ornaments to the style of the landscape. In a formal setting, classically themed sculptures—mythological figures, emperors and queens, warriors, goddesses—or columns with Doric, Ionic, or Corinthian capitals, and large urns can all work beautifully. If the house is contemporary, more abstract pieces, such as nonrepresentational sculpture or polished stone spheres, would be more fitting.

Finding the right accessory for your garden is only half the battle. Just as important as acquiring the perfect piece is putting it in the perfect spot. When you arrive home with a newly purchased piece, place it with care. Think about the vantage points from which the piece will be viewed, and orient it to the best viewing angle. Put yourself in each vantage point to try it out. Sit on the bench from which the statue will be visible. Walk the path and turn the corner that will reveal the piece. Go inside the house and look out of the window at the border in which the ornament will rest. When the piece is in position, check it out from every angle, and move or adjust it until it looks just right.

A row of concrete columns makes a formal statement in this garden of hostas, boxwood, and white-flowered oakleaf hydrangea (*Hydrangea quercifolia*).

Large boulders are essential parts of many Japanese-style gardens. It takes a discerning eye to place each rock in the ideal position.

Water Features

Water animates a garden and brings it to life. Moving water brings its quiet music as it gurgles and splashes or shoots into the air and falls back into a pool below. Still water is hypnotic—a mirror that reflects the sky and trees overhead, then ripples and dances to scatter the image when touched by a breeze, only to re-form it once more. Either way, water in the garden draws and holds your attention. Water is an entirely delightful addition to the garden, especially when used with its inherent natural characteristics in mind.

In nature, water is drawn by gravity to run downhill and pool in low spots. For the most successful design, use these inherent qualities when incorporating water features into the garden. An old gardening axiom directs us to "plant the hills and flood the hollows," and that is still good advice to follow. Locate a pool or pond in a low spot where water would naturally collect. A pool on top of a slope will look somehow strange and out of place, no matter how carefully you shape it or how beautifully you plant around it. But placed at the foot of the hill, the pool will make a lot more sense. Similarly, a cascade needs to run from high ground to low; it would seem odd running across ground level.

Water, both moving and still, is an essential element in Japanese gardens. The garden is not complete without some sort of water feature. In fact, where there is no natural water, the Japanese create the look of it with "rivers" and "pools" of raked stones. Water can bring magic to your garden, too.

Here are some guidelines for incorporating water features into your garden.

Still Water

If you want to have a reflecting pool, be sure to locate it where it will have something to reflect. Still water mirrors the clouds above and nearby plants, too. The glistening surface draws and holds your attention. We can all take a lesson in water garden design from Italy, which has a long history of glorious water gardens. In the grand Italian water gardens, pools are surrounded with balustrades and ornamented with statuary. Their reflections in the water surface draw the eye like a magnet. You gaze at the reflections, and suddenly you can see through the water to the fish and plants below the surface.

Pools can be formal or informal, as the style of your landscape dictates. You might not think about it, but a pool, especially a formal one, is going to be the center of attention—the focal point—for the part of the garden in which it is located. In cold-winter climates, the pool will be especially dominant in winter, when all but evergreen plants are dormant. The pool may be dry then—in climates where a thick layer of ice is likely to form, the pool may need to be drained in winter—so its shape and the materials from which it is made need to be chosen with care. A pool in a prominent location must have crisp, well-defined lines and good proportions.

A water feature can be as simple as this lotus (*Nelumbo nucifera*) or a waterlily in a crock of water.

A formal rectangular pool suits this walled courtyard garden perfectly. Colorful pansies and other plants soften the hard edges of the pool.

A garden pool need not be deep to work its magic. If you do not plan on having fish, a garden pool can be quite shallow—2 feet is plenty, and many pools are not even that deep. If you do want fish, 2 feet is probably a minimum depth. Many aquatic plants can grow in shallow water. A shallow pool will be less work to dig and easier to maintain than a deep one. If young children are present, you definitely will want to keep the pool shallow. (And always keep an eye on little ones; toddlers can drown in just a few inches of water.)

A pool with a dark bottom (or liner) will have the most reflective surface, and the dark depths below will look mysterious. On the other hand, a light-colored undersurface lets you see right to the bottom of the pool, which can be a design feature in itself if you have a mosaic or other design on the bottom. You can add interest to a pool, if you want to, by including statuary, plants in or near it, or a fountain. Alongside a pool is an especially good place for a specimen tree or shrub (weeping ones that seem to stretch their branches toward the water are especially lovely). Waterlilies, water cannas, lotus, and other aquatics in a pool or pond can be quite striking with their bold, sculptural forms and beautiful flowers. Rocks and ferns have a special affinity for water and make natural partners; they look right at home along the edges of pools and streams. The waterside also is a congenial place for a bench on which to sit and contemplate the depths or watch the clouds reflected in the surface.

You can contain a pool with a preformed hard plastic or fiberglass liner, or with a flexible liner. The best flexible liners are made of butyl (synthetic) rubber or ethylene propylene diene monomer (EPDM). These liners are durable and long-lasting, but they are expensive. Polyvinylchloride (PVC) liners are less costly but don't last as long. Polyethylene liners are the cheapest and have the shortest life. Flexible liners are generally best used in informal pools with curved edges. (And by the way, curves are easier to keep clean than right angles.) Preformed rectangular or oval liners can work well for formal pools of geometric shape. Cover the top edge of the liner with a coping to conceal it and also to protect it from ultraviolet damage that could cause the liner to crack or otherwise deteriorate.

If your budget permits, you can have a garden pool custom-built with a Gunite or vinyl lining like those used in swimming pools. This is the most expensive way to go, but it gives you the most design flexibility.

Whether formal or informal in design, a pool in a partly shaded location will be easiest to manage. A location in full sun will encourage algae growth. A pool in a spot surrounded by lots of trees will fill up with leaves, which will have to be removed before they decay.

Informal pools: These can work beautifully in a naturalistic garden. Remember, if you live where winters are cold, your pool will be empty in winter; site it carefully. Instead of setting it in the middle of a lawn, seek out a less conspicuous spot in a corner or at the bottom of a slope, where the pool can blend more easily into its setting and not be so noticeable in winter.

Formal pools: A flat rectangle of water looks inherently formal. In a formal garden, put a pool where

A rock-edged pool in a woodland garden looks peaceful and a little mysterious. Waterlilies, lotus, and pickerelweed (*Pontederia cordata*) grow in the water, and ajuga carpets the ground alongside.

it fits into the geometry of the overall design. Use a simple geometric shape—round or oval, rectangular or square. The water itself is the whole point of a formal pool. The shape of the pool frames the water and turns it into a design element in the landscape. The pool is meant to be noticed; it's not supposed to look natural. Raising the pool above ground level makes it stand out even more. A formal pool can be situated in the middle of the space, unconnected to other immediate features or structures.

A raised pool can have sides of concrete, stone, brick, or tile. Use formal materials to edge the pool and cover the top of the liner: flagstone, brick, tile, or cast concrete pavers all can work beautifully. A raised pool works especially well when tucked into a city courtyard garden.

Round and rectangular pools are inherently formal. This one gets a touch of drama from an abstract fountain positioned off-center in the water.

This pool is strictly formal. It is round, raised above ground level, and contained within a brick wall, and it sits in the center of a formal garden. Even the fountain is classically styled.

Moving Water

Moving water animates the garden with its motion and musical sounds. Moving water can be as subtle as a slow trickle from a bamboo waterspout into a stone basin, or as dramatic as a fountain shooting a jet up toward the sky. Moving water is an important feature in the landscape that commands attention, but it does not dominate in quite the same way that a formal pool does. The sound of moving water can, to a degree, mask traffic noise and other intrusive neighborhood racket. At the very least, it can provide a welcome distraction from ambient noise. Moving water also generates negative ions in the air, which have a soothing effect and promote a sense of well-being.

You can introduce moving water into the landscape in any number of ways. The quietest form, and the one that takes up the least amount of space, is a simple waterspout that trickles into a catch basin below. There are single-unit, wall-mounted or freestanding waterspouts that emanate from the head of a lion or cherub or another source and fall into a basin below. These pieces can be had in natural stone, cast or cultured stone, or lighter-weight resin. There are also small bubblers to install in a large olive jar, urn, or other vessel. All of these devices use pumps to recirculate the water through the system. You can find a wide variety of fountains, too, in many sizes and designs. There are also delicate-looking creations that emit beads of water to trickle down nylon strings, looking for all the world like a curtain of dewdrops. And, of course, waterfalls allow streams or curtains of water to cascade over rocks.

An elegant waterspout trickles gently, the centerpiece of a magnificent espaliered jasmine (*Jasminum polyanthum*) in this sophisticated formal garden.

Streams and Channels

Water can trace a path across the landscape, too. If you are lucky enough to have a stream running through your property, make the most of it. You might even want to partially dam it and make a pool. If you don't have a natural stream but wish that you did, you can create a similar look by building a channel or a cascade and pumping water to circulate through it. For design purposes, you can treat this kind of linear water feature as an axis in the garden, and design around it. In a formal garden, the course of the water should run straight and fit into the

A water channel runs from the fountain along an axis line through this formally structured garden.

overall grid. The edges should be neat and well defined. In an informal garden, a stream or channel can run diagonally, or it can flow in sweeping curves. Do not, though, plan a stream with lots of tight bends and loops—it'll look silly and overdone. An informal stream can have rougher banks than a formal channel, perhaps overhung with rocks or plants in places.

You can have water moving in a more or less linear way by constructing a channel or a fake streambed. Or you can take a simpler and more imaginative—but more occasional—path by channeling runoff water from your rain gutters and sending it through a series of connected spouts, gutters, and half-pipes down a grade to collect at the bottom in a catch basin or just to flow into the ground. Stand outside with your umbrella (or run the water course through an awning-protected patio) when it rains, and listen to the water playfully gurgling and splashing around you.

The speed at which the water flows will influence the best type of garden to have alongside. For a slow-moving, gently flowing stream or channel, you might create a tranquil viewing spot with a bench surrounded by grasses and native flowers. Landscape a faster-moving stream more simply, perhaps with rocks and ferns, and let the water be the main attraction.

Waterfalls

A waterfall can be a simple trickle of water around stones or a dramatic cascade over a rock ledge. The water can be a thin stream or thread, or a sheet. Kits are available with all the parts you need if you're a do-it-yourselfer, or you can have the feature designed and built by a landscaping company.

A waterfall makes the most sense on sloping ground. If you want to build one on flat land, make the changes in level very gradual, not sharp, to appear more natural.

Fountains

A fountain captures the interplay of water and light. It can be small and subtle or big and dramatic, but it is not supposed to look like a natural feature. The only natural fountains are the geysers found in volcanic areas such as Yellowstone National Park and Iceland. Fountains demand your attention. Whether the water bubbles gently or leaps skyward in a concentrated jet, its sound and motion draw you to it.

Fountains can be as grand and glorious as the Italian Water Garden at Longwood Gardens in Pennsylvania or the Basin of Apollo at Versailles. Or they can be as quiet and unassuming as a bamboo spout in a Japanese garden, trickling water into a hollowed-out stone below. Between these two extremes, you'll find all sorts of fountains suited to the home landscape.

Many fountains incorporate a second point of interest (besides the water) in the form of sculptures. These may provide the source of the water, or they may have a purely ornamental value. Statuary is mounted on a submerged pedestal to look as if it is rising from the water or floating upon it.

A fountain should, of course, work with the style and character of your landscape. If the garden is simply designed, with clean lines and lots of open space, you can accommodate a more complex water display. In a more complicated and densely planted garden, or in a small space, a simpler fountain will work better.

Consider viewing angles when choosing a location for a fountain. A jet or spray is sublime when backlit by the sun. Also pay some heed to sightlines: How high, and at what angle, should the water rise into the air in order to be visible from your chosen vantage point?

Be mindful of scale and proportion, too. The basin or pool into which the water falls should be in scale with the rest of the landscape. Then, select a fountainhead that's in scale with the pool. Generally, the larger the pool, the higher the water can go. A formal fountain looks best when centered in the pool; but in an informal garden, it can go either in the middle or off to one side.

Probably the most versatile kind of fountain is one that shoots a single jet of water vertically upward from the surface. A solitary jet can look equally fine in a formal or informal setting.

The universe of fountain designs is far larger than what can be catalogued in a book of this size, but here are some examples of what's available. There are fountains that sit at ground level or in a pool, and fountains that mount on a wall or tabletop. Wall-mounted fountains take up the least space, but small floor and tabletop units can be moved around. There are fountains in formal, Romanesque, Italianate, French, Asian, Mediterranean, contemporary, old-fashioned, naturalistic, and rustic styles. They may be made of concrete, stone, cast stone, tile, cast iron, aluminum, copper, bronze, fiberglass, acrylic, or resin. There are figurative designs and abstract styles, such as polished stone or clear acrylic globes that bubble water out of the top and let it flow down over the sides.

Fountains may be powered by electricity or by the sun. One solar model floats atop a pool and needs no pumps, hoses, or wires. It even turns itself on when the sun is bright enough. But if you will want to operate the fountain at night or in a shady location, don't choose a solar-powered design.

Water spouts for fountains may be simple tubes of bamboo, plastic, or metal; or they may emerge from the mouths of sculpted lions, fish, birds, cherubs, angels, frogs, nymphs, or children. Spray patterns for jets and sprays include single and multiple jets, trumpets, fans or fishtails, bells, arcs, geysers, and whirling or multitiered forms. Each pattern looks and sounds different.

Small spraying and bubbling fountains can be made in ceramic pots, natural or artificial rock formations, real or faux millstones, stone troughs, and a host of other garden-worthy objects.

Maintaining Water Features

Like most parts of the garden, your water feature will need to be maintained in order to work properly. First and foremost, never let the water in your water feature get too low. That means checking the water level in a small feature every day in hot, dry weather. Submersible pumps are made to operate underwater, and when they get dry, they become damaged.

In a pool or pond of any appreciable size, you will need to have fish and plants to keep the system healthy and prevent algae growth. A smaller pool will need a fountain or other aeration device to keep the water oxygenated and to discourage algae.

If you notice the flow of water in a fountain decreasing over time, check the pump for mineral deposits, and clean it if necessary. In a system without plants or fish, periodically add a small amount of bleach or vinegar to the water to prevent algae from growing. The instruction manual with the unit should provide information on cleaning. If you have plants and fish, use a bubbler or head with larger holes to prevent algae.

A triple-jet fountain enlivens this formal pool with its musical bubblings and splashings.

Here are some good plants for water gardens. Some will grow in a pool or pond, others in the boggy soil around the edges of a pond.

PLANT	DESCRIPTION	LIGHT NEEDS	WATER NEEDS	GROWING RANGE
Acorus gramineus 'Variegatus', variegated Japanese rush	Tender perennial to 12 in. high, with pointed, irislike leaves striped with creamy white.	Sun to partial shade.	Bog to 6 in. of water.	Zones 10–11; elsewhere grow as annual
Canna Longwood Hybrids, Longwood water canna	Upright plants to 6 ft high, with slender leaves and spikes of flowers in warm shades of red, orange, and yellow.	Full sun.	Bog to 6 in. of water.	Zones 7–11
Carex spp., sedges	Grassy plants of varying height, with a tuft of narrow leaves.	Sun to partial shade.	Bog.	Hardiness varies with species
Colocasia esculenta 'Black Magic', elephant's ear, taro	Upright perennial to 4 ft high, with large, heart-shaped leaves that open green and mature to deep purple-black.	Sun to partial shade.	Bog to 12 in. of water.	Zones 9–11; elsewhere grow as annual
Cyperus alternifolius, umbrella palm	Whorls of narrow leaves atop clumps of slender, upright stems to 5 ft high.	Sun to partial shade.	Bog to 6 in. of water.	Zones 9–11; elsewhere grow as annual
Equisetum hyemale, horsetail	Spreading evergreen perennial with slender, jointed, canelike stems to 2 ft high (grow in containers).	Sun to partial shade.	Bog to 6 in. of water.	Zones 3–11
Hydrocleys nymphoides, water poppy	Submerged perennial with rounded, floating leaves and yellow flowers.	Sun to partial shade.	4 to 12 in. of water.	Zones 9–10; elsewhere grow as annual
Iris ensata, Japanese iris	Upright perennial to 3 ft high, with sword-shaped leaves and broad-petaled flowers in various colors.	Full sun.	Bog to 2 in. of water.	Zones 4–11
Iris pseudacorus, yellow flag	Vigorous perennial with sword-shaped leaves and yellow flowers.	Full sun.	Bog to 10 in. of water.	Zones 5–8
Iris versicolor, blue flag	Upright perennial to 2½ ft high, with sword-shaped leaves and narrow-petaled blue-violet flowers.	Full sun.	Bog to 6 in. of water.	Zones 3–9
Lobelia cardinalis, cardinal flower	Clumping perennial to 3 ft high, with oblong leaves and spikes of brilliant red flowers.	Sun to partial shade.	Bog to about 2 in. of water.	Zones 3–9

PLANT	DESCRIPTION	LIGHT NEEDS	WATER NEEDS	GROWING RANGE
Lysimachia nummularia 'Aurea', golden creeping Jenny	Mat-forming perennial to 2 in. high, with rounded, greenish yellow leaves on long stems and yellow flowers.	Full sun to partial shade.	Bog to 2 in. of water.	Zones 4–8
Myriophyllum aquaticum, parrot's feather	Trailing perennial to 6 in. high, with floating, branched stems with feathery leaves.	Full sun to partial shade.	3 to 12 in. of water.	Zones 6–11
Nelumbo lutea, American lotus	Perennial with floating, rounded leaves and yellow flowers on tall stems.	Full sun.	2 to 18 in. of water.	Zones 4–11
Nelumbo nucifera, sacred lotus	Perennials with floating, rounded leaves and large flowers in white and shades of pink on tall stems.	Full sun.	1 to 2 ft of water.	Zones 4–11
Nymphaea cvs., hardy waterlilies	Perennials with floating, heart-shaped leaves and day-blooming, pointed-petaled flowers in many warm colors.	Full sun.	6 to 18 in. of water.	Zones 3–11
Nymphaea cvs., tropical waterlilies	Perennial with heart-shaped, floating leaves and day- or night-blooming flowers in many warm colors.	Full sun.	1 to 2 ft of water.	Zones 10–11; elsewhere grow as annual or store indoors over winter
Nymphoides cristata, white snowflake	Perennial with floating, heart-shaped, brown-mottled leaves and fragrant white flowers.	Sun to partial shade.	4 to 12 in. of water.	Zones 6–11
Pontederia cordata, pickerelweed	Perennial with lance-shaped leaves and spikes of violet-blue flowers.	Sun to partial shade.	Bog to 12 in. of water.	Zones 4–11
Sagittaria latifolia, arrowhead	Upright perennial to 2 ft high, with arrow-shaped leaves and spikes of white flowers.	Sun to partial shade.	Bog to 6 in. of water.	Zones 5–11
Typha minima, dwarf cattail	Perennial to 2½ ft high, with slender, grassy leaves and fat brown spikes of minute flowers.	Full sun to partial shade.	Bog to 12 in. of water.	Zones 3–11
Zantedeschia aethiopica, calla lily	Clump-forming perennial to 3 ft high, with large, arrow-shaped leaves and white spathe flowers with yellow spadices.	Full sun.	Bog to 12 in. of water.	Zones 8–10; elsewhere in pots moved indoors over winter

Outdoor Lighting

If you're going to be outdoors at night, you're going to need lights in the landscape, on decks, and on patios. Lighting is a practical concern, of course. You need it to see where you're going and to do what you need to do. But lighting can be dramatic or fanciful, too. Lighting the landscape, deck, or patio will make it seem bigger at night. And inspired and sensitive lighting is artistry that can reveal qualities in your landscape that you never knew it possessed, and transform it into another world at night. You will need different kinds of lighting for different uses outdoors.

In nature, light is ever-changing. Natural light doesn't stay the same over the course of a day, a season, or a year. It brightens and dims, and it strikes the ground at a different angle at different times of the day and the year, casting different shadows. Your outdoor lighting will be more successful if it, too, can change and adapt to different situations. Outdoor lighting works best—and looks best—when it is not the same all over. Here are some things to think about when planning lighting for your outdoor spaces.

Reasons for Lighting

There are three main reasons you need light outdoors at night: for safety, for utilitarian purposes (to do things), and for purely aesthetic visual qualities. The techniques and locations of each kind of lighting are a bit different.

Solar lamps come in a host of attractive styles and are easy to install. They need no electrical wiring, so you can place them wherever you need them, as long as sunlight can reach and recharge them.

Lighting for Safety

Foremost among the goals of lighting is safety. Walkways, driveways, and stairs need to be lit at night so that they can be navigated without injury. This kind of lighting needs to be even and reasonably bright, but not glaring. Lights for safe walking mostly light the ground level. For a primary path, you may want the light to be brighter than other paths, to point out that this is the path to take to the door (or other important destination). In this case, you might use lampposts in a style that suits the landscape. For other paths, the ground lights will do the job.

One good solution is low lights mounted on 12- to 18-inch-high posts with caps or deflectors that direct the light down toward the ground. Another option is bollarded lights, which are embedded inside the posts and shine out the sides. Along the edge of a path, these low lights will illuminate the path surface and the plants along the edge of the garden. Low-voltage and solar-powered systems work well—they emit a soft, but not bright, light and they can be very decorative; some solar fixtures look like small lanterns. Low-voltage systems are the safest for do-it-yourselfers to install. The cables can be laid right on top of the ground if you wish.

To light stairs, you can mount lamps right on the stair risers (if there's enough room), on the undersides of railings, on a wall next to the steps, or, less desirably, in overhead fixtures.

When lighting a driveway, the natural tendency is to install a row of lights along one or both sides. This arrangement is certainly functional, but it's also pretty boring. There are more creative options avail-

A lantern illuminates stone steps in a Japanese-style garden.

Candles cast a soft, romantic glow on evening gatherings.

able, if the landscape is suited to them. One possibility is to mount down-facing spotlights in trees located conveniently near the driveway. Another option might be to put spike-mounted upward-facing lights in a bed of groundcovers alongside the drive, or at the base of a tall hedge next to the driveway (you need a tall hedge for this to make visual sense).

For a driveway, a lamppost at the beginning, near the street, is a classic. Farther from the street, you could use lanterns on poles to illuminate a major path. Japanese rice paper lanterns offer a wonderfully soft glow that can light the way to a party, but don't leave them out in the rain. You can line a drive or path with low-voltage lights that sit close to the ground. Solar lights need no wiring and work quite well, except in climates where cloudy, rainy weather is frequent. Low-level driveway and path lights take many forms—they can be shaped like mushrooms, domes, or little pagodas, among other things.

Lighting for Utility and Comfort

On decks and patios and in other outdoor living spaces, you need to arrange for light that is bright enough to cook by, if that is what you're going to do, to play games by, or perhaps even to read. You can light spaces for gathering and socializing or relaxing for mood and ambience.

In a cooking or other utility area, use even flood lighting to wash the area, or spotlighting to focus on the grill or stovetop and preparation areas. You might be able to mount lights on nearby trees, strategically placed poles or railings, and tabletops or work surfaces.

Mood or ambient lighting can be softer than the focused task lighting. The part of the deck or patio used for socializing does not need to be as bright as day. In these areas, a softer, more appealing light will be better. Sometimes, the simplest solution can be

the best. Candlelight flatters everyone; place candles inside hurricane globes and lanterns to protect the flame from passing breezes, and to enhance the decorative quality. Line them up on a low wall or set them on tabletops, or place them at the heads of stairs or along a path for soft halos of warm light. See "Outdoor Party Lights" on page 199 for ideas for festive touches from candles and other ambient lighting. Candles aren't the only kind of soft lighting;

A beautifully crafted lantern amid luxuriant bougainvillea lights the way to the front door and extends a gracious welcome.

DIGGING DEEPER

LANDSCAPE LIGHTING TECHNIQUES

Lighting designers use these techniques to turn gardens into theatrical realms at night. You can use them, too, when you think about how you want to light your outdoor world, and discuss your ideas with a designer or electrical contractor.

Uplighting: Light shines up from below to highlight trees, statuary, fountains, and other landscape features. Uplighting is dramatic; don't overuse it.

Downlighting: Light shines down from above. Downlights can come from a large single source, such as a floodlight, or from several smaller sources, such as pinpoint spots. Lampposts and hanging fixtures with hoods and shades also create downlighting.

Contour lighting: A specialized kind of downlighting that uses lights with hoods or covers to define the edges of things with light. They can illuminate the edges of a pool, a garden border, or a patio.

Moonlighting: Fixtures concealed in trees create interesting patterns of light and shadow on the ground, like moonlight shining through the canopy.

Spotlighting: Concentrated light focused to light a small area. Spotlights are dramatic and best used in a limited way for exciting accents.

Background lighting: Used along with other kinds of lighting, it washes or punctuates the background of the scene, such as a hedge behind a statue. It can be very dramatic or soft and subtle.

Silhouetting: Casts a shadow on a background surface. A bright light hidden behind a piece of sculpture or an interestingly formed tree can throw its shadow onto a wall or other flat surface.

Grazing light: This light flows softly across a surface to point out its texture and create interesting patterns of light and shadow. Grazing light might be used to illuminate a complicated pavement pattern or, perhaps, the interesting texture of a dry stone wall.

there are many kinds of fixtures to stand, hang, or sit atop tables that can supply a gentle, friendly glow.

To create gentle ambient lighting, try mounting hooded spotlights in adjacent trees (for down-lighting), under the eaves of the house, or on top of stakes in garden beds around the perimeter. Freestanding torchères and floor lamps made with weather-resistant materials bring a homey, roomlike feeling to the outdoor space. And of course there are lanterns in every style imaginable, lit with candles, lamp oil, or electric bulbs. Outdoor lights also can sit atop a table or hang from overhead. On a porch, a hanging lantern or other suspended fixture is the usual choice. Or, mount one on the wall to either side of the door.

Aesthetic Lighting

Lights can be purely decorative, too, especially out in the landscape. Lights in the landscape can add drama, spotlighting a sculptural plant with boldly shaped leaves or contorted branches, for instance. Or the lamps can create mystery and intrigue with the shadows they create, perhaps a silhouette of fo-liage patterns against a wall. Tiny white lights can make magic, peeping out from the depths of a border or the branches of a tree. You can light plants and garden ornaments to define their shapes, enhance their features, or distort them to look exotic and a little bit otherworldly, different from their usual forms.

Practically any landscape feature you want to be noticed can be enhanced by lighting. You can illumi-nate trees, statuary, fountains, structures such as arbors and gazebos, or beds of white or night-blooming flowers. Use pinpoint spotlights on statues

---

OUTDOOR PARTY LIGHTS

Festive lighting helps set the mood for outdoor par-ties. Candles, of course, are hard to beat. Even if you like to use candles outdoors on ordinary nights, set-ting them out en masse turns a deck or patio into a party place. For a soft, warm glow, line paths and steps with luminarias made with votive candles set atop a layer of sand in small paper bags. Candles set inside hurricane globes are safer—and more likely to stay lit in the night breeze—than unprotected candles.

For a theatrical touch, remove the wiring from an old chandelier and put candles in the light sockets, then hang the fixture over a table or in a corner of the deck or patio. Or have the chandelier rewired for out-door use, if possible, and use it with light bulbs.

For more drama, line the path and surround the patio with torches. Torches range in style from sleek copper cylinders to disc-shaped ceramic birds, frogs, and fish, and to the cheap but fun bamboo models found in discount stores.

Strings of special lights or Japanese lanterns add a lighthearted note to outdoor festivities. Wrap tree trunks, umbrella poles, or arbors with strings of tiny white lights. Interweave strands of ivy or other vines for a lusher look. Drape strings of your favorite lights in tree branches or overhead across a patio, let them dangle from arches, or wrap them around deck rail-ings—you can find strings of small colored globes, chili peppers, Halloween pumpkins, flowers, hearts, butterflies, or practically anything else you fancy. Small, luminous dragonflies on stakes can stand in pots of flowers, around a buffet table, out on the lawn, or in out-of-the-way corners.

Outdoors on a summer evening, let your imagina-tion guide your choice of party lights.

and ornaments. Use softer lights to make water features shimmer.

Trees can be lit from above or below. You can mount downlights up high in the branches of large old trees; or, on smaller trees, clamp uplights on lower limbs. Well lights recessed into the ground beneath trees can create mysterious and dramatic effects, especially in an orchard or grove of old trees, or amid a group of younger trees in a bed or border.

One note of caution about lighting trees: Consider the needs of the trees as well as your needs for design effects. Too many, too-bright lights can interfere with the daylength needs and growth/dormancy cycles of the trees and damage them. Many woody plants need to experience natural seasonal cycles of daylight and darkness in order to maintain healthy growth. Too much light can encourage trees to hold on to their leaves too long in autumn and continue growing later in the season than they normally would, putting them at risk for winter damage—late growth that isn't able to harden properly before cold weather sets in. Ordinary landscape lighting does not usually cause problems, but if you need brighter lights, such as high-pressure sodium lamps, for security purposes, aim them away from plants and don't turn them on unless you need to. (If you're into naturalistic gardening, also keep in mind that nighttime lighting could interfere with your ecosystem.)

A flower-shaped downlight illuminates a path alongside a bed of blue pride of Madeira (*Echium candicans*), pink *Watsonia*, and yellow daylilies.

Getting the Most from Containers

Wooden barrels and tubs full of geraniums and petunias sprout on decks and patios from Maine to California every summer. They're fun and colorful, especially in informal settings, but usually they're an afterthought. You can do a lot more with containers. There's a world of pots from which to choose, and creative ways to plant them.

Decorating with Containers

Setting a couple of pots of impatiens on a deck will give you small spots of color, but containers situated and planted for visual impact can make major contributions to the design of outdoor space. To achieve the most visual bang for your potscaping buck, use large containers (planted or empty) or group collections of smaller pots together. In a grouping of pots, using containers of varying heights or placing some of them on stands or shelves will provide color on several different levels, much as in a garden in the ground. Multiple levels allow all the plants to be immediately visible, too.

Creating visual impact with containers does not necessarily mean using fancier or brighter-colored pots. Elaborately decorated and unusually shaped pots can be striking, but they do call attention to themselves and they are harder to fit seamlessly into decorating schemes. A simple pot lets the plants be the stars of the show; a fancy pot may compete with the plants inside it. And a planting of multicolored

Containers have myriad uses in the garden. *Above:* Group containers of plants on decks or patios to make a garden of their own, or to augment a bed or border. *Right:* You can also use an attractive, interesting oil jar, urn, jug, or other vessel, planted or unplanted, as an accent or focal point in the garden.

flowers in an elaborate container can easily look too frenetic and even garish. A good rule of thumb to follow is, the fancier the pot, the simpler the planting should be. Or don't plant such a pot at all, but instead use it empty for its architectural or decorative value.

Use pots in the same ways you would use statuary and other garden ornaments. Large pots can signal the beginning or end of an important path, the main entry to the house, or the top or bottom of a staircase. Use a pair of matched pots planted with topiaries or neatly clipped shrubs flanking the entry for a formal look. Or set out a single large container, or several grouped together to one side, and fill them to overflowing with a profusion of plants.

Pots can also call attention to features in the garden or to matters of safety. You can place a pot to mark a change of level on a deck, or the locations of benches and swings. Or place them at the intersections of axial paths in a formal garden of geometric beds. A pot can function purely as an architectural accent, too. You might like the look of an antique urn in a shady corner of a garden near a Victorian house. Or perhaps a glazed ceramic oil jar color-coordinated with the flowers growing in a sunny Mediterranean-style garden would add the perfect focal point. See "Statuary and Ornaments" on page 184 for more ideas about how to use pots.

Window boxes are charmingly romantic and a lovely way to soften the look of a severe or un-adorned façade. On a house without much in the way of architectural detail, window boxes can add colorful grace notes to the structure. Window boxes can work their magic not only on house facades but also on deck and porch railings, and below the windows of garages, sheds, and outbuildings.

Hanging baskets have a multiplicity of uses, too. You can suspend them from arbors and pergolas,

Left: A tree-form musk rose (*Rosa* 'Penelope') in a large pot adds a vertical accent (and heavenly fragrance) to a container garden near a fence. *Below:* Group pots full of flowers on steps leading to the front door to dress up the entry and add a festive, welcoming note.

Window boxes are charmers, especially when they're full of summer annuals. This one dresses up a garden shed.

and from the ceiling of a porch or breezeway. Hanging a group of baskets at different heights can create a flowery screen between the porch railing and the ceiling. Hang baskets in the cutouts in gazebo walls. Hang them from lampposts or poles, or even from the branches of trees.

Kinds of Pots

Everyone is familiar with terra-cotta and plastic flowerpots, and with the half-barrels and tubs that are widely available at garden centers. But there are many other styles of pots, large and small, to consider using in your outdoor space. Here is a rundown of some traditional pot styles.

Bowls are low, wide, rounded containers. Some are shallower than others and some have rims, but all are suited only for shallow-rooted plants.

Boxes are square or rectangular and traditionally made of wood, usually with a natural or white (or sometimes hunter green) finish. A classic design is the Versailles box, which was used in that most splendid of French gardens to hold topiaries and citrus trees. Round finials on the corners give the box a formal look, and short legs or feet keep the bottom of the box off the floor. Wooden planters last longer when lined with metal or plastic. Many boxes are sold with removable liners that make end-of-season cleanup easier.

The **citrus pot** was originally designed to hold citrus trees in gardens of the Italian Renaissance. These pots are large and heavy, with a wide, rolled rim. They are often decorated with a garland pattern in relief. Look for them in unglazed terra-cotta.

A **long tom** is a tall, narrow pot that the Victorians used for plants with long root systems. These pots make interesting containers for long-stemmed plants such as topiary standards, but they are also top-heavy and at risk of toppling over in strong winds.

Containers for plants come in many shapes and sizes in addition to the standard flowerpot. Make a grouping of potted plants more interesting by using a variety of containers.

An **oil jar,** or olive jar, also called an amphora, is the kind of jug recovered from ancient shipwrecks in the Mediterranean. These clay vessels were used in past times to hold olive oil or wine. Modern versions can be found in unglazed terra-cotta or glazed in different colors. They come in different sizes and may or may not have handles. Oil jars often come without drainage holes in the bottom. Check when you buy one, and if necessary, ask whether the seller can drill a hole for you. Alternatively, you can put a layer of gravel and charcoal, topped by a layer of sand, in the bottom of the pot before you add potting mix, to provide drainage.

You've probably seen a **strawberry jar** but may not have known what it was called. This is the kind of tall pot that has little pockets in the sides. The pockets are there to accommodate the baby plants formed on runners of the strawberry plants growing in the top of the jar. Strawberry jars look charming planted with annuals (use small plants such as sweet alyssum and lobelia in the pockets), and some gardeners like to grow herbs in them. You can find these pots in unglazed terra-cotta and glazed clay styles.

Troughs are shallow pans, usually longer than they are wide, which are generally used to grow alpine and rock garden plants, or small succulents and cacti. Many are made of stone, faux stone, or hypertufa. They may be simple and rough-textured or ornately detailed and formal.

An **urn** is an old-fashioned, chalice-shaped container that usually has a footed base or a pedestal. Urns may sit atop a column or plinth in styles including Queen Anne, Georgian, Regency, and Gothic. Some urns are wide and squat; others are taller and narrower. Urns have a rolled-back rim that is often fluted, scalloped, or incised with an egg-and-dart motif or other historical pattern. The Victorians loved to put cascading plants in cast-iron urns. You can still find antique iron urns, but good-looking imitations in fiberglass and other materials will serve you well. There are also concrete models. Urns generally work best in formal settings, even when they are planted informally with ornamental grasses or tropicals.

This lovely, graceful, glazed oil jar is the perfect ornament for a bed of pink wallflowers (*Erysimum* 'Bowles' Mauve').

Pedestal urns have a classic look. This formal planting of neat, white kalanchoe is coolly elegant.

A **vase** has a top that is wider than its base, and it often has a rolled rim. Vases come in many sizes and shapes, and they may be plain or ornate. Many are decorated with simple moldings around the middle and the base. You can find vases of terra-cotta, glazed clay, metal, stone, and faux stone. You can plant directly in a vase or use it as a cachepot to hold an ordinary terra-cotta or other pot, which in turn holds the plants. Make sure when you select urns and vases for planting that they are intended for outdoor use.

Container Materials

Terra-cotta is *the* classic material for pots. Terra-cotta containers come in a vast assortment of sizes, shapes, and styles. Terra-cotta pots also vary in color, from the familiar orange-brown to lighter pink and sandy shades, depending on where the clay comes from. Pot-making companies have always tended to spring up where particularly good clay is found. Italy is the capital of terra-cotta—many of the finest clay pots in the world are made there. The United States also boasts some top-quality clay pieces, many from small artisanal companies around the country. Clay pots are manufactured in Mexico, too, and these pots are often less expensive but also not as strong due to the kind of clay available there.

Terra-cotta planters will age with time spent outdoors, or you can buy them distressed or pre-aged, with a sanded surface, a whitish bloom, or moss already growing on them. Antique unglazed clay pieces are also on the market, but they are pricey. Clay pots fired at very high temperatures are frost re-

Terra-cotta chimney flue liners hold spring annuals.

Blue delphiniums pick up the blue glaze of this pot.

sistant, though perhaps not entirely frostproof. Many pots are not fired this way, however, so it's safest to move them indoors over winter unless you live in a mild climate. Clay is porous, and the walls of the pot absorb moisture that expands when it freezes and cracks the pot.

Stone and concrete are most often used for urns, vases, and troughs. These containers are often quite elegant and beautifully suited to formal gardens. Limestone, granite, and marble are all used to make containers. The pieces are also extremely heavy. Once you have them in place, you won't want to move them. But you can find very attractive imitation pieces that are lighter in weight and more portable. See "Fabulous Fakes" on page 206.

Metal containers have a sleek, elegant look. Copper, zinc, galvanized steel, brushed stainless steel, and aluminum pieces look very formal and modern. Antique cast-iron pieces are better suited to traditional formal and Victorian landscapes. Metal containers are not porous and so retain more moisture than clay. They also heat up in full sun and can cook the plants inside them; use metal containers in shady locations if you want to grow plants in them. Copper containers tarnish, but they can be given a preventive coating to hold their luster.

Glazed clay pieces add their own colors to the garden and, like terra-cotta, they come in a huge assortment of styles, shapes, and sizes. In addition to solid-color glazes, you can find elaborately detailed pots and jardinieres with oriental designs, blue-and-white delft patterns, Southwestern motifs, folk art flower designs, and lots more. If you want to use pots with colored designs, pick up or contrast one of the colors with the flowers you plant in the pot, or use a simple, elegant plant in each, or an all-green combination of foliage textures.

Solid-color glazes are far easier to work with, especially when they are earthy tones—the colors of soil, foliage, water, and sky. Key the colors of the containers to your garden color scheme and to the trim on your house.

Neutral-colored containers are easiest of all to work with and are comfortable with a lot of different color schemes. Beige, tan, gold, and brown glazes are very versatile in the landscape. They work especially well with warm-colored flowers—reds, oranges, yellows, and creams. Grays beautifully set off cool pinks, blues, and purples, and pastel salmon and peach tints. Black is dramatic and can look spare and oriental, or chic and modern.

Greens, since they relate to the most prevalent color in any garden, are also easy to work with. Glazes range from palest mint to emerald, sage, and olive, or deep forest shades.

You can find blue pots in light cerulean, aqua, rich turquoise, teal, royal blues, deep marine, and navy. Yellow and orange flowers contrast with blue pots, while pinks and purples harmonize.

Red pots are probably the trickiest colors to work with, but they, too, adapt to a variety of color schemes when the glazes are warm, brownish brick and mahogany shades, or deep burgundy tones.

If you find all this decorating talk too ponderous,

you can simply ignore it. Go out and get yourself some acrylic pots in neon-bright pink, electric blue, lime, or a shiny metallic finish, and just have some fun with your pots.

Fabulous Fakes

A surprising diversity of composite materials that resemble natural, often much heavier, materials is finding its way into containers for plants. Cast stone looks remarkably real and can be molded with intricate patterns that would be impossible to hand-carve on a large scale today. Cast stone can resemble marble, limestone, or even concrete. Plastic colored to look like terra-cotta comes in different shades and looks more realistic than it used to. Some of the most amazing pieces are made of fiberglass and resin materials that look like cast iron, zinc, or stone. There are cement/plastic blends that mimic concrete. Cast silicone can be made in various colors. Many of these faux materials hold up better outdoors than their genuine counterparts, and they're often a lot lighter and easier to move around.

Choosing and Planting Pots

If your pots coordinate with the style and colors of your house and garden, they will enhance the unified, all-of-a-piece look. In a formal garden, use classically styled pots in traditional shapes, perhaps with smooth glazes. In a more modern setting, opt for containers with austere, elegant lines. Topiaries in pots make a supremely sophisticated statement in a

This cast-resin urn looks an awful lot like cast iron, but it's lightweight and long lasting.

formal garden. Choose from standards (lollipops), spirals, rings, pyramids, and more. Neatly clipped small shrubs and vines trained on elegant tuteurs and scrolled iron supports also work beautifully in formal settings.

In an informal garden, you can, really, use just about any kind of container if you plant it lavishly. A pot overflowing with flowers and greenery will look

Growing plants in pots is not a difficult proposition, if you choose plants suited to the available growing conditions and take care of them after you plant them.

Rule number one is to learn what growing conditions are available where a container will be located. Conditions will most likely be different for pots in different places. Here's what to look for:

Light. Is the area in full sun all day? Is it partly shaded, receiving sun in the morning or afternoon and shade the rest of the day? Does it get dappled sun and shade all day? Is the shade deeper than that? Many plants will grow just fine in partial shade. But for dappled to moderate shade, look for shade-tolerant plants.

Moisture. Water is a big concern for container plants. In hot, dry, windy weather, plants in pots—especially small to medium-size pots—will need water every day, and perhaps even twice a day. If you live where summer weather is likely to be dry, or if you will not be home to water every day, mix a moisture-holding polymer gel into the potting mix, and use drought-tolerant plants.

Temperature. Many of the annuals that bloom so lavishly all summer are tender and cannot tolerate temperatures below about 50°F. It's tempting to get all the pots planted by a certain date—say, Memorial Day. But if you live where springs are late and cool, hold off on planting tender annuals until the weather is warm enough and nighttime temperatures remain above 50°F. If you want to have earlier color, use cold-tolerant annuals such as osteospermum and pansies, and replant the pots when the hot weather arrives.

Soil. Most plants grow best in a light, porous, well-drained potting mix. Plants can grow in either a soil-based or a soilless mix, but for outdoor plants I personally prefer a potting mix that contains soil. One good, all-purpose mix is a blend of 2 parts of good potting soil or garden loam, 1 part compost, and 1 part peat moss or vermiculite. Mix a packaged organic all-purpose fertilizer into the potting mix when you blend it.

Container plants will thrive when you give them a little basic care:

Water. Regular watering is essential. Check your pots every day, and water when the potting mix is dry $1/2$ to 1 inch below the soil surface. To check hanging baskets without taking them down, place one hand underneath the basket and lift up just enough to feel the pot's weight in your hand. If the pot has weight to it, the soil is still moist. When it feels very light, it's time to water. A long-handled watering wand makes watering potted plants a snap.

Fertilize. Container plants, especially annuals, need lots of nutrients to fuel their growth and flowering. The easiest way to fertilize them is to mix a liquid seaweed and fish fertilizer or compost tea into the water once a week for annuals, or every other week for other plants, when you water. Dilute the fertilizer as directed on the package. If the package contains directions for fertilizing container plants, follow the manufacturer's directions.

Deadhead. Deadheading—removing faded and dead flowers—is the other basic component of care for potted plants. Regular deadheading keeps plants looking neat, and it keeps annuals blooming.

informal no matter what kind of container it's in. To complement a naturalistic garden, for instance, you might seek out containers covered in birchbark, or use twig baskets as cachepots. A Mediterranean garden would be beautifully complemented by terracotta pots full of sun-loving plants. For a formal landscape with geometric beds or even parterres, elegant urns with lots of detail and scalloped rims would have the right look.

When you plant your pots, fill them up. Professionals stuff pots with as many plants as they can shoehorn into them, which makes for instant impact but allows no room for growth. Professionals also dig fatigued and overgrown plants out of those pots as the season progresses, in a continual process of renewal and replenishment. If you want to do less work, allow some room for the plants to grow when you put them in.

Still, there are basic guidelines to follow to create a container planting that looks great. Depending on the size of the pot, you'll need to include one or more tall plants for height and vertical line. Around the tall plants, put bushy plants for volume. Fill in gaps with small-leaved, delicate-textured filler plants. Finish off the pot with trailing or cascading plants to spill over the edges.

Whether you are planting formal or informal containers, remember, above all, that plants grow and you have to allow room for that. Even the most carefully clipped shrub will eventually outgrow its pot and need to be removed and replanted someplace else. Otherwise, the plant will finally become too pot-bound to support itself, and it will die.

Perennials will grow well in a large enough container for a year or two, but for longer-term health, most perennials will do better in the ground. Also bear in mind that perennials of borderline hardiness are less likely to survive a hard winter in a pot than they would in the ground. The smaller volume of soil in the pot provides less protection for roots; it's more likely to thaw in mild weather, then quickly refreeze when the temperature drops. Freezing/thawing/refreezing cycles can cause perennial roots to heave out of the soil, where they'll be damaged by the cold and wind.

Here's a trick for planting a very large, tall container such as an olive jar or a tall, narrow vase. If you will be planting just annuals or other shallow-rooted plants in the pot, you won't need all that deep root space below. To avoid sinking your life savings into filling the entire container with potting mix, fill some of the unneeded space in the bottom with upside down smaller pots or crumbled newspaper. Fill in around and over the filler material with sand, then fill the upper third or so (depending on the depth of the pot) with potting mix.

Pots of citrus trees line a stone balustrade in a very formal, polished design.

Plant Finders

These Plant Finder tables are designed to supplement Chapter 1. For each style of garden described in that chapter, you will find a corresponding Plant Finder in this section listing some of the plants that are suited to that particular kind of garden.

Each Plant Finder provides botanical and common names and description of each plant, along with preferred growing conditions, the growing range, and useful comments.

PLANT	DESCRIPTION	GROWING CONDITIONS	COMMENTS	GROWING RANGE
Acanthus spinosus, bear's breech	Dark green, deeply cut, spiny-edged leaves on plants 4 to 5 ft high; tall spikes of white flowers with purple bracts in summer.	Sun to partial shade; prefers moist but well-drained, fertile soil but adapts to many soils.	Bold, sculptural plant for back of garden.	Zones 5–9
Aconitum spp., monkshoods	Perennials to 5 ft high, with lobed, rich green leaves and, in mid- to late summer, spikes of helmet-shaped blue flowers.	Sun to partial shade; moist, fertile soil.	Mulch to keep roots cool.	Zones 3–8; varies with species
Agapanthus africanus, African lily	Tender evergreen perennial with strap-shaped leaves and, in late summer, spherical clusters of blue trumpet flowers atop tall stems.	Full sun; moist but well-drained, fertile soil.	Where not hardy, grow in pots and bring indoors over winter to bright, cool spot.	Zones 9–10
Ageratum houstonianum, flossflower	Neat, compact plant 6 to 12 in. high, depending on cultivar, with broadly oval leaves and clusters of small, blue, powder-puff flowers.	Full sun to partial shade; moist but well-drained, fertile soil.	Prone to disease in hot, dry or cool, wet climates.	Tender annual
Alchemilla mollis, lady's mantle	Low, mat-forming perennial to 2 ft high, with lobed, pleated, light green leaves that capture dewdrops; loose, airy clusters of tiny chartreuse flowers in early summer.	Sun to light shade; moist, humusy soil of average fertility.	Use in front of garden.	Zones 4–8
Allamanda cathartica, golden trumpet vine	Evergreen climber that can be trained as a standard. Large, yellow trumpet flowers; oval green leaves.	Full sun; moist, fertile soil.	Sap may irritate skin. Overwinter indoors.	Tender; grow as annual
Allium spp., flowering onions	Bulbous perennial with grassy or strap-shaped leaves and, in spring or summer, globe-shaped heads of starry flowers in purple, pink, yellow, or white.	Full sun; well-drained soil of average to good fertility.	Heights and bloom times vary with species.	Zones 4–9; varies with species
Alternanthera ficoidea, Joseph's coat	Neat, mat-forming plant 8 to 10 in. high, with small, pointed leaves marked with green, red, orange, yellow, and pink.	Full sun to partial shade; moist but well-drained soil.	Clip to keep plants small and neat.	Tender; grow as annual
Angelonia angustifolia, summer snapdragon	Upright plants to 18 in. high, with lance-shaped leaves and narrow spires of lipped flowers in purple, pink, white, or bicolors.	Full sun; moist but well-drained soil.	Good vertical accent in containers or garden beds.	Zones 9–10; elsewhere grow as annual
Asarum spp., wild gingers	Elegant, slow-spreading groundcovers with glossy green, heart-shaped leaves and hard-to-see, jug-shaped, brownish flowers in spring.	Partial to full shade; humusy, moist but well-drained soil.	Slow to establish but worth the wait.	Zones 4–9; varies with species

PLANT	DESCRIPTION	GROWING CONDITIONS	COMMENTS	GROWING RANGE
Begonia semperflorens, wax begonia	Group of hybrids with compact habit, 6 to 12 in. tall; glossy, rounded leaves of green or bronze; clusters of pink, red, or white flowers all summer.	Full sun to light shade; rich, humusy, well-drained soil.	Deer-resistant plants for front of garden or pots.	Tender; grow as annuals
Bergenia cvs., heartleaf bergenias	Evergreen perennial 10 to 18 in. high, with rosette of broad, glossy green leaves and, in spring, clusters of pink, red, or white flowers.	Full sun to partial shade; moist but well-drained, humusy soil.	Spreads to form clumps.	Zones 4–8
Buxus spp., boxwoods	Slow-growing evergreen shrubs of rounded, pyramidal, or upright habit with small, aromatic, glossy dark green leaves.	Partial to light shade; moist but well-drained, fertile soil.	Take shearing well.	Zones 6–9; varies with species
Camellia spp.	Evergreen shrubs to 20 ft, with glossy, deep green leaves and single or double flowers in pink, red, or white.	Partial shade; humusy, moist but well-drained soil with an acid pH.	Not sheared like other formal evergreens, but the elegant flowers earn them a place in formal gardens. Benefit from mulch.	Zones 7–8
Campanula spp., bellflowers	Perennials of upright, clumping, or spreading habit, with oval to lance-shaped leaves and flowers that may be bell-shaped, tubular, or starlike, in white, blue, or violet.	Full sun to partial shade; moist but well-drained, fertile soil of neutral to alkaline pH.	Heights and bloom times vary with species.	Zones 3–8; varies with species
Clematis cvs.	Deciduous or evergreen vines with flowers in a variety of forms and colors, including white, pink, red, blue, and purple.	Full sun to partial shade; moist but well-drained, rich, humusy soil.	Mulch or locate where roots are shaded.	Zones vary with species
Consolida ajacis, larkspur	Branching plant 1 to 4 ft high, with ferny leaves and, in late spring in the North, or winter in the South, spikes of single or double purple, pink, or white flowers.	Full sun; light, moist but well-drained, fertile soil.	Tall varieties need staking.	Hardy annual
Dahlia cvs.	Tender, tuberous roots produce flowers in many forms, from single and daisylike to round pompoms, in a host of warm colors; plant sizes range from several in. to 6 ft.	Full sun; well-drained, fertile, humusy soil.	Stake tall plants. Dig and store tubers in Zones 7 and north after first frost.	Zones 8–11; elsewhere tender
Delphinium spp.	Spikes of blue, purple, pink, or white flowers on plants 2 to 7 ft high, depending on species or cultivar.	Full sun; rich, humusy soil, even moisture.	Tall stems need staking.	Zones 3–7

(continued)

PLANT	DESCRIPTION	GROWING CONDITIONS	COMMENTS	GROWING RANGE
Dianthus spp., garden pinks	Mat-forming plants 4 to 12 in. high, with narrow, blue-green leaves and flowers with notched petals in shades of red, pink, and white, many clove-scented.	Full sun; well-drained soil of neutral to mildly alkaline pH.	Deadhead to prolong bloom.	Zones 4 or 5 to 9
Dictamnus albus, gas plant	Perennial to 3 ft high, with spikes of white to pinkish flowers on tall stems in summer above a clump of divided, deep green, lemon-scented leaves.	Full sun to light shade; well-drained, average to fertile soil.	Durable, long-lived plant that needs little maintenance.	Zones 3–9
Ferns	Many species and sizes. Foliage plants in various shades of green, most with fronds divided into many oblong or rounded leaflets.	Partial to full shade; humusy, moist soil.	Neat and clump-forming or running and creeping, ferns are at home in formal or woodland gardens.	There are ferns for every zone
Fuchsia cvs.	Upright or cascading plants with slender to broad, dangling, bell-shaped flowers in pink, red, orange, white, and bicolors; oblong green leaves.	Partial shade; moist but well-drained, fertile soil; best where summers are cool.	Plants trained as standards work well in formal gardens and pots.	Zones 7–10; elsewhere grow as annual
Heuchera spp., coralbells, alumroots	Perennials 1 to 2 ft high, with mounds of scalloped or lobed leaves of green or purple, marbled, veined or flushed with silver, cream, purple, or chocolate; tiny bell flowers on tall, slender stems, white, pink, or red, rise above the foliage in summer.	Sun to light shade; moist but well-drained, fertile soil of neutral pH.	Foliage is attractive even when plants are not in bloom.	Zones 4–8
Hibiscus rosa-sinensis, Chinese hibiscus	Tropical shrubs to 8 to 12 ft high in frost-free areas, 4 to 6 ft where used for summer color; glossy, deep green, pointed leaves and funnel-shaped flowers of red, pink, orange, yellow, and white; available trained as standards.	Full sun; moist but well-drained, fertile soil of neutral to mildly alkaline pH.	Rich summer color, beautiful in large containers.	Zones 10–11; elsewhere grow as annual
Hosta spp. and cvs., plantain lilies	Many varieties, from a few inches to 3 ft high; lance-shaped to rounded leaves in many shades of green and combinations of green, white, gold, and chartreuse; spikes of trumpet-shaped white to lavender flowers, some fragrant, in summer.	Partial to full shade; moist but well-drained, humusy, fertile soil.	Indispensable for shady gardens.	Zones 3–8
Hydrangea macrophylla, bigleaf hydrangea	Elegant deciduous shrubs to about 5 ft tall, with big flowerheads in summer of either round snowball or flattened "lacecap" form, in blue, pink, or white; broadly oval green leaves.	Full sun to partial shade; moist but well-drained, rich, humusy soil.	Flowers tend to be blue in acid soil, pink in alkaline soil; white flowers do not change color.	Zones 6–9

PLANT	DESCRIPTION	GROWING CONDITIONS	COMMENTS	GROWING RANGE
Hyssopus officinalis, hyssop	Aromatic perennial to 2 ft high, with lance-shaped to oblong green leaves and, in summer, spikes of deep violet-blue flowers.	Full sun; well-drained, fertile soil of neutral to alkaline pH.	Can be clipped for low hedge.	Zones 3–10
Ilex spp., hollies	Evergreen shrubs of upright, pyramidal, or rounded form, and various leaf sizes and shapes. Glossy, deep green leaves, variegated with gold or cream in some cultivars. Female plants produce red, orange, yellow, or black berries as long as male plants grow nearby.	Full sun to partial shade; rich, humusy, moist but well-drained soil.	Elegant specimen plants; some can be used for hedging.	Zones vary with species
Impatiens walleriana cvs., bedding impatiens	Widely grown mounded plants with single or double flowers in shades of pink, orange, red, or white, blooming all summer into fall; oval green leaves.	Partial to full shade; adapts to wide range of soils.	Hard to beat for massing in beds or containers. New Guinea impatiens has larger flowers in tropical colors, longer leaves, needs brighter light.	Tender annual
Iris cvs., bearded irises	Classic garden flowers with 3 upright and 3 drooping petals with a hairy "beard" in center of each; fan of sword-shaped leaves. Heights vary from 3 in. to 4 ft; early summer blossoms come in all colors of the rainbow.	Full sun to partial shade; fertile, moist but well-drained soil of mildly acid to neutral pH.	Plant with top of rhizome exposed at soil level.	Zones 3–9
Leucanthemum x*superbum*, Shasta daisy	Classic yellow-centered white daisy, available with single or double flowers, heights from 10 in. to 3 ft; lance-shaped green leaves.	Full sun to partial shade; moist but well-drained soil of average to good fertility.	Taller varieties may need staking.	Zones 3–10
Lilium spp. and cvs., lilies	Bulbous plants with tall, straight stems lined with narrow leaves and, in summer, trumpet-shaped flowers, some fragrant, some with reflexed petals, in many warm colors and sizes.	Filtered sun to partial shade; light, loamy, well-drained soil; average moisture, but even moisture during bloom.	Stems may need staking.	Zones 4–8
Liriope spp., lilyturfs	Evergreen or semi-evergreen plants with grassy leaves and spikes of tiny violet or white flowers in late summer or fall.	Sun or shade; moist but well-drained, humusy soil.	Tolerates drought; damaged by cold winter winds.	Zones 5–10
Lupinus cvs., lupines	Bushy perennials to 3 ft high, with compound leaves and spikes of pealike flowers in red, pink, violet, yellow, white, or bicolors in summer.	Full sun to partial shade; light, fertile, moist but well-drained soil of mildly acid to neutral pH.	Does best where summers are not too hot.	Zones 4–8

(continued)

PLANT	DESCRIPTION	GROWING CONDITIONS	COMMENTS	GROWING RANGE
Paeonia spp., peonies	Large single or double summer blossoms, some fragrant, in shades of red, rose, pink, and white on large, bushy plants about 3 ft high, with lobed and divided leaves.	Full sun to partial shade; humusy, well-drained soil; average moisture.	Long-lived; may not bloom if planted too deeply.	Zones 2–8
Papaver orientale, oriental poppy	Large, cup-shaped flowers in shades of red, orange, pink, and white on tall stems to 3 ft above a mound of hairy, divided leaves.	Full sun (partial shade in warm climates); light, humusy soil; average moisture.	Plants die back to ground after blooming.	Zones 3–9
Phlox paniculata, garden phlox	Conical to rounded clusters of fragrant, disc-shaped flowers in shades of pink, purple, and white on clumps of stems 2 to 4 ft tall, with lance-shaped leaves.	Full sun; rich, moist, humusy soil.	Prone to mildew; needs good air circulation.	Zones 4–9
Phormium tenax, New Zealand flax	Tender perennial with clumps of sword-shaped green or bronze leaves, striped with cream, red, pink, yellow, or orange in some varieties.	Full sun; moist but well-drained, fertile soil.	Elegant plants for containers or accents.	Zones 9–11; elsewhere grow as annual
Physostegia virginiana, false dragonhead	Upright perennial to 4 ft high, with lance-shaped, toothed leaves and, in late summer to early fall, spires of tubular lavender, pink, or white flowers.	Full sun to partial shade; moist soil of average fertility.	Tolerates poor soils; easy to grow.	Zones 4–9
Picea glauca 'Alberta Conica', dwarf Alberta spruce	Bushy, cone-shaped evergreen shrub growing slowly to as high as 20 ft, with bluish green needle-like leaves.	Full sun; moist but well-drained soil of average fertility.	Classic plant for containers.	Zones 3–6
Platycodon grandiflorus, balloon flower	Clumping perennial with oval, bluish green leaves and, in mid- to late summer, clusters of balloon-shaped buds opening to bell-shaped violet to purple flowers.	Full sun to partial shade; moist but well-drained soil of average to good fertility.	Slow to emerge in spring; be patient.	Zones 4–9
Salvia xsylvestris 'Mainacht', 'May Night' salvia	Upright, branched perennial 2½ ft high, with oblong leaves and, through most of summer, slender spikes of small violet-blue flowers.	Full sun; moist but well-drained, humusy soil of average fertility.	Deadhead regularly for season-long bloom.	Zones 5–9
Santolina chamaecyparissus, lavender cotton	Branched small shrub 1½ to 2 ft high, with aromatic, small, oblong, toothed gray leaves and, in mid- to late summer, yellow button flowers.	Full sun; well-drained soil of average to poor fertility.	Clip for low hedges and knot gardens.	Zones 6–9
Stachys byzantina 'Silver Carpet', 'Silver Carpet' lamb's ears	Low, mat-forming perennial about 1 ft high, with thick, oval leaves covered with soft silver-white fuzz.	Full sun to partial shade; well-drained soil of average fertility.	Will rot in soggy soil.	Zones 4–8

PLANT	DESCRIPTION	GROWING CONDITIONS	COMMENTS	GROWING RANGE
Taxus spp., yews	Pyramidal, upright, or rounded evergreen trees, with glossy, deep green, flat needles, and small red fruits in fall. Size varies with cultivar.	Sun or shade; well-drained soil of good fertility.	Grow as hedge or individual specimens. May suffer winter wind burn in colder climates. Toxic if eaten.	Zones 5–8; varies with species
Teucrium chamaedrys, germander	Woody perennial to 1½ ft high, with small, oblong, toothed, aromatic dark green leaves and, in summer, small spikes of purple-pink flowers.	Full sun; well-drained soil of average to poor fertility, with neutral to mildly alkaline pH.	Grow as low hedges or in knot gardens.	Zones 5–10
Tulipa cvs., tulips	Bulbous plant with pointed, oblong, light green leaves and, in spring, cup-shaped flowers in many shades of red, rose, pink, purple, yellow, orange, and white atop tall, straight stems.	Full sun in the North, partial to light shade in the South; moist but well-drained fertile soil, with mildly acid to neutral pH.	Hybrid tulips are not reliably perennial; plant bulbs deeply and fertilize yearly to encourage longer life.	Zones 4–7; farther south, grow as annual
Veronica spicata, spike speedwell	Spreading perennial to 2 ft high, with oblong to lance-shaped leaves and, in mid- and late summer, tapered spikes of blue or white flowers.	Full sun to partial shade; moist but well-drained soil of average to good fertility.	Deadhead to prolong bloom.	Zones 3–8

PLANT	DESCRIPTION	GROWING CONDITIONS	COMMENTS	GROWING RANGE
Achillea spp., yarrows	Clump-forming perennials 2 to 4 ft high, with divided, fernlike, grayish green leaves and, in summer, flat-topped clusters of yellow, pink, orange, red, or white flowers.	Full sun; moist but well-drained soil of average fertility.	Tolerates dry conditions when established.	Zones 3–9; varies with species and cultivar
Anemone x*hybrida*, Japanese anemone	Upright perennial to 4 ft high, with 3-lobed, toothed leaves and, in late summer to early fall, clusters of single or semidouble white or pink flowers on slender stems.	Full sun to partial shade; moist but well-drained, humusy soil.	Excellent source of late-season color.	Zones 5–8
Artemisia spp., wormwoods	Upright or bushy perennials of varying sizes from a few inches to 3 ft, with aromatic, divided, gray-green or silver leaves and, in summer, small yellow or white flowers.	Full sun; well-drained soil of average fertility.	Versatile foliage accent plants.	Zones 3–9; varies with species
Aruncus dioicus, goat's beard	Clumping perennial to 6 ft high, with compound, fernlike leaves with toothed leaflets and, in summer, loose, feathery clusters of tiny white flowers.	Full sun to partial shade; moist but well-drained soil of average to good fertility.	Looks like astilbe, but bigger.	Zones 3–7
Aster novae-angliae, *A. novi-belgii*	Clumping perennials to 4 ft high, with oblong leaves and, in late summer and fall, clusters of narrow-rayed daisy flowers in shades of pink, rose, purple, red, or white.	Full sun to partial shade; moist but well-drained soil of good fertility.	Need moisture while growing but dislike soggy soil in winter.	Zones 4–8
Astilbe cvs., false spireas	Clumping perennials from 1 to 3 ft high, with compound fernlike leaves with toothed leaflets, and, in summer, airy branched clusters or plumes of tiny red, rose, pink, lavender, or white flowers.	Filtered sun to light shade; moist soil of average to good fertility, with mildly acid to neutral pH.	Deer resistant and attractive all season.	Zones 4–9; varies with cultivar
Calamagrostis x*acutiflora*, feather reed grass	Clumping perennial grass with slender, arching leaves to 3 ft long and, in late summer, narrow, airy seedheads of silvery brown to bronzy purple.	Full sun to partial shade; moist, humusy soil of average fertility.	Adapts to a range of soils.	Zones 5–9
Cimicifuga racemosa, black cohosh	Upright perennial to 6 ft high, with divided, lobed leaves and, in mid- to late summer, tall wands of small white flowers.	Full sun to partial shade; moist but well-drained, humusy soil.	Good for late-season interest in back of garden.	Zones 3–8
Coleus cvs. (*Solenostemon scutellarioides*)	Branched tender perennials grown as foliage annuals, with scalloped oval to pointed leaves in many combinations of green, lime, chartreuse, gold, cream, orange, red, pink, and brown; spikes of small blue flowers in summer.	Sun to light shade; moist, humusy soil of average fertility.	Perennial in frost-free climates. Pinch back stems for bushier growth.	Tender annual

PLANT	DESCRIPTION	GROWING CONDITIONS	COMMENTS	GROWING RANGE
Coreopsis grandiflora, C. verticillata, tickseed	Upright perennials 1½ to 3 ft high, with oblong or finely divided, threadlike leaves and, through much of summer, golden, light yellow, or pink daisy flowers.	Full sun to partial shade; moist but well-drained soil of good fertility.	Deadhead regularly to extend bloom.	Zones 3 or 4 to 9
Cosmos spp.	Upright, branched annuals 1 to 5 ft high, depending on cultivar, with divided to threadlike leaves and yellow-centered daisy flowers in shades of pink, red, white, yellow, and orange that bloom all summer.	Full sun; well-drained soil of average fertility.	Deadhead to extend bloom, but allow some late-season flowers in place to self-sow.	Tender annual
Dianthus chinensis, China pink	Bushy, tender perennial usually grown as annual, to 2 ft high, with narrow, light green leaves and, in summer, clusters of fringed red, pink, or white flowers, some bicolored.	Full sun; well-drained soil of average fertility, with neutral to mildly alkaline pH.	Heat tolerant and easy to grow.	Zones 7–10; elsewhere grow as annual
Echinacea purpurea, purple coneflower	Upright perennial 1 to 3 ft high, with coarse, oval leaves and, in mid- to late summer, purple-pink or white daisy flowers with drooping petals and conical bronze-orange centers.	Full sun to partial shade; well-drained, humusy soil.	Deadhead to prolong bloom and prevent rampant self-sowing.	Zones 3–9
Echinops ritro, globe thistle	Clumping perennial to 5 ft high, with spiny, pointed leaves and, in late summer, prickly, steel blue, globe-shaped flowerheads.	Full sun; well-drained soil of average fertility.	Very attractive to bees.	Zones 3–9
Epimedium grandiflorum, bishop's hat	Spreading perennial groundcover to 1 ft high, with heart-shaped leaves and, in mid- to late spring, spurred white, purple, pink, or yellow flowers.	Partial to full shade; moist but well-drained, humusy soil.	Takes some drought when established.	Zones 5–8
Gaura lindheimeri, butterfly flower	Clumping perennial to 3 ft or more, with oblong leaves on thin stems and, through much of summer, white or pink flowers with pointed petals, resembling butterflies.	Full sun to partial shade; moist but well-drained soil of average to good fertility.	Exceptionally long blooming, but often short-lived.	Zones 6–9
Geranium spp., cranesbills	Spreading perennials 4 in. to 2 ft high, depending on species, with lobed or deeply cut leaves and, in summer, 5-petaled flowers in shades of pink, rose, blue, and white.	Full sun to partial shade; moist but well-drained, humusy soil of average fertility.	Quietly charming plants for front to middle of garden.	Zones 3–9; varies with species
Gypsophila paniculata, baby's breath	Branched perennial to 3 ft high, with lance-shaped dark green leaves and, in mid- to late summer, airy masses of little white or pink flowers.	Full sun; moist but well-drained, humusy soil with neutral to mildly alkaline pH.	Good for cutting or drying.	Zones 4–9

(continued)

PLANT	DESCRIPTION	GROWING CONDITIONS	COMMENTS	GROWING RANGE
Helenium cvs., sneezeweeds	Clumping upright perennials 2 to 5 ft high with ob-long to lance-shaped leaves and, in mid- or late summer to early fall, daisy flowers in yellow, orange, or red.	Full sun to partial shade; moist but well-drained soil of av-erage fertility.	Tall varieties need staking.	Zones 4–8
Hemerocallis cvs., daylilies	Upright perennials from 1 to 4 ft high, with narrow, arching leaves and, in early to late summer, large trumpet-shaped flowers in many shades of yellow, peach, orange, red, purple, and white.	Full sun to partial shade; moist but well-drained, humusy soil of average to good fertility.	Twist off old flowers to keep plants looking neat.	Zones 3–10, de-pending on variety
Hibiscus moscheutos, rose mallow	Tropical-looking plant 4 to 8 ft high, with a clump of upright stems, broad leaves, and huge, cup-shaped flowers in shades of pink, red, and white in summer.	Full sun; moist but well-drained, fertile soil of neutral to mildly alkaline pH.	Big, dramatic plants for big gardens.	Zones 5–10
Ipomoea spp., morning glories	Annual vines with heart-shaped or lobed leaves and, from midsummer to frost, broad-petaled trumpet flowers of pink, rose, purple, blue, red, and white, some flushed or streaked with a second color.	Full sun; moist but well-drained soil of average fertility.	Heirloom varieties often self-sow. Soak seeds before planting.	Tender annual
Lantana camara cvs.	Tender shrubs to 4 ft high, grown as annuals in most places, with oval leaves and, from late spring to fall, round flowerheads in pink, yellow, red, orange, and white, often in bicolored combinations.	Full sun; moist but well-drained soil of average fertility.	Bloom in winter in warm climates.	Zones 8–11; else-where grow as annual
Ligularia stenocephala 'The Rocket'	Clumping perennial to 5 ft high, with large, trian-gular, toothed leaves and, in summer, tall spires of bright yellow flowers.	Full sun to light shade; moist, humusy soil of average to good fertility.	Bold, imposing plant for back of garden.	Zones 4–8
Lonicera heckrottii 'Gold Flame', goldflame honeysuckle	Twining perennial vine with oval to oblong leaves and, in summer, clusters of tubular, 2-lipped flowers of yellow and pink.	Full sun to partial shade; moist but well-drained soil of av-erage to good fertility.	Long-blooming and adaptable.	Zones 6–9
Miscanthus spp., maiden grasses, eulalia grasses	Perennial grasses 3 to 10 ft high, depending on cul-tivar, with narrow, arching leaves, striped or banded with gold or cream in some varieties, and, in late summer, airy, fanlike seedheads of white to shiny bronze or purplish brown that fade to tan or beige.	Full sun to partial shade; moist but well-drained soil of av-erage fertility; tolerates a range of soils.	Cut back to ground in late fall or early spring. Can be invasive in good soil.	Zones 4–9; varies with species

PLANT	DESCRIPTION	GROWING CONDITIONS	COMMENTS	GROWING RANGE
Monarda didyma, beebalm	Clumping perennial to 3 ft high, with soft, oval, grayish green, fragrant leaves and, in mid- to late summer, clusters of tubular red, pink, or purple flowers.	Full sun to partial shade; moist, rich, humusy soil.	Attracts humming-birds and bees. Prone to mildew; needs good air circulation.	Zones 4–9
Narcissus spp. and cvs., daffodils	Bulb plants with spring flowers in shades of yellow, orange, pink, and white, consisting of central cup surrounded by flat petals (perianth), followed by clump of narrow leaves.	Full sun to partial shade; moist but well-drained soil of av-erage fertility.	Diverse range of flower sizes, heights, and bloom times.	Zones 3–9; varies with species
Nepeta x*faassenii*, catmint	Sprawling perennial 1 to 1½ ft high, with aromatic, oblong, toothed and wrinkled grayish green leaves and, through summer into fall, spikes of lavender-blue flowers.	Full sun to partial shade; well-drained soil of average fertility.	Prune when plants get straggly to promote continued blooming and neater appearance.	Zones 3–8
Nicotiana alata, flowering tobacco	Branching tender perennial grown as annual 2 to 4 ft high, with oblong leaves and, in summer, wide-mouthed tubular flowers of white, pink, red, or lime green, some fragrant at night.	Full sun to partial shade; moist but well-drained soil of av-erage fertility.	Tall, old-fashioned varieties are most fragrant.	Zones 10–11; else-where grow as annual
Oenothera speciosa, showy primrose	Spreading perennial to 1½ ft high, with lance-shaped leaves and, in summer, cup-shaped light pink flowers.	Full sun to partial shade; well-drained soil.	Drought tolerant when established.	Zones 5–9
Pennisetum alopecuroides, fountain grass	Perennial grass 10 in. to 5 ft high, depending on cul-tivar, with slender, pointed leaves and, in late summer, pale grayish brown, white, or pinkish, bristly, bottlebrush seedheads.	Full sun; moist but well-drained soil; tolerates a range of soils.	Smaller varieties are handsome in con-tainers.	Zones 6–9
Perovskia atriplicifolia, Russian sage	Upright woody perennial to 4 ft high, with aromatic, feathery, gray-green leaves and, in late summer, airy spires of tiny, silvery, lavender-blue flowers.	Full sun; well-drained soil of average to poor fertility.	Tolerates drought.	Zones 5–9
Persicaria spp. (*Polygonum* spp.), knotweeds	Clumping or mat-forming perennials 1 to 4 ft high, with oblong leaves and, in summer, dense spikes of tiny pink, red, or white flowers.	Full sun to partial shade; moist soil of average fertility.	Most are spreaders.	Zones 3–8; varies with species

(continued)

PLANT	DESCRIPTION	GROWING CONDITIONS	COMMENTS	GROWING RANGE
Petunia cvs.	Branched plants 6 in. to 1½ ft high, some trailing, depending on cultivar, with oval leaves and, throughout summer, funnel-shaped flowers in many shades of red, rose, pink, purple, and violet, as well as yellow and white, some bicolors, some ruffled or fringed.	Full sun to partial shade; light, moist but well-drained soil of average fertility.	Deadhead to prolong bloom.	Half-hardy annual
Rudbeckia spp., black-eyed Susans	Branched perennials to 3 ft, depending on variety, with oval to oblong leaves and, in late summer and fall, golden or orangey yellow daisy flowers with brown centers.	Full sun to partial shade; well-drained soil of average fertility.	Plants self-sow and spread.	Zones 3–9; varies with species
Salvia farinacea, mealycup sage	Bushy perennial, often grown as annual, to 2½ ft high, with lance-shaped leaves and, throughout summer, slender spikes of rich blue, white, or blue-and-white flowers.	Full sun to partial shade; light, moist but well-drained, humusy soil of average fertility.	Dependable and long-blooming. 'Victoria' is especially floriferous.	Zones 8–10; elsewhere grow as annual
Sedum 'Autumn Joy' (*S.* 'Herbstfreude')	Upright, clumping perennial to 2 ft high, with fleshy, toothed, oval leaves on thick stems and, in late summer, flat-topped clusters of small, starry flowers that open pink, turn salmony bronze, then reddish.	Full sun to partial shade; well-drained soil of average fertility, with neutral to mildly alkaline pH.	Tolerates drought.	Zones 3–10
Solidago spp., goldenrods	Upright perennial with narrow, oblong leaves and, in late summer, branched clusters or sprays of tiny, bright yellow flowers.	Full sun to partial shade; well-drained soil of average to poor fertility.	Does not cause hay fever.	Zones 5–9
Thalictrum rochebrunianum, meadowsweet	Upright clumping perennial to 5 ft high, with a mound of lobed leaves and, in mid- to late summer, branched, airy clusters of lilac-pink to lavender flowers with yellow stamens on tall, slender stems.	Full sun to light shade; moist but well-drained, humusy soil of average to good fertility.	Lovely vertical accent for back of garden.	Zones 5–10
Zinnia elegans, Z. haageana	Bushy plants 4 in. to 3 ft high, depending on cultivar, with lance-shaped to oblong leaves and, throughout summer, single or double daisy flowers in many shades of red, orange, rose, pink, yellow, and white.	Full sun to partial shade; well-drained, humusy soil of average fertility.	Prone to mildew; needs good air circulation.	Tender annual

PLANT	DESCRIPTION	GROWING CONDITIONS	COMMENTS	GROWING RANGE
Alcea rosea, hollyhock	Biennial or short-lived perennial to 6 or more ft high, with rounded, lobed, hairy leaves and, in summer, tall spikes of large single or double flowers in shades of red, pink, purple, yellow, white, and near-black.	Full sun; well-drained, humusy soil of average fertility.	Grow as annual to avoid rust disease. Often self-sows.	Zones 3–10
Amaranthus caudatus, love-lies-bleeding	Bushy plant to 5 ft high, with oval, light green leaves and, through summer, drooping tassellike clusters of tiny purple-red, blood red, or green flowers.	Full sun to partial shade; moist, humusy soil of average to poor fertility.	Grows best in northern climates.	Tender annual
Amaranthus tricolor, Joseph's coat	Bushy plant to 3 ft high, with brilliantly colored leaves in combinations of red, rose, bronze, gold, copper, yellow, brown, and green, depending on cultivar.	Full sun in the North, partial shade in the South; moist, humusy soil of average fertility.	Brilliant color for containers or garden beds.	Tender annual
Antirrhinum majus, snapdragon	Upright perennial in range of heights to 4 ft, with lance-shaped leaves and, in midsummer to fall, spikes of tubular, 2-lipped flowers in shades of red, rose, pink, orange, yellow, and white.	Full sun; well-drained soil of good fertility.	Cut back spent spikes to keep plants blooming. Plant in fall for winter flowers south of Zone 7.	Grow as hardy annual
Aquilegia spp. and cvs., columbines	Graceful plants with a rosette of divided, scalloped leaves and, in spring or early summer, nodding, spurred flowers of blue, lavender, pink, red, yellow, salmon, white, or bicolors on thin stems.	Partial to light shade; well-drained, humusy soil of average to good fertility.	May self-sow.	Zones 3–9; varies with species
Calendula officinalis, pot marigold	Upright plant to 2½ ft high, with oblong leaves and single or double daisy flowers in shades of yellow, orange, or cream.	Full sun to partial shade; moist but well-drained soil of average fertility.	Best in cool weather. Plant in fall in the South, early spring in the North.	Hardy annual
Campanula medium, Canterbury bells	Upright biennial or hardy annual to 3 ft high, with oblong to lance-shaped leaves and, in spring and summer, spikes of single or double bell-shaped flowers in pink, blue, or white.	Full sun to partial shade; moist but well-drained soil of average to good fertility, with neutral to alkaline pH.	Best in cool climates.	Zones 5–8
Centaurea cyanus, bachelor's button	Upright annual to 2½ ft high, with lance-shaped leaves and rounded heads of tiny tubular florets of rich blue, pink, white, purple, or red.	Full sun; well-drained soil.	Best in cool weather.	Hardy annual
Centranthus ruber, Jupiter's beard	Clumping upright perennial to 3 ft high, with oblong to lance-shaped leaves and, through much of summer, clusters of crimson to rose-pink flowers.	Full sun; well-drained soil of average to poor fertility, with neutral to alkaline pH.	Often self-sows.	Zones 4–8

(continued)

PLANT	DESCRIPTION	GROWING CONDITIONS	COMMENTS	GROWING RANGE
Cleome hassleriana, spider flower	Upright plant to 5 ft high, with hairy stems, lobed leaves with a thorn at the base, and, in summer, rounded clusters of rose, pink, or white flowers with long stamens.	Full sun to partial shade; well-drained soil of average fertility.	Often self-sows.	Half-hardy annual
Consolida ajacis, larkspur	Upright plant to 4 ft high, with fine-textured ferny leaves and, in summer, dense spikes of single or double purple, lavender, pink, or white flowers.	Full sun to partial shade; light, moist but well-drained, humusy soil of good fertility.	Often self-sows. Plant in fall in the South.	Hardy annual
Convallaria majalis, lily-of-the-valley	Rhizomatous, spreading perennial to 9 in. high, with pointed oval to oblong leaves and, in late spring, clusters of richly fragrant, drooping, white bell flowers on thin stems.	Full sun to full shade; moist, humusy soil of average fertility.	Can be invasive in good soil.	Zones 3–9
Cosmos spp.	Upright, branched annuals 1 to 5 ft high, with oblong or finely divided, threadlike leaves and yellow-centered daisy flowers in shades of pink, red, white, yellow, and orange that bloom all summer.	Full sun; well-drained soil of average fertility.	Deadhead to extend bloom, but allow some late-season flowers in place to self-sow.	Tender annual
Dianthus barbatus, sweet William	Bushy, upright biennial to 2 ft high, with narrow leaves and, in late spring or early summer, dense, flat-topped clusters of flowers in shades of red, rose, pink, and white, many with a contrasting band or eye, atop straight stems.	Full sun; well-drained soil of average fertility, with neutral to mildly alkaline pH.	Often self-sows.	Zones 3–9
Dicentra spectabilis, bleeding heart	Clumping perennial to 3 ft high, with pointed-lobed, light green leaves and, in late spring, heart-shaped pink or white flowers dangling from slender horizontal stems.	Partial to light shade; moist, humusy soil of average to good fertility, with neutral to mildly alkaline pH.	Plants die back in summer after blooming.	Zones 3–9
Digitalis purpurea, foxglove	Biennial to 5 ft high, depending on cultivar, with a rosette of oblong, toothed leaves and, in late spring to early summer, tall spikes of tubular flowers in shades of purple, pink, rose, red, yellow, or white, often with purple or burgundy spots inside.	Full sun to partial shade; moist but well-drained soil of average fertility.	Adapts to a range of conditions. Self-sows. Poisonous if eaten.	Zones 4–8
Fritillaria imperialis, crown imperial	Bulb plant to 3 ft high, with lance-shaped leaves and, in late spring, clusters of drooping orange, red, or yellow bell flowers surmounted by a crown of upright green bracts, atop tall, straight stems.	Full sun; well-drained soil of good fertility.	Plant bulb on its side to prevent rot.	Zones 5–9

PLANT	DESCRIPTION	GROWING CONDITIONS	COMMENTS	GROWING RANGE
Heliotropium arborescens, heliotrope	Bushy, tender perennial to 1½ ft high, with oval, dark green, textured leaves and, throughout summer, dense, rounded clusters of small, vanilla-scented, deep violet or white flowers.	Full sun in the North, partial shade in the South; well-drained, humusy soil of average fertility.	Deadhead to keep plants blooming.	Grow as tender annual
Hemerocallis lilioasphodelus, lemon lily	Perennial to 3 ft high, with narrow leaves and, in early summer, fragrant, lemon yellow, narrow-petaled trumpet flowers that open in the evening on tall stems.	Full sun; moist but well-drained soil of good fertility.	Plant near patios or paths.	Zones 3–10
Hesperis matronalis, dame's rocket	Biennial to 3 ft high, with oval, deep green leaves in late spring and, in early summer, clusters of pinkish purple or white flowers.	Full sun to partial shade; moist but well-drained soil of average fertility, with neutral to mildly alkaline pH.	Flowers are fragrant in the evening.	Zones 4–9
Hibiscus syriacus, rose of Sharon	Deciduous shrub to 10 ft high, with oblong, lobed and toothed leaves and, in late summer and early fall, pink, rose, lavender, light blue, or white flowers with prominent stamens.	Full sun; moist but well-drained soil of average fertility, with neutral to mildly alkaline pH.	Self-sows readily; pull up unwanted seedlings.	Zones 5–9
Impatiens balsamina, balsam impatiens	Upright plant to 2 ft high, with oblong leaves and, through summer, cup-shaped double flowers in shades of pink, red, purple, yellow, or white.	Partial shade; moist but well-drained, humusy soil of average fertility.	Self-sows.	Tender annual
Ipomoea alba, moonflower	Vigorous vine with heart-shaped leaves and, from late summer to frost, large, fragrant, wide-petaled, tubular white flowers that bloom at night.	Full sun to partial shade; moist but well-drained soil of average fertility.	Soak seeds before planting. Craves hot weather.	Tender annual
Ipomoea purpurea, common morning glory	Twining vine with lobed leaves and, from mid-summer to frost, trumpet flowers in purple, rose, pink, or white, some streaked with another color.	Full sun; moist but well-drained soil of average fertility.	Self-sows readily. Soak seeds before planting.	Tender annual
Iris cvs., bearded irises	Perennials in a range of heights to 4 ft, with fan of sword-shaped leaves and, in early summer, flowers in all colors of the rainbow, with 3 upright and 3 drooping petals with a hairy "beard" in center of each.	Full sun to partial shade; fertile, moist but well-drained soil of mildly acid to neutral pH.	Plant with top of rhizome exposed at soil level.	Zones 3–9
Lathyrus odoratus, sweet pea	Tendrilled vine climbing to 6 ft, with oval leaves and, in late spring and early summer, clusters of sweetly fragrant, pealike flowers in shades of purple, rose, pink, red, blue, and white.	Full sun; moist but well-drained, humusy soil of good fertility, with mildly alkaline pH.	Grows best in cool weather. In the South, plant in fall for winter flowers. Deadhead regularly.	Hardy annual

(continued)

PLANT	DESCRIPTION	GROWING CONDITIONS	COMMENTS	GROWING RANGE
Lavandula angustifolia, English lavender	Bushy small shrub to 3 ft high, with narrow, gray-green leaves and, in midsummer, wands of fragrant, tiny purple flowers on slender stems.	Full sun; well-drained soil of average fertility.	Loves hot, sunny weather.	Zones 5–8
Lilium lancifolium (*L. tigrinum*), tiger lily	Clumping bulbous perennial to 5 ft high, with lance-shaped leaves and, in late summer, red-orange flowers with backcurved petals and purple spots grouped on tall stems.	Full sun to partial shade; moist but well-drained soil of average to good fertility, with mildly acid pH.	Adaptable and vigorous, forms clumps.	Zones 2–7
Lunaria annua, money plant	Upright biennial or annual to 3 ft high, with heart-shaped leaves, clusters of rosy purple or white flowers in late spring, and, in summer, flat seedpods whose outer skin opens to reveal silvery, papery inner capsules.	Full sun to partial shade; moist but well-drained soil of average to good fertility.	Self-sows readily. Seed capsules dry well.	Zones 4–9
Mirabilis jalapa, four o'clock	Bushy, tender perennial to 2 ft high, with oval leaves and, throughout summer, fragrant, tubular, red, rose, pink, yellow, or white flowers that open in the afternoon.	Full sun; moist but well-drained soil of average fertility.	Self-sows readily.	Zones 8–11; elsewhere grow as annual
Myosotis sylvatica, forget-me-not	Biennial to 1 ft high, with soft, oblong, grayish green leaves and, in late spring, many clusters of small, sky blue flowers.	Full sun to light shade; moist but well-drained soil of average to poor fertility.	Happily self-sows.	Zones 5–9
Narcissus spp., daffodils	Bulbous plants in a range of sizes from 4 in. to nearly 2 ft with narrow leaves, and flowers consisting of a central cup backed by flat petals, in shades of yellow, orange, cream, and pink, some fragrant.	Full sun; moist but well-drained soil of average fertility.	Bloom from late winter to late spring, depending on variety.	Zones 3–10; varies with cultivar and type
Nigella damascena, love-in-a-mist	Branching annual to 1½ ft high, with finely divided, feathery, threadlike leaves; soft-looking saucer-shaped blue, pink, or white flowers in summer; and interesting, inflated bronze seedpods.	Full sun; moist but well-drained soil of average fertility.	Seed capsules dry well for use in arrangements.	Hardy annual
Papaver rhoeas, corn poppy	Upright, branched annual to 3 ft high, with deeply cut oblong leaves and, in early summer, single or semidouble, bowl-shaped flowers in shades of red, pink, yellow, lilac, or white.	Full sun; well-drained soil of good fertility.	Grows best in cool weather. Deadhead to keep plants blooming. Often self-sows.	Hardy annual
Petunia ×*hybrida* Multiflora types	Bushy plants 8 to 12 in. high, with oval, sticky-haired leaves and, throughout summer, single flowers to 2 in. across in shades of red, rose, pink, blue, purple, and white.	Full sun to partial shade; well-drained soil of average fertility.	Floriferous and tolerates some drought.	Half-hardy annual

PLANT	DESCRIPTION	GROWING CONDITIONS	COMMENTS	GROWING RANGE
Philadelphus coronarius, mock orange	Deciduous shrub to 10 ft high, with oval leaves, and, in early summer, clusters of fragrant, white, cup-shaped flowers.	Full sun to partial shade; moist but well-drained soil of average fertility.	Double-flowered hybrids are available.	Zones 5–8
Portulaca grandiflora, rose moss	Sprawling, low-growing plant about 6 in. high, with fleshy, needlelike leaves and, throughout summer, single or double, cup-shaped flowers in many warm colors, with a satiny sheen.	Full sun; well-drained soil of average to poor fertility.	Often self-sows. Tolerates drought.	Tender annual
Reseda odorata, mignonette	Upright plant to 2 ft high, with oblong leaves and, through summer, loose cone-shaped clusters of fragrant but not showy greenish to white, tiny flowers.	Full sun to partial shade; well-drained soil of average fertility, with alkaline pH.	Grows best in cool weather. Attracts bees.	Hardy annual
Rosa spp. and cvs., shrub roses	Upright shrubs 4 to 12 ft high, with arching, thorny canes and flowers in shades of red, rose, pink, lavender, yellow, and white, many very fragrant, some repeat-blooming or long-blooming.	Full sun to partial shade; well-drained, humusy soil of average to good fertility.	Try old-fashioned varieties or modern ones such as Austin English roses. Provide good air circulation.	Zones 3–9; varies with cultivar
Syringa vulgaris, lilac	Spreading shrub to 20 ft high, with oval to heart-shaped leaves and, in late spring or early summer, cone-shaped clusters of very fragrant lilac, purple, deep red, pink, or white flowers.	Full sun; well-drained, humusy soil of neutral to alkaline pH. Adapts to range of soils.	Deadhead or prune within a month after blooming.	Zones 3–9; varies with cultivar
Tropaeolum majus, nasturtium	Trailing annual to 10 ft long or high, if trained upward, with rounded, bluish green leaves and, in summer to fall, lightly fragrant, spurred flowers in red, orange, mahogany, yellow, salmon-pink, and cream.	Full sun to partial shade; well-drained soil of average to poor fertility.	Grows best in cool weather. Flowers, leaves, and buds are edible.	Tender annual
Viola tricolor, Johnny jump-up	Branched, sprawling annual, biennial, or perennial to 6 in. high, with oblong, scalloped leaves and, in summer, 2- or 3-tone flowers in shades of purple, blue, yellow, and near-black.	Moist but well-drained, humusy soil of average to good fertility.	Self-sows readily.	Zones 4–8

PLANT	DESCRIPTION	GROWING CONDITIONS	COMMENTS	GROWING RANGE
Acer griseum, paperbark maple	Deciduous tree growing slowly to 30 ft, with 3-lobed leaves that turn orange and red in fall, and peeling cinnamon brown bark.	Full sun to partial shade; moist but well-drained soil of good fertility; adapts to a range of soils.	Attractive tree; good for small gardens.	Zones 4–8
Acer japonicum 'Aconitifolium', full moon maple	Deciduous tree to 15 ft high, with deeply lobed, toothed leaves that turn red in fall.	Full sun to light shade; moist but well-drained, humusy soil of average to good fertility.	Small tree; ideal for small gardens.	Zones 5 to 7 or 8
Acer palmatum, Japanese maple	Rounded deciduous tree to 25 ft high, with lobed green or burgundy leaves, finely dissected in some varieties, that turn orange, yellow, or red in fall.	Full sun to light shade; moist but well-drained, humusy soil of average to good fertility.	Many cultivars available.	Zones 5–8
Actaea rubra, red baneberry	Clumping perennial to 1½ ft high, with compound, toothed leaves and, in spring to early summer, clusters of white flowers followed by spikes of red berries.	Partial to light shade; moist, cool, humusy soil of average fertility.	North American native.	Zones 3–8
Amelanchier arborea, downy serviceberry	Deciduous tree to 25 ft high, with oval leaves that turn yellow or red in fall, and, in spring, dangling clusters of fragrant white flowers, followed by purple fruits.	Full sun to partial shade; moist but well-drained soil of average to good fertility, with acid pH.	North American native.	Zones 4–9
Arctostaphylos uva-ursi, bearberry	Low, mat-forming shrub about 4 in. high, with small, rounded, leathery, dark green evergreen leaves; pink-tinged white flowers in spring; and red fruits in fall.	Full sun to partial shade; well-drained, sandy soil of average fertility, with acid pH.	Use as a groundcover.	Zones 3–7
Arisaema spp.	Perennials 1 to 3 ft high, depending on species, with oblong or lobed leaves and, in spring or summer, hooded spathe-and-spadix flowers.	Partial to light shade; moist but well-drained, humusy soil with acid to neutral pH.	Susceptible to slug damage.	Zones 4–9; varies with species
Asarum spp., wild gingers	Elegant, slow-spreading groundcovers with glossy green, heart-shaped leaves and hard-to-see, jug-shaped brownish flowers in spring.	Partial to full shade; humusy, moist but well-drained soil.	Slugs and snails love these plants.	Zones 4–9; varies with species
Athyrium filix-femina, lady fern	Deciduous fern to 3 ft high, with lacy fronds composed of divided leaflets.	Partial to full shade; moist, humusy soil of average to good fertility, with neutral to mildly acid pH.	Japanese painted fern (*A. nipponicum* 'Pictum') is another good choice; see "Plants for Woodland Gardens" on page 231.	Zones 3–8

PLANT	DESCRIPTION	GROWING CONDITIONS	COMMENTS	GROWING RANGE
Camellia japonica, Japanese camellia	Evergreen shrub to 20 ft, with glossy, deep green leaves and single or double flowers in pink, red, or white.	Partial shade; humusy, moist but well-drained soil with an acid pH.	Benefits from mulch.	Zones 7–8
Carex spp., sedges	Grasslike plants ranging from a few inches to several feet high, with narrow, pointed leaves, yellow, brownish, or striped with cream in some species and varieties, and slender, catkinlike brown flower spikes in spring or summer.	Sun to partial shade; soil needs vary with species—some prefer moist to wet soil, others need good drainage.	Many choices available.	Zones vary with species
Chamaecyparis obtusa, Hinoki cypress	Conical evergreen to 70 ft high, with flat sprays of scalelike deep green leaves. Many cultivars offer a range of sizes and foliage colors from golden to blue-green.	Full sun; moist but well-drained soil with mildly acid to neutral pH. *C. pisifera*, sawara cypress, is also recommended.	Variety of sizes, shapes, and colors available.	Zones 4–8
Chionanthus virginicus, fringe tree	Deciduous shrub or small tree to 12 ft high, with shiny, oval, dark green leaves and, in summer, drooping sprays of tiny white, fragrant flowers followed by small, dark fruits.	Full sun; moist but well-drained soil of good fertility, with mildly acid pH.	Native to the eastern United States.	Zones 4–9
Cryptomeria japonica, Japanese cedar	Pyramidal to cone-shaped evergreen tree to 60 ft high (some cultivars are smaller) with deep green, needlelike leaves and peeling reddish brown bark.	Full sun to partial shade; moist but well-drained, humusy soil of average to good fertility with acid pH. Tolerates a range of soils.	Needs shelter from strong winds.	Zones 5–9
Darmera peltata	Clumping perennial to 4 ft high, with large, rounded, lobed and toothed deep green leaves and, in late spring, round clusters of pink flowers atop tall stems.	Full sun to partial shade; moist to wet soil.	Northwest native. Grow near streams and ponds.	Zones 5–9
Disporum spp., fairy bells	Clumping perennials 1 to 3 ft high, depending on species, with oblong to lance-shaped leaves; clusters of drooping, bell-shaped flowers in spring; and orange or black berries in fall.	Partial to light shade; moist but well-drained, humusy soil of average fertility.	Subtle and charming.	Zones 4–9
Dryopteris filix-mas, male fern	Clumping deciduous fern to 3 ft high, with glossy, deep green fronds composed of divided leaflets.	Partial to light shade; moist but well-drained, humusy soil of average fertility, with acid pH.	Interesting cultivars available.	Zones 3–9

(continued)

PLANT	DESCRIPTION	GROWING CONDITIONS	COMMENTS	GROWING RANGE
Franklinia alatamaha, Franklin tree	Deciduous tree to 15 ft high, with oblong, glossy green leaves that turn red in fall, and fragrant, white, cup-shaped flowers in late summer.	Full sun; moist but well-drained, humusy soil with mildly acid to neutral pH.	Believed extinct in the wild; found only in cultivation.	Zones 6–9
Hakonechloa macra 'Aureola', hakone grass	Perennial grass about 1 ft high, with narrow, pointed, yellow leaves striped in green, and, in late summer, airy, light green flower clusters.	Full sun to partial shade; moist but well-drained, humusy soil of good fertility.	Glows in shady spots.	Zones 5–9
Hamamelis ×intermedia, witch hazel	Deciduous shrub to 12 ft high, with broadly oval leaves that turn yellow in fall, and, in winter, fragrant yellow, orange, or red flowers with narrow, ribbony petals.	Full sun to partial shade; moist but well-drained, humusy soil with acid to neutral pH.	One of the first harbingers of spring.	Zones 5–9
Hosta spp. and cvs., plantain lilies	Many varieties from a few inches to 3 ft high, with lance-shaped to rounded leaves in many shades of green and combinations of green, white, gold, and chartreuse; spikes of trumpet-shaped white to lavender flowers, some fragrant, in summer.	Partial to full shade; moist but well-drained, humusy, fertile soil.	Indispensable for shady gardens.	Zones 3–8
Ilex crenata, Japanese holly	Evergreen shrub to 10 ft high, with rounded, upright, spreading, or pyramidal form depending on cultivar; small, oval, glossy, deep green leaves; and small black fruits on female plants in fall.	Full sun to light shade; light, moist but well-drained soil with mildly acid pH.	Takes pruning and shearing well.	Zones 5–7
Ilex glabra, inkberry	Upright evergreen shrub to 8 ft high, with oblong, glossy, deep green leaves, and black fruits on female plants in fall and winter.	Full sun to light shade; moist soil with acid pH.	Durable and adaptable.	Zones 5–9
Ilex opaca, American holly	Upright evergreen shrub or tree to 40 ft high, with spiny-toothed, oval, glossy, dark green leaves, and red berries on female plants in fall.	Full sun to partial shade; light, moist but well-drained soil of good fertility, with acid pH.	Both male and female plants needed for berries.	Zones 5–9
Illicium floridanum, Florida anisetree	Aromatic evergreen shrub to 10 ft high, with narrow oval, glossy, deep green leaves and, in late spring, starlike purplish red flowers.	Partial to full shade; moist but well-drained, humusy soil with acid pH.	Native to the Southeast.	Zones 7–9
Iris ensata, Japanese iris	Perennial to 3 ft high, with narrow leaves and, in early summer, beardless, broad-petaled flowers in shades of purple, burgundy, and red-violet.	Full sun to partial shade; moist soil of good fertility, with acid pH.	Yellow flag (*I. pseudacorus*) and blue flag (*I. versicolor*) also grow well along pond edges.	Zones 5–8

PLANT	DESCRIPTION	GROWING CONDITIONS	COMMENTS	GROWING RANGE
Kalmia latifolia, mountain laurel	Evergreen shrub to 8 ft high, with glossy, deep green, oval leaves and, in early summer, clusters of small cup-shaped flowers in shades of rose, pink, or white.	Full sun to light shade; moist, humusy soil of good fertility, with acid pH.	Poisonous if eaten.	Zones 5–9
Mahonia aquifolium, Oregon grapeholly	Evergreen shrub to 6 ft high, with spiny, glossy green leaves similar to holly; yellow flowers in spring; and dark blue fruits in summer to fall.	Light to full shade; moist but well-drained, humusy soil with acid pH.	Does not tolerate hot sun and drying winds.	Zones 5–9
Malus cvs., crabapples	Deciduous trees 10 to 20 ft high, with oval leaves; clusters of white, pink, or red flowers, some fragrant, in spring; and small red or yellow fruits in summer.	Full sun; moist but well-drained soil of average fertility.	Many cultivars are available.	Zones 4–8; varies with cultivar
Ophiopogon japonicus, mondo grass	Perennial to 1 ft high, with narrow, grassy, arching dark green leaves and, in summer, short spikes of little bell-shaped white flowers.	Full sun to partial shade; moist but well-drained, humusy soil of average to good fertility, with mildly acid pH.	Farther north, grow *Liriope* instead.	Zones 7–10
Osmunda cinnamomea, cinnamon fern	Vase-shaped fern to 4 ft high, with glossy green fronds and deep green fertile fronds in the center that turn rich brown as they mature.	Partial to medium shade; moist, humusy soil with acid pH.	Elegant, tall fern for back of garden.	Zones 3–10
Phyllostachys spp., bamboos	Spreading bamboos to 20 or more ft high, with up-right, hollow, jointed stems and lance-shaped leaves.	Full sun to light shade; moist but well-drained, humusy soil or good all-purpose potting mix.	Best grown in large containers to prevent spreading.	Zones 6–10; varies with species
Pinus bungeana, lacebark pine	Evergreen tree to 50 ft, with stiff needles and smooth, peeling bark with patches of grayish green, mahogany, cream, and pale green.	Full sun; any well-drained soil.	Site where the bark can be seen.	Zones 4–8
Pinus contorta var. *contorta*, shore pine	Western evergreen tree to 30 ft high, with deep green needles, irregular trunk, and twisted branches.	Full sun; moist to wet soil.	Interesting gnarled form.	Zones 6–8
Pinus rigida 'Sherman Eddy', pitch pine	Compact evergreen tree to 15 ft high, with tufts of dark green needles and interestingly twisted trunk and branches.	Full sun; light, moist but well-drained, sandy soil with acid pH.	Tolerates poor soil and salt.	Zones 4–7
Platycodon grandiflorus, balloon flower	Clumping perennial with oval, bluish green leaves and, in mid- to late summer, clusters of balloon-shaped buds opening to bell-shaped violet to purple flowers.	Full sun to partial shade; moist but well-drained soil of average to good fertility.	Not well-suited to the Southeast.	Zones 3–8

(continued)

PLANT	DESCRIPTION	GROWING CONDITIONS	COMMENTS	GROWING RANGE
Prunus mume, Japanese apricot	Deciduous tree to 25 ft high, with toothed, oval leaves; fragrant, single or double, pink or white flowers in spring; and sour yellow fruit in summer.	Full sun; moist but well-drained soil of average to good fertility, with acid pH.	Attractive spreading form.	Zones 6–9
Prunus serrulata, *P. subhirtella*, flowering cherries	Deciduous trees 15 to 30 ft high, depending on cultivar, some weeping, with oval leaves; and single or double white or pink flowers in spring.	Full sun; moist but well-drained soil of average fertility.	Classic trees; numerous cultivars available.	Zones 5–8; varies with cultivar
Rhododendron spp. and cvs., azaleas	Deciduous or evergreen shrubs of varying size and hardiness, with small, oval leaves and, in spring, tubular to funnel- or bell-shaped flowers in shades of red, rose, pink, orange, yellow, and white, some fragrant.	Full sun to partial shade; moist but well-drained, humusy soil with acid pH.	Mulch to protect shallow roots.	Zones vary with species and cultivar
Rhododendron spp. and cvs., rhododendrons	Evergreen shrubs 2 to 20 ft high, with oblong, leathery, dark green leaves and, in spring, large clusters of lavender, pink, rose, red, yellow, or white flowers.	Partial to light shade in the North, medium to full shade in the South; moist but well-drained, humusy soil with acid pH.	Deer usually avoid them	Zones 4–9; varies with species and cultivar
Sciadopitys verticillata, Japanese umbrella pine	Cone-shaped evergreen tree to 70 ft high, with whorls of glossy, deep green needles and peeling reddish brown bark.	Partial shade; moist but well-drained soil of good fertility, with mildly acid to neutral pH.	Beautiful specimen tree.	Zones 5–9
Shibataea kumasasa	Clumping bamboo to 5 ft high, with slender canes and lance-shaped, deep green leaves.	Partial shade; moist but well-drained soil of average fertility.	Grow in containers to prevent spreading.	Zones 6–10
Sisyrinchium graminoides (*S. angustifolium*), blue-eyed grass	Clumping perennial to 1½ ft high, with narrow, grassy leaves and, in summer, violet flowers resembling tiny irises.	Full sun; well-drained soil of average fertility, with neutral to mildly alkaline pH.	Self-sows readily.	Zones 5–8
Spartina pectinata, cord grass	Perennial grass to 5 ft high, with slender, arching leaves that turn yellow in fall, and, in late summer, narrow, brownish flower spikes.	Full sun; moist but well-drained soil.	Spreads quickly to form clumps.	Zones 4–9
Thelypteris noveboracensis, New York fern	Deciduous fern to 2 ft high, with creeping rhizomes and upright bright green fronds with pairs of narrow leaflets, turning yellow in fall.	Full sun to light shade; moist, humusy soil of average fertility, with mildly acid to neutral pH.	Native to eastern North America.	Zones 3–8
Thuja spp., arborvitaes	Evergreen trees to 70 ft (size varies widely with cultivar), with thin, flat, scalelike leaves.	Full sun; moist but well-drained soil of average fertility.	Many cultivars available in a host of sizes and forms.	Zones 2–9; varies with species

Trees, Shrubs, and Vines

PLANT	DESCRIPTION	GROWING CONDITIONS	COMMENTS	GROWING RANGE
Acer griseum, paperbark maple	Deciduous tree growing slowly to 30 ft, with 3-lobed leaves turning bronze to orangey red in fall, and attractive, peeling bark.	Partial shade to sun; moist but well-drained, humusy soil.	Does not tolerate drought.	Zones 5–8
Acer palmatum, Japanese maple	Graceful deciduous tree to 25 ft high, with 5-part leaves of green or burgundy, finely cut in some varieties, with rich red fall color.	Partial to light shade; moist but well-drained, humusy soil.	Many cultivars available.	Zones 5–9
Aesculus parviflora, bottlebrush buckeye	Clumping deciduous shrub to 10 ft high, with compound leaves having 5 oval leaflets, turning yellow in fall, and, in summer, bottlebrush clusters of small white flowers.	Partial to light shade; moist but well-drained soil of average to good fertility.	Suffers in soggy soil.	Zones 5–9
Amelanchier arborea, downy serviceberry	Deciduous tree 15 to 25 ft high, with oval leaves turning red, yellow, and orange in fall; drooping clusters of fragrant white flowers in spring; and edible purple-black fruits in fall.	Partial to light shade or sun; moist but well-drained soil with acid pH.	North American native.	Zones 4–9
Calycanthus floridus, Carolina allspice	Bushy deciduous shrub to 9 ft high, with oval, dark grayish green leaves and sweet-scented reddish brown flowers.	Light shade to sun; moist but well-drained, humusy soil.	Unusual flowers release scent when crushed.	Zones 4–9
Camellia japonica, Japanese camellia	Broad-leaved evergreen shrub to 15 ft high, with glossy, deep green, oval leaves and large red, pink, or white flowers in late fall to early spring.	Partial shade; moist but well-drained, humusy soil with acid pH.	Classic in southeastern gardens; many cultivars available.	Zones 7–9
Clethra alnifolia, sweet pepperbush	Clumping deciduous shrub to 8 ft high, with toothed, oval leaves and, in late summer, slender spikes of fragrant white flowers.	Partial to medium shade; moist, humusy soil with acid pH.	Tolerates range of soil as long as it stays moist.	Zones 3–9
Cornus x*rutgersensis,* hybrid dogwood	Deciduous tree to 30 ft high, with oval leaves turning red to purplish in fall, and white or pink flowers in spring.	Partial to light shade or sun; moist but well-drained, humusy soil with acid pH.	Resists anthracnose. Mulch in summer to keep roots cool.	Zones 5–8
Corylopsis pauciflora, buttercup winterhazel	Deciduous shrub to 6 ft high, with broadly oval leaves, and fragrant yellow flowers in early spring.	Partial to light shade; moist but well-drained, humusy soil with acid pH.	Compact and free-blooming.	Zones 6–9

(continued)

Trees, Shrubs, and Vines—*Continued*

PLANT	DESCRIPTION	GROWING CONDITIONS	COMMENTS	GROWING RANGE
Gaultheria shallon, salal	Bushy, clumping shrub to 4 ft high, with broad, pointed, glossy deep green leaves and, in late spring to early summer, arching clusters of pinkish white flowers followed by purple fruits.	Partial shade; moist, humusy soil with acid to neutral pH.	Best in western gardens.	Zones 6–8
Halesia carolina, Carolina silverbell	Spreading tree or large shrub to 25 ft high, with oval leaves turning yellow in fall, preceded in late spring by drooping clusters of bell-shaped white flowers.	Partial shade to sun; moist but well-drained, humusy soil of good fertility, with acid to neutral pH.	Native to the Southeast.	Zones 5–8
Hamamelis x*intermedia*, hybrid witch hazel	Spreading, upright, deciduous shrub to 15 to 20 ft high, with broadly oval leaves turning yellow in fall, and fragrant, ribbony yellow, orange, or red flowers in late winter to early spring.	Medium to light shade or sun; moist but well-drained, humusy soil with mildly acid pH.	Among the earliest bloomers.	Zones 5–9
Hydrangea petiolaris, climbing hydrangea	Deciduous, clinging, woody vine to 50 ft high, with dark green, oval leaves; clusters of white lacecap flowers in summer; and peeling cinnamon brown bark.	Partial to light shade or sun; moist but well-drained, fertile, humusy soil.	Lovely climbing a tree trunk.	Zones 4–9
Hydrangea quercifolia, oakleaf hydrangea	Deciduous shrub to 6 ft high, with large, lobed leaves resembling oak leaves, turning purple-bronze in fall, and large conical white flower clusters in summer.	Partial shade or sun; moist but well-drained, humusy soil.	Mulch in summer to keep roots cool.	Zones 5–9
Ilex verticillata, winterberry	Deciduous, clumping shrub to 10 ft tall, with dark green, toothed, oval leaves and bright red fruits on female plants in fall and winter.	Partial shade to sun; moist, humusy soil with acid pH.	Need both male and female plants for the berries, which birds love.	Zones 3–9
Kalmia latifolia, mountain laurel	Evergreen shrub 6 to 15 ft high, with dark green, oval leaves and, in late spring, clusters of cup-shaped pink, rose, red, or white flowers.	Full shade to sun; moist but well-drained soil with acid pH.	Mulch in summer to keep roots cool.	Zones 5–9
Kerria japonica, Japanese kerria	Dense, arching, deciduous shrub to 8 ft high, with toothed, oval leaves and many bright golden yellow flowers in spring.	Partial to full shade; moist but well-drained soil of average fertility.	Bright shot of color in the shade.	Zones 4–9
Leucothoe fontanesiana, fetterbush	Evergreen shrub to 6 ft high, with glossy green, oval leaves turning purplish in winter, and drooping wands of small, white flowers in spring.	Partial to full shade; moist but well-drained soil with acid pH.	Does not tolerate drought or very windy locations.	Zones 4–8

PLANT	DESCRIPTION	GROWING CONDITIONS	COMMENTS	GROWING RANGE
Magnolia x*loebneri*, hybrid magnolia	Deciduous tree or large shrub to 30 ft high, with fragrant, star-shaped white flowers flushed with pink or purple in spring, and oblong leaves.	Partial shade to sun; moist but well-drained, humusy soil with acid pH.	One of the most beautiful magnolias.	Zones 5–9
Mahonia aquifolium, Oregon grapeholly	Evergreen shrub to 6 ft high, with spiny, glossy green leaves similar to holly; yellow flowers in spring; and dark blue fruits in summer to fall.	Light to full shade; moist but well-drained, humusy soil with acid pH.	Does not tolerate hot sun and drying winds.	Zones 5–9
Rhododendron catawbiense, catawba rhododendron	Evergreen shrub to 10 ft high, with oblong, leathery, dark green leaves and, in spring, large clusters of lavender, pink, rose, red, yellow, or white flowers.	Partial to light shade in the North, medium to full shade in the South; moist but well-drained, humusy soil with acid pH.	Native to eastern North America.	Zones 4–8
Stewartia pseudocamellia, Japanese stewartia	Deciduous tree to 70 ft high, with dark green oval leaves turning yellow, orange, and red in fall; cup-shaped white flowers in summer; and peeling gray and pink to reddish brown bark.	Partial to light shade or sun; moist but well-drained, humusy soil of average fertility, with acid to neutral pH.	Truly beautiful in all seasons.	Zones 5–8
Styrax japonicus, Japanese snowbell	Spreading deciduous tree to 30 ft high, with oval green leaves and, in late spring, dangling bell-shaped white flowers.	Partial shade or sun; moist but well-drained, humusy soil of good fertility, with acid to neutral pH.	Needs protection from strong winds.	Zones 6–8
Symphoricarpos albus var. *laevigatus*, snowberry	Bushy, clumping, deciduous shrub to 6 ft tall, with oval, dark green leaves; clusters of small pinkish white flowers in summer; and round white fruits in fall.	Medium shade to sun; tolerates a range of soils.	Forms a thicket over time.	Zones 3–7
Viburnum acerifolium, mapleleaf viburnum	Deciduous shrub to 6 ft high, with lobed leaves similar to maple leaves, and clusters of creamy white flowers in late spring, followed by purple-black fruit.	Medium shade to sun; moist but well-drained soil of average to good fertility, with mildly acid to mildly alkaline pH.	Good for naturalizing in very shady spots.	Zones 3–8

(*continued*)

Perennials

PLANT	DESCRIPTION	GROWING CONDITIONS	COMMENTS	GROWING RANGE
Actaea pachypoda, A. rubra, baneberries	Bushy perennials with compound leaves, and small spikes of little white flowers followed in summer by white or red berries that are poisonous.	Medium to full shade; moist but well-drained soil.	Mulch in summer to keep roots cool.	Zones 2–8
Adiantum pedatum, northern maidenhair	Perennial fern to 3 ft high, with oblong fronds composed of wing-shaped leaflets with notched edges.	Partial to full shade; moist, humusy soil with pH near neutral.	The southern maidenhair, *A. capillaris-veneris*, bears triangular fronds with light green, fan-shaped leaflets; Zones 6–9.	Zones 3–9
Aquilegia spp. and cvs., columbines	Graceful plants with a rosette of divided, scalloped leaves and, in spring or early summer, nodding, spurred flowers of blue, lavender, pink, red, yellow, salmon, white, or bicolors on thin stems.	Partial to light shade; well-drained, humusy soil of average to good fertility.	May self-sow.	Zones 3–9; varies with species
Arum italicum 'Pictum', Italian arum	Tuberous-rooted perennial to 1½ ft high, with arrow-shaped leaves patterned in white; yellow spathe-and-spadix flowers in spring; and an upright cluster of red berries in late summer.	Medium shade to sun; moist, humusy soil.	Excellent choice for late-season interest.	Zones 6–11
Aster divaricatus, white wood aster	Clumping perennial to 2 ft high, with oblong leaves on dark stems, and, from summer into fall, white daisy flowers with yellow centers.	Partial to light shade to sun; moist, humusy soil of good fertility.	Lights up a shady spot.	Zones 4–8
Astilbe xarendsii	Perennial 2 to 3 ft high, with a low clump of compound, fernlike leaves and, in spring or summer, feathery or fluffy plumes of tiny red, pink, or white flowers on thin, upright stems.	Partial to light shade; moist, humusy soil of good fertility.	Foliage is attractive all season.	Zones 4–8
Athyrium nipponicum 'Pictum', Japanese painted fern	Deciduous fern to 2 ft high, with triangular green fronds overlaid with shimmering silvery gray, with reddish veins.	Partial to light shade, full shade in the South; moist but well-drained, humusy soil with moderately acid to neutral pH.	Silvery fronds gleam in the shade.	Zones 4–8
Chrysogonum virginianum, green-and-gold	Mat-forming perennial 4 to 10 in. high, with rich green, oval leaves, evergreen in the South; and, in summer, 5-petaled bright gold flowers.	Medium shade to sun; moist but well-drained soil of average fertility.	Attractive as ground-cover or edging.	Zones 5–9

PLANT	DESCRIPTION	GROWING CONDITIONS	COMMENTS	GROWING RANGE
Dicentra eximia, fringed bleeding heart	Perennial 12 to 18 in. high, with a mound of finely cut leaves and, in late spring and much of summer, loose clusters of narrow, heart-shaped flowers of red, pink, or white.	Medium shade to full sun; moist but well-drained, humusy soil.	Does not tolerate soggy or very dry soil.	Zones 3–9
Epimedium grandiflorum, bishop's hat	Spreading perennial to 1 ft high, with heart-shaped, light green leaves and, in spring, drooping, spurred pink, yellow, white, or purple flowers.	Partial to light shade; moist but well-drained, humusy soil of good fertility.	Use as groundcover in woodland gardens.	Zones 5–8
Erythronium americanum, yellow trout lily	Bulbous perennial to 6 in. tall, with oblong leaves splotched with purplish brown and, in spring, yellow flowers with reflexed petals.	Partial to medium shade, with some sun in spring; moist but well-drained, humusy soil.	A western species, *E. revolutum*, has pink, yellow, or white flowers.	Zones 4–8
Galium odoratum, sweet woodruff	Spreading perennial groundcover to 1 ft high, with whorls of small, lightly scented, oblong leaves and, in late spring and early summer, starry white flowers.	Partial to light shade; moist, humusy soil of average fertility; adapts to a range of soils.	Attractive and free-spreading.	Zones 5–8
Helleborus cvs., hellebores	Evergreen perennials 1½ to 2 ft high, with toothed, oblong leaves and, in early spring, cup-shaped flowers of maroon, pink, pinkish white, or chartreuse.	Partial to medium shade; moist but well-drained, fertile soil with neutral to alkaline pH.	Very early blooming.	Zones 4–9
Heuchera americana, alumroot	Perennial with a mound of decorative, pointed-lobed leaves and, in late spring to early summer, sprays of tiny white flowers.	Partial to light shade; sandy, well-drained, humusy soil.	North American native; numerous cultivars available.	Zones 5–7
Hosta spp. and cvs., plantain lilies	Perennials ranging from a few inches to 3 ft high, with a clump of pointed to oval to rounded leaves in various shades of green, many with edging, stripes, or flushes of a contrasting green, creamy white, or yellow, some with puckered, quilted, or deeply veined leaves. In early to late summer, trumpet-shaped lavender or white flowers, some fragrant, bloom on upright stems.	Partial to full shade; moist but well-drained soil of average fertility.	Deer love them.	Zones 3–9
Matteucia struthiopteris, ostrich fern	Vase-shaped, clump-forming fern to 5 ft high, with tapered, upright, deciduous fronds.	Partial to full shade; moist, humusy soil with pH near neutral.	Spreads by rhizomes.	Zones 2–8

(continued)

Perennials—*Continued*

PLANT	DESCRIPTION	GROWING CONDITIONS	COMMENTS	GROWING RANGE
Osmunda cinnamomea, cinnamon fern	Vase-shaped fern to 4 ft high, with glossy green fronds and deep green fertile fronds in the center that turn rich brown as they mature.	Partial to medium shade; moist, humusy soil with acid pH.	Native to eastern North America.	Zones 3–10
Phlox divaricata, wild sweet william	Spreading, semi-evergreen perennial about 1 ft high, with a mat of oval leaves and, in spring, clusters of lavender-blue or white flowers.	Partial to light shade; moist but well-drained, humusy soil.	Grow this or the smaller *Phlox stolonifera* as groundcover in a woodland garden.	Zones 4–9
Polygonatum odoratum 'Variegatum', variegated Solomon's seal	Spreading perennial to 2 ft high, with a clump of upright, arching stems bearing white-edged oval leaves and, in late spring, dangling, white, tubular flowers.	Partial to full shade; moist but well-drained, humusy soil, but adapts to a range of soils.	Spreads freely; may become invasive in good conditions.	Zones 5–9
Polystichum acrostichoides, Christmas fern	Clump-forming, upright, evergreen fern to 3 ft high, with stiff, leathery green fronds with toothed leaflets.	Partial to full shade; moist but well-drained, humusy soil with acid pH.	The similar western sword fern, *P. munitum*, grows to 5 ft; Zones 5–9.	Zones 3–9
Primula japonica, Japanese primrose	Perennial to 1½ ft high, with rosette of oblong, scalloped leaves and, in spring, clusters of rosy purple, pink, or white flowers atop straight stems.	Partial shade; moist, humusy soil with mildly acid to neutral pH.	Polyanthus Group primrose is shorter, with longer leaves and larger flowers in many colors.	Zones 3–8
Smilacina racemosa, false Solomon's seal	Perennial to 2½ ft high, with a clump of upright or arching stems lined with oblong leaves, and, in spring, spikes of tiny white flowers followed by red berries.	Partial to full shade; moist but well-drained, humusy soil with mildly acid pH.	Western gardeners can grow the similar *S. racemosa* var. *amplexicaulis*.	Zones 3–8
Tiarella cordifolia, foamflower	Small, spreading perennial 6 to 12 inches high, evergreen in mild climates, with lobed leaves and, in late spring to early summer, airy wands of tiny white flowers.	Partial to full shade; moist, humusy soil with mildly acid pH.	Spreads but is not aggressive.	Zones 3–7
Tricyrtis hirta, toad lily	Perennial to 2½ ft high, with lance-shaped green leaves and, in fall, purple-splashed white flowers resembling small orchids.	Partial to full shade; moist but well-drained, humusy soil.	Good source of late-season color.	Zones 4–9
Vinca minor, periwinkle, myrtle	Trailing evergreen perennial groundcover with glossy, dark green, oblong leaves and, in early spring, 5-petaled lavender-blue flowers.	Partial to medium shade; adapts to practically any soil.	Carefree and attractive.	Zones 4–9

PLANT	DESCRIPTION	GROWING CONDITIONS	COMMENTS	GROWING RANGE
Achillea millefolium, yarrow	Finely divided gray-green leaves, flat-topped clusters of tiny white flowers in summer on mat-forming plants to 2 ft tall.	Full sun; well-drained soil of average fertility.	Cultivars available in various warm colors.	Zones 3–9
Asclepias incarnata, swamp milkweed	Perennial to 4 ft tall, with narrow, oblong leaves, clusters of purple-pink flowers midsummer to fall.	Full sun; moist soil; good near a stream or pond.	Attracts butterflies.	Zones 3–8
Asclepias tuberosa, butterfly weed	Perennial to 2 ft tall, with oblong leaves and clusters of small, bright orange flowers from midsummer to fall.	Full sun; well-drained soil. Drought tolerant.	Attracts butterflies. Slow to reappear in spring. Deadhead to promote rebloom.	Zones 4–9
Aster novae-angliae, New England aster	Branched plants 3 to 5 ft tall depending on variety, with narrow leaves and clusters of narrow-rayed, yellow-centered daisy flowers in shades of pink, rose, and purple in autumn.	Full sun to partial shade; reasonably moist, fertile soil.	Attracts butterflies.	Zones 4–8
Aster novi-belgii, New York aster	Branched perennial to 4 ft tall, with lance-shaped leaves and clusters of yellow-centered, narrow-rayed flowers in shades of pink, purple, red, and white in autumn.	Full sun to partial shade; moist, fertile soil.	American native; many cultivars available.	Zones 4–8
Aster oblongifolius, aromatic aster	Branched perennial to 1½ ft tall, covered with light purple, thin-petaled daisy flowers in fall.	Full sun to light shade; well-drained soil of average fertility.	Forms sizable clumps.	Zones 3–8
Boltonia asteroides	Tall, branched perennial to 6 ft high, with lance-shaped leaves and masses of thin-rayed, yellow-centered white flowers in late summer and fall.	Full sun to partial shade; rich, moist but well-drained soil.	Tall and weedy but lots of flowers.	Zones 4–9
Camassia cusickii, camass	Bulbous western wildflower to 4 ft tall, with sword-shaped leaves and with upright spikes of starry light blue flowers in spring.	Full sun to light shade; moist but well-drained, humusy soil.	*C. quamash* has white or light blue blossoms.	Zones 5–8
Centaurea cyanus, bachelor's button, cornflower	Self-sowing annual with lance-shaped leaves on upright stems 1 to 2 ft tall, with rich blue fringed-looking flowers in summer.	Full sun; well-drained soil of average fertility.	Good cut flower.	Hardy annual
Consolida ambigua, larkspur	Cool-weather annual with finely cut leaves and spikes of flowers in shades of purple, blue, pink, and white on upright plants.	Full sun; moist but well-drained soil.	Deadhead to extend bloom, or let self-sow. Excellent cut flower.	Hardy annual. Plant for spring flowers in cool climates, winter bloom in the South.

(continued)

PLANT	DESCRIPTION	GROWING CONDITIONS	COMMENTS	GROWING RANGE
Coreopsis lanceolata, tickseed	Perennial 2 ft high, with lance-shaped leaves and, from late spring to midsummer, golden yellow daisy flowers with jagged edges.	Full sun to partial shade; well-drained soil of average to good fertility.	Tolerates drought.	Zones 4–9
Cosmos bipinnatus	Upright, branched plant 2 to 3 ft high, with thread-like leaves and wide-petaled daisy flowers in shades of pink, red, and white all summer.	Full sun; well-drained soil of average fertility.	Deadhead to prolong bloom, but allow to self-sow late in season.	Annual
Echinacea purpurea, purple coneflower	Upright perennial 3 ft tall, with coarse oval leaves and, in midsummer to fall, purplish pink daisy flowers with drooping petals and domed orange centers.	Full sun to partial shade; well-drained, fertile soil.	Cut back stems as flowers fade to promote rebloom and prevent rampant self-sowing, but leave some late seedheads for birds to enjoy.	Zones 3–9
Eschscholzia californica, California poppy	Mat-forming annual or perennial to 1 ft tall, with finely cut bluish green leaves and cup-shaped orange flowers in late spring to summer.	Full sun, well-drained soil.	Self-sows. Very drought tolerant.	Zones 9–10; elsewhere grow as annual
Eupatorium maculatum, Joe Pye weed	Tall, clump-forming perennial to 7 ft high, with oval leaves and, in late summer to early fall, large, domed clusters of tiny purple-pink flowers on upright stems.	Full sun to partial shade; moist, fertile soil.	Statuesque plant for late-season interest.	Zones 3–9
Filipendula rubra, queen-of-the-prairie	Clump-forming perennial to 6 ft or more, with divided, toothed leaves and, in summer, plumy clusters of tiny deep pink flowers	Full sun to partial shade; moist or even boggy soil.	Don't deadhead; seedheads add late-season interest to garden.	Zones 3–9
Helenium autumnale, sneezeweed	Upright perennial to 5 ft tall, with oblong leaves and, in late summer, brown-centered yellow daisy flowers	Full sun; moist but well-drained, fertile soil.	May need staking. Deadhead to prolong bloom.	Zones 4–8
Heliopsis helianthoides subsp. *scabra*	Perennial to 3 ft high, with hairy oval leaves and yellow daisy flowers in midsummer to early fall.	Full sun; moist but well-drained, humusy soil.	North American native.	Zones 4–9
Koeleria macrantha, June grass	Clumping cool-season perennial grass to 1½ ft high, with slender, bluish green leaves and, in early to midsummer, narrow, upright, green flower spikes that dry to golden brown.	Full sun to partial shade; light, well-drained soil.	May go dormant in late summer.	Zones 4–9

PLANT	DESCRIPTION	GROWING CONDITIONS	COMMENTS	GROWING RANGE
Lagurus ovatus, hare's tail grass	Annual grass to 20 in. high, with narrow, arching leaves and softly hairy, oval, white to pale beige seedheads.	Full sun; light sandy soil of average fertility.	Nice in garden, and for cutting and drying.	Annual
Leucanthemum vulgare, oxeye daisy	European perennial naturalized here, with leathery dark green leaves and classic yellow-centered white daisy flowers in early to midsummer; to 2 ft high.	Full sun to partial shade; moist but well-drained, fertile soil.	Good cut flower.	Zones 3–8
Lilium canadense, meadow lily	Native bulb plant 3 to 5 ft high, with narrow leaves and graceful yellow trumpet flowers with slightly curved-back petals.	Full sun to partial shade; moist but well-drained, fertile soil.	Flowers face downward.	Zones 2–6
Lilium superbum, Turk's cap lily	Vigorous native to 5 or more ft tall, with whorls of lance-shaped leaves and, in late summer, branched clusters of maroon-spotted orange flowers with backswept petals.	Full sun to partial shade; moist soil with acid pH.	Late-blooming; spreads to form clumps.	Zones 4–7
Lobelia cardinalis, cardinal flower	Perennial to 3 ft high, with narrow oblong leaves and, in late summer to early fall, spikes of brilliant red, tubular flowers.	Sun or shade; moist to wet soil.	Self-sows readily. Do not mulch or allow leaves to cover plants in winter. Attracts hummingbirds.	Zones 3–9
Lupinus perennis, wild lupine	Upright perennial to 2 ft tall, with palmately lobed leaves and, in late spring to early summer, spikes of deep blue to purple pealike flowers.	Full sun; light, well-drained soil of average fertility.	Cannot tolerate heavy, wet soils.	Zones 4–9
Monarda didyma, beebalm	Clump-forming perennial to 3 ft tall, with soft oval leaves of grayish green, with a citrusy fragrance, and, in mid- to late summer, clusters of tubular red, pink, or purple flowers.	Full sun to partial shade; moist, rich, humusy soil.	Attracts hummingbirds and bees. Prone to mildew; needs good air circulation.	Zones 4–9
Oenothera fruticosa, sundrops	Upright perennial to 3 ft high, with oblong leaves and cup-shaped yellow flowers through much of the summer.	Full sun; well-drained soil of moderate fertility.	Day-blooming cousin of evening primrose.	Zones 4–8
Panicum virgatum, switch grass	Clump-forming perennial grass 4 to 7 ft tall, with slender, grayish green leaves and, in late summer to autumn, fine-textured arching clouds of tiny spikelets, aging to gold and then beige.	Full sun; moist but well-drained soil of average fertility.	Tolerates both wet and dry conditions.	Zones 5–9

(continued)

PLANT	DESCRIPTION	GROWING CONDITIONS	COMMENTS	GROWING RANGE
Papaver rhoeas, Flanders poppy	Cool-weather plant to 2½ ft high, with divided light green leaves and, in spring, rich red flowers with dark centers.	Full sun to partial shade; rich, well-drained soil.	Sow late fall in the South, early spring in the North. Direct-sow; does not transplant well.	Annual
Rudbeckia fulgida, black-eyed Susan	Branching perennial to 3 ft tall with oblong leaves and, in mid- to late summer, brown-centered orange-yellow daisy flowers.	Full sun; moist but well-drained soil of average fertility.	Self-sows and spreads.	Zones 4–9
Schizachyrium scoparium, little bluestem	Tufted, clump-forming perennial grass about 3 ft tall, with slender light green leaves that turn bronze to orangey red in fall, and slender, fluffy seedheads in late summer and fall.	Full sun; well-drained soil of average fertility.	Drought-tolerant. Self-sows and spreads.	Zones 4–10
Sisyrinchium graminoides, blue-eyed grass	Clump-forming perennial 1½ ft high, with narrow, grassy leaves and, in summer, deep blue flowers resembling small irises.	Full sun; well-drained soil of average fertility, with neutral to mildly alkaline pH.	Does not tolerate wet winter conditions.	Zones 5–8
Solidago odora, sweet goldenrod	Upright plant to 4 ft; oblong leaves, fragrant when crushed, pyramidal clusters of tiny, bright yellow flowers in late summer.	Full sun; average to good soil. Tolerates some drought.	Self-sows and spreads.	Zones 6–8
Solidago rigida, stiff goldenrod	Upright perennial to 5 ft high, with oval leaves and flat-topped clusters of yellow flowers somewhat larger than most other goldenrods.	Full sun; well-drained, average to poor soil.	Does poorly in shade or fertile soil. Tolerates both heat and cold when established.	Zones 3–9
Trifolium incarnatum, crimson clover	Bushy plant about 1 ft high, with 3-part leaves and, in spring, oblong red flowerheads.	Full sun; moist but well-drained soil with neutral pH; adapts to range of soils.	Very vigorous; may crowd out less aggressive flowers.	Annual
Vernonia noveboracensis, ironweed	Branching perennial to 6 ft high, with long, lance-shaped leaves and, from late summer to fall, loose, fluffy clusters of small, purple-pink or white flowers.	Full sun to partial shade; loose, light, moist soil of average to good fertility.	Deadhead often.	Zones 5–9

PLANT	DESCRIPTION	GROWING CONDITIONS	COMMENTS	GROWING RANGE
Andropogon gerardii, big bluestem	Perennial grass to 6 ft high, with clumps of arching blue-green leaves and, in autumn, clusters of little spikelets of deep reddish purple.	Full sun; light, well-drained soil, especially in winter.	Cut back to ground in early spring.	Zones 2–7
Bouteloua curtipendula, sideoats grama	Warm-season perennial grass to 2 ft high, with clumps of bluish green leaves and, in summer, wands of flat reddish spikelets.	Full sun; well-drained soil, especially in winter.	Tolerates drought, heat, and cold. Cut back to ground in early spring.	Zones 5–9
Callirhoe involucrata, wine cups	Sprawling taprooted perennial to 1 ft high, with lobed leaves and, in late spring and summer, cup-shaped wine-red flowers with white bases.	Full sun; well-drained soil, especially in winter.	Native to the Midwest.	Zones 4–8
Coreopsis tinctoria, Plains coreopsis	Upright plant to 3 ft tall, with oblong leaves and, in summer, bright yellow daisies with deep red base and central disk.	Full sun; well-drained soil of average fertility; adapts to range of conditions.	Vigorous and easy to grow. Nitrogen-rich soil hinders bloom.	Annual
Dalea (*Petalostemon*) *candida,* white prairie clover	Perennial to 2 ft high, with 3-part leaves and tight, conical spikes of white flowers in early summer.	Full sun to light shade; moist, humusy soil.	Adapts to a range of conditions and tolerates drought. Fixes nitrogen in soil, like all legumes.	Zones 3–9
Dalea (*Petalostemon*) *purpurea,* purple prairie clover	Perennial to 2 ft high, with narrow, fuzzy, gray-green leaves and, in summer, short, conical spikes of rosy purple flowers.	Full sun; moist but well-drained soil of average fertility.	Tolerates drought, attracts butterflies and bees.	Zones 3–9
Echinacea pallida, pale purple coneflower	Upright perennial to 4 ft tall, with lance-shaped leaves and, in summer, daisy flowers with orange-brown centers and drooping, pale rose rays.	Full sun to partial shade; humusy, well-drained soil of average to good fertility.	Tolerates drought.	Zones 4–8
Eryngium yuccifolium, rattlesnake master	Taprooted perennial with spiny-edged blue-green leaves and, in summer, clusters of whitish flowers surrounded by gray-green bracts.	Full sun; moist but well-drained, fertile soil.	Midwestern native.	Zones 4–8
Gaillardia pulchella, Indian blanket	Bushy plant to 1½ ft high, with oblong leaves and yellow-tipped red daisy flowers all summer.	Full sun; well-drained soil.	Adaptable and drought tolerant. Water occasionally to prolong bloom.	Annual
Geum triflorum, prairie smoke	Spreading perennial about 1 ft high, with fuzzy stems with 3 nodding, rosy pink flowers above a basal mat of divided grayish leaves in summer.	Full sun to partial shade; well-drained soil of average fertility.	Good groundcover.	Zones 1–8

(continued)

PLANT	DESCRIPTION	GROWING CONDITIONS	COMMENTS	GROWING RANGE
Helianthus salicifolius, willow-leaved sunflower	Upright perennial 4 or more ft high with narrow, bright green leaves and, in summer, yellow daisy flowers.	Full sun; well-drained soil of average to good fertility.	Good vertical accent; forms clumps.	Zones 5–9
Heliopsis helianthoides, oxeye sunflower	Upright perennial to 6 ft high, with oval to lance-shaped leaves and large-centered yellow daisy flowers from midsummer into fall.	Full sun; in moist but well-drained soil of average to good fertility.	American native; numerous cultivars available.	Zones 4–9
Koeleria macrantha, prairie June grass	Cool-season clumping grass to 1½ ft high, with narrow blue-green leaves and, in early summer, slender green flower spikes that turn golden brown as they dry.	Full sun; well-drained, sandy or rocky soil.	Tolerates light shade but not heavy, wet, or fertile soil. May go dormant in late summer.	Zones 4–9
Liatris pycnostachya, Kansas gayfeather	Upright perennial to 5 ft high, with narrow, grassy leaves and tall spikes of feathery bright purple flowers in late summer.	Full sun; moist but well-drained soil.	Plants may need staking to support heavy flower stems.	Zones 4–9
Liatris spicata, dense blazing star	Upright perennial to 5 ft high, with narrow, grassy leaves and tall spires of feathery pinkish purple flowers in late summer.	Full sun; moist but well-drained, humusy soil.	Plants often need staking to support heavy flower stems.	Zones 4–9
Melampodium leucanthum, blackfoot daisy	Small taprooted plant with mound of narrow, gray-green leaves and yellow-centered white daisy flowers all summer.	Full sun; in well-drained soil of average to poor fertility.	Self-sows. Will rot in soggy soil.	Zones 7–9
Panicum virgatum, switch grass	Clumping, upright, warm-season grass to 7 ft high, with slender leaves and, in late summer, airy, delicate flower panicles that turn golden in fall and dry to soft beige.	Full sun to light shade; moist soil of average to good fertility.	Tolerates a variety of soils and some drought when established.	Zones 5–9
Ratibida columnifera, Mexican hat	Upright perennial to 2½ ft high, with finely divided green leaves and, throughout summer, yellow or red daisy flowers with backswept petals and columnar green centers that turn brown.	Full sun to light shade; well-drained, humusy soil of neutral to mildly alkaline pH.	Drought resistant; tolerates heat and humidity. Sometimes grown as an annual.	Zones 3–8
Ratibida pinnata, gray-headed coneflower	Perennial 4 to 5 ft high, with divided leaves; yellow daisy flowers have drooping petals and ovoid reddish brown centers that turn gray in fall.	Full sun.	Drought resistant.	Zones 3–8
Rudbeckia amplexicaulis, clasping coneflower	Hardy plants to 2 ft tall, with toothed oblong leaves and golden daisy flowers with backswept petals and conical brown centers.	Full sun; moist but well-drained soil of average fertility.	Adapts to a range of soils. Self-sows and forms colonies.	Annual

PLANT	DESCRIPTION	GROWING CONDITIONS	COMMENTS	GROWING RANGE
Rudbeckia hirta, black-eyed Susan	Short-lived perennial often grown as an annual, to 1½ ft high, with oblong leaves and, in mid- to late summer into fall, orangey yellow daisy flowers with brown centers.	Full sun; moist but well-drained soil of average fertility.	Spreads readily; tolerates neglect.	Zones 4–7
Rudbeckia submentosa, sweet black-eyed Susan	Upright perennial to 1½ ft high, with oval gray-green leaves and, in fall, yellow daisy flowers with conical brown centers.	Full sun; moist but well-drained soil of average fertility.	Late blooming.	Zones 4–7
Silene armeria, catchfly	Upright plant to 2 ft high, with lance-shaped gray-green leaves, sticky stems, and clusters of deep rose-pink flowers all summer.	Full sun to partial shade; well-drained soil of average to good fertility, with neutral to mildly alkaline pH.	May self-sow.	Annual
Silphium laciniatum, compass plant	Taprooted perennial to 5 ft tall, with hairy, fernlike leaves and, in late summer to early fall, clusters of huge yellow daisy flowers on tall stems. Leaves and flowers face east.	Full sun to partial shade; moist, fertile soil with neutral to mildly alkaline pH.	Spreads readily.	Zones 4–8
Solidago rigida, stiff goldenrod	Clump-forming perennial to 5 ft high, with oval leaves and, in late summer, flat-topped clusters of small golden flowers.	Full sun; well-drained soil of average to poor fertility.	Self-sows.	Zones 3–9
Sorghastrum nutans, Indian grass	Clump-forming warm-season grass to 3 ft tall, with slender bluish green leaves and, in late summer, delicate, airy spikes of long-bristled brownish flowers. In fall, plants turn yellow, then brownish orange.	Full sun; moist, fertile soil.	Tolerates light shade, a variety of soils, and drought when established.	Zones 4–8
Spartina pectinata, prairie cord grass	Warm-season grass to 5 or 6 ft, with arching leaves and, in midsummer, arching, brownish flower spikes. Leaves turn rich gold in fall.	Full sun; moist but well-drained, fertile soil.	Tolerates drought once established. Spreads readily, especially in moist soil.	Zones 4–8
Sporobolus heterolepis, prairie dropseed	Clump-forming grass behaving like an early warm-season grass, to 3 ft tall, with thin, arching leaves and, in late summer, airy, fragrant flower panicles on drooping stems. Leaves turn yellow and orangey in fall, fading to creamy tan when dry.	Full sun; well-drained, rocky soil.	Tolerates heat, drought, and a range of conditions. Slow growing.	Zones 3–9
Veronicastrum virginicum, Culver's root	Upright perennial to 6 ft high, with toothed, lance-shaped, dark green leaves and, in late summer, slender spikes of white flowers.	Full sun to partial shade; moist, humusy soil of average fertility.	Tall midwestern native for back of garden.	Zones 3–8

PLANT	DESCRIPTION	GROWING CONDITIONS	COMMENTS	GROWING RANGE
Arabis caucasica, wall rock cress	Mat-forming evergreen perennial to 6 in. high, with a basal mound of oblong, grayish green leaves and, in the spring, clusters of fragrant white flowers atop upright stems.	Full sun; well-drained soil, especially in winter.	Nice draping over top of wall. Vigorous spreader.	Zones 4–8
Armeria maritima, sea thrift	Clumping perennial to 8 in. high, with narrow, grassy leaves and, in late spring to early summer, globe-shaped heads of small rose-pink flowers on stiff stems.	Full sun; well-drained soil of average to poor fertility.	Grow in scree bed, wall, or crevice.	Zones 3–9
Aubrieta ×cultorum (*A. deltoidea*), purple rock cress	Mat-forming perennial 2 to 6 in. high, with small, oval, grayish green leaves and, in spring, single or double flowers in shades of purple or rose-pink.	Full sun; well-drained soil of average fertility, with neutral to mildly alkaline pH.	Cut back lightly after bloom. Short-lived where summers are hot and humid.	Zones 5–7
Aurinia saxatilis, basket-of-gold	Mounding evergreen perennial 8 to 12 in. high, with grayish green leaves and, in late spring, clusters of tiny, bright yellow flowers.	Full sun; well-drained soil of average fertility.	Cut back lightly after blooming. Often self-sows.	Zones 4–8
Calluna vulgaris, Scotch heather	Small evergreen shrub to 2 ft high, with needlelike dark green leaves and spikes of tiny bell-shaped flowers in white or shades of pink or purple, in mid- to late summer or fall.	Full sun; humusy, well-drained soil with acid pH.	Mulch during winter. Best in cool climates.	Zones 4–7
Campanula carpatica, Carpathian harebell	Clumping perennial 6 to 12 in. high, with broadly oval to heart-shaped leaves and bell-shaped blue, purple, or white flowers through much of summer.	Full sun to partial shade; moist but well-drained soil of average fertility.	Grow in an alpine meadow.	Zones 4–7
Crocus tommasinianus, tommies	Small early bulb to 6 in. high, with slender cup-shaped silvery lavender to reddish purple flowers in late winter to early spring, followed by narrow, grassy leaves.	Full sun; well-drained soil of average to poor fertility.	Will naturalize and spread. Grow in alpine meadow.	Zones 3–8
Cyclamen coum	Tuberous-rooted perennial with rounded leaves, sometimes patterned with deep green or silver, and, in late winter or early spring, pink, purple-red, or white flowers with backswept petals.	Partial to light shade; well-drained, humusy soil of reasonable fertility.	Grow in woodland rock garden.	Zones 5–9
Daphne ×burkwoodii 'Carol Mackie'	Semi-evergreen shrub 3 to 4 ft high, with whorls of narrow, oblong green leaves edged in yellow to creamy white, and, in late spring, clusters of fragrant white flowers.	Full sun to partial shade; well-drained, humusy soil of reasonable fertility, with pH near neutral.	Grow in woodland rock garden. Poisonous if eaten.	Zones 5–8

PLANT	DESCRIPTION	GROWING CONDITIONS	COMMENTS	GROWING RANGE
Deutzia crenata var. *nakaiana* 'Nikko'	Bushy dwarf shrub 1 to 2 ft high, with lance-shaped leaves and, in spring to early summer, spikes of fragrant white flowers.	Full sun; well-drained soil of average fertility.	Leaves turn wine red in fall.	Zones 5–8
Dianthus deltoides, maiden pink	Mat-forming perennial to 8 in. high, with slender dark green leaves and, in summer, fringe-petaled flowers of deep pink, red, or white.	Full sun; well-drained soil of average fertility, with neutral to mildly alkaline pH.	Self-sows readily.	Zones 3–10
Dianthus gratianopolitanus, cheddar pink	Mat-forming perennial to 6 in. high, with narrow, grayish green leaves and, in summer, deliciously fragrant, dark pink flowers with toothed petals.	Full sun; well-drained soil of average fertility, with neutral to mildly alkaline pH.	Deadhead to prolong bloom. Grow in wall.	Zones 3–8
Euphorbia myrsinites, myrtle spurge	Evergreen perennial to 4 in. high, with small, broadly oval, bluish green leaves and, in spring, clusters of greenish yellow flowers at the stem tips.	Full sun; light, well-drained soil of average fertility.	Grow on outcrops or ledges.	Zones 5–8
Geranium dalmaticum, Dalmatian cranesbill	Usually evergreen perennial to 6 in. high, with divided, light green leaves and light pink flowers in summer.	Full sun to partial shade; well-drained, humusy soil of average fertility.	Grow in woodland rock garden.	Zones 5–7
Geranium sanguineum var. *striatum*, Lancaster geranium	Spreading perennial to 6 in. high, with 5- to 7-part leaves and, through much of summer, light pink flowers with darker pink veins.	Full sun to partial shade; well-drained, humusy soil of average fertility.	Grow in alpine meadow, scree bed, crevices, or wall.	Zones 4–8
Gypsophila repens, creeping baby's breath	Mat-forming perennial to 8 in. high, with narrow leaves and, in summer, loose clusters of small white or pink flowers.	Full sun; light, very well-drained soil with alkaline pH.	Grow in wall, crevices, or scree bed.	Zones 4–7
Hypericum olympicum, Olympic St. John's wort	Small shrub about 10 in. high, with oblong, grayish green leaves and clusters of golden yellow flowers in summer.	Full sun; very well-drained soil of average fertility.	Grow on ledge or outcrop, in scree bed, or in a wall.	Zones 6–8
Iris cristata, crested iris	Small iris just 4 to 6 in. high, with fans of sword-shaped leaves and, in spring, lavender-blue, violet, or white flowers with a white patch on each petal.	Full sun to partial shade; moist, humusy soil.	Grow in woodland rock garden.	Zones 4–8
Iris reticulata, netted iris	Small bulb plant to 6 in. high, with narrow leaves and, in late winter or early spring, purple, blue, or violet flowers.	Full sun; well-drained soil of average fertility, with neutral to alkaline pH.	Blooms very early; hardy and long-lived.	Zones 5–8

(continued)

PLANT	DESCRIPTION	GROWING CONDITIONS	COMMENTS	GROWING RANGE
Juniperus procumbens 'Nana', Japanese garden juniper	Mat-forming dwarf evergreen shrub about 1 ft high, with sprays of branches in layers, lined with bluish green, needlelike leaves in groups of 3.	Full sun to light shade; any well-drained soil.	Compact and adaptable.	Zones 5–9
Lewisia Cotyledon Hybrids	Clumping evergreen perennials 6 to 12 in. high, with rosettes of oblong green leaves and, in spring and summer, clusters of funnel-shaped flowers in shades of pink, rose-pink, apricot, orange, and some striped.	Partial to light shade; humusy, well-drained soil with acid pH.	Can't tolerate wet soil in winter. Grow in scree bed or crevices.	Zones 3–9
Narcissus bulbocodium, hoop petticoat daffodil	Small bulb plant to 6 in. tall, with slender leaves and, in spring, bright yellow flowers with a flared cup backed by pointed petals.	Full sun to partial shade; well-drained soil of average fertility with acid pH.	Grow on ledges and outcrops or in alpine meadow.	Zones 6–7
Paxistima canbyi, cliff green	Spreading shrub to 1½ ft high, with narrow, toothed, glossy dark green leaves and, in summer, drooping clusters of small white flowers.	Full sun to light shade; moist but well-drained, humusy soil.	Grow in woodland rock garden.	Zones 3–7
Petrorhagia saxifraga, tunic flower	Mat-forming perennial 6 to 10 in. high, with needle-like leaves and, in summer, clusters of small white or pink flowers.	Full sun; well-drained soil of average to poor fertility.	Shear back lightly in midsummer if plants look ratty.	Zones 5–7
Phlox subulata, moss pink	Mat-forming evergreen perennial to 6 in. high, with needlelike leaves and spring flowers in shades of pink, rose, lavender, and white.	Full sun; well-drained soil of average fertility.	Grow in scree bed or crevices.	Zones 3–8
Picea glauca 'Conica', dwarf Alberta spruce	Conical evergreen tree with bluish green needles, growing very slowly to 10 ft.	Full sun; moist but well-drained soil of average fertility, with acid to neutral pH.	Popular tree for rock gardens and containers.	Zones 3–6
Potentilla fruticosa 'Abbotswood', shrubby cinquefoil	Deciduous shrub about 2½ ft high, with dark green leaves divided into 5 to 7 oblong leaflets and white flowers in summer.	Full sun; well-drained soil of average to poor fertility.	Many other cultivars available.	Zones 3–7
Primula auricula, auricula primrose	Evergreen perennial 6 to 8 in. high, with a rosette of oblong leaves and, in spring, clusters of fragrant yellow flowers atop slender stems.	Full sun to partial shade; moist but well-drained, humusy soil.	Grow in woodland rock garden.	Zones 3–8
Rhododendron 'Purple Gem', *R. catawbiense* 'Compactum', *R. mucronulatum* 'Nana', dwarf rhododendrons	Evergreen shrubs 2 to 3 ft high, with oblong leaves and, in spring, clusters of purple or pink flowers.	Partial to light shade; moist but well-drained, humusy soil with acid pH.	Grow in woodland rock garden.	Zones 5–8

PLANT	DESCRIPTION	GROWING CONDITIONS	COMMENTS	GROWING RANGE
Saponaria ocymoides, rock soapwort	Mat-forming perennial about 4 in. high, with spoon-shaped leaves and, in late spring to summer, many clusters of purplish pink flowers.	Full sun; well-drained soil of average fertility with neutral to mildly alkaline pH.	Cut back after blooming to keep plants in bounds. Grow on ledges or outcrops, or let spill over a wall.	Zones 4–8
Saxifraga paniculata	Mat-forming perennial 6 in. high, with rosettes of oblong leaves and, in early summer, clusters of white, pale yellow, or pink flowers on slender stems.	Partial shade; moist but well-drained soil of average fertility.	Grow in crevices, walls, or scree beds.	Zones 1–6
Sedum acre, golden carpet sedum	Mat-forming evergreen perennial 2 in. high, with small triangular leaves and, in summer, many clusters of tiny yellow flowers.	Full sun; well-drained soil of average fertility, with neutral to mildly alkaline pH.	Drapes itself over rocks.	Zones 4–9
Sedum cauticola	Trailing perennial 3 in. high, with oblong to rounded leaves and, in late summer to early fall, clusters of purple-pink flowers.	Full sun; well-drained soil of average fertility, with neutral to mildly alkaline pH.	Attractive late bloomer.	Zones 5–9
Spiraea japonica 'Nana', dwarf Japanese spirea	Small deciduous shrub 1½ ft high, with small leaves and clusters of deep pink flowers in early summer.	Full sun to partial shade; moist but well-drained soil of average to good fertility.	'Goldmound' has yellow leaves; 'Limemound' has yellow-green leaves.	Zones 4–9
Syringa meyeri 'Palibin', dwarf Korean lilac	Deciduous shrub growing slowly to 4 to 5 ft tall, with oval leaves and clusters of fragrant lilac-pink flowers in late spring.	Full sun; well-drained, humusy soil of average fertility, with neutral to mildly alkaline pH.	Compact and hardy.	Zones 4–7
Thymus pseudolanuginosus, woolly thyme	Mat-forming perennial a few inches high, with tiny, oval, aromatic, hairy, gray-green leaves and, in summer, clusters of tiny pink flowers.	Full sun; well-drained soil of average fertility, with neutral to mildly alkaline pH.	Grow in walls or scree bed.	Zones 6–9
Thymus serpyllum, mother-of-thyme	Mat-forming perennial 6 to 10 in. high, with thin, trailing stems lined with tiny, oval, aromatic leaves and, in summer, clusters of little rosy purple flowers.	Full sun; well-drained soil of average fertility, with neutral to mildly alkaline pH.	Grow in walls, scree bed, or alpine meadow.	Zones 4–9

PLANTS FOR DESERT GARDENS

PLANT	DESCRIPTION	GROWING CONDITIONS	COMMENTS	GROWING RANGE
Abronia villosa, desert sand verbena	Trailing plant about 2 in. high, with small, oval leaves and round clusters of fragrant, purple-pink flowers in summer.	Full sun; well-drained, sandy soil of average fertility.	Southwestern native for front of garden.	Annual
Achillea spp., yarrows	Clump-forming perennials 2 to 3½ ft high, with fern-like grayish green leaves and, in summer, flat-topped clusters of tiny yellow, gold, pink, red, orange, or white flowers.	Full sun; well-drained soil of average fertility, with some moisture.	Many cultivars available.	Zones 3–9
Agave spp.	Succulent perennials with a rosette of sword-shaped leaves of varying heights and shades of green. Clusters of tubular flowers, mostly white or yellow, on tall stalks in summer.	Full sun; very well-drained soil of average fertility.	Native to the Southwest and Mexico.	Zones vary with species, but all need 40°F or higher.
Aloe spp.	Succulent perennials of varying sizes with a rosette of pointed, triangular to lance-shaped leaves with toothed edges, striped or spotted with white in some species. Spikes or clusters of red, orange, yellow, or white tubular to bell-shaped flowers in summer or fall.	Full sun; well-drained soil of average to good fertility.	Need temperatures above 50°F.	Zones 10–11
Antennaria dioica, pussytoes	Mat-forming perennial 2 in. high, with spoon-shaped leaves and, in summer, fuzzy clusters of small pink or white flowers.	Full sun to partial shade; well-drained soil of average fertility.	Flowers can be cut and dried.	Zones 5–9
Anthemis tinctoria, golden marguerite	Clump-forming perennial to 2½ ft high, with oblong, grayish green leaves and, in summer, many small yellow-centered white daisy flowers.	Full sun; well-drained soil of average fertility.	Cut back after blooming to promote rebloom and longer life.	Zones 3–7
Baileya multiradiata, desert marigold	Perennial to 1½ ft high, with hairy gray-green leaves, and yellow daisy flowers through much of summer.	Full sun; well-drained, sandy soil of average fertility.	Southwestern native; can't take humidity.	Zones 7–11; elsewhere grow as annual
Bougainvillea spp.	Evergreen vines to 15 ft or more, with oval green leaves and clusters of tiny flowers surrounded by colorful bracts in shades of red, pink, magenta, purple, orange, or white in summer to fall.	Full sun; well-drained soil of good fertility.	Breathtaking trained on a wall, fence, or arbor.	Zones 9–11
Cerastium tomentosum, snow-in-summer	Vigorous mat-forming perennial to 3 in. high, with narrow silver leaves and many clusters of starry white flowers in late spring and summer.	Full sun; well-drained soil of average to poor fertility.	Spreads readily and can be a pest.	Zones 3–7

PLANT	DESCRIPTION	GROWING CONDITIONS	COMMENTS	GROWING RANGE
Cercidium floridum, blue palo verde	Deciduous tree to 30 ft high, with bluish green leaves divided into pairs of tiny leaflets and, in spring, clusters of small yellow flowers.	Full sun; well-drained soil of average fertility.	Drought tolerant, but looks best with some water.	Zones 9–10
Cercis occidentalis, western redbud	Deciduous shrub or small tree to 15 ft high, with rounded bluish green leaves that turn yellow in fall, and, in spring, clusters of bright purplish pink flowers.	Full sun to light shade; well-drained soil of good fertility.	Water during first 2 years until established.	Zones 7–9
Chilopsis linearis, desert willow	Upright shrub or tree to 25 ft high, with slender leaves and clusters of trumpet-shaped flowers in white, pink, or lavender in spring and summer.	Full sun; well-drained soil of average fertility.	Southwestern native not suited to other places.	Zones 8–9
Delosperma cooperi, ice plant	Mat-forming perennial to 5 in. high, with succulent, oblong leaves, and pinkish purple daisy flowers all summer.	Full sun; very well-drained soil.	Very drought-tolerant groundcover.	Zones 7 or 8–10
Forestiera neomexicana, desert olive	Deciduous shrub to 8 ft high, with oval green leaves and small blue-black fruits.	Full sun; well-drained soil of average fertility.	Tolerates drought but grows faster if watered. Good screening plant.	Zones 8–10
Fouquiera splendens, ocotillo	Deciduous shrub to 25 ft high, with clump of upright, thorny stems; oblong leaves that drop after rainy season; and bright red flowers in spring or summer.	Full sun; very well-drained soil of average fertility.	Use as specimen, barrier, or screen.	Zones 8–10
Gaillardia spp., blanketflowers	Bushy perennials or annuals 1 to 2½ ft high, with oblong leaves and yellow or red daisy flowers with red centers.	Full sun; well-drained soil of average fertility.	Tolerates some drought. Deadhead regularly to prolong bloom.	Zones 3–8
Gomphrena globosa, globe amaranth	Upright annual to 2 ft high, with oblong leaves, and round to egg-shaped pink, purple, red, or white flowerheads all summer.	Full sun; well-drained soil of average fertility.	Good for cutting or drying.	Annual
Kniphofia uvaria, red-hot poker	Upright perennial with narrow, grassy leaves and, in early fall, spikes of tubular red-orange flowers that age to yellow.	Full sun to partial shade; moist but well-drained soil of average to good fertility.	Tolerates drought and heat.	Zones 6–9

(continued)

PLANT	DESCRIPTION	GROWING CONDITIONS	COMMENTS	GROWING RANGE
Lagerstroemia indica, crape myrtle	Large upright shrub to 25 ft high, with oblong, deep green leaves; smooth, peeling brown and gray bark; and, in late summer, large, conical clusters of pink, magenta, purple, red, or white flowers.	Full sun; well-drained soil of average fertility.	Many cultivars available.	Zones 7–9
Lampranthus spectabilis, trailing ice plant	Spreading perennial to 1 ft high, with succulent, narrow, grayish green leaves, and many pink, magenta, red, or purple flowers in spring or summer.	Full sun; very well-drained soil of average fertility.	Drought-tolerant groundcover.	Zones 8–10
Larrea tridentata, creosote bush	Upright shrub to 8 ft high, with glossy green, aromatic leaves divided into pairs of tiny leaflets; yellow flowers; and rounded, hairy fruit.	Full sun to light shade; moist but well-drained soil.	Grows taller and denser when watered and fertilized.	Zones 8–10
Lavandula angustifolia, English lavender	Small shrub 1 to 3 ft high, with narrow gray-green leaves and, in summer, wands of tiny, wonderfully fragrant purple flowers.	Full sun; well-drained soil of average fertility, with neutral to mildly alkaline pH.	Can be clipped and used as low hedge.	Zones 5–8
Leucophyllum frutescens, Texas ranger	Compact deciduous shrub to 8 ft high, with fuzzy silver leaves, and purple-pink flowers in summer.	Full sun; well-drained, sandy soil of average to poor fertility.	Tolerates heat and wind.	Zones 8–9
Mammillaria spp.	Group of round to columnar cacti in a range of sizes, covered with thin spines. Produce funnel-shaped pink, red, yellow, or white flowers in a ring around the top of the plant in spring or summer.	Full sun; very well-drained soil of average to poor fertility.	Many species; most form clumps of offsets.	Zones 9–10
Mimulus aurantiacus, bush monkey flower	Branching small shrub to 4 ft high, with sticky, oblong green leaves and, in late summer and fall, clusters of yellow or orange trumpet flowers.	Full sun; well-drained soil of average fertility.	Can be grown from seed.	Zones 7–10
Nerium oleander, oleander	Upright evergreen shrub to about 12 ft high, with glossy, deep green, lance-shaped leaves and, in summer, clusters of red, pink, salmon, or white flowers, some fragrant.	Full sun; adapts to many soils.	Tolerates heat and drought. Poisonous if eaten.	Zones 9–10
Phacelia campanularia, California bluebell	Upright plant to 1½ ft high, with dark green, oval leaves and clusters of bell-shaped, dark blue flowers in spring or summer.	Full sun; well-drained soil of average fertility.	California native.	Annual
Prosopis glandulosa, honey mesquite	Spreading deciduous tree to 25 ft high, with leaves divided into pairs of small oblong leaflets and, in spring, clusters of fragrant white flowers.	Full sun; very well-drained, sandy soil.	Attractive to bees.	Zones 10–11

PLANT	DESCRIPTION	GROWING CONDITIONS	COMMENTS	GROWING RANGE
Robinia hispida, rose acacia	Upright shrub to 8 ft high, with dark green leaves divided into pairs of oval leaflets and, in late spring to early summer, drooping clusters of rose-pink flowers.	Full sun; moist but well-drained soil of average fertility.	Tolerates poor soil and much drought when established.	Zones 6–10
Rosmarinus officinalis, rosemary	Dense, bushy shrub to 5 ft high, with aromatic, dark green, needlelike leaves, and clusters of light blue flowers in spring or summer.	Full sun; well-drained soil of average fertility.	Can be clipped for topiaries or hedges.	Zones 8–10
Salvia gregii, autumn sage	Bushy, woody perennial or small shrub to 3 ft high, with oblong leaves and spikes of 2-lipped cherry red, purple, or pink flowers in late summer and fall or winter.	Full sun; well-drained soil of average fertility.	Southwestern native.	Zones 7–9
Santolina chamaecyparissus, lavender cotton	Small shrub to 2 ft high, with slender, toothed, gray-green leaves and, in summer, yellow button flowers.	Full sun; well-drained soil of average fertility.	Can be clipped as a small hedge.	Zones 6–9
Sedum spathulifolium, Pacific or broadleaf stonecrop	Mat-forming perennial with rosettes of purplish-tinged, spoon-shaped, evergreen leaves and, in summer, clusters of small, bright yellow flowers.	Full sun to light shade; well-drained soil of average fertility, with neutral to mildly alkaline pH.	Native to western North America.	Zones 5–9
Teucrium chamaedrys, germander	Shrubby perennial to 1½ ft high, with oblong, toothed, dark green leaves and, in summer, loose spikes of small pink to purple flowers.	Full sun; well-drained soil with neutral to alkaline pH.	Can be clipped for a low hedge.	Zones 5–9
Yucca filamentosa, Adam's needle	Shrub forming clumps of stiff, sword-shaped leaves to 2½ ft high, with white threads along the edges, and, in summer, clusters of bell-shaped white flowers on tall stalks.	Full sun; any well-drained soil.	Grows well in eastern gardens.	Zones 5–10
Zauschneria californica, California fuchsia	Woody-based perennial to 2 ft high, with lance-shaped grayish green leaves and, in late summer and early fall, clusters of bright scarlet, tubular flowers.	Full sun; well-drained soil of average fertility.	Tolerates drought, attracts hummingbirds.	Zones 8–10
Zinnia grandiflora, desert zinnia	Perennial to 1 ft high, with narrow leaves and orange-centered yellow flowers all summer.	Full sun; well-drained, sandy soil of average fertility.	Tolerates heat, drought, and alkaline soil.	Zones 6–10

[Recommended Reading]

Books

Cullina, William. *The New England Wild Flower Society Guide to Growing and Propagating Wildflowers of the United States and Canada*. New York: Houghton Mifflin, 2000.

DiSabato-Aust, Tracy. *The Well-Designed Mixed Garden: Building Beds and Borders with Trees, Shrubs, Perennials, Annuals, and Bulbs*. Portland, OR: Timber Press, 2003.

Druse, Ken. *The Natural Habitat Garden*. Portland, OR: Timber Press, 2004

Gilmer, Maureen. *Gaining Ground: Dramatic Landscape Solutions for Reclaiming Lost Spaces*. New York: McGraw-Hill/Contemporary Books, 2000.

Gilmer, Maureen, and Michael Glassman. *Water Works: Creating a Splash in the Garden*. New York: McGraw-Hill/Contemporary Books, 2002

Hobhouse, Penelope. *Color in Your Garden*. Boston: Little, Brown and Company, 1985.

Johnson, Hugh. *The Principles of Gardening: The Practice of the Gardener's Art*. New York: Simon & Schuster, 1997.

Loewer, Peter. *The Evening Garden*. Portland, OR: Timber Press, 2002.

Van Sweden, James, and Thomas Christopher. *Architecture in the Garden*. New York: Random House, 2003.

Magazines

Fine Gardening
63 South Main Street, P.O. Box 5506
Newtown, CT 06470
(203) 426-8171
www.finegardening.com

Garden Design
460 North Orlando Avenue, Suite 200
Winter Park, FL 32789
(407) 628-4802
www.gardendesignmag.com

Horticulture
98 North Washington Street
Boston, MA 02114
(877) 860-9146 (United States and Canada only)
www.hortmag.com

[Resources]

Furnishings and Accessories

Outdoor furnishings are a big business, with a pretty staggering array of choices for homeowners. Many chain stores sell outdoor furniture and accessories, and there are many other sources. Investigate the products offered by companies such as Pier One Imports, Crate and Barrel, Restoration Hardware, Smith and Hawken, Target, and Home Depot, depending on your budget. The listings below will give you some other places to search for the perfect stuff to furnish your yard and patio, but the universe is vast. Go forth and explore it.

Allison Armour-Wilson
Baldhorns Park
Rusper, West Sussex RH12 4QU
England
+44 1293 871 575
www.allisonsgarden.com

Garden art and water features created by a sculptor in the United Kingdom

Brown Jordan International
1801 North Andrews Avenue
Pompano Beach, FL 33069
www.brownjordan.com

Designers, manufacturers, and marketers of fine outdoor furnishings under several brand names

Garden Accents
4 Union Hill Road
West Conshohocken, PA 19428
(800) 296-5525
www.garden-accent.com

Good selection of garden ornaments

Haddonstone (USA) Ltd.
www.haddonstone.com

Several locations in the United States:

- 201 Heller Place
  Bellmawr, NJ 08031
  (856) 931-7011

- 15591 Computer Lane
  Huntington Beach, CA 92649
  (714) 894-3500

- 32207 United Avenue
  Pueblo, CO 81001
  (719) 948-4554

Many kinds of containers, ornaments, architectural stonework, fountains, and lighting, in cast stone with three different-colored finishes

Hoover Fence Company
PO Box 563
5531 McClintocksburg Road
Newton Falls, OH 44444
(800) 355-2335
www.hooverfence.com

All sorts of fences and gates, plus the
necessary hardware

The Intimate Gardener
Chicago, IL 60613
(800) 240-2771; in Illinois only: (773) 472-7066
www.theintimategardener.com

Outdoor furniture, accessories, water features,
and gardening supplies

Plow & Hearth
PO Box 6000
Madison, VA 22727
(800) 494-7544
www.plowhearth.com

Furniture, accessories, and gardening
supplies

Laura Spector Rustic Design
786 Westport Turnpike
Fairfield, CT 06430
(203) 254-3952
www.lauraspectorrusticdesign.com

Fanciful furniture of twined bittersweet vines

Spirit Elements
6672 Gunpark Drive, #200
Boulder, CO 80301
(800) 511-1440
www.spiritelements.com

Furniture, structures, water features, and
accessories

Stone Manor Lighting
(800) 534-0544
www.stonemanorlighting.com

Outdoor light fixtures in a range of beautifully
crafted styles

Summer Classics
PO Box 390
7000 Highway 25
Montevallo, AL 35115
(205) 987-3100
www.summerclassics.com

Furnishings and accessories

Sunbrella
www.sunbrella.com

Weather-resistant fabrics for cushions, umbrellas,
and other outdoor furnishings

Trex Company
www.trex.com
(800) 289-8739 (800-BUY-TREX)

Decking boards made from recycled plastic

Walpole Woodworkers
Many locations in the eastern United States
(800) 343-6948
www.walpolewoodworkers.com

Structures, furniture, accessories, fencing,
and lighting

Seed Sources
for Meadows and Prairies

American Meadows
223 Avenue D, Suite 30
Williston, VT 05495
(802) 951-5812
www.americanmeadows.com

Lady Bird Johnson Wildflower Center
4801 La Crosse Avenue
Austin, TX 78739
(512) 292-4100
www.wildflower.org

Moon Mountain Wildflowers
PO Box 725
Carpinteria, CA 93013
(805) 684-2565

Prairie Moon Nursery
31837 Bur Oak Lane
Winona, MN 55987-9515
(866) 417-8156
www.prairiemoon.com

Prairie Nursery
PO Box 306
Westfield, WI 53964
(800) 476-9453 (800-GRO-WILD)
www.prairienursery.com

Clyde Robin Seed Co.
PO Box 2366
Castro Valley, CA 94546-0366
(510) 785-0425
www.clyderobin.com

Seed Savers Exchange
3076 North Winn Road
Decorah, IA 52101
(563) 382-5990
www.seedsavers.org

Wildseed Farms, Inc.
425 Wildflower Hills
PO Box 3000
Fredericksburg, TX 78624
(800) 848-0078
www.wildseedfarms.com

[Photo Credits]

Photo Locations

Both the author and principal photographer offer special thanks to the homeowners and designers listed below for allowing us to use photos of their gardens in this book.

Page ii Private garden, St. Helena, California; design by Elizabeth Tjader

Page ix Moss Garden, Mendocino, California; design by Gary Ratway

Page xii Jo Wunderlich—Dennis Stradford Garden, Bolinas, California

Page 2 (left) John Alexander Garden, Santa Barbara, California

Page 4 James Morton Garden, Savannah, Georgia

Page 5 Gennaro Prozzo Garden, Putney, Vermont; design by Gordon Hayward

Page 6 Terry Garden, Franklin, Tennessee

Page 10 Erica Shank Garden, Amagansett, New York

Page 12 (left) Joanne Woodle Garden, Peconic, New York

Page 17 Private Garden, Napa, California; design by Sabrina and Freeland Tanner

Page 19 Thomas Garden, Ketchum, Idaho

Page 20 Gennaro Prozzo Garden, Putney, Vermont; design by Gordon Hayward

Page 178 Cathy Fitzgerald Garden, Palo Alto, California

Page 181 Roger Raiche Garden, Berkeley, California

Page 182 (bottom) Craig Luna Garden, Riverdale, Georgia

Page 184 Marcia Donohue Garden, Berkeley, California

Page 185 Nancy Schibanoff Garden, Del Mar, California

Page 186 Bob Dash Garden, Sagaponack, New York

Page 187 (top) Virginia Bissell Garden, Birmingham, Alabama **(bottom)** Maud Siljestron Garden, Milwaukee, Wisconsin

Page 188 (right) Porter Carswell Garden, Savannah, Georgia

Page 190 (right) Garden Valley Center, Petaluma, California

Page 192 Diane and Johnathan Spieler Garden, Lafayette, California

Page 193 Nancy and Ray Retzlaff Garden, River Hills, Wisconsin

Page 196 Terry Garden, Franklin, Tennessee

Page 197 (right) Ryan Gainey Garden, Decatur, Georgia

Page 201 (bottom) Private Garden, Napa, California; design by Sabrina and Freeland Tanner

Page 202 (right) The late Orene Horton Garden, Columbia, South Carolina

Page 204 (left) Helie Robertson Garden, San Anselmo, California; vase by Gladding McBean

[Index]

Underscored page references indicate boxed text and tables. **Boldface references indicate photographs.**

A

Abelia, glossy, 128
Abelia ×grandiflora, 128
Abeliophyllum distichum, 60
Abronia villosa, 248
Acacia, rose, 251
Acanthus spinosus, 210
Accent colors of house, coordinating
 garden colors with, 73, 77, **77**
Acer campestre, 128
Acer griseum, 226, 231
Acer japonicum, 226
Acer palmatum, 226, 231
Achillea, 216, 248
Achillea millefolium, 237
Aconitum, 210
Acorus gramineus, 194
Actaea pachypoda, 234
Actaea rubra, 226, 234
Actinidia kolomikta, 160
Adam's needle, 251
Adiantum capillusveneris, **38**
Adiantum pedatum, 234
Adirondack chairs, 173–74, **173**
Adobe homes
 informal gardens for, 19, 21
 naturalistic gardens for, 35
Aesculus parviflora, 231
Agapanthus africanus, 210
Agave, 248
Ageratum houstonianum, 210
Ajuga, **98**

Ajuga reptans, 99
Alcea rosea, 221
Alchemilla alpina, 99
Alchemilla mollis, 210
Allamanda cathartica, 22, 117, 210
Allium, 210
Allspice, Carolina, 231
All-white garden
 greenery with, 80
 plants for, 60
Aloe, **49**, 248
Alpine meadow, 44–45, 48, 49
Alternanthera ficoidea, 210
Aluminum outdoor furniture, 169, **172**
Alumroot, 212, 235
Alyssum, sweet, 60
Amaranth, globe, 249
Amaranthus caudatus, 221
Amaranthus tricolor, 221
Amelanchier arborea, 226, 231
Analogous colors, 62, 62, **62**
Andropogon gerardii, 40, 241
Anemone, Japanese, 60, 216
Anemone blanda, 60
Anemone ×hybrida, 60, 216
Angelonia angustifolia, 210
Anisetree, Florida, 228
Annuals, color palettes for, 66, 67–68,
 69, 70–71, 71–72
Antennaria dioica, 99, 248
Anthemis tinctoria, 248
Antigonon leptopus, 160
Antirrhinum majus, 60, 221
Apricot, Japanese, 230

Aquilegia, 60, 221, 234
Arabis caucasica, 244
Arbors
 for decks, 144, 148
 for desert gardens, 51
 location of, 156, **156**
 paint color for, 159
 for patios, 133
 plants for, 159, 160–61, 162
 near shed, 165
 structure styles of, 156, 157–58, **158**
 uses for, 131, 152, 154–55, **155**, **157**
Arborvitae, 230
 American, 127
Arches
 location of, 156, **157**
 paint color for, 159
 plants for, 159, 160–61, 162
 structure style of, 156, 157
 uses for, 154–55, **155**
Arctostaphylos uva-ursi, 226
Argyranthemum frutescens, 60
Arisaema, 226
Aristolochia durior, 160
Aristolochia elegans, 160
Armchairs, outdoor, 173–74
Armeria maritima, 244
Arrowhead, 195
Artemisia, 216
Artisan wood houses, informal gardens
 for, 21
Arts and Crafts houses, colors for, 73
Arum, Italian, 234
Arum italicum, 234

Aruncus dioicus, 216
Asarum, 210, 226
Asclepias incarnata, 237
Asclepias tuberosa, 237
Aster, 60
 aromatic, 237
 in informal gardens, 27
 New England, 237
 New York, 237
 white wood, 234
Aster divaricatus, 234
Aster novae-angliae, 216, 237
Aster novi-belgii, 216, 237
Aster oblongifolius, 237
Astilbe, 27, 60, 216
Astilbe ×arendsii, 234
Athyrium filix-femina, 226
Athyrium nipponicum, 234
Aubrieta ×cultorum, **108**, 244
Aubrieta deltoidea, 244
Aurinia saxatilis, **48**, 244
Awnings, 133, 144, 152
Axes, in formal gardens, 9, 11, **11**
Azalea, 33, 60, 230

B

Baby's breath, 27, 60, 217
 creeping, 245
Baby's tears, 100
Bachelor's button, 221, 237
Background lighting, as lighting
 technique, 198

Baileya multiradiata, <u>248</u>
Balance
    in formal gardens, 9, 12, **12**, **13**
    in Japanese-style gardens, 31
Balloon flower, <u>214</u>, <u>229</u>
Bamboo, <u>229</u>
    containing, <u>31</u>
    in Japanese-style gardens, 34
Baneberry, <u>234</u>
    red, <u>226</u>
Barberry, **75**, 126
    Mentor, <u>128</u>
Bars, outdoor, 177
Bases, umbrella, 176
Basket-of-gold, **48**, <u>244</u>
Bearberry, <u>226</u>
Bear's breech, <u>210</u>
Beds (flower)
    balanced, in formal gardens, 12, **12**, **13**
    circular, in formal gardens, 6, 11
    curved, in informal gardens, 20, 22
    around decks, 149
    geometric, in formal gardens, 11, **11**, **13**
    laying out, in informal gardens, 5, **5**,
        20, 23–24
    around patio, 134
Beds, outdoor (furniture), 183–84
Beebalm, <u>219</u>, <u>239</u>
Begonia, wax, <u>211</u>
Begonia semperflorens, <u>211</u>
Beige houses, garden colors for, 80, <u>80</u>, **80**
Bellflowers, <u>211</u>
Benches
    deck, 147, **147**
    garden, 181
        metal, 183
        stone, **181**, 182–83
        wooden, 181–82, **182**
Bengal clock vine, <u>118</u>
Berberis, 126
Berberis ×*mentorensis*, <u>128</u>
Berberis thunbergii, **75**
Bergenia, <u>211</u>
    heartleaf, <u>211</u>
Birdbaths, **185**

Bishop's hat, <u>217</u>, <u>235</u>
Bistro chairs, 173, **180**
Bistro table, **180**
Black-eyed Susan, <u>220</u>, <u>240</u>, <u>243</u>
    in informal gardens, 27
    in meadow gardens, **34**
    sweet, <u>243</u>
Black-eyed Susan vine, <u>118</u>
Blanketflower, <u>249</u>
Blazing star, dense, <u>242</u>
Bleeding heart, 27, <u>222</u>
    fringed, <u>235</u>
Blue
    houses, garden colors for, 84, <u>84</u>, **84**
    plants, <u>70</u>
    qualities of, 25, 56, **56**
Bluebell, California, <u>250</u>
Bluestem
    big, 40, <u>241</u>
    little, <u>240</u>
Bluestone flags, for patios, 139, **139**
Board-on-board fences, **112**, 114–15, **114**,
Boltonia, <u>60</u>
Boltonia asteroides, <u>60</u>, <u>237</u>
Borders
    in formal gardens, 11
    in informal gardens, 22, 23–24
    in modified formal gardens, 18–19
Bougainvillea, **121**, <u>160</u>, <u>248</u>
Boulders
    in Japanese-style gardens, 31
    placement of, **187**
    in rock gardens, 45
Bouteloua curtipendula, 40, <u>241</u>
Bowls, 203, **203**
Boxes, 203, **203**
Boxwood, <u>127</u>, <u>211</u>
    in formal garden, **7**, 12, 16
    Korean, **4**
Brass buttons, New Zealand, <u>99</u>
Brick
    edging, for paths, 98
    paths, 90, 91–92, **91**, **92**
    patios, 137, 139, **140**
    walls, 105–6, **105**

Bridal wreath, <u>128</u>
Bridges, in Japanese-style gardens, 31,
    32
British country gardens, modified
    formal style in, 18
Brown, Lancelot "Capability," 6
Brown houses, garden colors for, 81,
    <u>81</u>, **81**
Bruxus microphylla var. *koreana*, **4**
Buchloe dactyloides, 40
Buckeye, bottlebrush, <u>231</u>
Bugbane, <u>60</u>
Bugleweed, <u>99</u>
Bulbs, color palettes for, <u>66</u>, <u>67–68</u>, <u>69</u>,
    <u>70–71</u>, <u>71–72</u>
Bungalows
    colors for, <u>73</u>
    informal gardens for, 19, <u>21</u>, **21**
    integrating landscape elements with,
        <u>153</u>
Burning bush, <u>128</u>
Butterfly flower, <u>217</u>
Butterfly weed, <u>237</u>
Buxus, <u>211</u>
Buxus sempervirens, <u>127</u>

C

Cabins, naturalistic gardens for, 35
Cacti, for desert gardens, 51
Calamagrostis ×*acutiflora*, <u>216</u>
Calendula officinalis, <u>221</u>
Calico flower, <u>160</u>
Callirhoe involucrata, <u>241</u>
Calluna vulgaris, <u>244</u>
Calocedrus decurrens, <u>129</u>
Calycanthus floridus, <u>231</u>
Camass, <u>237</u>
Camassia cusickii, <u>237</u>
Camellia, <u>211</u>
    Japanese, <u>227</u>, <u>231</u>
Camellia japonica, <u>227</u>, <u>231</u>
Campanula, <u>211</u>
Campanula carpatica, <u>244</u>

Campanula medium, <u>221</u>
Campsis radicans, <u>22</u>, <u>160</u>
Canary creeper, <u>118</u>, <u>161</u>
Candlelight, **197**, 198, <u>199</u>
Candytuft, perennial, <u>60</u>
Canna, Longwood water, <u>194</u>
Canna Longwood Hybrids, <u>194</u>
Canopy, in woodland garden, 35
Canterbury bells, <u>221</u>
Cardinal climber, <u>117</u>
Cardinal flower, <u>194</u>, <u>239</u>
Cardiospermum halicacabum, <u>117</u>
Carex, <u>194</u>, <u>227</u>
Carex siderosticha, **33**
Carpinus betulus, <u>128</u>
Catchfly, <u>243</u>
Catmint, <u>219</u>
Cattail, dwarf, <u>195</u>
Cedar (plant)
    incense, <u>129</u>
    Japanese, <u>227</u>
Cedar (wood)
    as deck material, 148
    for outdoor furniture, 170
Centaurea cyanus, <u>221</u>, <u>237</u>
Centranthus ruber, <u>221</u>
Cephalotaxus fortunei, <u>127</u>
Cerastium tomentosum, <u>99</u>, <u>248</u>
Cercidium floridum, <u>249</u>
Cercis occidentalis, <u>249</u>
Chaenomeles speciosa, 126
Chain-link fencing, 116
Chairs, outdoor, 173
    armchairs and side chairs, 173–74
    cushions and pillows for, 173, 175
    dining chairs, 173
    hanging chairs, 183
    lounge chairs, 174, **174**
    sling chairs, 174, 183
Chamaecyparis nootkanensis,
    <u>129</u>
Chamaecyparis obtusa, <u>227</u>
Chamaemelum nobile, <u>99</u>
Chamomile, Roman, <u>99</u>
Channels, 191–92, **192**

Cherries
  flowering, 60, 230
  Japanese, 34
Chilopsis linearis, 249
Chiminea, for outdoor heating, 178
Chionanthus virginicus, 227
Chrysanthemum, 60
Chrysogonum virginianum, 99, 234
Cimicifuga, 60
Cimicifuga racemosa, 216
Cinquefoil, shrubby, 246
Circular beds, in formal gardens, 6, 11
Citrus pot, 203
Clematis, 60, **110**, 117, 160, 211
  sweet autumn, 60
Clematis terniflora, 60
Cleome hassleriana, 222
Clethra alnifolia, 128, 231
Cliff green, 246
Climbing roses, 118, **122**, 161, 162
Clover
  crimson, 240
  purple prairie, 241
  white prairie, 241
Cobaea scandens, 117, 160
Cohosh, black, 216
Coleus, 216
Colocasia esculenta, 194
Colonial-style houses
  colors for, 73
  formal gardens for, 7, 8
  integrating landscape elements with, 153
Color(s)
  for architectural styles, 73
  from foliage, 59, **59**
  garden
    for blue houses, 84, 84, **84**
    for brown houses, 81, 81, **81**
    coordinating, with house color, 73–77
    for gray houses, 78, 78, **78**
    for green houses, 82, 82, **82**
    personal responses to, 54–55
    for red houses, 83, 83, **83**

for taupe and tan houses, 79, 79, **79**
uses for, 53–54
for white, off-white, and beige houses, 80, 80, **80**
for yellow houses, 85, 85, **85**
psychological qualities of, 56–57, **56**, **57**
visual qualities of, 55–56
Color palettes for plants
  blues, 70
  oranges, 68
  pinks, 67–68
  purples, 70–71
  reds, 66
  violets, 70
  whites, 71–73
  yellows, 69
Color schemes
  contrasting, **63**, 64–65, 64
  in formal gardens, 15
  harmonious, 62, 62, **62**
  in informal gardens, 25, **25**
  in modified formal gardens, 18–19
  monochromatic, 58, **58**, 60
  polychromatic, 65, **65**
Color wheel, 58, **58**
Columbine, 60, 221, 234
Columns
  garden, 186, **187**
  porch, 154
Compass plant, 243
Concrete
  block and stucco, for walls, 107–8
  containers, 205
    faux, 206
  for edging paths, 98
  pavers, for paths, 90, 94, **94**
  poured
    for paths, 94
    for patios, 137–38, **138**
  wall blocks, 108–9
Coneflower
  clasping, 242
  gray-headed, 242

in meadow and prairie gardens, **34**, **41**
  pale purple, 241
  purple, 217, 238
Consolida ajacis, 211, 222
Consolida ambigua, 237
Container plants
  deck, 149–50, **149**, **150**, 150
  in Japanese-style garden, 29
  porch, 154
  shade, 151
Containers
  choosing, 206, 208
  decorating uses for, 201–3, **201**, **202**, **203**
  faux materials for, 206
  for formal gardens, 16, **17**, 206
  for informal gardens, 206, 208
  kinds of, 203–5, **203**, **204**
  materials for, 205–6
  planting in, 207, 208
Contemporary houses
  colors for, 73
  formal gardens for, 8
  integrating landscape elements with, 153
  naturalistic gardens for, 34
Contour lighting, as lighting technique, 198
Contrasting color schemes, **63**, 64–65, 64
Convallaria majalis, 60, 222
Convertible furniture, outdoor, 174
Cooking systems, outdoor, 176
Cool colors, effects of, 25
Coralbells, 212
Coral vine, 160
Coreopsis
  in informal gardens, **5**, **27**
  plains, 241
Coreopsis grandiflora, 217
Coreopsis lanceolata, 238
Coreopsis tinctoria, 241
Coreopsis verticillata, 217
Cornflower, 237
Cornus ×rutgersensis, 231

Corylopsis pauciflora, 231
Cosmos, 217, 222
Cosmos bipinnatus, 238
Cotoneaster multiflorus, 128
Cottage gardens, 27, 28
  plants for, 221–25
Cottages
  informal gardens for, 19, 21
  integrating landscape elements with, 153
Cotton, lavender, 214, 251
Cotula (Leptinella) squalida, 99
Country gardens, modified formal style in, 18
Country settings, influencing garden style, 4–6
Crabapples, 60, 229
Craftsman homes, informal gardens for, 21
Cranesbill, 217
  Dalmatian, 245
Crataegus, 126
Creeping Jenny, 100
  golden, 195
Creosote bush, 250
Crevices
  plants for, 46, 49
  as rock gardens, 45
Crimson glory vine, 161
Crocus tommasinianus, 244
Crown imperial, 222
Crushed stone, for paths, 94, 96
Cryptomeria japonica, 227
Culver's root, 243
Cup-and-saucer vine, 117, 160
Curves, in informal gardens, 5, **5**, 20, 22
Cushions, chair, 173, 175
Cyclamen coum, 244
Cymbalaria muralis, 99
Cyperus alternifolius, 194
×*Cypressocyparis leylandii,* 127
Cypress (plant)
  Hinoki, 227
  Leyland, 127
  Nootka false, 129

Cypress (wood), as deck material, 148
Cypress vine, 117, 161

D

Daffodil, 219, 224
  hoop petticoat, 246
Dahlia, 60, 211
Daisy
  blackfoot, 242
  oxeye, 239
  Shasta, 60, 213
Dalea (Petalostemon) candida, 241
Dalea (Petalostemon) purpurea, 241
Dame's rocket, 223
Daphne ×burkwoodii, 244
Darmera peltata, 227
Daylily, 60, 218
Deciduous plants, for hedge or plant
  screen, 125
Deck(s)
  features and accessories
    benches, 147, **147**
    fireproofing, 148
    hot tub, 148
    lighting, 197–99
    planter boxes, 147
    window boxes, 147
  function of, 131, 143, **144**
  furnishings
    choosing materials for, 169–71
    choosing types of, 171, 173–75
    cleaning, 176
    cushions and fabrics, 175–76, **175**
    heaters, 177–79, **178**
    kitchen and service pieces, 176–77
    planning for, 168–69
    umbrella, 176
  hanging basket plants for, 150
  integrating, with house and
    landscape, 146
  landscaping for, 144, **144**, 149–51
  locations of, 143–44
  materials for, 148–49

multilevel, 145
planning, 144–45
railings on, 146, 147
screening, for shade and privacy, 144,
  152
second-story, 145
shapes of, 145
shelter for, 144, **144**
size of, 145
stair risers on, 146, 147
steps on, 147
surface patterns of, 145, **146**
window box plants for, 148
Decorating, outdoor
  with containers, 201–8
  with deck and patio furnishings,
    168–79
  with lawn and garden furnishings,
    179–84
  with lighting, 196–200
  principles of, 167–68
  with statuary and ornaments, 184–86
  with water features, 187–95
Deer, in desert gardens, 51
Deer fencing, 119
Delosperma cooperi, 249
Delphinium, 16, 211
Dendrathema, 60
Desert gardens, 2
  characteristics of, 49, 50, 51
  design tips for, 51
  planting and maintenance tips for, 51
  plants for, 51, 248–51
  river of stone in, 101
Deutzia crenata var. *nakaiana*, 48, 245
Diagonals, in informal gardens, 20
Dianthus, 60, 212
Dianthus barbatus, 222
Dianthus chinensis, 217
Dianthus deltoides, 245
Dianthus gratianopolitanus, 245
Dicentra eximia, 235
Dicentra spectabilis, 27, 222
Dichondra micrantha, 99
Dictamnus albus, 212

Digitalis purpurea, 222
Dining chairs, 173
Dining tables, 168, 171
Disporum, 227
Dogwood, hybrid, 231
Dolichos lablab, 117
Doors, directing attention to, 185
Downlighting, as lighting technique,
  198, 199, **200**
Dragonhead, false, 214
Drainage, in desert gardens, 51
Drifts, in informal gardens, 20, 24,
  24
Driveway
  color of, 77
  lighting for, 196–97
  screening, 77
Dropseed, prairie, 243
Dry-laid stone walls, 106–7, **107**
  planting pockets in, 108, **108**
  plants for, 46
  as rock gardens, 45
Dryopteris filix-mas, 227
Dutchman's pipe, 160

E

Echinacea, **34**
Echinacea pallida, 241
Echinacea purpurea, 41, 217, 238
Echinops ritro, 217
Edgings, for paths, 98, 101
Elephant's ear, 194
Ephemerals, in woodland garden, 2
Epimedium grandiflorum, 217, 235
Equisetum hyemale, 194
Eryngium yuccifolium, 241
Erysimum cheiri, **108**
Erythronium americanum, 235
Eschscholzia californica, 238
Euonymous alatus, 128
Euonymus fortunei, 99
Eupatorium maculatum, 43, 238
Euphorbia myrsinites, 245

Evergreen(s)
  foliage, effects of, 59
  for hedge or plant screen, 125
  in Japanese-style gardens, 33–34

F

Fabrics, for outdoor use, 175–76
Fairy bells, 227
Fallopia aubertii, 117, 160
Farmhouses
  informal gardens for, 19, 21
  naturalistic gardens for, 35
Faux materials, for containers, 206
Federal-style houses
  colors for, 73
  formal gardens for, 7, 8
  integrating landscape elements with,
    153
Feijoa sellowiana, 127
Fences
  in desert gardens, 51
  design considerations for, 111–12,
    111
  function of, 102–3, 110–11, **110**, **119**,
    131
  installing, 119
  for privacy, **152**
  trying out, 119
  types of, 112
    board-on-board fences, **112**,
      114–15, **114**
    metal fences, 112, 116, **116**, 119
    panel fences, 114, **114**
    picket fences, 27, 112–13, **112**,
      113
    post-and-rail fences, **112**, 115
    stockade fences, 115, **115**
  on uneven or sloping terrain, 120,
    120
  vines to train on, 117–18
Fern(s), 212
  Christmas, 236
  cinnamon, 229, 236

Japanese painted, 234
in Japanese-style gardens, 34
lady, 226
maidenhair, **38**
male, 227
New York, 230
ostrich, 235
Fetterbush, 232
Fibonacci numbers, in landscape
    design, 13
Fieldstone
    paths, 93–94, **97**
    patios, 137, 139, 141, **141**
Filipendula rubra, 238
Firepit, for outdoor heating, 177–78
Fireplaces, outdoor, **178**, 179
Fireproofing, outdoor, 148, 176
Flag
    blue, 194
    yellow, 194
Flag-of-Spain, 118
Flagstone
    paths, 90, 93
    patios, 137, 139, **139**, **142**
Flat-sided pot, **203**
Flax, New Zealand, 214
Flossflower, 210
Flower forms and textures, variety of,
    61, **61**
Foamflower, 236
Foliage color, effects of, 59, **59**
Forestiera neomexicana, 249
Forget-me-nots, 27, **122**, 224
Formal gardens
    characteristics of, 2, **2**
    circular beds in, 6, 11
    comeback of, 7
    containers in, 16, **17**, 206
    design elements of, **4**, 9, 10, **10**
        axes, 9, 11, **11**
        balance and symmetry, 9, 12, **12**,
            13
        formal pavements, 12, **12**, **13**
        geometric beds and borders, 11,
            11, **13**

neatly groomed plants, 14–15, 16, **16**
restrained color scheme, 15
statuary and ornaments, 16, **17**, 18
topiaries, 15, 206
water features, 16
designs for flower plantings in, 24
history of, 6–7
house styles suited to, 7–9
integrating landscape elements with,
    153
modified, 18–19, **19**
paths in, 89, **89**, **93**
plants for, 210–15
in urban settings, 4
variety of, 9
Forsythia, Korean, 60
Fountains, 192–93, **193**
    in formal gardens, 16
    patio, 134, **134**
Fouquiera splendens, 249
Four o'clock, 224
Foxglove, 222
Fragrant plants, 134, **135**, 136
Franklinia alatamaha, 60, **228**
Franklin tree, 60, 228
Freestanding walls, **103**, 103–4
Fringe tree, 227
Fritillaria imperialis, 222
Fuchsia, 212
    California, 251
Furnishings, outdoor, 133
    cleaning, 176
    cushions and fabrics for, 175–76, **175**
    garden, 168
        beds, 183–84
        benches and seats, 179, 181–83,
            181, **182**
        guidelines for, 179–80
        hammocks, swings, and hanging
            chairs, 179, 183
        gazebo, 164
        heaters, 177–79, **178**
        materials for
            aluminum, 169, **172**
            plastics, 170–71

vinyl, 169
wicker, 170, **171**
wood, 169–70, **170**
wrought iron, 170
porch, 154
quality of, 169
types of, for decks and patios
    chairs, 173–74
    dining tables, 171
    kitchen and service pieces, 176–77
    modular and convertible pieces,
        174–75
    occasional tables, 173

G

Gaillardia, 249
Gaillardia pulchella, 241
Galium odoratum, 235
Garden colors. *See* Colors, garden
Garden structures
    arbors, 131, 154–56, 157–58
    arches, 154–57, 159
    decks, 131, 143–52 (*see also* Decks)
    gazebos, 131, 162–64
    patios, 131, 132–43, 152 (*see also*
        Patios)
    pavilions, 163
    pergolas, 131, 158–59
    porches, 154
    sheds, 131, 165
Garden styles, 1–2. *See also* Formal
        gardens; Informal gardens;
        Naturalistic gardens
    house style influencing, 2
    settings influencing
        country, 4–6
        natural, 6
        urban, 4
Gas log sets, for outdoor heating, 179
Gas plant, 212
Gates, 121–22, **121**, **122**, 185
Gaultheria shallon, 232
Gaura lindheimeri, 217

Gayfeather, Kansas, 242
Gazebos
    construction tips for, 164
    function of, 131
    furnishings for, 164
    history of, 162
    locations of, 163, **163**, **164**
    plants for, 164
    structure style of, 162–63
Gazing globes, **179**
Gelsemium sempervirens, 160
Georgian-style houses
    colors for, 73
    formal gardens for, 7
Geranium, 217
    Lancaster, 245
Geranium dalmaticum, 245
Geranium sanguineum var. *striatum,*
    245
Germander, 215, 251
Geum triflorum, 241
Gift plants, grown in cottage garden, 27
Gingers, wild, 210, 226
Glass, recycled, for paths, 96
Glazed clay containers, 205–6
Gleditsia triacanthos, 126
Goat's beard, 27, 216
Gold, as sunset color, 76
Golden foliage, effects of, 59
Golden hop vine, 160
Goldenrod, 27, 220
    stiff, 240, 243
    sweet, 240
Goldenstar, 99
Gomphrena globosa, 249
Gothic-style houses
    colors for, 73
    formal gardens for, 8
Granite
    containers, 205
    flagstones, 93
Grass(es)
    blue-eyed, 230, 240
    buffalo, 40
    cord, 230

Grass(es) *(cont.)*
  dwarf mondo, 100
  eulalia, 218
  feather reed, 216
  fountain, 219
  hakone, 228
  hare's tail, 239
  Indian, **43**, 243
  June, 238
  maiden, **75**, 218
  mondo, 229
  ornamental, 27, 34
  for paths, 97, **97**
  prairie, 40
  prairie cord, 243
  prairie June, 242
  side-oats grama, 40, 241
  switch, 40, 239, 242
Gravel
  in Japanese-style gardens, 32
  for paths, 90, 94, **95**, 96
Gray
  foliage, effects of, 59
  houses, garden colors for, 78, 78, **78**
  qualities of, 56–57
Grazing light, as lighting technique, 198
Greek Revival-style houses
  colors for, 73
  formal gardens for, 7, 8
Green
  foliage, effects of, 59
  houses, garden colors for, 82, 82, **82**
  qualities of, 25, 56
Green-and-gold, 234
Grills, outdoor, 176
Groomed plants, in formal gardens,
    14–15, 16, **16**
Grottoes, in early formal gardens, 6
Groundcovers
  in Japanese-style gardens, 34
  for paths, 98, **98**, 99–100
  in woodland garden, 2
Guava, pineapple, 127
Gypsophila paniculata, 60, 217
Gypsophila repens, 245

H

Hakonechloa macra, 228
Halesia carolina, 232
Hamamelis ×intermedia, 228, 232
Hammocks, 179, 183
Hanging baskets
  for decks, 150, **150**, 152
  for gazebos, 164
  for patios, 152
  plants for, 150
  uses for, 202–3
Hanging chairs, 183
Hardscape
  elements of, 87–88
    fences, 102–3, 110–20
    gates, 121–22
    hedges and plant screens, 123–29
    paths, 88–102 (*see also* Paths)
    walls, 102–9
  function of, 88
Harebell, Carpathian, 244
Harmonious color schemes, 62, *62*, **62**
Hawthorn, 126
Hearths, outdoor, 178–79
Heaters, outdoor, 133, **133**, 177–79, **178**
Heather, Scotch, 244
Heating
  gazebo, 164
  patio, 133, **133**
Hedges
  choosing plants for, 125, 127
  in cottage gardens, 27
  around deck, 152
  in formal gardens, 12, **13**, 15
  function of, 123, **123**, 131
  in informal gardens, 23
  maintenance of, 123
  around patio, 134, 152
  as windbreak, 126
Heirloom plants, in cottage gardens, 27
Helenium, 218
Helenium autumnale, 238
Helianthus salicifolius, 242

Heliopsis helianthoides, 242
Heliopsis helianthoides susp. *scabra*,
    238
Heliotrope, 27, 223
Heliotropium arborescens, 223
Hellebores, 235
Helleborus, **40**, 235
Hemerocallis, 60, 218
Hemerocallis lilioasphodelus, 223
Hemlock, eastern, 125
Herbaceous plants, in woodland
    garden, 37
Hesperis matronalis, 223
Heuchera, 212
Heuchera americana, 235
Hibiscus, Chinese, 212
Hibiscus moscheutos, 218
Hibiscus rosa-sinensis, 212
Hibiscus syriacus, 223
Holly, 129, 213
  American, 228
  Chinese, 126, 127
  Japanese, 228
  Oregon grape, 229, 233
Hollyhock, 221
Honeysuckle, 118, 161
  boxleaf, 127
  goldflame, 218
Hoop support, for plants, **14**
Hornbeam, fastigiate European, 128
Horsetail, 194
Hosta, **75**, 212, 228, 235
Hot tub
  on deck, 148
  on patio, 134
House color. *See also* Color(s), garden;
    specific colors
  coordinating garden colors with,
    73–77
  daylight affecting, 73
  size of house affecting, 73–74
House styles. *See also specific styles*
  integrating landscape elements with,
    153
  suited to formal gardens, 2, 7–9

suited to informal gardens, 19, 21
suited to naturalistic gardens, 2,
    34–35
Hues, 55
Hularo, for covering wicker, 175
Humulus lupulus, 160
Hyacinth bean, 117
Hydrangea, 60
  bigleaf, 212
  climbing, 160, 232
  oakleaf, 232
Hydrangea macrophylla, 212
Hydrangea petiolaris, 160, 232
Hydrangea quercifolia, 232
Hydrocleys nymphoides, 194
Hypericum olympicum, 245
Hyssop, 213
Hyssopus officinalis, 213

I

Iberis sempervirens, 60
Ice plant, 249
  trailing, 250
Ilex, 126, 129, 213
Ilex cornuta, 126, 127
Ilex crenata, 228
Ilex glabra, 228
Ilex opaca, 228
Ilex verticillata, 232
Illicium floridanum, 228
Impatiens
  balsam, 223
  bedding, 213
Impatiens balsamina, 223
Impatiens walleriana, 213
Indian blanket, 241
Informal gardens
  characteristics of, 2, **2**, **5**
  color schemes in, 25, **25**
  containers for, 206, 208
  in country settings, 5
  design elements of, 20, 22–23, **23**
  designs for flower plantings in, 24

drifts in, **20**, 24, **24**
house styles suited to, 19, <u>21</u>
integrating landscape elements with, <u>153</u>
laying out beds and borders in, 23–24
paths in, 89, **89**
plants for, **5**, **26**, 27, <u>216–20</u>
types of
cottage garden, 27, <u>28</u>
Japanese-style garden, 23, 29–34
Inkberry, <u>228</u>
Intensity of color, 55–56
Ipomoea, <u>161</u>, <u>218</u>
Ipomoea alba, <u>117</u>, <u>223</u>
Ipomoea ×multifida, <u>117</u>
Ipomoea purpurea, <u>117</u>, <u>223</u>
Ipomoea quamoclit, <u>117</u>, <u>161</u>
Iris, <u>60</u>, <u>213</u>, <u>223</u>
bearded, <u>213</u>, <u>223</u>
crested, <u>245</u>
in formal gardens, 14, 16, **16**
Japanese, <u>194</u>, <u>228</u>
netted, <u>245</u>
Iris cristata, <u>245</u>
Iris ensata, <u>194</u>, <u>228</u>
Iris pseudacorus, <u>194</u>
Iris reticulata, <u>245</u>
Iris versicolor, <u>194</u>
Ironweed, <u>240</u>
Island beds, in informal gardens, 5
Italianate-style houses, formal gardens for, <u>8</u>
Italian Renaissance-style houses, formal gardens for, <u>8</u>
Ivy, 22
Boston, <u>161</u>
Kenilworth, <u>99</u>

J

Japanese moon gates, 122
Japanese-style gardens, 23
characteristics of, 29, 31
containers in, 16, 18, <u>29</u>

elements of, <u>30</u>
paths, 32, 90
rocks, 31–32
water, 32, 187
lighting in, 31, **197**
plants for, <u>226–30</u>
choosing, 33–34
pruning tips for, <u>33</u>
river of stone in, <u>101</u>
Jasmine, <u>118</u>, <u>161</u>
Confederate, <u>161</u>
Jasminum, <u>118</u>, <u>161</u>
Jekyll, Gertrude, 18–19
Jessamine, Carolina, <u>160</u>
Joe Pye weed, **43**, <u>238</u>
Johnny jump-up, 27, <u>225</u>
Joseph's coat, <u>210</u>, <u>221</u>
Juniper, <u>129</u>
Japanese garden, <u>246</u>
Juniperus, <u>129</u>
Juniperus procumbens, <u>246</u>
Jupiter's beard, <u>221</u>

K

Kalmia latifolia, <u>229</u>, <u>232</u>
Kerria, Japanese, <u>232</u>
Kerria japonica, <u>232</u>
Kitchens, outdoor, 176–77, <u>177</u>
Knifophia, **54**
Kniphofia uvaria, <u>249</u>
Knotweed, <u>219</u>
Koeleria macrantha, <u>238</u>, <u>242</u>
Kolomikta vine, <u>160</u>

L

Lablab purpurea, <u>117</u>
Lady's mantle, <u>210</u>
alpine, <u>99</u>
Lagerstroemia indica, <u>250</u>
Lagurus ovatus, <u>239</u>
Lamb's ears, <u>214</u>

Lampposts
for driveway, 197
for paths, 196
Lampranthus spectabilis, <u>250</u>
Landscape elements, integrating, with house styles, <u>153</u>
Landscape lighting techniques, <u>198</u>
Landscape movement, influencing formal gardens, 6
Lantana, in cottage garden, 27
Lantana camara, <u>218</u>
Lanterns
in Japanese-style gardens, 31, **197**
for parties, <u>199</u>
for paths, 197, **198**
styles of, 199
Larkspur, <u>211</u>, <u>222</u>, <u>237</u>
Larrea tridentata, <u>250</u>
Lath houses, for desert gardens, 51
Lath strips, as screening, 152
Lathyrus odoratus, <u>223</u>
Lattice screens, 51, 152
Laurel
cherry, <u>129</u>
mountain, <u>229</u>, <u>232</u>
Lavandula angustifolia, <u>224</u>, <u>250</u>
Lavender (color), effects of, 25
Lavender, English (plant), <u>224</u>, <u>250</u>
Lawn
converting, to meadow or prairie garden, 42
shape, curved beds and, 5, **5**
Leucanthemum ×superbum, <u>60</u>, <u>213</u>
Leucanthemum vulgare, <u>239</u>
Leucophyllum frutescens, <u>250</u>
Leucothoe fontanesiana, <u>232</u>
Lewisia Cotyledon Hybrids, <u>246</u>
Liatris pycnostachya, <u>242</u>
Liatris spicata, <u>242</u>
Lighting, outdoor
gazebo, 164
in Japanese-style garden, 31, **197**
for parties, <u>199</u>

for paths, 196
patio, 133
porch, 199
reasons for
aesthetics, 199–200
safety, 196–97
utility and comfort, 197–98
on statuary, 199–200
techniques with, <u>198</u>
Ligularia stenocephala, <u>218</u>
Ligustrum ovalifolium, <u>127</u>
Lilac, <u>60</u>, <u>225</u>
dwarf Korean, <u>247</u>
Lilium, <u>213</u>
Lilium canadense, <u>239</u>
Lilium lancifolium, <u>224</u>
Lilium superbum, <u>239</u>
Lily, <u>213</u>
African, <u>210</u>
calla, **56**, <u>195</u>
in formal gardens, 16, **16**
lemon, <u>223</u>
meadow, <u>239</u>
plantain, <u>212</u>, <u>228</u>, <u>235</u>
tiger, <u>224</u>
toad, <u>236</u>
Turk's cap, <u>239</u>
yellow trout, <u>235</u>
Lily-of-the-valley, <u>60</u>, <u>222</u>
Lilyturf, <u>213</u>
Limestone
containers, 205
paths, 93
patios, 139
Liriope, <u>213</u>
Lobelia cardinalis, <u>194</u>, <u>239</u>
Lobularia maritima, <u>60</u>
Locust, honey, 126
Log homes
informal gardens for, 19, <u>21</u>
naturalistic gardens for, 34
Long tom, 203, **203**
Lonicera, <u>118</u>, <u>161</u>
Lonicera heckrottii, <u>218</u>
Lonicera nitida, <u>127</u>

Lotus, **188**
   American, 195
   sacred, 195
Lounge chairs, 174, **174**
Love-in-a-mist, **65**, 224
Love-in-a-puff, 117
Love-lies-bleeding, 221
Low lights, 196
Lunaria annua, 224
Lupine, 213
   wild, 239
Lupinus, 213
Lupinus perennis, 239
Lysimachia nummularia, 100,
   195

M

Maclura pomifera, 128
Magnolia, 60
   hybrid, 233
Magnolia ×loebneri, 233
Mahonia aquifolium, 229,
   233
Maidenhair, northern, 234
Mallow, rose, 218
Malus, 229
Mammillaria, 250
Mammillaria zeilmanniana, **49**
Mandevilla ×amabilis, 118
Maple
   full moon, 226
   hedge, 128
   Japanese, 34, 226, 231
   paperbark, 226, 231
Marble containers, 205
Marguerite, 60
   golden, 248
Marigold
   desert, 248
   pot, 221
Matteucia struthiopteris, 235
Mauve, qualities of, 25, 57
Mazus reptans, 100

Meadow gardens
   characteristics of, 40, 41, 42
   establishing, 42
   maintaining, 42
   mowing, 43–44
   plants for, **34**, 42–43, 43, **43**, 237–40
   seeds for, 43
   weed removal in, 43–44
Meadows, characteristics of, 40
Meadowsweet, 220
Melampodium leucanthum, 242
Mentha requienii, 100
Mesquite, honey, 250
Metal
   benches, 183
   containers, 205
   edging, for paths, 101
   fences, 112, 116, **116**, 119
Mexican hat, 242
Mignonette, 225
Milkweed, swamp, 237
Mimulus aurantiacus, 250
Mina lobata, 118
Mint, Corsican, 100
Mirabilis jalapa, 224
Mirrors, garden, 186, **186**
Miscanthus, 218
Miscanthus sinensis, 34, **75**
Mixed media, for patios, 142, **142**
Modern houses. *See* Contemporary
   houses
Modular furniture, outdoor, 174–75
Monarda didyma, 219, 239
Money plant, 224
Monkey flower, bush, 250
Monkshoods, 210
Monochromatic gardens, 58, **58**, 60
   varied forms and textures in, 61, **61**
Moonflower, 117, 223
Moon gates, Japanese, 122
Moonlighting, as lighting technique,
   198
Morning glory, 117, 161, 218
   common, 223
Mortared stone walls, 106, **106**

Moss
   Irish, 100
   in Japanese-style gardens, 34
   rose, 225
Mother-of-thyme, 100,247
Moving water, 191
   fountains, 192–93, **193**
   streams and channels, 191–92, **192**
   waterfalls, 192
Mowing strips, for plant protection, 5
Mulch, for paths, 96–97
Myosotis sylvatica, 224
Myrica cerifera, 129
Myriophyllum aquaticum, 195
Myrtle, 236
   crape, 250
   wax, 129

N

Narcissus, 60, 219, 224
Narcissus bulbocodium, 246
Nasturtium, 225
Native plants
   in cottage gardens, 27
   in naturalistic gardens, 34, 35
Naturalistic gardens
   characteristics of, 2, **2**, 34–35, 35
   houses suited to, 34–35
   in informal gardens, 23
   integrating landscape elements with,
     153
   in natural settings, 6
   types of
     desert gardens, 49–51
     meadow and prairie gardens, **34**,
      40–44
     rock gardens, 4449
     woodland gardens, 34, 35–40
Natural settings, influencing garden
   style, 6
Nelumbo lutea, 195
Nelumbo nucifera, **188**, 195
Nepeta, in informal gardens, **5**

Nepeta ×faassenii, 219
Nerium oleander, 129, 250
Nicotiana alata, 219
Nigella damascena, 65, 224
Night-blooming flowers, 141
Nummularia, golden, **98**
Nymphaea, 195
Nymphoides cristata, 195

O

Obelisks, 18, **184**
Occasional tables, outdoor, 173
Ocotillo, 249
Oenothera fruticosa, 239
Oenothera speciosa, 219
Off-white houses, garden colors for, 80,
   80, **80**
Oil (or olive) jar, **203**, 204, **204**, 208
Old-fashioned plants, in cottage
   gardens, 27
Oleander, 129, 250
Olive
   desert, 249
   holly, 126
Onion, flowering, 210
Ophiopogon japonicus, 100, 229
Orange (color)
   in plant palette, 68, 75
   qualities of, 57
   as sunset color, 76
Orange (plant)
   mock, 225
   Osage, 128
Ornamental grasses
   in informal gardens, 27
   in Japanese-style gardens, 34
Ornaments
   in formal gardens, 16, **17**, 18
   garden, 184–86, **184**, **185**, **186**
   lighting on, 199–200
Osmanthus heterophyllus, 126
Osmunda cinnamomea, 229, 236
Outcrops, as rock gardens, 45, 48

Outdoor decorating. *See* Decorating, outdoor
Outdoor furnishings. *See* Furnishings, outdoor
Outdoor lighting. *See* Lighting, outdoor
Oxydendrum arboreum, 60

P

Paeonia, 60, 214
Paint colors
    for arches, arbors, and pergolas, 159
    for deck, 148
Palm, umbrella, 194
Palo verde, blue, 249
Panel fences, 114, **114**
Panicum virgatum, 40, 239, 242
Papaver orientale, 214
Papaver rhoeas, 224, 240
Papaver somniferum, **65**
Parrot's feather, 195
Parterres, in early formal gardens, 6
Parthenocissus tricuspidata, 161
Party lights, outdoor, 199
Passiflora, 118, 161
Passionflowers, 118, 161
Pastels, effects of, 25
Paths
    edgings for, 98, 101
    in formal gardens, 12, **12**, **13**, 89, **89**, **93**
    function of, 88, 131
    hillside, steps in, 90
    in informal gardens, 89, **89**
    installing, 91, 101–2, **102**
    in Japanese-style gardens, 32, 90
    lighting for, 196
    locations for, 88–89
    in naturalistic gardens, 35
    in rock gardens, 47
    safety considerations for, 90
    softening edges of, **86**
    stepping stones in, 90, 91, **91**, **93**, **97**, 102, **102**

style of, 90–91
surface materials for, 89–90
    brick, 90, 91–92, **91**, **92**
    choosing, 90–91
    concrete pavers, 90, 94, **94**
    fieldstone, 93–94, **97**
    flagstone, 90, 93
    grass, 97, **97**
    gravel, pebbles, and crushed rock, 90, **91**, 94, **95**, 96
    groundcovers, 98, **98**, 99–100
    natural materials, 96–97
    poured concrete, 94
    recycled glass, 96
    tile, 90, 91, 96
    temporary, 98
    tricks for lengthening, 185
    width of, 90
    in woodland gardens, 38, **38**
Patio(s)
    construction tips, 142
    features
        arbors, 133
        awnings, 133
        fountains, 134, **134**
        heaters, 133, **133**, 177–79, **178**
        hot tub, 134
        lighting, 133, 197–99
    function of, 131, 132
    furnishings
        choosing materials for, 169–71
        cleaning, 176
        cushions and fabrics, 175–76, **175**
        kitchen and service pieces, 176–77
        planning for, 168–69
        tables and chairs, 171, 173–75
        umbrella, 176
    integrated into landscape, **132**
    locations, 132
    plantings, **142**, 143
        fragrant plants, 134, **135**, 136
        garden beds, 134
        hedges, 134
        night-blooming flowers, 141
        trees, 134, 137

screening, for shade and privacy, 152, **152**
shapes, 133
size, 132–33
sunken, 132
surfaces
    brick, 137, 139, **140**
    fieldstone, 137, 139, 141, **141**
    flagstone, **133**, 137, 139, **139**, **142**
    mixed media, 142, **142**
    poured concrete, 137–38, **138**
    stone pavers, 137, 138–39, **138**
    tile, 137, 141
Pavements, in formal gardens, 12, **12**
Pavers
    for paths, 90, 94, **94**
    for patios, 137, 138–39, **138**
Pavilions, 163
Paxistima canbyi, 246
Pebbles
    in Japanese-style gardens, 32
    for paths, 91, 96
Pedestal, **185**
Pennisetum alopecuroides, 219
Peony, 14, 16, 60, 214
Pepperbush, sweet, 128, 231
Perennials
    color palettes for, 66, 67–68, 69, 70–71, 71–72
    in containers vs. ground, 208
    for woodland gardens, 38, 234–36
Pergolas
    for desert gardens, 51
    location of, 156
    paint color for, 159
    plants for, 159, **159**, 160–61, 162
    structure style of, 156, 158–59
    uses for, 131, 152, 154–55, **158**
Periwinkle, 236
Perovskia atriplicifolia, 219
Persicaria, 219
Petrorhagia saxifraga, 246
Petunia, 220
Petunia ×*hybrida,* 224
Phacelia campanularia, 250

Philadelphus coronarius, 225
Phlox
    garden, 214
    summer, 60
Phlox divaricata, **38**, **40**, 236
Phlox paniculata, 60, 214
Phlox subulata, 246
Phormium tenax, 214
Phyllostachys, 229
Physostegia virginiana, 214
Picea glauca, 125, 214, 246
Pickerelweed, 195
Picket fences, 112–13, **112**, **113**
Pieris, 60
Pillows, chair, 173, 175, 183
Pine
    Japanese black, 33
    Japanese umbrella, 230
    lacebark, 229
    pitch, 229
    Scotch, 33–34
    shore, 34, 229
    Swiss stone, 129
    white, 34
    yew, 127
Pink (color)
    in plant palette, 67–68
    qualities of, 25, 57
Pink (plant)
    cheddar, 245
    China, 217
    garden, 212
    maiden, 245
    moss, 246
Pinus bungeana, 229
Pinus cembra, 129
Pinus contorta var. *contorta,* 34, 229
Pinus rigida, 229
Pinus strobus, 34
Pinus sylvestris, 34
Pinus thunbergii, 33
Planter boxes, for deck, 147
Planting pockets, in stone wall, 45, 46, 47, 108, **108**

Plants. *See also specific plants*
for all-white garden, 60
for arbors, arches, and pergolas, 159,
160–61, 162
color palettes for, 66–73
container, for shade, 151
for cottage gardens, 221–25
for desert gardens, 51, 248–51
for formal gardens, 210–15
fragrant flowers, 134, **135**, 136
for gazebos, 164
groundcover, for paths, 99–100
hanging basket, 150, **150**
hedge, 127
for informal gardens, 216–20
for Japanese-style gardens, 226–30
for meadows, 237–40
night-blooming flowers, 141
patio, 134, **135**, 137, 143
for prairies, 241–43
for rock gardens, 46, 48–49, 244–47
screening, 128–29
for sunset garden, 76
vines for arbors, 160–61
vines for fences, 117–18
for walls and crevices, 46
for water gardens, 194–95
window box, 148
for woodland gardens, 39, 231–36
Plastic
for edging paths, 101
for outdoor furniture, 170–71
Platycodon grandiflorus, 214, 229
Podocarpus macrophyllus, 127
Polychromatic gardens, 65, **65**
Polygonatum, 60
Polygonatum odoratum, 236
Polygonum aubertii, 117
Polystichum acrostichoides, 236
Polywood outdoor furniture, 171
Ponds
locations for, 187
maintaining, 193
ornaments in, 185
Pontederia cordata, 195

Pools, garden
locations for, 187
ornaments in, 185
reflecting, 188–90, **188**, **189**, **190**,
193
Poppy, **65**
California, 238
corn, 224
Flanders, 240
oriental, 214
water, 194
Porches, 154, 199
Portulaca grandiflora, 225
Post-and-beam houses, informal
gardens for, 21
Post-and-rail fences, **112**, 115
Postmodern homes, informal gardens
for, 21
Potentilla fruticosa, 246
Pots. *See also* Containers
choosing, 206, 208
materials for, 205–6
planting in, 207, 208
types of, 203–5, **203**, **204**
uses for, 201–2, **202**
Poured concrete
for paths, 94
for patios, 137–38, **138**
Prairie gardens
characteristics of, 41, 42
establishing, 42
maintaining, 42
mowing, 43–44
plants for, 42–43, **43**, 43, 241–43
seeds for, 43
weed removal in, 43–44
Prairies, characteristics of, 40
Prairie smoke, 241
Primrose
auricula, 246
Japanese, 236
showy, 219
Primula auricula, 246
Primula japonica, 236
Privet, California, 127

Proportions, in landscape designs, 13
Prosopis glandulosa, 250
Pruning, in Japanese-style gardens, 33,
33
Prunus laurocerasus, 129
Prunus mume, 230
Prunus serrulata, 230
Pueblo Revival homes, informal
gardens for, 19, 21
Purple
foliage, effects of, 59
qualities of, 25, 56, **56**
Purple bell vine, 118
Purple plants, 70–71
Pussytoes, 99, 248
Pyramids, in formal gardens, 18

Q

Queen Anne-style houses, formal
gardens for, 8
Queen-of-the-prairie, 238
Quince, common flowering, 126

R

Rabbits, in desert gardens, 51
Railings, deck, 146, 147
Ranch houses
informal gardens for, 19, 21, **21**, **22**
integrating landscape elements with,
153
Ratibida columnifera, 242
Ratibida pinnata, 242
Rattlesnake master, 241
Recycled glass, for paths, 96
Red
foliage, effects of, 59
houses, garden colors for, 83, **83**, **83**
plants, 66
qualities of, 25, 57, **57**
as sunset color, 76
Redbud, western, 249

Red-hot poker, **54**, 249
Redwood, as deck material, 148
Reflecting pools, 188–90, **188**, **189**,
190, 193
Renaissance-style houses, formal
gardens for, 8
Reseda odorata, 225
Retaining walls, 104–5, **104**
Rhodochiton atrosanguinea, 118
Rhododendron, 60, 129, 230, 246
catawba, 233
dwarf, 246
Rhododendron catawbiense, 233,
246
Rhododendron mucronulatum,
246
Robinia hispida, 251
Robinson, William, 18
Rock cress, **108**
purple, 244
wall, 244
Rock gardens
characteristics of, 44, **45**
paths in, 47
plants for, 46, 48–49, 244–47
sites for, **44**, 46–47
soil in, 47–48
soil mixes for, 48
types of
alpine meadow, 44–45
dry stone walls, 45
rock outcrops, boulders, and
crevices, 45
rocky woodland, 45–46
screes, 45
Rocks
in Japanese-style gardens, 31–32
tips for working with, 47
Rocky woodland, 45–46, 49
Romanesque-style houses, formal
gardens for, 8
Roof color, coordinating garden with,
77
Rosa, 118, 161, 202, 225
Rosa rugosa, 126

Rosemary, 251
Rose of Sharon, 223
Roses
    climbing, 118, **122**, **161**, 162
    Iceberg, in formal garden, **7**, **15**
    musk, **202**
    rugosa, 126
    shrub, 225
Rosmarinus officinalis, 251
Rudbeckia, **34**, 220
Rudbeckia amplexicaulis, 242
Rudbeckia fulgida, 240
Rudbeckia hirta, 243
Rudbeckia submentosa, 243
Ruins, in early formal gardens, 6
Rush, variegated Japanese, 194
Russet, as sunset color, 76

S

Sage
    mealycup, 220
    Russian, 219
Sagina subulata, 100
Sagittaria latifolia, 195
Salal, 232
Salmon, as sunset color, 75, 76
Saltbox houses
    informal gardens for, 19, 21
    integrating landscape elements with,
        153
    naturalistic gardens for, 35
Salvia, **56**, **65**, 214
Salvia farinacea, 220
Salvia gregii, 251
Salvia ×sylvestris, 214
Santolina chamaecyparissus, 214,
    251
Saponaria, **45**
Saponaria ocymoides, 247
Saxifraga paniculata, 247
Scandent plants, 162
Schizachyrium scoparium, 240
Sciadopitys verticillata, 230

Screens
    lattice, 51, 152
    plant, **124**, 125, 128–29
        for driveway, 77
        function of, 123, 126, 126
        maintenance of, 123
Screes, 45
    plants for, 49
    soil mix for, 48
Sculpture. *See* Statuary
Sea thrift, 244
Second Empire-style houses, formal
        gardens for, 7, 8
Sedge, variegated, in Japanese-style
        gardens, **33**
Sedges, 194, 227
Sedum, 220
    golden carpet, 247
    goldmoss, 100
Sedum acre, 100, 247
Sedum cauticola, 247
Sedum spathulifolium, **108**, 251
Seeds, for meadow and prairie gardens,
    43
Serviceberry, downy, 226, 231
Service pieces, outdoor, 177
Shade
    arbors providing, 144, 148
    container plants for, 151
    for decks, 152
    in desert gardens, 51
    for patios, 133, 152
    types of, 37
    from window trellises, 162
Sheds, 131, 165, **165**
Shibataea kumasasa, 230
Shrubs
    color palettes for, 66, 68, 69, 70, 71,
        73
    around decks, 149, 152
    in informal gardens, 23
    around patios, 152
    in woodland garden, 2, 39, 231–33
Silene armeria, 243
Silhouetting, as lighting technique, 198

Silphium laciniatum, 243
Silverbell, Carolina, 232
Silver foliage, effects of, 59
Silver lace vine, 117, 160
Single-color gardens, 58, **58**, 60
Sisyrinchium graminoides, 230, 240
Sling chairs, 174, 183
Smilacina racemosa, 236
Snapdragon, 60, 221
    summer, 210
Sneezeweed, 218, 238
Snowbell, Japanese, 233
Snowberry, 233
Snowflake, white, 195
Snow-in-summer, 99, 248
Soapwort, rock, 247
Soil
    color, coordinating plants with, 77
    mixes, for rock gardens, 48
    in rock gardens, 47–48
    in woodland gardens, 37–38
Solar lights, **196**, 197
Soleirolia soleirolii, 100
Solenostemon scutellarioides, 216
Solidago, 220
Solidago odora, 240
Solidago rigida, 240, 243
Solomon's seal, 60
    false, 236
    variegated, 236
Sorghastrum nutans, **43**, 243
Sourwood, 60
Space management, 88
Spartina pectinata, 230, 243
Speedwell, spike, 215
Spheres, in formal gardens, 18
Spider flower, 222
Spiraea japonica, 247
Spiraea ×vanhouttei, 128
Spirea
    dwarf Japanese, 247
    false, 216
Sporobolus heterolepis, 243
Spotlighting, as lighting technique,
    198

Spruce
    dwarf Alberta, 214, 246
    white, 125
Spurge, myrtle, 245
St. John's wort, Olympic, 245
Stachys byzantina, 214
Stains, deck, 148
Stair risers, deck, 146, 147
Stairs. *See* Steps
Stakes, types of, **14**
Statuary
    in formal gardens, 18, **18**
    fountain, 192
    garden, 184–86, **184**, **185**, **186**
    lighting on, 199–200
Stephanandra, cut-leaf, 128
Stephanandra incisa, 128
Stepping stones, 90, 91, **91**, **93**, **97**,
    102, **102**
Steps
    deck, 147
    in formal gardens, 12
    for hillside paths, 90
    lighting for, 196
    porch, 154
Stewartia, Japanese, 60, 233
Stewartia pseudocamellia, 60, 233
Still water, **188**, 188–90, **189**, **190**
Stone(s)
    benches, **181**, 182–83
    containers, 205
        faux, 206
    crushed, for paths, 94, 96
    for edging paths, 98
    in Japanese-style gardens, 32
    pavers, for patios, 137, 138–39, **138**
    for suggesting look of river, 101
    walls, 45, 106–7, **106**, **107**
Stonecrop
    broadleaf, 251
    Pacific, 251
Storage units, outdoor, 177
Strawberry, barren, 100
Strawberry jar, 204
Streams, 191–92

String lights, for parties, 199
Stucco
    homes, informal gardens for, 19, 21
    walls, 107–8, **109**
Styrax japonicus, 233
Sunbrella fabrics, 175
Sundials, 18, **185**
Sundrops, 239
Sunflower
    oxeye, 242
    willow-leaved, 242
Sunset colors
    for coordinating house and garden
        colors, 75, **75**
    plants with, 76
Sweet pea, 27, 223
Sweet William, **38**, **40**, 222
    wild, 236
Swings, 179, 183
Symmetry, in formal gardens, 9, 12, **12**,
    13
Symphoricarpos albus var. *laevigatus*,
    233
Syringa meyeri, 247
Syringa vulgaris, 60, 225

T

Tables, outdoor
    dining, 171
    occasional, 173
Tall hoop, for supporting plants, **14**
Tan houses, garden colors for, 79, 79,
    79
Taro, 194
Taupe houses, garden colors for, 79, 79,
    79
Taxus, 215
Taxus ×media, 127
Teak, for outdoor furniture, 169–70,
    170, 174, 181
Terraces, 104–5
Terra-cotta pots, 205
    faux, 206

Teucrium chamaedrys, 215, 251
Texas ranger, 250
Thalictrum rochebrunianum, 220
Thelypteris noveboracensis, 230
Thistle, globe, 27, 217
Thuja, 230
Thuja occidentalis, 127
Thunbergia alata, 118
Thunbergia grandiflora, 118
Thyme, woolly, 100, 247
Thymus pseudolanuginosus, 100, 247
Thymus serpyllum, 100, 247
Tiarella cordifolia, 236
Tickseed, 217, 238
Tile
    for paths, 90, 91, 96
    for patios, 137, 141
Tobacco, flowering, 219
Tommies, 244
Topiaries
    in formal gardens, 15
    in pots, 206
Torches, for party lighting, 199
Trachelospermum jasminoides, 161
Transitional plantings, 6, **6**, 22–23
Trees
    color palettes for, 66, 68, 69, 70, 71,
        73
    in informal gardens, 23
    in Japanese-style gardens, 34
    lighting on, 200
    patio, 134, 137
    pruning, in Japanese-style gardens,
        33, **33**, **33**
    root systems of, 38
    in woodland gardens, 2, 38, 39,
        231–33
Trellises, window, for shade, 162
Trelliswork, as screening, 152
Trex, as deck material, 148–49
Triangular grid, for supporting plants, **14**
Tricyrtis hirta, 236
Trifolium incarnatum, 240
Trim color of house, coordinating garden
    colors with, 73, 74–75, **74**

Tropaeolum majus, 225
Tropaeolum peregrinum, 118, 161
Troughs, 204
Trumpet creeper, 22, 160
Trumpet vine, golden, 22, 117, 210
Tsuga canadensis, 125
Tulipa, 215
Tulips, 215
Tunic flower, 246
Turkey wire fencing, 116
Twig stakes, for supporting plants, **14**
Typha minima, 195

U

Umbrellas, deck and patio, 176
Understory, in woodland garden, 35
Uplighting, as lighting technique,
    198
Urban settings, influencing garden
    style, 6
Urns, 16, **203**, 204, **204**, **206**

V

Value of color, 55
Variegated foliage, effects of, 59
Vases, 204, 208
Verbena, **56**
    desert sand, 248
Vernonia noveboracensis, 240
Veronica, **5**
Veronica spicata, 215
Veronicastrum virginicum, 243
Viburnum
    doublefile, 128
    mapleleaf, 233
Viburnum acerifolium, 233
Viburnum plicatum var. *tomentosum*,
    128
Victorian-style houses
    colors for, 73
    formal gardens for, **8**, 9, **9**

informal gardens for, 9, 19
integrating landscape elements with,
    153
Vinca minor, 236
Vines
    arbor, 133, 159, 160–61, 162
    for arches, 159, 160–61, 162
    Bengal clock, 118
    black-eyed Susan, 118
    climbing methods of, 159
    color palettes for, 66, 68, 69, 70, 71,
        73
    coral, 160
    crimson glory, 161
    cup-and-saucer, 117, 160
    cypress, 117, 161
    for fences, 117–18
    fence supporting, **110**
    for gazebos, 164
    golden hop, 160
    golden trumpet, 22, 117, 210
    in informal gardens, 23
    kolomikta, 160
    for pergolas, 159, 160–61,
        162
    purple bell, 118
    on screening structures, 152
    silver lace, 117, 160
    uses for, 22
    in woodland gardens, 231–33
Vinyl outdoor furniture, 169
Viola tricolor, 27, 225
Violet (color)
    in plant palette, 70
    qualities of, 25, 56, **56**
Vitis coignetiae, 161

W

Waldsteinia ternata, 100
Walkways. *See* Paths
Wall color of house, coordinating
    garden colors with, 73, 74
Wallflower, **108**

Walls
  in desert gardens, 51
  function of, 102–3, 131
  materials for
    brick, 105–6, **105**
    calculating amount of, <u>109</u>
    choosing, 105
    concrete, 107–9
    stone, 45, 106–7, **106**, **107**
    stucco, 107–8, **109**
  planting pockets in, 45, <u>46</u>, 49, <u>108</u>,
    108
  softening edges of, **86**
  types of
    freestanding walls, 103–4, **103**
    retaining walls, 104–5, **104**
Warm colors, effects of, 25
Waterfalls, 192
Water features
  in formal gardens, 16
  function of, 187
  in Japanese-style gardens, 32, 187
  lighting on, 200
  maintaining, 193
  moving water, 191–93
  patio, 134, **134**
  still water, 188–90, **188**, **189**, **190**
Water gardens, plants for, <u>194–95</u>

Waterlilies
  hardy, <u>195</u>
  tropical, <u>195</u>
Waterspout, 191, **191**
Waverly fabrics, 175
Weathervane, 164
Weeds, in meadow and prairie gardens,
  43–44
White
  houses, garden colors for, 80, <u>80</u>, **80**
  plants, 60, <u>71–73</u>
  qualities of, 56, **56**
Wicker, for outdoor furniture, 170, **171**,
  175
Wildflowers
  in Japanese-style gardens, 34
  in meadow gardens, **34**, **41**
  in prairie gardens, **41**
  in woodland gardens, 38
Wildlife, attracting, to naturalistic
  gardens, 35
Willow, desert, <u>249</u>
Windbreaks, 51, <u>126</u>
Windflower, Grecian, <u>60</u>
Window boxes
  for deck, 147
  for gazebo, 164
  plants for, <u>148</u>

for shed, 165
  uses for, 202, **203**
Window trellises, for shade, <u>162</u>
Wine cups, <u>241</u>
Winterberry, <u>232</u>
Wintercreeper, <u>99</u>
Winterhazel, buttercup, <u>231</u>
Wisteria, <u>161</u>
Witch hazel, <u>228</u>
  hybrid, <u>232</u>
Wood
  benches, 181–82, **182**
  decks, 146, 148
  for edging paths, 101
  fences, 112–15
  for outdoor furniture, 169–70, **170**
Woodland gardens
  design tips for, 38
  elements of, 35, <u>36</u>, 37–38
  planting and care tips for, 38, 40
  plants for
    perennials, 38, <u>234–36</u>
    trees, shrubs, and vines, 2, 38, <u>39</u>,
      <u>231–33</u>
Woodruff, sweet, <u>235</u>
Wood-shingle houses, informal gardens
  for, <u>21</u>
Wormwood, <u>216</u>

Wrought iron
  benches, 183
  fences, 116, **116**
  gates, 122
  outdoor furniture, 170

Y

Yarrow, <u>216</u>, <u>237</u>, <u>248</u>
Yellow
  houses, garden colors for, 85, <u>85</u>,
    85
  plants, <u>69</u>, 75
  qualities of, 57
Yew, <u>127</u>, <u>215</u>
  Chinese plum, <u>127</u>
Yucca filamentosa, <u>251</u>

Z

Zantedeschia aethiopica, **56**, <u>195</u>
Zauschneria californica, <u>251</u>
Zinnia, desert, <u>251</u>
Zinnia elegans, <u>220</u>
Zinnia grandiflora, <u>251</u>
Zinnia haageana, <u>220</u>

[USDA Plant Hardiness Zone Map]

This map is recognized as the best indicator of minimum temperatures available. Look at the map to find your area, then match its pattern to the key below. When you've found your color, the key will tell you what hardiness zone you live in. Remember that the map is a general guide; your particular conditions may vary.

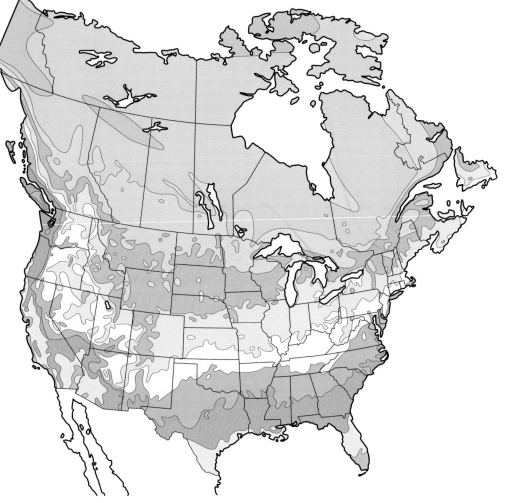

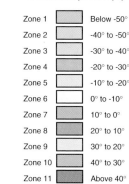

Average annual minimum temperature (°F)

Zone 1		Below -50°
Zone 2		-40° to -50°
Zone 3		-30° to -40°
Zone 4		-20° to -30°
Zone 5		-10° to -20°
Zone 6		0° to -10°
Zone 7		10° to 0°
Zone 8		20° to 10°
Zone 9		30° to 20°
Zone 10		40° to 30°
Zone 11		Above 40°